Competing in the

SECOND EDITION

EDITED BY Jerry N. Luftman

Information Age

ALIGN IN THE SAND

OXFORD
UNIVERSITY PRESS

2003

OXFORD

UNIVERSITY PRESS

Oxford   New York
Auckland   Bangkok   Buenos Aires   Cape Town   Chennai
Dar es Salaam   Delhi   Hong Kong   Istanbul   Karachi   Kolkata
Kuala Lumpur   Madrid   Melbourne   Mexico City   Mumbai   Nairobi
São Paulo   Shanghai   Taipei   Tokyo   Toronto

Copyright © 2003 by Oxford University Press, Inc.

Published by Oxford University Press, Inc.
198 Madison Avenue, New York, New York 10016

www.oup.com

Library of Congress Cataloging-in-Publication Data

Competing in the information age : align in the sand / [edited by] Jerry
N. Luftman.—2nd ed.
p. cm.
Includes bibliographical references and index.
ISBN 0-19-515953-5
1. Organizational change.   2. Strategic planning.   3. Information
technology—Management.   4. Competition.   I. Luftman, Jerry N.
HD58.8 .C646 2003
004'.068'4—dc21   2003004709

2 4 6 8 9 7 5 3 1

Printed in the United States of America
on acid-free paper

Preface

Since the release of "Competing in the Information Age: Strategic Alignment in Practice" in 1996, a substantial shift has taken place in our industry. Businesspeople are beginning to understand the importance of information technology (IT). Many suggest that those competitors with the best information systems and intelligence will be the winners. In numerous cases it is impossible to distinguish business strategies from IT strategies. About half of all investments in information technology are driven by functional (line-of-business; e.g., marketing, finance, research and development) executives. Many CIOs (chief information officers) sit at executive board meetings where information technology is translated into business value. Other significant changes that have affected corporations and our lives since 1996 include the implications of terrorism and security, the focus on morals and ethics, and the dynamics of our economy. In all of these cases, it is clear that information technology will provide the driving force behind business transformation in the information age.

There are large numbers of articles, books, case studies, and anecdotes that discuss what is being done by IT to affect all aspects of a firm's competitive strategy. More and more industries are recognizing that information technology can be instrumental in both integrating cross-organizational resources and shaping core business capabilities. Ignoring the Internet as a fundamental part of the business strategy is simply not an option. Having a website is not enough. The information age has opened new channels for selling products. Empowered by evolving technologies, customers are unforgiving. Misfortune awaits the organization that does not meet the challenge. Business is moving from technology as supporting the business to technology as an integral part of the business. As with all transformations, these changes do not come easily. Executives must take charge of their organizations' future in the information age. At a minimum, having a harmonious IT-business relationship is key. One thing that has not changed is the challenge of aligning IT and business strategies.

The purpose of this book is to present a new set of practical and powerful tools to help ensure that businesses get the full benefit from their investments in IT. Senior executives are provided with an understanding of how to manage the new ways of doing business in an innovation-driven information economy. We have learned a lot from applying the tools presented in the initial book. The strategic alignment model still is an essential vehicle for clarifying and ordering the process of bringing an organization's business strategic plan into harmony with the information technology that is necessary to make that plan work. Our experiences have helped identify and measure the key elements that facilitate the important relationship that must exist among IT and business organizations. Defining what will be demanded of managers and firms to survive and succeed in the information age remains a major challenge. This book prepares organizations to meet the challenge.

Acknowledgments

This book has its origins in research that began in the mid-1980s. Much of the original work has been published and presented around the world. A great deal has changed. A lot has been learned. The demand to align business and IT strategies, however, remains a top issue facing management today.

The chapters in this book present an evolution of the original research and initial book. An international team of authoritative leaders, researchers, consultants, and teachers make up the authors of this important book. Vita of the contributing authors follow the Contents.

While researching, writing, and editing this book, I have become indebted to a large number of individuals and organizations, only a few of whom can be mentioned here. I am greatly appreciative to The Conference Board and Society of Information Systems (SIM) for sponsoring this important research. IBM, especially the Advanced Business Institute, will always be a part of me. Recognition is due to Stevens Institute of Technology for giving me time to research and teach these important ideas to the future leaders of industry, including the participants in the executive information management programs.

Of course, a large degree of thanks is due to the hundreds of organizations that have been used in creating, developing, and advancing the application of the Strategic Alignment Model. This includes the thousands of students attending the Stevens graduate programs, where thought-provoking discussion has led to many of the new insights.

This book is dedicated to the families of all of the contributors. I especially want to dedicate it to my wife, Vivian, who has shown me for over 33 years that being aligned is not just an IT-business thing.

Contents

Sheryl Axline's areas of expertise include team learning, organizational learning, large-scale change, sociotechnical systems and the changing nature of work and careers. Her clients have ranged from long established Fortune 50 corporations to Internet start-ups. Currently, Sheryl assists nonprofit executives with continuous improvement and organizational development. Previously, Sheryl provided consulting and conducted research on human learning, technology, and process change in approximately 50 organizations in North America and Europe. Sheryl holds a Ph.D. in applied psychology and an M.B.A. from Claremont Graduate University and a B.A. in psychology and business administration from UCLA.

Glenn J. Browne is an associate professor of information systems and director of the Institute for Internet Buyer Behavior (IB2) at Texas Tech University. He received his Ph.D. from the Carlson School of Management at the University of Minnesota. As Director of IB2, he manages and conducts research concerning consumer behavior and decision making, business process analysis, and analysis and design considerations for e-business. His other research interests include information requirements determination and behavioral decision-making processes.

Carol V. Brown is an associate professor of information systems in the Kelley School of Business at Indiana University. She holds an A.B. from Vassar College, an M.M. from Northwestern University, and both an M.B.A. and Ph.D. from Indiana University. During 1998–2000, she served on the executive board of SIM International, and she currently is the president of the SIM-Indianapolis chapter and serves as an associate editor for *MIS Quarterly* and *MIS Quarterly Executive*.

Carol's research on IT management issues has been published in major academic journals such as *MIS Quarterly, Organization Science,* and *Information Systems Research*. Her coauthored publications for practitioners include *Repositioning the IT Organization to Enable Business Transformation* (Pinnaflex, 1999) and *Managing Information Technology* (4th edition, Prentice Hall, 2002), and she is the editor of the 7th edition of the *IS Management Handbook* (Auerbach, 2000).

Yolande E. Chan is an associate professor of management information systems at Queen's University. She holds a Ph.D. from the University of Western

Ontario, an M. Phil. in management studies from Oxford University, and S.M. and S.B. degrees in electrical engineering and computer science from the Massachusetts Institute of Technology. She is a Rhodes Scholar. Prior to joining Queen's, Dr. Chan worked with Andersen Consulting (now Accenture) as an information systems consultant. Dr. Chan conducts research on knowledge management, the alignment of information systems strategy and business strategy, and business and societal impacts of information technology investments. She has published her research in a number of refereed books and journals.

Dr. Eric K. Clemons is a professor of operations and information management at the Wharton School, University of Pennsylvania. He is a pioneer in the study of the impacts of information on business strategy. Dr. Clemons is the founder and Project Director for the Reginald H. Jones Center's Sponsored Research Project on Information: Strategy and Economics, area coordinator of the School's major in Information: Strategy, Systems, and Economics, and director of the School's MBA eCommerce major. Dr. Clemons focuses on helping clients anticipate the impacts of information technology on the structure of their industries and the strategies available to their firms.

Thomas H. Davenport is director of the Accenture Institute for Strategic Change and a Distinguished Scholar in Residence at Babson College. He is a widely published author and speaker on the topics of information and knowledge management, reengineering, enterprise systems, and electronic business. Tom's latest book—coauthored with John Beck—is *The Attention Economy* (Harvard Business School Press), which describes how individuals and organizations can manage "the new currency of business." Prior to this, Tom wrote, coauthored, or edited eight other books, including the first books on business process reengineering, knowledge management, and enterprise systems. He has written over 100 articles for such publications as *Harvard Business Review, Sloan Management Review, California Management Review,* the *Financial Times,* and many other publications, and has been a columnist for *Information Week, CIO,* and *Darwin* magazines.

Michael J. Earl is dean of Templeton College, Oxford, and also chairman of the Centre for the Network Economy at London Business School. He works at the intersection of business strategy and IT and is concerned especially with the strategic management of information resources. His recent research has been on the role of the CIO, cross-cultural aspects of information management, the impact of e-commerce on IT, and strategies for knowledge management. He has published in journals such as *Harvard Business Review, MIS Quarterly, Sloan Management Review,* and the *Journal of Management Information Systems.*

Dana Edberg is an associate professor of computer information systems at the University of Nevada, Reno. Her work experience includes software engineering project management in government and industry as well as consulting and training experience in IS organizational management and software design processes. Dr. Edberg's research projects have included evaluations of large-scale information systems projects for government, methods of systems acquisition, development of data warehouses, and application of organizational learning methodologies. Her areas of expertise include software engineering, knowledge management, and database design. She holds a Ph.D. from the School of Information Science at Claremont Graduate University.

Harvey G. Enns is an assistant professor of information systems in the MIS, Operations Management, and Decision Sciences Department at the University of Dayton. He received his Ph.D. from the Richard Ivey School of Business at the University of Western Ontario. His research focuses on the exercise of influence by information technology professionals and the diffusion of IT innovations in developing countries. He has published in the *Journal of Strategic Information Systems* and the *Journal of Global Information Technology Management* as well as presented papers at conferences such as the International Conference on Information Systems and the Academy of Management.

David Feeny is a Fellow of Templeton College, University of Oxford, and director of the Oxford Institute of Information Management. His teaching and research interests center on the connections between strategy, organization, and information technology. He contributes to a large proportion of the College's programs for senior executives, whose participants are drawn from a wide range of industries. His work has won international recognition, and he has published a number of articles in the MIT Sloan Management Review in recent years—on CIOs, IT Sourcing, Core IS Capabilities, CEOs for the Information Age, and E-Business Opportunity.

David is a Fellow of the Royal Society of Arts and Commerce. He holds an M.A. from Oxford University and an M.B.A. from Harvard Business School. He was vice president of Templeton College from 1995 to 1999, and is currently an Advisory Board Member of two new venture companies.

Sid Huff is professor and Ericsson Chair of information systems at Victoria University of Wellington, New Zealand, and is the head of the School of Information Management. He has been teaching and researching in the information systems field for over 25 years. His current research focuses on electronic commerce, IS strategy, and senior management roles in IT. He has taught at universities in the United States, Canada, and New Zealand, and has published extensively in the leading information systems journals. He has also written over 50 teaching cases, and is the lead author of *Cases in Electronic Commerce*, the second edition of which was recently published by Irwin/McGraw-Hill.

Blake Ives holds the C. T. Bauer Chair in Business Leadership at the University of Houston. He is president of the Association for Information Systems and one of its first Fellows. He holds the MISQ's Distinguished Researcher Award and is a past MISQ editor-in-chief. He has held research Fellowships at IBM, the Harvard Business School, and Oxford University. His work has been published in *MISQ, Sloan Management Review, Management Science, Information Systems Research, CACM, IBM Systems Journal, Journal of MIS, Academy of Management Executive,* and *Decision Sciences.* He is a past member of the board of directors for SIM International and the founder of ISWorld Net.

Sirkka L. Jarvenpaa is the James Bayless/Rauscher Pierce Refsnes Chair in business administration at the University of Texas at Austin. At the University of Texas at Austin, she serves as codirector of the Center for Business, Technology, and Law, and a track leader in the cross-functional Customer Insight Center. Her current research projects focus on mobile business and managing knowledge and intelligence in network structures.

C. Timothy Koeller is professor of economics in the Wesley J. Howe School of Technology Management at Stevens Institute of Technology. His research in labor economics, industrial relations, and industrial economics has appeared in a number of journals, including *The Quarterly Journal of Economics, Industrial Relations (Berkeley), Managerial and Decision Economics, Small Business Economics,* and the *Journal of Labor Research,* on which he also is a member of the editorial board. The National Science Foundation, the U.S. Small Business Administration, the U.S. Department of Labor, and the N.J. Department of Higher Education have supported his research. He earned A.B., M.A., and Ph.D. degrees in economics from Rutgers University, an M.S. in economics from Auburn University, and held a University Fellowship in economics at Washington University in St. Louis.

Jerry Luftman is the executive director of graduate information systems programs and professor of information systems at Stevens Institute of Technology. His career includes strategic positions in management (information technology, including being a CIO, and consulting), management consulting, information systems, and education. After a notable 22-year career with IBM, and over 10 years at Stevens, Dr. Luftman's experience combines the strengths of practitioner, consultant, and academic. His framework for applying the strategic alignment model and assessing alignment maturity is key in helping companies around the world understand, define, and scope an appropriate strategic planning direction that leverages information technology.

M. Lynne Markus is professor (chair) of electronic business at the City University of Hong Kong (on leave from the Peter F. Drucker Graduate School of Management, Claremont Graduate University). Professor Markus has over 20 years' experience teaching, conducting research, and consulting in the information systems field. Her current research interests include the strategic positioning of electronic marketplaces, the challenges of B2B systems integration, and interorganizational change management around B2B e-business initiatives. Markus holds a B.S. in industrial engineering from the University of Pittsburgh and a Ph.D. in organizational behavior from Case Western Reserve University.

Ephraim R. McLean is a professor and holder of the George E. Smith Eminent Scholar's Chair. Prior to joining the GSU faculty in 1987, he was on the faculty at UCLA for 18 years; and before that he worked for seven years for Procter and Gamble, primarily doing manufacturing management and information systems work. He has published over 125 articles in publications such as the *Harvard Business Review, Sloan Management Review, California Management Review, MIS Quarterly, Information Systems Research, Management Science, Journal of MIS, Communications of the ACM,* and the *Proceedings* of ICIS, ECIS, HICSS, and AMCIS. He is the coauthor or coeditor of seven books.

Jeff Nickerson is an associate professor of technology management at Stevens Institute of Technology, and director of the e-commerce program. Before he went to Stevens, Dr. Nickerson held several industry positions, including electronic publishing work at Time Inc., image processing at AT&T, and pioneering work in distributed systems on Wall Street, with associate director and vice president positions at Bear Stearns and Salomon Inc. As a partner at PricewaterhouseCoopers, he led the firm's thinking on issues related to Internet technology. He holds a Ph.D. in computer science from New York University. Dr. Nickerson's current research interests include workflow, web services, and resilient systems.

David Petrie is a Ph.D. candidate at the School of Information Science, Claremont Graduate University. He has studied the business value of, and IT architectural issues around, ERP system implementations since 1997 and has 20 years of practical IS experience with manufacturing, financial services, and telecommunications firms. David's dissertation research concerns how companies deal with technological discontinuities such as that created by the Internet and business-to-business electronic commerce. He teaches at California State University, Fullerton.

Gabriele Piccoli is assistant professor of information technology at the School of Hotel Administration at Cornell University. His research interests relate to strategic deployment of information systems and the business application of network and Internet technologies in support of external activities, such as customer service, and internal activities, such as training and teamwork. His research has appeared in *MIS Quarterly, Information Technology,* and *Management and Communications of the AIS.*

Scott L. Schneberger, Computer Information Systems Department, J. Mack Robinson School of Business, Georgia State University, is a visiting professor from the Richard Ivey School of Business at the University of Western Ontario, where he taught information systems and e-commerce to M.B.A.s and executive M.B.A.s. Scott has published in the areas of information system complexity, educational technology, e-commerce, and software maintenance.

James A. Senn is professor and former chair of the Department of Computer Systems at Georgia State University in Atlanta. Under his leadership, the department's programs in information systems were ranked second only to the Massachusetts of Information Technology. Senn speaks and consults extensively on successful technology and business strategies and on the development, implementation, and management of information technology applications. His client list includes many well-known "blue chip" firms from Europe, Asia, and the Americas. He is also a highly regarded facilitator at corporate and technology planning sessions.

Professor Edward A. Stohr holds a Bachelor of Civil Engineering degree from Melbourne University, Australia, and M.B.A. and Ph.D. degrees in Information Science from the University of California, Berkeley. He is currently associate dean for research and academics at the Howe School of Technology Management, Stevens Institute of Technology, Hoboken, New Jersey. His research interests are centered on the problems of developing computer systems to support work and decision making in organizations. He is the editor of two books on decision support systems and has published articles in many leading journals. In 1992, Professor Stohr served as chairman of the executive board of the *International Conference on Information Systems (ICIS)*. He is on the editorial board of a number of leading journals in the information systems field and also has acted as consultant to a number of major corporations.

Kerem Tomak is an assistant professor in the MSIS Department of the McCombs School of Business. His primary research is in the area of economics of information systems. His recent projects focus on economics analysis of online auctions, business-to-business network formation, and online purchasing behavior. He received his Ph.D. from Purdue University. He is a member of INFORMS, IEEE, AEA, and ACM.

James C. Wetherbe is the Stevenson Chair of information technology and executive director of the Institute for Internet Buyer Behavior at Texas Tech University. He is the author of 18 books and over 200 articles on systems analysis and design, strategic use and management of information systems, information requirements determination, and cycle time reduction. He is quoted often in leading business and information systems journals, and was ranked by *Information Week* as one of the top dozen information technology consultants. He was the first recipient of the MIS Quarterly Distinguished Scholar Award.

Competing in the Information Age

Jerry Luftman

Introduction

Alignment is the perennial chart topper on top-ten lists of information technology (IT) issues. For at least 15 years, it has been at or near number one in studies conducted by academics, consultants, and research firms. Educating line management on information technology's possibilities and limitations is hard; so is setting IT priorities for projects, developing resources and skills, and integrating systems with corporate strategy. It is even tougher to keep business and IT aligned, as business strategies and technologies evolve. Economic shifts caused by events such as innovative entrepreneurial ideas, regulatory changes, new technology, war, and scandals bring dramatic swings in how to appropriately respond. The endless, quicksilver shifting of business strategies and technology makes aligning them as difficult as surveying sand dunes in the Sahara. Organizations must draw "a line" in the sand, however, and continuously ensure that the process for aligning IT and business is appropriately managed.

Why has this important issue remained for so long on the top of so many surveys? Is it as difficult as drawing a line in the sand? One of the biggest reasons has been the continuous pursuit of a silver bullet—the one answer that will ensure IT-business alignment. The experts contributing to the insights presented in this book recognize that there is *no one* answer. They present many ideas and approaches. Some are new; some are not. IT-business alignment is a continuous process that comprises many contributing factors. A dominant theme of this book is that *all* of these factors must be understood and regularly worked on to ensure alignment and the innovative business transformations that it can deliver.

At the corporate level, IT—by improving communications and reducing the bureaucratic costs associated with managing the relationships between corporate headquarters and divisions, among divisions, and among external strategic partners—has allowed organizations to be more effective and efficient. IT facilitates the sharing of knowledge and information not just inside business units but also among business units and external partners and customers. IT improves the base of knowledge that employees draw on when they engage in problem solving and decision making; IT provides a mechanism to promote collaboration and information sharing both inside and across business units and with external partners and customers. IT is changing organizational forms and promoting innovation inside global, virtual organizational forms. The real power of IT-enabled virtual organizations emerges when relationships among electronically connected people or firms produce new or qualitatively different communication that yields product/ service or process innovation.

The information age has opened new channels for selling products. The Internet is not just a vehicle for advertising. It is a place for a firm to conduct its marketing (e.g., advertising, selling, market research, forming relation-ships, branding, service delivery). IT's effect on interorganizational relation-ships such as joint ventures or strategic alliances is becoming an increasingly important topic, given the promise that business-to-business networks will provide increased organizational efficiency and innovation. IT also affects strategic alliances in other ways. For instance, aside from electronically link-ing backward with suppliers, firms may use IT to link forward in the value chain to connect their operations with those of customers and customers' customers. Increasingly, IT is being used in strategic alliances to break down barriers between industries and to link divergent value chains. New standards in customer service demand a comprehensive blend of customer relationship management and excellent products. Many suggest that those competitors with the best information systems and intelligence will be the winners. It is not surprising that these firms are quickly digitizing their business to achieve product and service innovation and cost savings.

This dynamic environment demands that organizations be agile and flexible. Often by the time a seemingly optimal solution is deployed, it is obsolete. Competing in the information age will require organizations con-tinuously not only to rethink their product offerings but also the very nature of how they provide value to customers.

Reading about or even experiencing this environment, however, still leaves executives with many unanswered questions:

- Is our organization leveraging its investments in IT?
- Are we achieving competitive advantage through IT?
- How can we achieve IT-business alignment?
- Is the alignment appropriate for our organization?
- How does it compare to other organizations?
- What can be done to improve IT-business alignment?

Although technology innovation cycles have shortened, computer adop-tion times have remained at about seven years. This is because of the time it takes to institutionalize the respective managerial, social, cultural, and organizational changes necessary to effectively deploy the technology and make related changes to the firm. Establishing trust is frequently overlooked. The often-missed message is that the technology is relatively easy to imple-ment, compared with the complexity of the organizational changes necessary to attain value.

Additionally, in the past, technology-differentiated organizations with deep pockets had a competitive buffer. Today, technology is within easy reach of any potential market entrant. If your organization perceives the Internet (you can substitute any information technology you desire; e.g., customer relationship management, wireless communication, data mining, virtual advisors) as an application tool, it will likely focus on building a good application. This probably will not provide much value because your competitors will be doing the same thing. If the technology is perceived as a strategic tool where you focus on differentiating your organization from competitors, however, your organization needs to build an aligned IT-business strategy.

Organizations should not be defined just as the sum of their parts (organizations that constitute the firm). They also must be defined by the interrelations that exist among and across these parts. This means that organizational characteristics must address the interactions across/among organizations. These complex interactions needed to integrate organizations, along with the expectations demanded by the relationships among stakeholders across/among organizations, define alignment. As They Hsieh (*Chinese Epigrams Inside Out, and Proverbs* [New York: Exposition Press, 1948]) appropriately said, "Harmony would lose its attractiveness if it did not have a background of discord."

Organizations need to understand what can be done to leverage IT so that it can be recognized as an enabler/driver of profits. The firm must be able to be responsive in its ability to quickly adapt to the ever-changing conditions. That is the objective of the maturity assessment discussed in chapter 1. My research has found that it is a combination of six components (communications, value measurement, governance, partnership, scope and architecture, and skills) that all must be done to attain mature alignment. There is no one silver bullet.

As an analogy: Providing a large income for your family is important. It is not the only thing, however, that ensures happiness. Other considerations include love, sensitivity, communications, partnership, and faithfulness. If any one of these elements is missing, so is the success of the family. All must be done to attain a successful family. There is no one silver bullet.

Alignment is like drawing a line in the sand, but achieving alignment is possible. Practitioners and researchers have found ways to look at alignment and turn their insights into action items. The results provide a surprise: Alignment is not just about vision statements. It is not even just about the goal that IT and non-IT executives are striving to attain. A decade of research has found that the key is building a consensus around the right relationships and processes that focus on the six maturity components. It takes success at all six to ensure mature IT-business alignment.

The six key components needed to assess an understanding of IT-business alignment are:

1. Communications
2. Competency/value measurement
3. Governance
4. Partnership

5. Scope and Architecture
6. Skills

A model has been developed and tested that involves assessing each of the six criteria listed above based on five levels of strategic alignment maturity. Figure I.1 illustrates the five levels, with level 1 the least mature, level 5 the most mature. The more mature IT-business relationships exist, as the alignment gap gets smaller. Figure 1.3 expands the six components of maturity. The model is based on practice validated with an initial evaluation of 25 Fortune 500 companies. As of this publication, over 50 Global 2,000 organizations and government agencies have successfully applied the assessment. The Conference Board and Society of Information Management (SIM) are continuing the sponsorship of this important benchmarking activity.

The strategic alignment maturity assessment (expanded in chapter 1) provides organizations with a vehicle to evaluate these activities. Knowing the maturity of its strategic choices and alignment practices makes it possible for a firm to see where it stands and how it can improve. In the past, methods have been introduced that address one or a few of the criteria. Focusing on anything less than all six components will put IT-business alignment at risk, as with the success of a family.

This book goes beyond what must be done. It addresses how IT and

Figure I.1. Climbing the Strategic Alignment Maturity Model

business organizations can work together to improve business performance. The book elaborates on the approach for assessing the maturity of business-IT alignment; once maturity is understood, an organization can identify opportunities for enhancing the harmonious relationship of business and IT.

The intent here is to provide a synthesis of the most recent work in the area of IT-business strategic alignment, emphasizing its practical application and maturity. The six components of the strategic alignment assessment will provide the framework for the chapters. The book is an evolution from *Competing in the Information Age: Strategic Alignment in Practice*, 1996, with all new chapters, contributed by the leading thinkers in IT business strategies.

The book provides business and IT professionals in the area of strategic planning and management information systems with a practical guide to aligning IT-Business strategies. It also will have a market in advanced M.B.A./M.S. and Ph.D. courses in strategy and the strategic use of information technologies.

The second dominant theme of the book will be the effective/efficient use of information technology as a response to a rapidly changing competitive business and technical environment. Lou Gerstner, the CEO of IBM, said, "There is no new economy . . . the wars haven't changed; it's just that somebody has invented gunpowder." Given the uncertainty, complexity, and dynamic nature of this environment, this effective response is no easy task. Specifically, these propositions are developed in the book as essential for firms' survival:

1. Continuous transformation of the business
2. Adoption of information/knowledge intensive management practices
3. Increasing the ability to effectively and efficiently process information/ knowledge
4. Improved maturity of the alignment of the business strategy and the information technology strategy

The book is divided into eight parts, with parts II–VII focusing on the six strategic alignment maturity assessment criteria.

⦂ *Align in the Sand*

I describe the strategic alignment maturity assessment in chapter 1. It is the foundation of this book. Mature alignment evolves into a relationship where IT and other business functions adapt their strategies together. It does not matter whether one considers business-IT alignment or IT-business alignment; the objective is to ensure that the organizational strategies adapt harmoniously. Once the maturity is understood, the assessment method provides the organization with a roadmap that identifies opportunities for enhancing the harmonious relationship of business and IT and for making IT a recognized enabler/driver of business value.

▪ Communications

Earl, in chapter 2, "Integrating Business and IT Strategy Reframing the Applications Development Portfolio," suggests that whether firms choose to integrate their formal business and IT strategies or not, they certainly need to integrate their business and IT thinking. As the theory and practice of strategy making in both the business and IT domains have evolved, it is useful to consider IT and business working together to assess portfolios of opportunities.

One perspective is time. In bad times organizations worry that the short term drives out the long term. In heady times, the emphasis seems often to be the reverse. Earl's T-Portfolio examines how a firm is competing for today and for tomorrow. It provides a tool to engage in executive discussion about the appropriate balance at different times.

In chapter 3, "Recognizing the Functionality of the Future," Wetherbe and Browne suggest that building sustainable competitive advantage (and products and services that approach perfection) in the future requires that organizations discover the functionality partners require and desire. To do this successfully, organizations will have to harness information technology to help gather requirements in new ways.

▪ Competency/Value Measurement

Ask 10 different IT or business leaders how best to measure the value of IT investments, and you will likely get at least 10 different approaches. In chapter 4, "Assessing the Value of IT," Koeller and Luftman argue that traditional financial techniques (e.g., Return on Investment, Discounted Cash Flows, Net Present Value) have shortcomings that need to be recognized.

It is the combination of getting IT and business to work together creating a Total Value of Ownership using a portfolio management, real options analysis, and a value management approach that is most effective.

The value management approach provides organizations seeking an IT-leveraged path to competitiveness with a model that can help to identify improvements in customer-focused processes. First, it enables understanding the business objectives and value. Second, the business process changes necessary to obtain the business value are reviewed. Finally, the information technologies necessary to change the business process that will bring the business value are defined. IT and business management must work together to identify these organizational benefits.

In chapter 5, "Sustainable Competitive Advantage Through IT," Feeny, Ives, and Piccoli introduce a framework for discussing the ways in which IT can enable/drive lasting benefits to the firm. They argue that competitive advantage generally does not stem from "visionary" initiatives but from "evolutionary" ones that begin with an IT-based response to perceived environmental pressure or opportunities and a commitment to continuous learning. Often organizational learning, a basis for sustainability, can only begin once the strategic initiative is enacted. This suggests that IT-enabled strategic initiatives can foster the development of capabilities that will evolve into strategies not readily envisioned at the start.

Jarvenpaa and Tomak, in chapter 6, "Competing With Mobile Technologies," contend that executives making decisions that aim to maximize the business value of their IT investments receive guidance from scholarly work on strategic alignment. Today, an increasing portion of their decisions involves investments in wireless technologies and coopting business resources. Wireless technologies extend a firm's transactions from a stationary virtual space to a mobile space. Mobility extends the access, reach, and richness of transactions, processes, knowledge, and relationships beyond those reached by wired information and communication technologies.

⦙ *IT Governance*

The complexities of information technology and business in the twenty-first century require organizations to make informed decisions about how best to leverage IT. Most important, organizations need to ensure that the decisions about deploying IT are aligned with the organization's strategic business objectives. Organizations also need to ensure that decisions about the strategic direction and deployment of IT are consistent across the firm and that they are in harmony with the organizational culture. Successful organizations in today's information economy integrate IT and business strategies and leverage customers and partners in a web of relationships that share information. But how should organizations make decisions about the deployment of IT? Which projects should be funded? Should organizations "make" or "buy" systems and software? Who should make these decisions? How should organizations make decisions about partners and alliances? Finally, what processes should organizations use to make these critical decisions? In chapter 7, "IT Governance," I answer these important questions.

In chapter 8, "IT Organization of the Future," Brown discusses three dimensions of governance: IT decision rights, IT coordination mechanisms, and IT sourcing arrangements. Each dimension is concerned with organizational design alternatives for achieving alignment across IT management, business partners, and IT service providers. The least-recognized IT governance dimension, IT coordination mechanisms, is often critical. For example, organizations faced with asking business units to relinquish IT decision rights can still maintain a strong IT-business lateral capability by implementing new structural overlays and informal mechanisms. Similarly, when IT functions are outsourced, a strong IT-business partnership can still be retained if coordination mechanisms are put in place to link the internal relationship managers for the outsourcer and the business unit. Today, these interpersonal networks also can be supplemented with media-rich technologies to communicate and collaborate across geographical boundaries. Each of these scenarios suggests that the ability to manage the three IT governance dimensions will be an important IT leadership capability in the information age.

: *Partnership*

Huff, Enns, and Schneberger, in chapter 9, "The Influential CIO: Establishing An IT-Business Partnership," maintain that it is not enough to just have excellent plans and strategies on paper. CIOs must be able to convince other peer executives of IT's contribution to the business. One key to this is the ability of the CIO to exert effective influence on their peers.

CIOs today are involved in shaping and supporting business strategy. They exert their influence in more areas than just IT projects. Consequently, it is important for CIOs to understand the nature and use of influence in organizations. Having power and effectively exercising influence are preconditions for accomplishing tasks in organizations The CIO who exercises influence well potentially can be more effective in future IT strategy planning, IT implementation, and business strategy planning efforts.

: *Scope and Architecture*

To attain the many benefits available in the information age demands the effective use of cutting edge technologies. These include individual technologies such as networks, knowledge, data, and applications. It also includes the integration of these technologies both across the firm and with external partners. Some readers might find the discussion in this section difficult to relate to alignment or perhaps too technical. Scope and architecture is the only technical criterion included in the alignment maturity assessment. It is important to recognize that, as with the other criteria, executives must have an appropriate understanding and strategy that addresses how the business can leverage these technologies.

Corporations grow and, as they grow, the need for integration across the enterprise increases. Integration, as presented by Stohr and Nickerson in chapter 10, "Intra Enterprise Systems Strategies," can be accomplished through various means. Integration is really a business need, and the technology mechanisms won't help without the proper organizational structures, goals, and incentives. Both organizational and technological integration is necessary. The objective of chapter 10 is to outline the major managerial issues and describe a range of technical approaches to integration. After a discussion of organizational integration, the chapter describes a new technology-based mechanism for coordination.

In chapter 11, "Toward The Future of Enterprise Integration: Inter-Enterprise Systems Integration," Markus, Edberg, and Petrie focus on external systems integration. External systems integration refers to IT-mediated transactions between independent business entities. For example, between a company and its customers, suppliers, or other business partners, such as coproducers and banks, and its importance to both economic and strategic business reasons. Leveraging these important relationships should be an important element of any firms' strategy.

In chapter 12, "Learning and Earning From E-Commerce," Earl argues that the discontinuity of e-commerce has left organizations with the promise of four IT management practices—strategic information systems planning, IT architecture planning, managing IT-user relationships, and systems development methodology—that should be captured, retained, and developed, and certainly not dismissed as freak practices of a dizzy time. Indeed, these practices might be elevated to the level of principles.

In chapter 13, "Attention and Knowledge Management Strategies," Davenport reasons that any ambitious initiative in business needs substantial attention from substantial people over substantial periods of time. Although humanity's information base is growing by revolutionary leaps and bounds, the ability of individual humans to absorb that knowledge has changed little, if at all. This situation leads to an obvious need not for more information but, rather, for more human attention—with no obvious way to fill it!

The management of attention in business is an entirely new subject. As the amount of information and knowledge that flows through organizations continues to grow, there is little doubt that creative new methods for allocating and even growing it will develop. By devoting some attention-to-attention, organizations can begin to focus on the information and knowledge that really matters to their success.

Clemons, in chapter 14, "Strategic IT Infrastructure Considerations," uses scenario analysis to help manage strategic uncertainty by anticipating possible future competitive environments. Anticipating possible alternative future environments will assist in identifying possible alternative future systems requirements. As noted in a military context, however, "he who defends everything defends nothing"; similarly, he who attempts to prepare for everything prepares for nothing. Thus, there is a need for a mechanism to determine which contingencies to prepare for and, thus, which investments to make. There is also a need to identify when to defer, when to proceed, and how to proceed rapidly and effectively when the time comes to act. This will, at worst, enable firms to avoid strategic disadvantage, and may indeed confer competitive advantage relative to other industry participants.

Senn, in chapter 15, "Business and IT Infrastructure Strategies In An Ever-Mobile World," examines the rapid growth of wireless devices and the current and emerging alternative technologies that underlie their use. He describes the different categories of emerging wireless networking applications and focuses on the specific issues that business and IT managers need to address to systematically capitalize on the potential benefits of deploying wireless networks. He argues that unless IT managers explicitly confront these issues, they will encounter difficult strategic challenges in the future.

Despite our differing viewpoints, few of us would disagree that, in the information age, astute information systems management is high on the list of credible responses. It seems that information—whether corporate, personal, or financial, or in individual pockets or massive databases—has become one of our most valuable commodities. Chan, in chapter 16, "Competing Through Information Privacy," discusses how personal (as contrasted with publicly available) information is managed, with whose interests in mind, and how these issues fit into the already complex information management challenges. She argues that privacy represents a significant challenge for businesses that needs to be addressed in terms of firm strategy and alignment.

: Skills

In chapter 17, "IT Personnel Strategies for the Future," McLean and Schneberger argue that competitive advantage in future business environments will come not from applying corporate capital to the right information technology but by applying the right *human* capital to information technology. This human capital includes all IT professionals as well as all corporate users of IT. Successful IT competitive strategies will depend more on *how* IT is applied than to *what* IT is applied. In some ways, applying the right human capital is more difficult than applying the right IT.

: Aligning This Book

In chapter 18, "Strategic Alignment As a Process," I explain how alignment evolves into a relationship in which IT and other business units adapt their strategies together. This ties—aligns—the chapters of this book together. Achieving alignment is evolutionary and dynamic. It requires strong support from senior management, good working relationships, strong leadership, appropriate prioritization, trust, and effective communication, as well as a thorough understanding of the business and technical environments. Chapter 18 brings together many of the ideas presented in this book to describe a process that maximizes the enablers and minimizes the inhibitors, with the purpose of cultivating alignment. This process has proven to help achieve and sustain a high level of alignment maturity. It is a continuous process.

I

Align in the Sand

1

Jerry Luftman

Assessing Strategic Alignment Maturity

▪ *Chapter Summary*

1. Alignment addresses both how IT is aligned with the business and how the business should or could be aligned with IT. When discussing business-IT alignment, terms such as harmony, linkage, fusion, fit, match, and integration are frequently used synonymously with the term alignment. Alignment is about a process to ensure that the organizational strategies adapt harmoniously.

2. Alignment of IT strategy with the organization's business strategy is a fundamental principle advocated for over 15 years. Why has something that has been considered so important for so many years taken so long to effectively address? The answer is that there are no silver bullets. By focusing on assessing six areas that have been identified as critical to the success of alignment, organizations can understand and improve the maturity of their organizations IT-business alignment.

3. Knowing the maturity of its strategic choices and alignment practices make it possible for a firm to see where it stands and how it can improve. Once the maturity is understood, the assessment method provides the organization with a roadmap that identifies opportunities for enhancing the business and IT relationship, and to make IT a recognized enabler/driver of business value.

4. Known enablers and inhibitors help and hinder alignment. Executives experience them daily. It is the processes applied that leverage the enablers and avoid the inhibitors that result in aligned IT business strategies. It is the effectiveness of the organizations alignment process that determines alignment maturity.

5. By referring to the characteristics of five maturity levels within each of the six strategic categories, companies can generate numeric scores that reflect the maturity of the organizations IT-business alignment. These scores are being used to benchmark organizations across industries and with exemplar firms. The scores also have been effective in measuring the progress (or lack of progress) of alignment improvement within an organization.

6. The methodology was validated and applied through studies of over 50 Global 2000 organizations. Thanks to the sponsorship by The Conference Board Inc. in New York and the Society for Information Management in Chicago, more organizations are participating.

: *Introduction*

Business-IT alignment refers to applying Information Technology (IT) in an appropriate and timely way, in harmony with business strategies, goals, and needs. It is still a fundamental concern of business executives. This definition of alignment addresses:

1. How IT is aligned with the business, and
2. How the business should or could be aligned with IT.

Mature alignment evolves into a relationship where IT and other business functions (internally and externally) adapt their strategies together. When discussing business-IT alignment, terms such as harmony, linkage, fusion, fit, match, and integration are frequently used synonymously with the term alignment. It does not matter whether one considers business-IT alignment or IT-business alignment; the objective is to ensure that the organizational strategies adapt harmoniously.

The evidence that IT has the power to transform whole industries and markets is strong (e.g., King, 1995; Luftman, 1996; Earl, 1993; Earl, 1996; Luftman, Lewis, & Oldach, 1993; Goff, 1993; Liebs, 1992; Robson, 1994; Luftman, Papp, & Brier, 1999; Luftman & Brier, 1999). Important questions that need to be addressed include the following:

- How can organizations assess alignment?
- How can organizations improve alignment?
- How can organizations achieve mature alignment?

The purpose of this chapter is to present an approach for assessing the maturity of a firm's business-IT alignment. Until now, none was available. The alignment maturity assessment described in this chapter provides a comprehensive vehicle for organizations to evaluate business-IT alignment in terms of where they are and what they can do to improve alignment. The maturity assessment applies previous research that identified enablers/inhibitors to achieving alignment (Luftman, Papp, & Brier, 1995; Luftman & Brier, 1999), and my consulting experience that applied the methodology (described in chapter 18) that leverages the most important enablers and inhibitors as building blocks for the evaluation. The maturity assessment is also based on the popular work done by the Software Engineering Institute (Humphrey, 1988), Keen's reach and range (Keen 1996) and an evolution of the Nolan and Gibson stages of growth (Nolan 1979).
This chapter is divided into five sections:

1. The Strategic Alignment Maturity Assessment Description—explains the essential components of the maturity assessment.
2. The Six Strategic Alignment Maturity Criteria—illustrates each of the six criteria that are evaluated in deriving the level of strategic alignment maturity. Examples from many of the previously conducted assessments are included.

3. Conducting a Strategic Alignment Maturity Assessment—describes the process applied in carrying out an evaluation. This section ties the respective assessment metrics together. Along with the examples in the appendix, the last section served as the vehicle for validating the model.
4. Conclusions—summarizes the strategic alignment maturity assessment research, to date.
5. Appendices. 1: Strategic Alignment Maturity Assessment Experiences—highlights the experiences with the original 25 Fortune 500 companies that participated in the initial strategic alignment maturity assessments. It also includes summaries of six assessments of Fortune 200 companies and a large university; 2: The Five Levels of Strategic Alignment Maturity—describes each of the five levels of strategic alignment maturity.

The components of the strategic alignment model are shown in figure 1.1 (which is reproduced from Luftman, 1996). The relationships that exist among the 12 components of this model further define business-IT alignment. The components of this model, in concert with the enablers/inhibitors research (Luftman et al., 1999), form the building blocks for the strategic alignment maturity assessment method. Aligning these components focuses on the activities that management performs to achieve cohesive goals across the information technology and other functional organizations (strategic business units; e.g., Finance, Marketing, H/R, Manufacturing).

Therefore, alignment addresses both how IT is in harmony with the business, and how the business should, or could be in harmony with IT. Alignment maturity evolves into a relationship in which the function of IT and other business functions (internal and external) adapt their strategies together. Achieving alignment is evolutionary and dynamic. IT requires strong support from senior management, good working relationships, strong leadership, appropriate prioritization, trust, and effective communication, as well as a thorough understanding of the business and technical environments. Achieving and sustaining alignment demands focusing on maximizing the enablers and minimizing the inhibitors that cultivate the integration of IT and business.

As previously discussed, known enablers and inhibitors help and hinder alignment. Executives experience them daily. Research under way since 1992 (Luftman et al., 1999; Luftman et al., 1995) identified these trends. Analysis of the research data shows that the six most important enablers and inhibitors, in rank order, are those shown in table 1.1. What is striking about table 1.1 is that the same topics (executive support, understanding the business, IT-business relations, and leadership) show up as both enablers and inhibitors. Research included as part of the maturity assessments suggests that these enablers/inhibitors have remained static.

The strategic alignment maturity assessment provides organizations with

I. **Business Strategy**
   1. **Business Scope**—Includes the markets, products, services, groups of customers/clients, and locations where an enterprise competes as well as the competitors and potential competitors that affect the business environment.
   2. **Distinctive Competencies**—The critical success factors and core competencies that provide a firm with a potential competitive edge. This includes brand, research, manufacturing and product development, cost and pricing structure, and sales and distribution channels.
   3. **Business Governance**—How companies set the relationship between management, stockholders, and the board of directors. Also included are how the company is affected by government regulations, and how the firm manages its relationships and alliances with strategic partners.

II. **Organization Infrastructure and Processes**
   4. **Administrative Structure**—The way the firm organizes its businesses. Examples include central, decentral, matrix, horizontal, vertical, geographic, federal, and functional.
   5. **Processes**—How the firm's business activities (the work performed by employees) operate or flow. Major issues include value added activities and process improvement.
   6. **Skills**—H/R considerations such as how to hire/fire, motivate, train/educate, and culture.

III. **IT Strategy**
   7. **Technology Scope**—The important information applications and technologies.
   8. **Systemic Competencies**—Those capabilities (e.g., access to information that is important to the creation/achievement of a company's strategies) that distinguishes the IT services.
   9. **IT Governance**—How the authority for resources, risk, conflict resolution, and responsibility for IT is shared among business partners, IT management, and service providers. Project selection and prioritization issues are included here.

IV. **IT Infrastructure and Processes**
   10. **Architecture**—The technology priorities, policies, and choices that allow applications, software, networks, hardware, and data management to be integrated into a cohesive platform.
   11. **Processes**—Those practices and activities carried out to develop and maintain applications and manage IT infrastructure.
   12. **Skills**—IT human resource considerations such as how to hire/fire, motivate, train/educate, and culture.

Figure 1.1 The twelve components of alignment

Table 1.1
Enablers and Inhibitors of Strategic Alignment (Luftman et al, 1999)

	Enablers	Inhibitors
1	Senior executive support for IT	IT/business lack close relationships
2	IT involved in strategy development	IT does not prioritize well
3	IT understands the business	IT fails to meet commitments
4	Business–IT partnership	IT does not understand business
5	Well-prioritized IT projects	Senior executives do not support IT
6	IT demonstrates leadership	IT management lacks leadership

a vehicle to evaluate these activities. Knowing the maturity of its strategic choices and alignment practices make it possible for a firm to see where it stands and how it can improve. Once the maturity is understood, the assessment method provides the organization with a road map that identifies opportunities for enhancing the harmonious relationship of business and IT, and to make IT a recognized enabler/driver of business value.

Several proposed frameworks assess the strategic issues of IT as a competitive weapon. They have not, however, yielded empirical evidence nor do they provide a road map to assess and enhance alignment. Numerous studies focus on business process redesign and reengineering (Rockart & Short, 1989; Davenport & Short, 1990; Hammer & Champy, 1993; Hammer & Stanton, 1995) as a way to achieve competitive advantage with IT. This advantage comes from the appropriate application of IT as a driver or enabler of business strategy.

Alignment of IT strategy and the organization's business strategy is a fundamental principle advocated for over 15 years (CSC Index studies, Robson, 1994; Rogers, 1997; Rockart, Earl, & Ross, 1996). IT investment has been increasing for years as managers are looking for ways to manage IT successfully and to integrate it into the organization's strategies. As a result, IT managers need to:

- Be knowledgeable about how the new IT technologies can be integrated into the business as well as among the different technologies and architectures
- Be privy to senior management's tactical and strategic plans
- Be present when corporate strategies are discussed
- Understand the strengths and weaknesses of the technologies in question and the corporate-wide implications (Rockart et al., 1996)

It is the processes applied that leverage the enablers and avoid the inhibitors that result in aligned IT business strategies. It is the effectiveness of the process that determines alignment maturity.

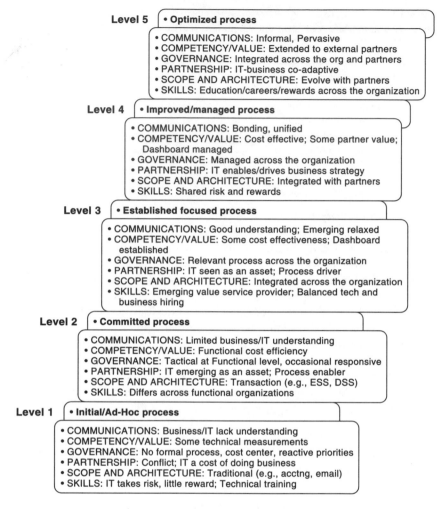

Figure 1.2. Strategic Alignment Maturity summary

▪ *Strategic Alignment Maturity Assessment*

As the summary of the maturity assessment in figure 1.2 illustrates, the model involves the following five levels of strategic alignment maturity:

1. Initial/Ad Hoc Process
2. Committed Process
3. Established Focused Process
4. Improved/Managed Process
5. Optimized Process

Each of the five levels of alignment maturity focuses, in turn, on a set of six criteria based on practice validated with an initial evaluation of 25 Fortune 500 companies. A consolidation of the evaluations is presented in appendix 1 of this chapter. The five levels of maturity are described in detail in appendix 2 of this chapter. A summary of all six components along with their respective five levels can be found at the end of appendix 2.

The six IT-business alignment criteria are illustrated in figure 1.3 and are described in the following section of this chapter. The remaining chapters of this book will be devoted to expanding each of the six criteria. The chapters present many new and previously discussed tools, ideas, and approaches. The important point to keep in mind is that there is *no* silver bullet. It is the appropriate application of these tools, ideas, and approaches while focusing on ALL six maturity criteria that will improve the maturity of IT-business alignment.

These six criteria are:

1. Communications Maturity
2. Competency/Value Measurement Maturity

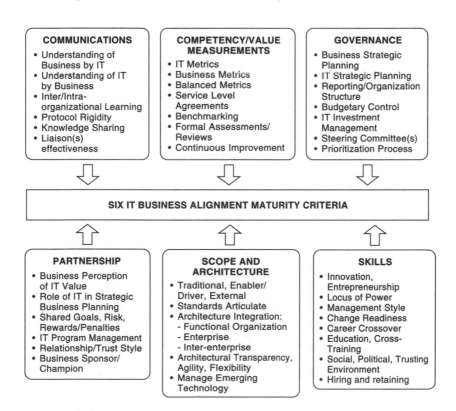

Figure 1.3. Alignment maturity criteria

3. Governance Maturity
4. Partnership Maturity
5. Scope and Architecture Maturity
6. Skills Maturity

The procedure for assessing maturity follows these six steps:

1. *Set the goals and establish a team.* Ensure that there is an executive business sponsor and champion for the assessment. Next, assign a team of both business and IT leaders. Obtaining appropriate representatives from the major business functional organizations (strategic business units; e.g., Marketing, Finance, R&D, Engineering) and IT is critical to the success of the process. The purpose of the team is to evaluate the maturity of the business-IT alignment. Once the maturity is understood, the team is expected to define opportunities for enhancing the harmonious relationship of business and IT. Assessments can be done via interviews, group discussions, questionnaires, or a combination of approaches. The time demanded depends on the number of participants, the approach selected (interviews, group discussions, questionnaires), the degree of consensus required, and the detail of the recommendations to carry out.

2. *Understand the business-IT linkage.* The Strategic Alignment Maturity Assessment is an important tool in understanding the business-IT linkage. The team evaluates each of the six criteria. Typically, they assess each criterion using a scale from one to five. A trained facilitator can be valuable in guiding the process.

3. *Analyze and prioritize gaps.* Recognize that the different opinions raised by the participants are indicative of the alignment opportunities that exist. Once understood, the group needs to converge on a maturity level. The team must remember that the purpose of this step is to understand the activities necessary to improve the business-IT linkage. The gap between where the organization is today and where the team believes it needs to be are the gaps that need to be prioritized. Apply the next higher level of maturity as a road map to identify what can be done to improve.

Attempts at skipping a level have proven ineffective. An organization must evolve through these levels sequentially, while establishing a strong base on which to build, before proceeding to the next higher level. An organization can put a plan in place that applies the maturity assessment as a road map to move forward, but without creating a firm foundation, skipping a level will more likely slow the process rather than expedite it.

4. *Specify the actions (project management).* Naturally, knowing where the organization is in regard to alignment maturity will drive what specific actions are appropriate to enhance IT-business alignment. Assign specific remedial tasks with clearly defined deliverables, ownership, timeframes, resources, risks, and measurements to each of the prioritized gaps.

5. *Choose and evaluate success criteria.* This step necessitates revisiting the

goals and regularly discussing the measurement criteria identified to evaluate the implementation of the project plans. The review of the measurements should serve as a learning vehicle to understand how and why the objectives are or are not being met.

6. *Sustain alignment.* Some problems just won't go away. Why are so many of the inhibitors IT related? Obtaining IT-business alignment is a difficult task, like drawing "a line" in the sand. This last step in the process is often the most difficult. To sustain the benefit from IT, an "alignment behavior" must be developed and cultivated. The criteria described to assess alignment maturity provides characteristics of organizations that link IT and business strategies. By adopting these behaviors, companies can increase their potential for a more mature alignment assessment and improve their ability to gain business value from investments in IT. Hence, the continued focus on understanding the alignment maturity for an organization and taking the necessary action to improve the IT-business harmony is key.

The research to derive the business-IT alignment maturity assessment has just begun. To date, over 50 Global 2000 firms have applied it. I would appreciate hearing from practitioners, researchers, and consultants, as the strategic alignment process and the alignment maturity assessment are applied. The intent is to enhance the alignment assessment tool and provide a vehicle to benchmark exemplar organizations.

This conceptual framework (qualities and attributes) is described in appendix 2. The process of conducting a Strategic Alignment Maturity Assessment is described in more detail in the second main section following. It should be noted that the maturity level is not as important as getting a good understanding of where the team believes they are and how they see the organization improving.

⦂ The Six Strategic Alignment Maturity Criteria

This section describes each of the six criteria (illustrated in figure 1.3) that are evaluated in deriving the level of strategic alignment maturity. Examples taken from actual assessment summaries illustrate the kinds of insights that can be identified. Appendix 1 includes a more complete description of seven of these studies, as well as the benchmark data attained from the first 25 organizations going through a formal assessment.

Most organizations today (from the over 50 Global 2000 companies and government agencies participating in the benchmark at the time of this writing) are at level 2, with some attributes of level 3. This is similar to what the Carnegie Mellon software models have found, identifying the comparable stage of application development. Naturally, the objective of the team applying the Strategic Alignment Maturity model is to identify how the organization can achieve a higher level of IT-business alignment.

Communications

Effective exchange of ideas and a clear understanding of what it takes to ensure successful strategies are high on the list of enablers and inhibitors to alignment. Too often there is little business awareness on the part of IT or little IT appreciation on the part of the business. Given the dynamic environment in which most organizations find themselves, ensuring ongoing knowledge sharing across organizations is paramount.

Many firms choose to draw on liaisons to facilitate this knowledge sharing. The key word is facilitate. Often I have seen facilitators whose role is to serve as the sole conduit of interaction among the different organizations. This approach tends to stifle rather than foster effective communications. Rigid protocols that impede discussions and the sharing of ideas should be avoided.

For example, a large aerospace company assessed its communications alignment maturity at level 2. Business-IT understanding is sporadic. The relationship between IT and the business function could be improved. Improving communication should focus on how to create the understanding of IT as a strategic business partner by the businesses it supports rather than simply a service provider. The firm's CIO made the comment that there was "no constructive partnership." In an interview with the firm's director of Engineering and Infrastructure, however, he said that he viewed his organization as a "strategic business partner." One approach to improve communications and, more important, understanding, would be to establish effective business function/IT liaisons that facilitate sharing of knowledge and ideas.

In a second case, a large financial services company's communication alignment maturity placed it in level 2 with some attributes of level 1. Business awareness within IT is through specialized IT business analysts, who understand and translate the business needs to other IT staff (i.e., there is limited awareness of business by general IT staff). Awareness of IT by the firm's business functions, is also limited, although senior and mid-level management is aware of the potential of IT. Communications are achieved through biweekly priority meetings attended by the senior and middle level management from both groups, where they discuss requirements, priorities, and IT implementation.

In a third example, a large utility company's communication alignment maturity places it at level 2−. Communications are not open until circumstances force the business to identify specific needs. There is a lack of trust and openness between some business units and their IT team. IT business partners tend to be bottlenecks in meeting commitments. Its poor performance in previous years left scars that have not healed.

Competency/Value Measurements

Too many IT organizations cannot demonstrate their value to the business in terms that the business understands. Frequently, business and IT metrics of value differ. A balanced "dashboard" that demonstrates the value of IT in terms of contribution to the business is needed. Chapter 4 describes an effective approach for IT and business to work together to demonstrate IT value.

Service levels that assess IT's commitments to the business often help. The service levels have to be expressed in terms that the business understands and accepts, however. The service levels should be tied to criteria (see the section on partnership in this chapter) that clearly define the rewards and penalties for surpassing or missing the objectives.

Frequently, organizations devote significant resources to measuring performance factors. They spend much less of their resources on taking action based on these measurements, however. For example, an organization that requires a Return on Investment (ROI) before a project begins, but that does not review how well objectives were met after the project was deployed, provides little to the organization. It is important to assess these criteria to understand (1) the factors that lead to missing the criteria and (2) what can be learned to improve the environment continuously.

For example, a large aerospace company assessed its competency/value measurements to be at level 2. IT operates as cost center. IT metrics are focused at the functional level, and Service Level Agreements (SLAs) are technical in nature. One area that could help to improve maturity would be to add more business-related metrics to SLAs to help form more of a partnership between IT and the business units. Periodic formal assessments and reviews in support of continuous improvement also would be beneficial.

A large software development company assessed its competency/value measurement maturity at level 3. Established metrics evaluate the extent of service provided to the business functions. These metrics go beyond basic service availability and help desk responsiveness, evaluating such issues as end-user satisfaction and application development effectiveness. The metrics are consolidated on to an overall dashboard. Because no formal feedback mechanisms are in place to react to a metric, however, the dashboard cannot be considered as well managed.

At a large financial services company, it competency/value was assessed at a level 2 because they use cost efficiency methods within the business and functional organizations. Balanced metrics are emerging through linked business and it metrics, and a balanced scorecard is provided to senior management. Service level agreements are technical at the functional level. Benchmarking is not generally practiced and is informal in the few areas where it is practiced. Formal assessments are done typically for problems and minimum measurements are taken after the assessment of failures.

Governance

The considerations for IT governance were defined briefly in figure 1.1. They are expanded in Luftman and Brier (1999) and in chapter 7. Ensuring that the appropriate business and IT participants formally discuss and review the priorities and allocation of IT resources is among the most important enablers/inhibitors of alignment. This decision-making authority needs to be clearly defined.

For example, IT governance in a large aerospace company is tactical at the core business level and not consistent across the enterprise. For this reason, they reported a level 2 maturity assessment. IT can be characterized as reactive to CEO direction. Developing an integrated enterprise-wide strategic business plan for IT would facilitate better partnering within the firm and would lay the groundwork for external partnerships with customers and suppliers.

A large communications manufacturing company assessed its governance maturity at a level falling between 1 and 2. IT does little strategic planning because it operates as a cost center and, therefore, cost reduction is a key objective. In addition, priorities are reactive to business needs as business managers' request services.

A large computing services company assessed their governance maturity at level 1+. A strategic planning committee meets twice a year. The committee consists of corporate top management with regional representation. Topics or results are not discussed or published to all employees. The reporting structure is federated with the CIO reporting to a COO. IT investments are traditionally made to support operations and maintenance. Regional or corporate sponsors are involved with some projects. Prioritization is occasionally responsive.

Partnership

The relationship that exists between the business and IT organizations is another criterion that ranks high among the enablers and inhibitors. Giving the IT function the opportunity to have an equal role in defining business strategies is obviously important. How each organization perceives the contribution of the other, the trust that develops among the participants, ensuring appropriate business sponsors and champions of IT endeavors, and the sharing of risks and rewards, however, are all major contributors to mature alignment. This partnership should evolve to a point where IT both enables *and* drives changes to both business processes and strategies. Naturally, this demands having a good business design, in which the CIO and CEO share a clearly defined vision.

For example, a large software development company assessed their partnership maturity at level 2. The IT function is mainly an enabler for the company. IT does not have a seat at the business table, either with the enterprise or with the business function that is making a decision. In the majority of cases, there are no shared risks because only the business will fail. Indications are that the partnership criterion will rise from level 2 to 3 as top management sees IT as an asset, and because of the very high enforcement of standards at the company.

Partnership for a large communications manufacturing company was assessed at level 1. IT is perceived as a cost of being in the communications business. Little value is placed on the IT function. IT is perceived only as help desk support and network maintenance.

For a large utility company, partnership maturity was assessed at level 1+. IT charges back all expenses to the business. Most business executives see IT as a cost of doing business. There is heightened awareness that IT can be a critical enabler to success, but there is minimal acceptance of IT as a partner.

Partnership for a large computing services company was assessed at level 2. Since the business executives pursued e-commerce, IT is seen as a business process enabler as demonstrated by the web development. Unfortunately, the business now assigns IT with the risks of the project. Most IT projects have an IT sponsor.

Scope and Architecture

This set of criteria tends to assess information technology maturity. The extent to which IT is able to:

- Go beyond the back office and the front office of the organization
- Assume a role supporting a flexible infrastructure that is transparent to all business partners and customers
- Evaluate and apply emerging technologies effectively
- Enable or drive business processes and strategies as a true standard
- Provide solutions customizable to customer needs

Chapters 10–16 provide excellent descriptions of current and emerging IT scope and architecture opportunities. Scope and Architecture is the only technical criterion included in the alignment maturity assessment. It is important to recognize that, as with the other criteria, executives must have an appropriate understanding and strategy that addresses how the business can leverage these technologies.

Scope and Architecture was assessed at a level of 2+ at a large software development company. This is another area in which the company is moving from level 2 to level 3. ERP systems are installed and all projects are monitored at an enterprise level. Standards are integrated across the organization and enterprise architecture is integrated. It is only in the area of interenterprise that there is no formal integration.

A large financial services company assessed their scope and architecture at level 1. Although standards are defined, there is no formal integration across the enterprise. At best, only functional integration exists.

Skills

Skills were defined in figure 1.1. They include all of the human resource considerations for the organization. Going beyond the traditional considerations such as training, salary, performance feedback, and career opportunities, are factors that include the organization's cultural and social environment. Is the organization ready for change in this dynamic environment? Do individuals feel personally responsible for business innovation? Can individuals and organizations learn quickly from their experience? Does the organization leverage innovative ideas and the spirit of entrepreneurship? These are some of the important conditions of mature organizations.

For example, a large aerospace company assesses their skills maturity at level 2. A definite command and control management style exists within IT and the businesses. Power resides within certain operating companies. Diverse business cultures abound. Getting to a nonpolitical, trusting environment between the businesses and IT, where risks are shared and innovation and entrepreneurship thrive, is essential to achieve improvements in each of the other maturity tenets.

Skills maturity at a large computing services company is assessed at level 1. Career crossover is not encouraged outside of top management. Innovation is dependent on the business unit, but in general is frowned upon. Management style is dependent on the business unit but is usually command and control. Training is encouraged but left up to the individual employee.

: *Conducting a Strategic Alignment Maturity Assessment*

As previously discussed, an essential part of the assessment process is recognizing that it must be done with a team including both business and IT executives. The convergence on a consensus of the maturity levels and the discussions that ensue are extremely valuable in understanding the problems and opportunities that need to be addressed to improve business-IT alignment. The most important part of the process is the creation of recommendations addressing the problems and opportunities identified, and working together to define and carry out steps to move the organization to a higher level of maturity. The most difficult step, of course, is actually carrying out the recommendations. This section ties the assessment metrics together. The examples and experiences provided in appendix 1 of this chapter, together with the procedure described here, served as the vehicle for validating the model.

Each of the criteria and levels, as illustrated in figure 1.2, are described by a set of attributes that allow a particular dimension to be assessed using a 1 to 5 Likert scale, in which:

1 = this does not fit the organization, or the organization is very ineffective

2 = low level of fit for the organization

3 = moderate fit for the organization, or the organization is moderately effective

4 = this fits most of the organization

5 = strong level of fit throughout the organization, or the organization is very effective

A sample tally sheet is provided at the end of appendix 1. Different scales can be applied to perform the assessment (e.g., good, fair, poor; 1, 2, 3). Whatever the scale, however, it is important to evaluate each of the six criteria with both business and IT executives to obtain an accurate assessment. The intent is to have the team of IT and business executives converge on a maturity level. Typically, the initial review will produce divergent results. This outcome is indicative of the problems/opportunities being addressed.

The relative importance of each of the attributes within the criteria may differ among organizations. For example, in some organizations, the use of SLAs (Service Level Agreements) might not be considered as important to alignment as the effectiveness of liaisons. Hence, giving SLAs a low maturity assessment should not significantly impact the overall rating in this case. It would be valuable, however to have the group discuss why the organization does not consider a particular attribute (in this example, SLAs) to be significant.

Using a Delphi approach with a Group Decision Support Tool (Luftman, 1997) often helps in attaining the convergence. My experience suggests that "discussions" among the different team members help to ensure a clearer understanding of the problems and opportunities that need to be addressed.

Keep in mind that the primary objective of the assessment is to identify specific recommendations to improve the alignment of IT and the business. The evaluation team, after assessing each of the six criteria from level 1 to 5, uses the results to converge on an overall assessment level of the maturity for the firm. They apply the next higher level of maturity as a roadmap to identify what they should do next.

Experience with 50 Global 2000 companies indicates that over 80 percent of the organizations are at level 2 maturity with some characteristics of level 3 maturity. Tables 1A.1–6 in appendix 1 illustrates the "average" results of the Strategic Alignment Maturity assessments for the 25 original organizations, which is the start of a Strategic Alignment Maturity Assessment benchmark repository. As the sample continues to grow (it has reached over 50 at the time of this writing), it is anticipated that exemplar benchmarks based on factors such as industry, company age, and company size will be available. The tables show the maturity attributes for each of the six maturity components. Tables 1A.1–6 (without the average numbers) can be used as the basis for determining an organizations maturity level. The tally sheet in figure 1A.1 at the end of appendix 1 is provided as a vehicle to capture the assessment responses.

The specific results of the maturity assessment for seven firms are also included in tables 1A.1–6. Keep in mind that the results of these maturity assessments were not the principal objective of this exercise. Rather, the goal is to provide the firm with specific insights regarding what it can do to improve the maturity level and thereby improving IT-business strategic alignment. Alignment is about process. Knowing the alignment maturity of an organization might not reveal immediate profits to the firm, but it will provide the organization with a road map to make IT a recognized enabler/driver of business value. The summary of the six components with their respective five levels of maturity at the end of appendix 2 can be applied as a convenient table to use during a maturity assessment as a vehicle for conducting:

√ Interviews
√ Group discussions
√ Surveys

▪ Conclusions

Achieving and sustaining IT-business alignment continues to be a major issue. Experience shows that no single activity will enable a firm to attain and sustain alignment. There are too many variables. The technology and business environments are too dynamic.

The strategic alignment maturity assessment provides a vehicle to evaluate where an organization is and where it needs to go to attain and sustain business-IT alignment. The careful assessment of a firm's alignment maturity is an important step in identifying the specific actions necessary to ensure IT is being used to appropriately enable or drive the business strategy. If you are interested in participating in the benchmarking of alignment maturity, please contact me. The journey continues.

▪ Appendix 1: Strategic Alignment Maturity Assessment Experiences

To validate the assessment, formal assessments of 25 Fortune 500 firms were completed. The last column in tables 1A.1–6 in this appendix illustrates the "average" evaluations (rated using a Likert scale) for the six criteria of the Strategic Alignment Maturity assessments for these 25 firms. The numbers are the average responses from all participants (e.g., IT, Finance, Marketing from all 25 firms) for each of the respective components of the six criteria. These results were the start of a Strategic Alignment Maturity Assessment benchmark repository. Future assessments will be included to provide exemplar benchmarks based on decisive factors such as industry, and company

Table 1A.1
Communications

	Seven assessments summarized							Initial
	1	2	3	4	5	6	7	25 firms
Understanding of business by IT								
1. IT management not aware	3	3	1	3	2	1	0	2
2. Limited IT awareness	4	3	3	2	2	4	2	4
3. Senior and mid-management	2	1	3	1	1	2	5	3
4. Pushed down through organization	0	0	1	0	0	0	1	1
5. Pervasive	0	0	0	0	0	0	0	1
Understanding of IT by business								
1. Business management not aware	2	3	2	3	2	2	2	3
2. Limited business awareness	4	3	4	2	3	4	3	4
3. Emerging business awareness	1	1	1	0	0	1	2	1
4. Business aware of potential	0	0	0	0	0	0	0	1
5. Pervasive	0	0	0	0	0	0	0	0
Inter/intra-organizational learning								
1. Casual, ad-hoc	3	2	2	3	2	1	0	4
2. Informal	3	4	3	2	3	4	5	4
3. Regular, clear	0	1	2	0	0	0	0	1
4. Unified, bonded	0	0	0	0	0	0	0	1
5. Strong and structured	0	0	0	0	0	0	0	0
Protocol rigidity								
1. Command and control	4	3	2	4	4	4	5	4
2. Limited relaxed	2	2	4	2	2	2	0	3
3. Emerging relaxed	0	0	1	0	0	1	0	1
4. Relaxed, informal	0	0	0	0	0	0	0	1
5. Informal	0	0	0	0	0	0	0	0
Knowledge sharing								
1. Ad-hoc	1	2	1	2	1	0	1	0
2. Semi structured	2	2	3	3	2	4	5	5
3. Structured around key processes	2	4	3	1	1	3	0	3
4. Institutionalized	0	0	0	0	0	1	0	1
5. Extra-enterprise	0	0	0	0	0	0	0	0
Liaison(s) breadth/effectiveness								
1. None or ad-hoc	4	2	1	2	1	1	1	2
2. Limited tactical technology based	1	2	3	3	4	4	4	4
3. Formalized, regular meetings	0	0	4	0	1	2	2	3
4. Bonded, effective at all internal levels	0	0	1	0	0	0	0	1
5. Extra-enterprise	0	0	0	0	0	0	0	0
Maturity level	2	2	2	2	2	2	2	2+

Table 1A.2
Competency/Value Measurements

	Seven actual assessments summarized							Initial
	1	2	3	4	5	6	7	25 firms
IT metrics								
1. Technical; not related to business	4	2	1	5	3	4	5	5
2. Cost efficiency	3	3	4	4	4	4	5	4
3. Traditional financial	3	4	4	3	4	3	3	3
4. Cost effectiveness	1	3	2	1	1	0	0	2
5. Extended to external partners	0	1	1	0	0	0	0	1
Business metrics								
1. Ad-hoc; not related to IT	4	2	2	4	4	2	5	4
2. At the functional organization	3	3	3	4	4	4	4	4
3. Traditional financial	2	4	4	4	4	4	5	4
4. Customer based	0	3	1	1	1	1	0	3
5. Extended to external partners	0	1	1	1	0	0	0	2
Balanced metrics								
1. Ad-hoc metrics unlinked	3	2	0	1	3	3	4	3
2. Business and IT metrics unlinked	4	3	2	5	5	4	4	4
3. Emerging business and IT metrics linked	0	2	4	0	0	2	0	3
4. Business and IT metrics linked	0	0	1	0	0	0	0	1
5. Business, partners, & IT metrics linked	0	0	0	0	0	0	0	1
Service level agreements								
1. Sporadically present	1	2	2	0	3	4	4	3
2. Technical at the functional level	5	3	5	5	4	2	3	4
3. Emerging across the enterprise	1	4	1	2	1	0	0	2
4. Enterprise wide	0	1	1	1	0	0	0	1
5. Extended to external partners	0	0	1	0	0	0	0	1
Benchmarking								
1. Not generally practiced	2	1	1	1	1	3	2	2
2. Informal	4	2	4	3	2	4	5	4
3. Focused on specific processes	2	4	3	4	4	3	1	3
4. Routinely performed	2	3	1	2	3	1	0	2
5. Routinely performed with partners	1	1	0	1	1	0	0	1
Formal assessments/reviews								
1. None	1	0	0	1	0	2	2	2
2. Some; typically for problems	4	2	4	4	4	5	4	4
3. Emerging formality	2	3	2	3	4	1	0	2
4. Formally performed	2	3	1	1	2	0	0	1
5. Routinely performed	0	0	0	1	1	0	0	0
Continuous improvement								
1. None	1	0	2	0	2	2	3	2
2. Minimum	3	2	3	3	3	3	3	3
3. Emerging	1	4	3	3	3	1	2	3
4. Frequently	1	1	1	2	2	0	0	2
5. Routinely performed	1	1	1	1	1	0	0	1
Maturity level	2	3	2	2	2	2	2	2+

Table 1A.3
Governance

	Seven assessments summarized							Initial 25 firms
	1	2	3	4	5	6	7	
Business strategic planning								
1. Ad-hoc	3	1	1	4	2	1	2	3
2. Basic planning at the functional level	5	3	5	3	4	5	3	5
3. Some inter-organizational planning	2	2	2	1	2	3	1	2
4. Managed across the enterprise	0	1	1	0	1	0	0	1
5. Integrated across & outside the enterprise	0	0	0	0	0	0	0	0
IT strategic planning								
1. Ad-hoc	3	1	1	4	5	4	4	3
2. Functional tactical planning	5	4	5	2	2	2	5	4
3. Focused planning, some inter-organizational	2	4	4	1	1	1	1	4
4. Managed across the enterprise	0	1	1	1	0	0	0	1
5. Integrated across & outside the enterprise	0	0	0	0	0	0	0	0
Reporting/organization structure								
1. Central/decentral; CIO reports to CFO	2	0	3	5	3	5	4	4
2. Central/decentral, some co-location; CIO reports to CFO	5	4	5	2	4	1	4	4
3. Central/decentral, some federation; CIO reports to COO	1	3	0	1	0	0	0	3
4. Federated; CIO reports to COO or CEO	0	4	0	0	0	0	0	2
5. Federated; CIO reports to CEO	0	2	0	0	0	0	0	2
Budgetary control								
1. Cost center; Erratic spending	2	2	3	3	4	4	5	3
2. Cost center by functional organization	5	5	5	5	3	1	3	5
3. Cost center; some investments	1	4	1	1	1	0	1	3
4. Investment center	0	0	0	0	0	0	0	1
5. Investment center; Profit center	0	0	0	0	0	0	0	1
IT investment management								
1. Cost based; erratic spending	4	2	3	5	5	5	5	4
2. Cost based; operations & maintenance focus	4	2	5	4	4	4	5	5
3. Traditional; process enabler	1	4	2	2	1	1	4	3
4. Cost effectiveness; process driver	0	0	1	0	0	0	0	1
5. Business value; extended to business partners	0	0	0	0	0	0	0	0

(continued)

Table 1A.3
Governance (*continued*)

	Seven assessments summarized							Initial
	1	2	3	4	5	6	7	25 firms
Steering committee(s)								
1. Not formal/regular	2	2	2	4	4	4	2	2
2. Periodic organized communication	5	4	3	3	2	3	5	4
3. Regular clear communication	0	2	1	0	0	0	1	1
4. Formal, effective committees	0	0	1	0	0	0	0	1
5. Partnership	0	0	0	0	0	0	0	0
Prioritization process								
1. Reactive	4	2	3	5	4	4	5	4
2. Occasional responsive	4	4	5	3	2	2	2	4
3. Mostly responsive	1	4	2	0	0	0	0	3
4. Value add, responsive	0	1	0	0	0	0	0	1
5. Value added partner	0	1	0	0	0	0	0	0
Maturity level	2	3	2	1+	1+	1	2	2+

size. As of the writing of this chapter, over 50 organizations have participated in the maturity assessment.

Tables 1A.1–6 in this appendix also includes the responses from six actual assessments of Fortune 200 companies and a large university. These seven assessments represent the average evaluations (rated using a Likert scale) that the multifunctional group (e.g., IT, Finance, Marketing) from each of the firms identified. They are a subset of the 25 firms.

Typically, after getting the individual responses from the participants for their perception of the level of maturity for each of the six criteria, a discussion was facilitated to obtain consensus on the respective maturity level for each of the six criteria. In one case, a Delphi was used to derive the consensus. The maturity level at the bottom of each column represents the consensus for the respective group. Most of the examples used in the main part of this chapter, especially in the section "The Six Alignment Maturity Criteria," come from these seven firms. Tables 1A.1–6 (without the average numbers) can be used as the basis for determining an organizations maturity level. The tally sheet in table 1A.7 is provided at the end of this appendix to be used as a vehicle to capture the assessment responses.

⦂ *Appendix 2: The Five Levels Of Strategic Alignment Maturity*

This appendix describes each of the five levels of strategic alignment maturity summarized in figure 1.3. Each of the six criteria described in the main part

	Seven assessments summarized							Initial
	1	2	3	4	5	6	7	25 firms
Business perception of IT value								
1. IT perceived as a cost of business	4	4	3	5	5	4	5	4
2. IT emerging as an asset	5	5	5	1	1	5	3	5
3. IT is seen as an asset	2	1	2	0	0	2	0	2
4. IT is part of the business strategy	1	0	1	0	0	0	0	1
5. IT-business co-adaptive	0	0	0	0	0	0	0	0
Role of IT in strategic business planning								
1. No seat at the business table	2	5	3	5	5	5	5	4
2. Business process enabler	5	5	5	2	2	5	4	5
3. Business process driver	0	0	0	0	0	0	0	1
4. Business strategy enabler/driver	0	0	0	0	0	0	0	0
5. IT-business co-adaptive	0	0	0	0	0	0	0	0
Shared goals, risk, rewards/penalties								
1. IT takes risk with little reward	5	5	3	5	5	5	4	4
2. IT takes most of the risk with little reward	4	5	5	2	2	4	3	5
3. Risk tolerant; IT some reward	1	0	1	0	0	0	3	1
4. Risk acceptance & rewards shared	0	0	0	0	0	0	0	0
5. Risk & rewards shared	0	0	0	0	0	0	0	0
IT program management								
1. Ad-hoc	2	1	1	1	2	2	4	2
2. Standards defined	5	5	5	4	4	3	4	4
3. Standards adhered	2	4	3	2	2	2	2	2
4. Standards evolve	2	3	3	2	0	0	0	2
5. Continuous improvement	0	0	1	0	0	0	0	0
Relationship/trust style								
1. Conflict/minimum	3	3	3	4	4	4	4	3
2. Primarily transactional	4	4	5	3	3	4	5	4
3. Emerging valued service provider	2	3	3	0	0	0	0	2
4. Valued service provider	1	1	1	0	0	0	0	0
5. Valued partnership	1	0	0	0	0	0	0	0
Business sponsor/champion								
1. None	2	4	3	5	4	3	4	4
2. Limited at the functional organization	2	4	4	2	4	3	4	4
3. At the functional organization	4	2	3	0	0	0	4	3
4. At the HQ level	1	1	1	0	0	0	0	1
5. At the CEO level	1	1	0	0	0	0	0	1
Maturity level	2	2	2	1	1+	2	2	2+

Table 1A.5
Scope and Architecture

	Seven assessments summarized							Initial 25 firms
	1	2	3	4	5	6	7	
Traditional, enabler/driver, external								
1. Traditional (e.g., accounting, email)	2	2	3	4	2	4	5	2
2. Transaction (e.g., ESS, DSS)	2	3	4	3	3	2	2	3
3. Expanded scope (e.g., business process enabler)	5	4	3	2	4	0	0	4
4. Redefined scope (business process driver)	1	0	0	1	0	0	0	1
5. External scope; business strategy driver/enabler	0	0	0	0	0	0	0	0
Standards articulation								
1. None or ad-hoc	0	0	4	4	0	4	3	2
2. Standards defined	5	4	3	2	4	1	4	4
3. Emerging enterprise standards	4	3	1	3	4	0	1	3
4. Enterprise standards	3	3	0	0	3	0	0	1
5. Inter-enterprise standards	0	0	0	0	0	0	0	0
Architectural integration								
Functional organization								
1. No formal integration	0	0	5	4	1	4	5	2
2. Early attempts at integration	3	3	2	2	2	3	1	5
3. Integrated across the organization	4	4	0	0	4	0	0	1
4. Integrated with external partners	1	0	0	0	0	0	0	0
5. Evolve with external partners	0	0	0	0	0	0	0	0
Enterprise								
1. No formal integration	1	2	5	5	1	4	4	3
2. Early attempts at integration	3	4	3	3	3	3	1	4
3. Standard enterprise architecture	4	3	2	1	4	1	1	3
4. Integrated with external partners	1	1	0	0	0	0	0	0
5. Evolve with external partners	0	0	0	0	0	0	0	0
Inter-enterprise								
1. No formal integration	2	3	5	4	3	4	4	3
2. Early concept testing	4	3	2	2	3	1	0	3
3. Emerging with key partners	3	1	0	0	1	0	0	2
4. Integrated with key partners	2	0	0	0	0	0	0	1
5. Evolve with all partners	0	0	0	0	0	0	0	0
Architectural transparency, agility, flexibility								
1. None	2	2	3	5	4	4	3	4
2. Limited	4	4	5	2	4	4	4	4
3. Focused on communications	5	3	2	3	3	1	2	3
4. Effective emerging technology management	3	2	0	2	2	0	0	2
5. Across the infrastructure	2	1	0	0	2	0	0	2
Maturity level	3	2+	1	1	2+	1	1	2+

Table 1A.6
Skills

	Seven assessments summarized							Initial 25 firms
	1	2	3	4	5	6	7	
Innovation, entrepreneurship								
1. Discouraged	3	3	4	3	4	5	3	4
2. Dependent on functional organization	4	5	5	4	5	3	4	3
3. Risk tolerant	1	2	0	0	1	1	2	2
4. Enterprise, partners, and IT managers	0	0	0	0	0	0	0	1
5. The norm	0	0	0	0	0	0	0	0
Locus of power								
1. In the business	3	2	4	2	2	5	3	3
2. Functional organization	4	4	2	4	4	2	4	4
3. Emerging across the organization	4	2	0	1	1	1	1	2
4. Across the organization	0	0	0	0	0	0	0	1
5. All executives, including CIO & partners	0	0	0	0	0	0	0	0
Management style								
1. Command and control	5	3	4	3	4	4	3	4
2. Consensus-based	2	4	2	3	3	1	2	3
3. Results based	1	2	2	2	2	1	3	2
4. Profit/value based	0	0	0	1	0	0	0	1
5. Relationship based	0	0	0	0	0	0	0	0
Change readiness								
1. Resistant to change	4	4	5	3	4	4	3	4
2. Dependent on functional organization	4	5	1	5	4	3	4	4
3. Recognized need for change	2	2	1	2	2	2	4	2
4. Programs in place at the corporate level	0	0	0	0	0	0	1	0
5. Proactive and anticipate change	0	0	0	0	0	0	0	0
Career crossover								
1. None	2	1	5	2	1	4	3	3
2. Minimum	5	5	3	5	4	2	4	4
3. Dependent on functional organization	1	3	2	1	3	2	1	2
4. Across the functional organization	0	0	0	0	0	0	0	0
5. Across the enterprise	0	0	0	0	0	0	0	0

(continued)

Table 1A.6
Skills (*continued*)

	Seven assessments summarized							Initial 25 firms
	1	2	3	4	5	6	7	
Education, cross-training								
1. None	3	2	1	1	3	4	4	3
2. Minimum	4	4	5	4	4	2	4	4
3. Dependent on functional organization	4	4	4	2	4	2	3	3
4. At the functional organization	0	0	0	0	0	0	1	1
5. Across the organization	0	0	0	0	0	0	0	0
Social, political, trusting environment								
1. Minimum	3	3	4	2	2	4	3	4
2. Primarily transactional	4	4	3	3	3	1	4	3
3. Emerging valued service provider	3	3	1	0	2	0	3	3
4. Valued service provider	0	0	0	0	0	0	0	1
5. Valued partnership	0	0	0	0	0	0	0	0
Maturity level	2	2	1	2	2	1	2+	2

of this chapter are evaluated in deriving the level of strategic alignment maturity. There is a summary at the end of this appendix of all six components with their respective five levels (table 1A.8).

Level 1—Initial/Ad Hoc Process

Organizations that meet many of the characteristics of the attributes in the six strategic alignment maturity criteria for level 1 can be characterized as having the lowest level of strategic alignment maturity. It is highly improbable that these organizations will be able to achieve an aligned IT business strategy, leaving their investment in IT significantly unleveraged.

Level 2—Committed Process

Organizations that meet many of the characteristics of the attributes in the six Strategic Alignment Maturity criteria for level 2 can be characterized as having committed to begin the process for Strategic Alignment Maturity. This level of Strategic Alignment Maturity tends to be directed at local situations or functional organizations (e.g., Marketing, Finance, Manufacturing, H/R) within the overall enterprise. Because of limited awareness by the business and IT communities of the different functional organizations use of IT, however, alignment can be difficult to achieve. Any business-IT

Table 1A.7
Tally sheet

Practice categories/practices	Averaged scores										Average category score	Your alignment score
Communication												
1 Understanding of business by IT	1	1.5	2	2.5	3	3.5	4	4.5	5			
2 Understanding of IT by business	1	1.5	2	2.5	3	3.5	4	4.5	5			
3 Organizational Learning	1	1.5	2	2.5	3	3.5	4	4.5	5			
4 Style and ease of access	1	1.5	2	2.5	3	3.5	4	4.5	5			
5 Leveraging intellectual assets	1	1.5	2	2.5	3	3.5	4	4.5	5			
6 IT business liaison staff	1	1.5	2	2.5	3	3.5	4	4.5	5			
Metrics												
7 IT metrics	1	1.5	2	2.5	3	3.5	4	4.5	5			
8 Business metrics	1	1.5	2	2.5	3	3.5	4	4.5	5			
9 Link between IT and business metrics	1	1.5	2	2.5	3	3.5	4	4.5	5			
10 Service level agreements	1	1.5	2	2.5	3	3.5	4	4.5	5			
11 Benchmarking	1	1.5	2	2.5	3	3.5	4	4.5	5			
12 Formally assets IT investments	1	1.5	2	2.5	3	3.5	4	4.5	5			
13 Continuous improvement practices	1	1.5	2	2.5	3	3.5	4	4.5	5			
Governance												
14 Formal business strategy planning	1	1.5	2	2.5	3	3.5	4	4.5	5			
15 Formal IT strategy planning	1	1.5	2	2.5	3	3.5	4	4.5	5			
16 Organizational structure	1	1.5	2	2.5	3	3.5	4	4.5	5			
17 Reporting relationships	1	1.5	2	2.5	3	3.5	4	4.5	5			
18 How IT is budgeted	1	1.5	2	2.5	3	3.5	4	4.5	5			
19 Rationale for IT spending	1	1.5	2	2.5	3	3.5	4	4.5	5			
20 Senior level IT steering committee	1	1.5	2	2.5	3	3.5	4	4.5	5			
21 How projects are prioritized	1	1.5	2	2.5	3	3.5	4	4.5	5			
Partnership												
22 Business perception of IT	1	1.5	2	2.5	3	3.5	4	4.5	5			
23 IT's role in strategic business planning	1	1.5	2	2.5	3	3.5	4	4.5	5			
24 Shared risks and rewards	1	1.5	2	2.5	3	3.5	4	4.5	5			
25 Managing the IT-business relationship	1	1.5	2	2.5	3	3.5	4	4.5	5			
26 Relationship/trust style	1	1.5	2	2.5	3	3.5	4	4.5	5			
27 Business sponsors/champions	1	1.5	2	2.5	3	3.5	4	4.5	5			

(*continued*)

Table 1A.7
Tally sheet (*continued*)

Practice categories/practices	Averaged scores									Average category score	Your alignment score
Technology											
28 Primary systems	1	1.5	2	2.5	3	3.5	4	4.5	5		
29 Standards	1	1.5	2	2.5	3	3.5	4	4.5	5		
30 Architectural integration	1	1.5	2	2.5	3	3.5	4	4.5	5		
31 How IT infrastructure is perceived	1	1.5	2	2.5	3	3.5	4	4.5	5		
Human Resources											
32 Innovative, entrepreneurial environment	1	1.5	2	2.5	3	3.5	4	4.5	5		
33 Key IT HR decisions made by	1	1.5	2	2.5	3	3.5	4	4.5	5		
34 Change readiness	1	1.5	2	2.5	3	3.5	4	4.5	5		
35 Career crossover opportunities	1	1.5	2	2.5	3	3.5	4	4.5	5		
36 Cross-functional training and job rotation	1	1.5	2	2.5	3	3.5	4	4.5	5		
37 Social interaction	1	1.5	2	2.5	3	3.5	4	4.5	5		
38 Attract and retain top talent	1	1.5	2	2.5	3	3.5	4	4.5	5		

alignment at the local level is typically not leveraged by the enterprise. The potential opportunities, however, are beginning to be recognized.

Level 3—Established Focused Process

Organizations that meet many of the characteristics of the attributes in the six Strategic Alignment Maturity criteria for level 3 can be characterized as having established a focused Strategic Alignment Maturity. This level of Strategic Alignment Maturity concentrates governance, processes, and communications toward specific business objectives. IT is becoming embedded in the business. Level 3 leverages IT assets on an enterprise-wide basis and applications systems demonstrate planned, managed direction away from traditional transaction processing to systems that use information to make business decisions. The IT extrastructure (leveraging the interorganizational infrastructure) is evolving with key partners.

Level 4—Improved/Managed Process

Organizations that meet many of the characteristics of the attributes in the six Strategic Alignment Maturity criteria for level 4 can be characterized as

Table 1A.8
Summary of the Six Components of Alignment Maturity With Their Respective Five Levels

	Level 1: without process (no alignment)	Level 2: beginning process	Level 3: establishing process	Level 4: improved process	Level 5: optimal process (complete alignment)
Assessing IT and business alignment in communication practices					
Understanding of business by IT	IT management lacks understanding	Limited understanding by IT management	Good understanding by IT management	Understanding encouraged among IT staff	Understanding required of all IT staff
Understanding of IT by business	Managers lack understanding	Limited understanding by managers	Good understanding by managers	Understanding encouraged among staff	Understanding required of staff
Organizational learning	Casual conversation and meetings	Newsletters, reports, group e-mail	Training, departmental meetings	Formal methods sponsored by senior management	Learning monitored for effectiveness
Style and ease of access	Business to IT only; formal	One-way, somewhat informal	Two-way, formal	Two-way, somewhat informal	Two-way, informal and flexible
Leveraging intellectual assets	Ad-hoc	Some structured sharing emerging	Structured around key processes	Formal sharing at all levels	Formal sharing with partners
IT-business liaison staff	None or use only as needed	Primary IT-business link	Facilitate knowledge transfer	Facilitate relationship-building	Building relationship with partners
Assessing IT and business alignment in metrics practices					
IT metrics	Technical only	Technical, cost; metrics rarely reviewed	Review, act on technical, ROI metrics	Also measure effectiveness	Also measure business ops, HR, partners

(continued)

Table 1A.8
Summary of the Six Components of Alignment Maturity With Their Respective Five Levels (*continued*)

	Level 1: without process (no alignment)	Level 2: beginning process	Level 3: establishing process	Level 4: improved process	Level 5: optimal process (complete alignment)
Business metrics	IT investments measured rarely, if ever	Cost/unit; rarely reviewed	Review, act on ROI, cost	Also measure customer value	Balanced scorecard, includes partners
Link between IT and business metrics	Value of IT investments rarely measured	Business, IT metrics not linked	Business, IT metrics becoming linked	Formally linked; reviewed and acted upon	Balanced scorecard, includes partners
Service level agreements	Use sporadically	With units for technology performance	With units; becoming enterprise wide	Enterprise wide	Includes partners
Benchmarking	Seldom or never	Sometimes benchmark informally	May benchmark formally, seldom act	Routinely benchmark, usually act	Routinely benchmark, act and measure results
Formally assess IT investments	Don't assess	Only when there's a problem	Becoming a routine occurrence	Routinely assess and act on findings	Routinely assess, act and measure results
Continuous improvement practices	None	Few; effectiveness not measured	Few, starting to measure effectiveness	Many, frequently measure effectiveness	Practices and measures well established
Assessing IT and business alignment in governance practices					
Formal business strategy planning	Not done, or done as needed	At unit functional level . . . slight IT input	Some IT input and cross-functional planning	At unit and enterprise with IT	With IT and partners

Formal IT strategy planning	Not done, or done as needed	At unit functional level . . . light business input	Some business input and cross-functional planning	At unit and enterprise, with business	With partners
Organizational structure	Centralized or decentralized	Central/decentral, some co-location	Central/decentral or federal	Federal	Federal
Reporting relationships	CIO reports to CFO	CIO reports to CFO	CIO reports to COO	CIO reports to COO or CEO	CIO reports to CEO
How IT is budgeted	Cost center, spending is unpredictable	Cost center by unit	Some projects treated as investments	IT treated as investment	Profit center
Rationale for IT spending	Reduce costs	Productivity, efficiency	Also as a process enabler	Process driver, strategy enabler	Competitive advantage, profit
Senior level IT steering committee	Don't have	Meet informally as needed	Formal committees meet regularly	Proven to be effective	Also includes external partners
How projects are prioritized	React to business or IT need	Determined by IT function	Determined by business function	Mutually determined	Partners' priorities are considered
Assessing IT and business alignment in partnerships practices					
Business perception of IT	Cost of doing business	Becoming an asset	Enables future business activity	Drives future business activity	Partner with business in creating value
IT's role in strategic business planning	Not involved	Enables business processes	Drives business processes	Enables or drives business strategy	IT, business adopt quickly to change
Shared risks and rewards	IT takes all the risks, receives no rewards	IT takes most risks with little reward	IT, business start sharing risks, rewards	Risks, rewards always shared	Managers incented to take risks
Managing the IT-business relationship	IT-business relationship isn't managed	Managed on ad hoc basis	Processes exist but not always followed	Processes exist and complied with	Processes are continuously improved

(continued)

43

Table 1A.8
Summary of the Six Components of Alignment Maturity With Their Respective Five Levels (continued)

	Level 1: without process (no alignment)	Level 2: beginning process	Level 3: establishing process	Level 4: improved process	Level 5: optimal process (complete alignment)
Relationship/trust style	Conflict and mistrust	Transactional relationship	IT becoming a valued service provider	Long-term partnership	Partner, trusted vendor of IT services
Business sponsors/champions	Usually none	Often have a senior IT sponsor/champion	IT and business sponsor/champion at unit level	Business sponsor/champion at corporate level	CEO is the business sponsor/champion
Assessing IT and business alignment in technology practices					
Primary systems	Traditional office support	Transaction oriented	Business process enabler	Business process driver	Business strategy enabler/driver
Standards	Not enforced	Defined, enforced at functional level	Emerging co-ordination across functions	Defined, enforced across functions	Also co-ordinated with partners
Architectural integration	Not well integrated	Within unit	Integrated across functions	Begins to be integrated with partners	Integrated with partners
How IT infrastructure is perceived	Utility run at minimum cost	Becoming driven by business strategy	Driven by business strategy	Beginning to help business respond to change	Enables fast response to changing market

Assessing IT and business alignment in human resource practices

Innovative, entrepreneurial environment	Discouraged	Somewhat encouraged at unit level	Strongly encouraged at unit level	Also at corporate level	Also with partners
Key IT HR decisions made by	Top business and IT management at corporate	Same, with emerging functional influence	Top business and unit management: IT advises	Top business and IT management across firm	Top management across firm and partners
Change readiness	Tend to resist change	Change readiness programs emerging	Programs in place at functional level	Programs in place at corporate level	Also proactive and anticipate change
Career crossover opportunities	Job transfers rarely occur	Occasionally occur within unit	Regularly occur for unit management	Regularly occur at all unit levels	Also at corporate level
Cross-functional training and job rotation	No opportunities	Deck led by units	Formal programs run by all units	Also across enterprise	Also with partners
Social interaction	Minimal IT-business interaction	Strictly a business-only relationship	Trust and confidence is starting	Trust and confidence achieved	Attained with customers and partners
Attract and retain top talent	No retention program; poor recruiting	IT hiring focused on technical skills	Technology and business focus retention program	Formal program for hiring and retaining	Effective program for hiring and retaining

having a managed Strategic Alignment Maturity. This level of Strategic Alignment Maturity demonstrates effective governance and services that reinforce the concept of IT as a value center. Organizations at level 4 leverage IT assets on an enterprise-wide basis and the focus of applications systems is on driving business process enhancements to obtain sustainable competitive advantage. A level 4 organization views IT as an innovative and imaginative strategic contributor to success.

Level 5—Optimized Process

Organizations that meet the characteristics of the attributes in the six Strategic Alignment Maturity criteria for level 5 can be characterized as having an optimally aligned Strategic Alignment Maturity. A sustained governance process integrates the IT strategic planning process with the strategic business process. Organizations at level 5 leverage IT assets on an enterprise-wide basis to extend the reach (the IT extra structure) of the organization into the supply chains of customers (and perhaps customers of customers) and external partners (e.g., vendors, outsourcers, franchises, suppliers).

References

Baets, W. (1996) "Some Empirical Evidence on IS Strategy Alignment in Banking," *Information and Management*, 30(4), 155–77.

Boynton, A., B. Victor, & B. Pine II. (1996) "Aligning IT with New Competitive Strategies," in J. N. Luftman (Ed.), *Competing in the Information Age*. New York: Oxford University Press.

Brancheau, J., & J. Wetherbe. (1987) "Issues In Information Systems Management," *MIS Quarterly*, 11(1), 23–45.

Broadbent, M., & P. Weill. (1993) "Developing Business and Information Strategy Alignment: A Study in the Banking Industry," *IBM Systems Journal*, 32(1), 162–79.

Chan, Y., & S. Huff. (1993) "Strategic Information Systems Alignment," *Business Quarterly*, 58(1), 51–6.

Davenport, T., & J. Short. (1990). "The New Industrial Engineering: Information Technology and Business Process Redesign," *Sloan Management Review*, 31(4), 11–27.

Davidson, W. (1996) "Managing the Business Transformation Process," in J. N. Luftman (Ed.), *Competing in the Information Age*. New York: Oxford University Press.

Dixon, P., & D. John. (1989). "Technology Issues Facing Corporate Management in the 1990s," *MIS Quarterly*, 13(3), 247–55.

Earl, M. J. (1993) *Corporate Information Systems Management*. Homewood, IL: Richard D. Irwin, Inc.

Earl, M. J. (1996). "Experience in Strategic Information Systems Planning," *MIS Quarterly*, 17(1), 1–24.

Faltermayer, E. (1994). "Competitiveness: How US Companies Stack Up Now," *Fortune*, 129(8), 52–64.

Foster, R. (1986) *Innovation: The Attacker's Advantage*. New York: Summit Books.

Goff, L. (1993). "You Say Tomayto, I Say Tomahto," *Computerworld*, Nov. 1, p. 129.

Hammer, M., & J. Champy. (1993). *Reengineering the Corporation: A Manifesto For Business Revolution*. New York: Harper Business.

Hammer, M., & S. Stanton. (1995). *The Reengineering Revolution*. New York: Harper Business.

Henderson, J., J. Thomas, & N. Venkatraman. (1992) *Making Sense Of IT: Strategic Alignment and Organizational Context*, Working Paper 3475–92. Cambridge, MA: Sloan School of Management, Massachusetts Institute of Technology.

Henderson, J., & J. Thomas. (1992) "Aligning Business and Information Technology Domains: Strategic Planning In Hospitals," *Hospital and Health Services Administrative*, 37(1), 71–87.

Henderson, J., & N. Venkatraman. (1990). *Strategic Alignment: A Model For Organizational Transformation Via Information Technology*, Working Paper 3223–90. Cambridge, MA: Sloan School of Management, Massachusetts Institute of Technology.

Henderson, J., & N. Venkatraman. (1996) "Aligning Business and IT Strategies," in J. N. Luftman (Ed.), *Competing in the Information Age: Practical Applications of the Strategic Alignment Model*. New York: Oxford University Press.

Humphrey, W. S. (1988) "Characterizing the Software Process: A Maturity Framework," *IEEE Software*, 5(2), 73–9.

IBM. (1981) *Business Systems Planning, Planning Guide, GE20–0527*. White Plains, NY: IBM Corporation

Ives, B., S. Jarvenpaa, & R. Mason. (1993) "Global Business Drivers: Aligning Information Technology To Global Business Strategy," *IBM Systems Journal*, 32(1), 143–61.

Keen, P. (1991) *Shaping the Future*. Boston, MA: Harvard Business School Press.

Keen, P. (1996) "Do You Need An IT Strategy?" in J. N. Luftman (Ed.), *Competing in the Information Age*. New York: Oxford University Press.

King, J. (1995) "Re-engineering Focus Slips," *Computerworld*, March 13.

Liebs, S. (1992) "We're All in This Together," *Information Week*, October 26, 1992.

Luftman, J., Ed. (1996) *Competing in the Information Age: Practical Applications of the Strategic Alignment Model*. New York: Oxford University Press.

Luftman, J. (1997). "Align in the Sand," *Computerworld*, Feb. 17.

Luftman, J., & T. Brier. (1999) "Achieving and Sustaining Business-IT Alignment," *California Management Review*, 1, 109–22.

Luftman, J., P. Lewis, & S. Oldach. (1993) "Transforming the Enterprise: The Alignment of Business and Information Technology Strategies," *IBM Systems Journal*, 32(1), 198–221.

Luftman, J., R. Papp, & T. Brier. (1995) "The Strategic Alignment Model: Assessment and Validation," *Proceedings of the Information Technology Management Group of the Association of Management (AoM) 13th Annual International Conference*, pp. 57–66. Vancouver, British Columbia, Canada, August 2–5.

Luftman, J., R. Papp, & T. Brier. (1999) "Enablers and Inhibitors of Business-IT Alignment," *Communications of the Association for Information Systems*, 1(11).

McLean, E., & J. Soden. (1977) *Strategic Planning for MIS*. New York: John Wiley & Sons.

Mills, P. (1986) *Managing Service Industries*. New York: Ballinger.

Niederman, F., J. Brancheau, & J. Wetherbe (1991) "Information Systems Management Issues For the 1990s," *MIS Quarterly*, 15(4), 475–95.

Nolan, R. L. (1979) "Managing the Crises In Data Processing," *Harvard Business Review*, March 1.

Papp, R. (1995) *Determinants of Strategically Aligned Organizations: A Multi-industry, Multi-perspective Analysis*. Ph.D. dissertation, Hoboken, NJ: Stevens Institute of Technology.

Papp, R., & J. Luftman. (1995) "Business and IT Strategic Alignment: New Perspectives and Assessments," in *Proceedings of the Association for Information Systems, Inaugural Americas Conference on Information Systems*, Pittsburgh, PA, August 25–27.

Parker, M., & R. Benson. (1988) *Information Economics*. Englewood Cliffs, NJ: Prentice Hall.

Robson, W. (1994) *Strategic Management and Information Systems: An Integrated Approach*. London: Pitman Publishing.

Rockart, J., & J. Short. (1989) "IT in the 1990s: Managing Organizational Interdependence," *Sloan Management Review*, 30(2), 7–17

Rockart, J., M. Earl, & J. Ross. (1996) "Eight Imperatives for the New IT Organization," *Sloan Management Review*, (38)1, 43–55.

Rogers, L. (1997). "Alignment Revisited." *CIO Magazine*, May 15.

Wang, C. (1997) *Techno Vision II*. New York: McGraw-Hill.

Watson, R., & J. Brancheau. (1991) "Key Issues In Information Systems Management: An International Perspective," *Information & Management*, 20, 213–23.

Weill, P., & M. Broadbent. (1998) *Leveraging the New Infrastructure*. Cambridge, MA: Harvard University Press.

Communications

Effective exchange of ideas and a clear understanding of what it takes to ensure successful strategies are high on the list of enablers and inhibitors to alignment. All too often there is little business awareness on the part of IT or little IT appreciation on the part of the business. Given the dynamic environment in which most organizations find themselves, ensuring ongoing knowledge sharing across organizations is paramount.

Many firms choose to draw on liaisons to facilitate this knowledge sharing. The key word is facilitate. Often I have seen facilitators whose role is to serve as

COMMUNICATIONS
- Understanding of Business by IT
- Understanding of IT by Business
- Inter/Intra organizational Learning/Education
- Protocol Rigidity
- Knowledge Sharing
- Liaison(s) effectiveness

COMPETENCY/VALUE MEASUREMENTS
- IT Metrics
- Business Metrics
- Balanced Metrics
- Service Level Agreements
- Benchmarking
- Formal Assessment/ Reviews
- Continuous Improvement

GOVERNANCE
- Business Strategic Planning
- IT Strategic Planning
- Organization Structure Reporting
- Budgetary Control
- IT Investment Management
- Steering Committee(s)
- Prioritization Process

IT BUSINESS ALIGNMENT MATURITY CRITERIA

PARTNERSHIP
- Business Perception of IT Value
- Role of IT in Strategic Business Shared Goals, Risk, Rewards/Penalties
- IT Program Management
- Relationship/Trust Style
- Business Sponsor/ Champion

SCOPE AND ARCHITECTURE
- Traditional, Enabler/ Driver, External
- Standards Articulate
- Architecture Integration:
  - Functional Organization
  - Enterprise
  - Inter-enterprise
- Architectural Transparency, Agility, Flexibility
- Manage Emerging Technology

SKILLS
- Innovation, Entrepreneurship
- Culture Locus of Power
- Management Style
- Change Readiness
- Career Crossover Training
- Social, Political, Trusting Interpersonal Environment
- Hiring and Retaining

the sole conduit of interaction among the different organizations. This approach tends to stifle rather than foster effective communications. Rigid protocols that impede discussions and the sharing of ideas should be avoided.

2

Michael J. Earl

Integrating Business and IT Strategy
Reframing the Applications Development Portfolio

: Chapter Summary

1. Whether firms choose to integrate their formal business and IT strategies or not, they certainly need to integrate their business and IT *thinking*.
2. As the theory and practice of strategy making, in both the business and IT domains have evolved, it is perhaps useful to consider IT and business working together to assess portfolios of opportunities. This important recommendation is elaborated on in the chapters on IT value and IT governance (chapters 4 and 7).
3. One perspective is time. In bad times, we worry that the short term drives out the long term. In heady times, the emphasis seems often to be the reverse. The T-Portfolio examines how a firm is competing for today and for tomorrow. It seeks to ensure that the other does not subjugate each timeframe. It provides a tool to engage in executive discussion about the appropriate balance at different times.
4. IT can both support and shape business strategy. Often it is the support aspect that dominates executive thinking in both business and IT strategy making. As a planning tool or an audit tool, the T-Portfolio may help ensure these twin-enabling contributions of IT are properly examined. It would seem able to accompany any style or process of strategy making.
5. Firms have to compete for both today and tomorrow and it seems likely that both the content and process of today's strategies differ from those of tomorrow's strategies. Thus, the T-Portfolio looks for a balance in investments that are competing for *today* and competing for *tomorrow*—or, put another way, for evidence that IT is both supporting business strategy and shaping it.

: Introduction

One obvious effect of e-commerce has been a reassessment of both the process and content of competitive strategy and IT strategy. In the e-commerce space, especially in pure play Internet businesses, both these strategy domains seem to be enacted as one, with an emphasis on strategy-making by teamwork and strategy implementation through rolling plans (Earl & Khan, 2001). More widely, it can be argued that to have business strategy separate from an IT strategy is folly (Earl, 2000). Not only do we need to ensure we are developing IT applications and building IT infrastructures to support the current business strategy; we also should be reexamining how the business strategy should change because of the threats and opportunities presented by IT—either in the way we do business or in the business positioning we choose. In other words (fig. 2.1), IT both shapes and supports business strategy.

Whether firms choose to integrate their formal business and IT strategies or not, they certainly need to integrate their business and IT *thinking*. We know that there are several methods, styles, or processes that firms adopt in strategy making (Mintzberg, 1973; Earl, 1993; Segars & Grover, 1999), and some are more likely to achieve such integration than others. So, one practical means of ensuring a degree of integration takes place is to devise and use a tool for either assessing an application development portfolio *ex ante* or reassessing it *ex post*—or both. In other words, the framework I will propose can be seen as a planning tool or as an audit tool. I call it the T-Portfolio.

The underlying premise of the T-Portfolio is that at all times, firms are competing on two time horizons. They are very much engaged in daily battles for, and current initiatives in, the present. Indeed, several theories and models of competitive strategy—for example, the work of Porter (1980)—are principally oriented toward visible and tangible timeframes. Likewise, as IT has evolved to the point where infrastructure and applications underpin business operations, there has to be a focus on the present and near-term in IT Strategy as well.

Not just because of the promise of ever-emerging new technologies that pose new business threats and opportunities, however, but also because other exogenous and endogenous factors change, too—demographics, politics, economics, consumer attitudes and behavior, management and organizational philosophies, innovation and creativity—businesses are competing for the future and longer term. Some more recent work on competitive strategy, for example (Hamel & Prahalad, 1994; Hamel, 1996) has been oriented toward the future and toward revolution rather than evolution. This has seemed especially relevant in the context of new media, e-business, and apparent indicators of a "new economy."

Figure 2.1. The IT-business strategy connections

In other words, firms have to compete for both today and tomorrow (Abell, 1999) and it seems likely that both the content and process of today's strategies differ from those of tomorrow's strategies. Thus, the T-Portfolio looks for a balance in investments that are competing for *today* and competing for *tomorrow*—or, put another way, for evidence that IT is both supporting business strategy and shaping it.

⁞ *Competing for Today*

In the "theory" and practice of IT strategy-making, there are different, or perhaps complementary, views on how to align the applications development portfolio with business strategy. The "top down" school usually has as its starting point explication of a firm's business strategy, followed by identifying applications to support the different strategic thrusts. Alternatively, candidate application ideas may be validated against the espoused business strategy. If, as argued earlier, most business strategies are framed in the current dynamics of competition, the result is essentially an applications development portfolio (Portfolio management is discussed further in the chapter 4) that meets today's needs, even if it implies a three-year (or longer) timeframe for implementation.

The "bottom up" school usually has as its starting point solicitation of user suggestions and ideas. The merit of this process is that such proposals are mostly grounded in the needs of daily business and the experience of using and deploying existing systems. As many managers learn by doing, or from experience, such a process can be a rich and relevant source of application ideas. Once again, however, the time orientation is the present.

A more emergent school of IT strategy-making, sometimes called "middle out" or "inside out," rests on local experimentation and innovation, the use of informal, *ad hoc* or formal teams to generate ideas, unplanned accidents and surprises, and evolutionary developments from existing systems. The results can be as much oriented toward the future as the present, possibly providing a mechanism of continuity that links the two. The "middle out" school, however, is not explicitly focused on the future.

In other words, most IT strategy-making tends to be grounded in the present rather than the future—or more graphically today rather than tomorrow. This is partly a function of executive and organizational mindsets and the focus on short-term performance as much as the orientation of most schools of IT strategy-making. If it were different, however, it would suggest misalignment rather than alignment with business strategy, because competitive strategy is rightly at least as much concerned with the daily battles of the marketplace and the current strengths of internal resources as it is with carving out a different or new future. Short-term survival is a precondition of longer-term renewal.

Indeed, when shocks arrive—business mistakes, economic recessions, political surprises, much as being experienced as I write this chapter—the need is to focus on the present, to ensure survival. So there are periods when a viable application development portfolio is dominated by today, not tomorrow. The left-hand side of figure 2.2, the T-Portfolio, therefore will have more content, where the emphasis is on IT supporting the business or competing for today.

▪ Today Investments

At any time, most business executives would have more confidence in an application development portfolio that had some short-term deliverables or quick wins. Most CIOs would want the same, because they know that their credibility—a key to survival (Earl & Feeny, 1994)—is improved by having a stream of deliverables. So ideas that generate rapid payback, help make life easier, or are a basic necessity should be present in every portfolio. They may be generated by any of the three "schools" outlined earlier, but are particularly likely to be outcomes of "bottom up" processes. These quick wins or essentials we can call *the basics* (fig. 2.3), or, more colloquially, "low hanging fruit." They are not "killer applications," but they are useful basic systems.

The crux of strategic alignment thinking, however, is to ensure there are IT applications that support the thrusts of competitive strategy. These

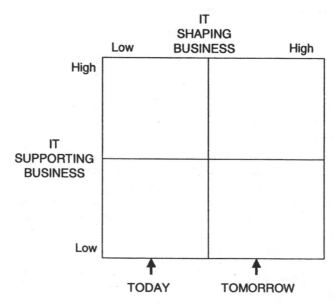

Figure 2.2. T-portfolio template

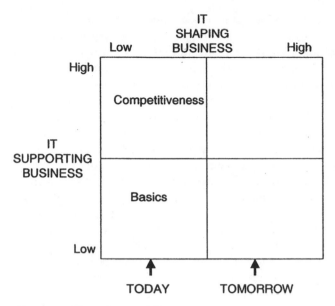

Figure 2.3. The today portfolio

are the killer applications. Here, "top down" processes do help in identifying and selecting them. Perhaps the critical success factors method (Rockart, 1979) is the obvious logic to employ because, in short, we seek a set of IT investments that enable achievement of operational goals critical to business success or superior performance. And if such seemingly strategic ideas happen to be generated by more "bottom up" or "middle out" processes, we can assess and rank them against a rubric of critical success factors.

Thus, the today side of the T-Portfolio also should have a set of IT projects that are seen as pillars of *competitiveness*. Earl's (1993) study of IS Strategic Planning suggested that successful IS/IT strategies comprised just three or four themes pursued over several years, and we might expect most of these themes to be ones of current competitiveness.

In allocating capital expenditure, the competitiveness cell should far outweigh the basics cell. This is where applications should be classified as either "competitive necessity" systems or "competitive advantage" systems (Clemons & Row, 1998).

▪ *Competing for Tomorrow*

The argument that IT can shape business strategy as well as support it has become more potent with the arrival of the Internet and e-commerce. Two claims often are made. First, potentially these "new technologies" can lead to firms repositioning themselves as industry boundaries change and value systems are reconfigured, and they can enable new ways of doing business by exploiting network structures and information richness. Second, because this is new territory, all the options are not yet known or understood; therefore, elements of both imagination and learning by doing are required.

The first claim suggests that any application development portfolio that claims to be strategic, or is also concerned with tomorrow, should comprise some investments that are carving out new positions and new ways of doing business. Otherwise, a firm may be blindsided by more perceptive and nimble players. The second claim suggests that necessarily some projects will have to be seen as "soft," either rather creative and speculative (options if you will), or more experimental in which the goal is as much about discovery and learning as about pursuit of a definitive commercial payoff.

Most IT strategy-making and the resultant strategies do not score highly on either creativity or experimentation. The same could be said for business strategies, although recently more attention has been paid to these issues—at least in the literature (Mintzberg & Lampel, 1999).

In the case of IT strategy-making, there often are calls for visions and visioning, but examples still tend to be grounded more in the present than in the future. If the intent is *shaping* business, this is where imagination, scenarios, brainstorming, and storyboards take over from analysis, success factors, continuous improvement suggestions, and feasibility studies. Of course, the scenarios or storyboards have to make business sense, but you are not likely to hit pon novel and different ideas by starting with business analysis. As one French designer1 puts it "virtuality can influence reality." To *imagine* futures may lead IT strategists, and business strategists, to discovering an exciting yet realistic strategic vision. Sometimes technology and new media may even mediate such imagination—as the above quotation suggests.

One rationale for an experimental approach as well is that the future, and thus viable strategies, are uncertain and unknowable and therefore may need to be discovered by doing. A related argument is that in rapidly changing times—for example, in the e-commerce boom—strategy is a race to learn. Therefore, learning devices such as experiments make sense. Indeed, experimentation is not entirely unknown in the information systems domain; prototyping is one obvious example. Here we are concerned, however, with prototyping the future. The tomorrow spirit is, "Let's see if we can change the paradigm and if it makes sense," rather than the more usual today spirit of prototyping, namely, "Let's see if this application will work and discover how to make it work."

So a balanced T-Portfolio will have some content on the right-hand side of figure 2.2, in which IT is being deployed to shape the business, ensuring today and the present do not background or drive out tomorrow and the future. One would not expect as many or even as large IT investments targeting tomorrow as those targeting today. After all, the future is more uncertain and portfolio approaches to strategic decisions are usually to do with managing risk. Nevertheless, in periods of excitement about the future, in which directions seem to be unfolding rapidly, one would hope to see some IT investments being made on the right-hand side of the T-Portfolio.

⁞ *Tomorrow Investments*

Experiments (fig. 2.4) are those projects that make some sense in today's context and may turn out to be really innovative and with further investment might shape the business of tomorrow. Therefore, they are low in both supporting today's business and, initially at least, in shaping tomorrow's business. They are not "bankers" in Return on Investment (R.O.I.) terms, nor are they "killer applications," because their impact or success is far from certain. They are experiments that may turn out to be winners, may suggest another experiment or incremental investment in due course, may turn out to be just mildly useful for a time at least, or may be short-lived and "written off to the learning budget." Accordingly, two or three true experiments may be the maximum any one business unit should tolerate, even in the best of times.

Visions are those projects that are bold moves to create new strategic positioning or some new source of competitive advantage. They are thus

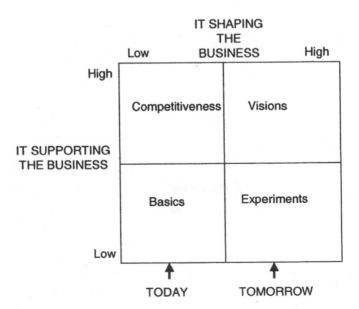

Figure 2.4. The today and tomorrow portfolio

high in potential for shaping the business of tomorrow. Unless there is no thread back to the current business or business context—and most strategic thrusts or visions *ex post* are seen to be connected to the present or past—they also will make increasing sense in terms of supporting today. At the least there is a good story to tell now. Because these are "big bets" or "strategic investments," however, any T-Portfolio would not contain more that one or two such visions.

⦙   *Retrofitting a Case Study*

British Airways (BA) has been pioneering ideas of e-business for some years (Earl, Anderson, & Perks, 2001). In early 2001, the e-business division of BA assessed its portfolio of projects, both completed and under development, looking for focus and seeing what it had learned so far. It can be imagined that with the severe shock faced by airlines in the fall of 2001 that BA *may* have wanted to assess the e-business portfolio once more as all investments and costs came under scrutiny. One way of doing this *could* be to use the T-Portfolio as an audit tool, no doubt emphasizing today and survival over tomorrow and industry leadership. Indeed, in teaching the BA case study (Earl et al.), this exercise can be done vicariously. While deeper knowledge of BA or the case study would help in understanding and evaluating the contents of figure 2.5, we can see how the exercise might work.

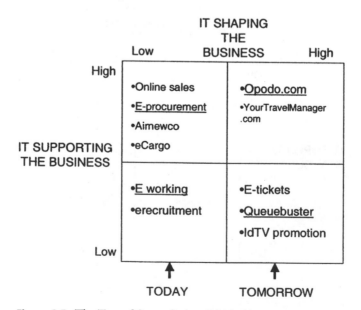

Figure 2.5. The T-portfolio applied to British Airways

The underscored projects or applications are those I select to justify the classification. E-working, in the basics cell, is about use of the Internet and BA's intranet to convey company information to employees, to provide answers to frequently asked questions, to automate training and so on. It should reduce administrative costs, simplify daily work activities, and improve information flow across the corporation. It is thus a basic investment, useful—probably valued over time—but probably will not make or break BA's competitiveness.

E-procurement, in the competitiveness cell, may promise more than it achieves, as others have found, but with potential to reduce costs in an industry in which profits are not easily made, to reduce spares and consumables replenishment time, and to improve coordination in the aircraft supply chain, it can be seen as an important defensive action in the daily battle for competitiveness.

"Queue Buster," in the experiments cell, is a new technology experiment in which a cybernaut-like check-in agent uses an around the body keyboard, display unit, and battery to complete on the spot check-ins. Sort of "wacky," it represents an experiment to reengineer a core subprocess with advanced technology and learn what might be possible, including user and customer reactions.

Opodo.com, in the visions cell, is an important joint venture across European airlines to create an online travel portal. I classify it in the vision cell because it attacks other nonairline portals in the Internet space, it is explicitly designed to exploit network structures to sell air travel related services as well as seats on planes, and it is one move, among others, to disintermediate travel agents.

BA might conclude from figure 2.5 that the portfolio has a good balance between today and tomorrow. Today-focused projects outnumber tomorrow-focused ones, which makes sense when the company is seeking to restore profitability in a highly competitive market place. As BA recognizes, however, that e-commerce and the Internet represent threats as much as opportunities in the next few years, they could be expected to maintain investment in some low-risk experiments and in one or two visions for changing their position in the marketplace. If capital becomes heavily rationed and today's performance and cash flow dominate the agenda, then a second hard look might be taken at the experiments and business performance targets set for the vision projects as well as the competitiveness ones.

: Conclusions

It is conventional wisdom and practice to think of the information systems plan as an applications development portfolio. The use of portfolios is included in chapter 4. Suggestions have been made over the year about the structure of these portfolios, for example, looking at project risks (McFarlan,

1981) or application types (Earl, 1989). As the theory and practice of strategy making, in both the business and IT domains, have evolved it is perhaps useful to revisit these ideas.

One perspective is time. In bad times, we worry that the short-term drives out the long term. In heady times, the emphasis seems often to be the reverse. The T-Portfolio attempts to explicitly and formally examines how a firm is competing for today and for tomorrow. It seeks both to ensure that the other does not subjugate each timeframe and to provide a tool to engage in executive discussion about the appropriate balance at different times.

It also recognizes that IT can both support and shape business strategy. Often it is the support aspect that dominates executive thinking in both business and IT strategy making. As a planning tool or an audit tool, the T-Portfolio may help ensure these twin-enabling contributions of IT are properly examined. It would seem able to accompany any style or process of strategy making.

: Note

1. I am grateful to Chafik Gasmi, Artistic Director of Sephora, for this insight.

: References

Abell, D. F. (1999) "Competing Today While Preparing for Tomorrow," *Sloan Management Review*, 40(3), 73–81.

Brown S. L., & K. M. Eisenhardt. (1998) *Competing on the Edge: Strategy and Structured Chaos*. Boston, MA: Harvard Business School Press.

Clemons E., & M. Row. (1998) "McKesson Drug Company: A Case Study of Economost—A Strategic Information System," *Journal of Management Information Systems*, 5(1), 36–50.

Earl, M. J. (1989) *Management Strategies for Information Technology*. Hemel Hempstead, UK: Prentice Hall.

Earl, M. J. (1993) "Experience in Strategic Information Systems Planning," *MISQuarterly*, 17(1), 1–24.

Earl, M. J. (2000) "IT Strategy in the New Economy," *Financial Times Mastering Management*, Dec. 18.

Earl M. J., J. Anderson, & T. Perks (2001). British Airways: Transitioning to e-business. London Business School Case Study LBS-CS-01-005.

Earl M. J., & D. F. Feeny. (1994) "Is Your CIO Adding Value?" *Sloan Management Review*, 35(3), 11–20.

Earl M. J., & B. Khan. (2001) "E-Commerce Is Changing the Face of IT," *Sloan Management Review*, 43(1), 64–72.

Hamel G., & C. K. Prahalad. (1994) *Competing for the Future*. Boston, MA: Harvard Business School Press.

Hamel G. (1996) "Strategy as Revolution." *Harvard Business Review*, 74, 69–82.

McFarlan, F. W. (1981) "Portfolio Approach to Information Systems," *Harvard Business Review*, 58(4), 142–50.

Mintzberg, H. (1973) "Strategy Making in Three Modes," *Californian Management Review*, 16(2), 44–53.

Mintzberg H., & J. Lampel. (1999) "Reflecting on the Strategy Process," *Sloan Management Review*, 40(3), 21–30.

Porter, M. E. (1980) *Competitive Strategy*. New York: Free Press.

Rockart, J. F. (1979) "Chief Executives Define Their Own Data Needs," *Harvard Business Review*, 57(2), 81–92.

Segars, A., & V. Grover. (1999) "Profiles of Strategic Information Systems Planning," *Information Systems Research*, 10(3), 199–232.

3

James C. Wetherbe and Glenn J. Browne

Recognizing the Functionality of the Future

⦂ *Chapter Summary*

1. Differentiating products and developing market niches achieve sustainable competitive advantage most effectively.
2. Information technologies provide valuable tools for differentiating products and developing market niches.
3. Using superior information gathering methods is critical for organizations in anticipating future consumer needs.
4. Technology usually advances more quickly than the techniques available to apply the technology successfully. Recognizing the needed functionality of the future requires that organizations align their information gathering methods with the technology available.
5. Ideally, organizations should aim to make their products or services available to customers any time, any place, and any way, and at a reasonable price.
6. Organizations that are able to utilize technology to gather useful information are more likely to anticipate future consumer needs and desires accurately and to build sustainable competitive advantage.

⦂ *Introduction*

Most organizations share three common concerns. First, they are overwhelmed by the rapidly growing amount of computing and network technology they know less and less about. To achieve and sustain competitive advantage, however, these organizations must apply technological innovations, including the Internet, effectively and efficiently. Second, organizations are under pressure to improve customer service while simultaneously reducing costs. This would appear to be contradictory. Yet computer technology, which has traditionally decreased in cost even while increasing in capability, can be used to achieve these apparently contradictory results. The third concern is a stronger than ever desire to achieve competitive advantage through product or service innovations. This requires that organizations accurately recognize the needs and desires of consumers of the future.

Over the past 40 years, most organizations have used computing technology to improve *existing* operations. In the future, technology will be used to innovate *new* businesses, products, and services. This chapter first briefly reviews strategies for achieving competitive advantage and harnessing the power of information technology. We then focus on discovering the functionality of the future through improved information gathering.

: Competitive Strategy

The seminal work on competitive advantage, Michael Porter's *Competitive Strategy* (Porter, 1980), presents three basic approaches for gaining competitive advantage:

- Be the low-cost producer
- Differentiate
- Fill a market niche

Of these three strategies, becoming the *low-cost producer* is the riskiest. If price is the only reason customers are doing business with you, lower prices from a competitor will result in fewer customers for you and possibly a price war. Ideally, a company does not want to be vulnerable to such actions from its competition. Competitive advantage can be achieved by some type of product or service differentiation or by filling a special niche in the marketplace. Perhaps one of the clearest examples of product differentiation is Harley-Davidson motorcycle. This product traditionally has a one- to two-year delay between order and delivery. Potential customers have the choice of buying an alternative product, such as a Japanese cruiser, with immediate delivery, a lower price, and, some would argue, a technically superior product. People wait for the Harleys, however, because of the look, sound, feel, and spirit—essentially the mystique that differentiates the product from all others. When someone feels so strongly about a product that they will tattoo the product name on their body, the company has achieved a high level of differentiation.

Continental Airlines has used aircraft cabin design to *differentiate* its product. Several years ago, Continental overhauled its international business class cabin, combining it with first class to create what it dubbed "BusinessFirst." Continental priced the cabin at the high end of the international business class range, but far below other carriers' first class sections. Because BusinessFirst was much better than other airlines' business cabins, Continental was able to attract strong bookings and win many quality and satisfaction awards from frequent flyers and independent consumer survey organizations. Although it is the fifth largest of the major full-service U.S. airlines, it has been the most consistently profitable over the past few years.

Progressive Insurance provides a good example of filling a *market niche*. Most insurance companies consider motorcyclists risky to insure and have what many consider unreasonable rates for this group. Progressive, by contrast, realized that Harley owners represented a unique market niche. The typical Harley owner is over 40 years old, earns a respectable income, and rides the motorcycle for recreational purposes only (owners spend more time polishing it than driving it). The most popular Harley-Davidson model is the Heritage Classic, a 1950s retro-styled motorcycle. Harleys have 65 horsepower with lots of torque for cruising at low speeds, which is what Harley owners enjoy most. Contrast the typical Harley owner to someone who would buy a high-performance Japanese sport bike, which has 150 horsepower, accelerates from 0 to 60 mph in 2.5 seconds, and has a top speed of 175 mph. The Japanese sport bike is popular among 19-year-old men who prefer models such as the Kawasaki "Ninja." Do the Harley owner and Japanese sport bike owner appear to be different insurance risks? Realizing the difference, Progressive offers very attractive insurance rates to Harley owners, whom they consider a special niche in the marketplace. Of course, Harley owners are grateful for the reasonable rates on their motorcycle insurance. As a result, Progressive is able to market insurance for automobiles, homes, and so on, to the Harley owner.

┇ Harnessing Information Technology

The Porter model has served many companies well in formulating their strategies. A traditional issue with computing technology is that most companies think of computers in terms of only one thing—to reduce costs (i.e., be a low-cost supplier). The innovative and clever company, however, can use information technology to differentiate its product or services or fill a niche in the marketplace (e.g., Progressive Insurance tracking new Harley registrations). The key difference in applying the Porter framework today is that competitive strategists no longer enjoy the long-term stability that they previously had. Strategies are much more dynamic with shorter life cycles.

As the pace of innovation has increased, so, too, has consumers' search for the next new advancement. A good example is using the World Wide Web for information or shopping. When the Web first achieved mainstream usage in the mid-1990s, and home computers were equipped with modems, the fact that people could communicate with each other, search vast sources of information, and even purchase products online overwhelmed any dissatisfaction with the speed of the modem. As broadband technologies have become available, however, people with modems are increasingly impatient with the speed of searches and transactions. Consumers now look for fast and continuous innovation and improvement, and are dissatisfied without it.

Organizations should be ready to act based on something their competition does. A good example of a recent strategic move is FedEx's action during the 1997 UPS strike. After UPS workers went on strike, thus increasing the demand for FedEx services, FedEx successfully increased its effort to provide world-class delivery. This accomplished two things. First, UPS customers forced to choose alternative carriers were impressed with FedEx service. Second, FedEx was able to accumulate a lot of extra cash because of the additional revenue. After the strike was over, FedEx used its "full pockets" to increase its ground delivery capacity through the acquisition of Caliber System to improve its competitiveness (FedEx has always had a larger air fleet than UPS, while UPS has always had the advantage of a larger ground fleet). FedEx used elements of speed and surprise to strengthen its position in the marketplace by making this strategic move, rather than just reaping the benefits of the cash flow during the strike.

⁝ *Gathering Information for Strategic Competitive Advantage*

The functionality of the future is what customers want and will pay for. We live in an increasingly consumer-driven economy, in which competition, ubiquitous information and comparison sources, and falling prices driven by technology and productivity gains all contribute to customer demands. To anticipate future functionality requirements and thereby gain competitive advantage, it is necessary to do a better job of gathering and organizing information. A useful starting point for anticipating future functionality is a framework known as the Customer Resource Life Cycle (Ives & Learmouth, 1984; Wetherbe & Vitalari, 1994), which is shown in figure 3.1. The life cycle describes a series of stages through which consumers pass in developing a relationship with a company. For purposes of understanding the functionality of the future, we will focus on the third step in the life cycle, that is, "Establish Requirements."

- Identify/Research/Profile
- Educate/Advertise/Market
- Establish Requirements
- Price/Order/Deliver/Payment
- Test/Accept
- Integrate/Monitor/Upgrade
- Maintenance/Dispose/Account For
- Feedback/Network

Figure 3.1 The customer resource life cycle

⦂ *Establishing Requirements*

The key to anticipating the functionality of the future is gathering, filtering, and organizing information. Understanding the requirements of customers is central to sustainable competitive advantage. Knowledge alone, however, no longer represents power. Rather, it is the right knowledge at the right time and appropriate cost that is key. Recognizing future functionality means gathering and organizing information proactively. This will require a significant investment in intelligence gathering capabilities. There are many ways to gather information effectively. Figure 3.2 presents a list of useful means of establishing customer requirements. We discuss each method later in this chapter.

Use Feedback

Feedback is critical to understanding customer needs and to fine-tuning products and services. Amazon.com always gathers feedback from customers when making changes to its website. For example, the company recently redesigned the menu tabs at the top of its pages in response to customer feedback about the usability of the tabs. Online auction company ebay has taken feedback to lofty heights. Not only does it provide its well-known feedback forum, which allows buyers and sellers to assess each other's reliability, it also monitors activity in items sold and creates new categories of items based on this indirect feedback. In this way, the indirect feedback allows the marketplace to drive the categories, and ebay is assured of categories that already have a strong level of demand.

Use Focus Groups

Focus groups are familiar means for gathering information from customers in a variety of domains, ranging from marketing to information systems development. Although sometimes derided recently as not "cutting edge" in

---

- · Use Feedback
- · Use Focus Groups
- · Use Prototyping
- · Share Knowledge
- · Build Trust and Personalize Experiences
- · Use Electronic Eavesdropping
- · Provide User Involvement Mechanisms

Figure 3.2 Information gathering methods

knowledge gathering, the method has shown surprising resiliency over the years. Focus groups take advantage of several proven methods for gathering information, including face-to-face contact and allowing knowledge to emerge from the interaction of the participants. United Airlines used focus groups to gather information for a redesign of the company's website in 1999. Based on information gathered, including the need to check flight status and monitor frequent-flyer accounts, the company implemented a redesigned website that has proven much more satisfying to customers ("Fix It and They Will Come," 2001). Internet discount fashion clothing seller Bluefly.com recently used focus groups to gather information about its core customers and to redesign its website to be more appealing to those customers ("Making the Sale," 2001).

Use Prototyping

Prototyping involves building a small-scale model of a process or system that shows basic functionality but is not overly costly to build. Similar processes to prototyping in other disciplines include "usability testing," "proof-of-concept," and "storyboarding." The advantage of using a prototype with customers is that it gives them an actual physical item to which they can respond rather than only an abstract description. Online travel agency Expedia.com employs widespread prototyping efforts to enhance its website's appearance. For instance, when redesigning the appearance of web pages displaying flight information, Expedia's designers build hundreds of possible page layouts and hold dozens of meetings with customers ("Testing, Testing, Testing," 2001). Paypal.com, the Internet payment site, builds prototypes of potential changes in their web pages and then videotapes customers as they navigate through the site ("Fix it and They Will Come," 2001). From the videotapes, the company learns what works well, what customers struggle with, and what features are candidates to be altered or eliminated.

Share Knowledge

Sharing knowledge across organizational functions or units within an organization, or between organizations, can often yield superlative results in refining products or services. For example, members of supply chains can use knowledge of scheduling practices or new products at other companies in the supply chain to adjust their own procedures to reduce cycle time. Companies downstream in a supply chain are customers whose requirements must be assessed to ensure that the supply chain works efficiently and effectively. Moen, Inc., a large faucet company, decreased cycle time in designing new faucets from 24 weeks to five days by posting new designs on the Internet and allowing suppliers to make design changes to the virtual products ("Opening the Spigot," 2001). Ford Motor Company has also leveraged knowledge sharing to improve designs. By sharing proposed design changes with its own engineers and external suppliers on the Internet, Ford has reduced the amount of time necessary to judge the impact of design changes on fuel economy from three days to less than a minute ("E-Biz: Down But Hardly Out," 2001). In another endeavor, Ford also reduced the number of people in its accounts payable and purchasing from 500 to 100 by sharing its production requirements with its suppliers and allowing them to automatically order, deliver, and keep in stock only necessary inventory.

Build Trust and Personalize Experiences

Building trust with customers can profoundly affect the ease with which information is gathered. If customers trust that the information they provide to an organization will be used properly, they will be much more inclined to give thoughtful, true, and useful information. Part of building trust is simply providing reasonable prices and consistently good service. In the current era, trust also can be enhanced dramatically by protecting customers' privacy and ensuring the security of transactions. In our studies of Internet shopping by members of Generation Y, the security of the transaction was the number one disadvantage people listed for shopping on-line (Browne & Wetherbe, 2002).

Unfortunately, reports of the inadvertent release of sensitive customer data by corporations worldwide continue to surface. Trust also can be engendered by personalizing experiences with customers, which help build relationships and loyalty. Amazon.com's well-documented personalization techniques include providing recommendations for customers based on past purchases. It also has introduced a feature that recommends products based on items a person clicks on at the Amazon website, even if he has never made a purchase. Finally, another effort to build trust and community by Amazon is its feature that allows people to write on-line reviews of products. These online reviews increase trust by providing unbiased (or at least not company-sponsored) judgments about products.

In a strategy combining elements of data mining (discussed later) and personalization, BrooksBrothers.com, a unit of the well-known clothier, analyzes the websites a person has visited in the past and develops a profile of that customer. The opening web page on the company's site seen by each visitor is based on the profile developed ("Making the Sale," 2001). The experience is thus personalized for a visitor, which may help the company convert more visitors into purchasers.

Use Electronic Eavesdropping

An important new method for assessing customer requirements is known as "electronic eavesdropping." With this method, companies pay people browsing websites, posting messages in chat rooms, and participating in online communities to allow them to monitor the users' behavior and to record their messages, clicks, and purchases. The goal is to use both ethnographic and standard quantitative techniques to understand consumers' behavior better. Companies such as Kraft Foods, Coca-Cola, Motorola, and Hallmark Cards have used electronic eavesdropping to gain insights into their customers' habits, needs, and shopping patterns ("Friendly Spies on the Net," 2001). This kind of data collection assesses needs by evaluating people's lifestyles and filling functionality niches that might otherwise go wanting. Coca-Cola, for example, launched a version of Powerade that contained B vitamins as a result of electronic eavesdropping efforts.

Provide Consumer Involvement Mechanisms

Psychologists have long understood that involvement with a brand increases both brand retention and brand loyalty. Consumer involvement is also a means for increasing information gathering. Some websites, for example, use online quizzes to involve the consumer, build brand retention, and gather information about preferences both directly and indirectly through the quiz questions. Chat rooms, bulletin boards, and promotions such as contests and coupons can also increase involvement and gather information. For example, to qualify for a promotion, a consumer might have to provide some basic demographic information. The website may then offer a choice of coupons and tabulate what demographics choose which coupons.

Use Data Mining

Data mining involves analyzing data for trends or insights not immediately apparent. Many times data are collected for a particular reason but can then be used later for additional information. Data collected at the point of purchase, for example, may later be used to market similar or complementary products to the purchasers. As another example, Paypal learned by analyzing click data that its sign-in process (requiring users to navigate through seven screens) was far too cumbersome, and that it lost 25 percent of its users at each screen ("Fix It and They Will Come," 2001). It used these data to reduce the sign-in to one screen.

Talk Directly to Your Customers

One of the authors has a good friend who is the CEO of a large building society (similar to a savings and loan in the United States) in Great Britain. Previously, as a high-ranking executive of a different building society, he spent a significant portion of his time visiting retail branches and hanging around the lobby area talking with customers. He asked them what they liked about doing business with the company and what they did not like. He asked them what they wished they could do but could not do currently. He asked them to imagine themselves as head of the company, and asked them what they would do differently. Talking to customers is fundamental to understanding the types of functionality that people would like to have and would be willing to pay for. This executive took many of the suggestions and complaints of customers and designed initiatives to improve customer service.

Talking directly with customers may sound obvious, but it is often neglected or forgotten in favor of more elaborate information gathering techniques. Encouraging employees to talk with customers and providing ways for information gathered to reach top management and strategic planners in organizations is fundamental, however, to continuous improvement efforts. Many, if not most, future needs are initially identified in a "bottom-up" fashion from people who use products and services rather than "top-down" from the supply side. Listening to customers and acting on what is heard can spur significant innovations.

All of these methods can provide insights into the functionality of the future by analyzing customer needs. Organizations are often slow to adopt new methods, however, for reasons we discuss next.

⁝ Technique Lags Technology

Technology is a great tool to gather information and improve relationships with customers. Unfortunately, the ideas described earlier are obvious *after* the fact. What organizations generally try to do, however, is to identify and capitalize on a technological innovation before someone else does.

One problem is that when we see new technologies we tend to use them in old ways. This is a real historical pattern. For example, automobiles were called horseless carriages for years, as if something were missing. In the eighteenth century, soldiers continued to line up shoulder-to-shoulder several layers deep in brightly colored uniforms and march in lines into open meadows, a very dysfunctional technique once rifle technology was developed. The old military technique was based on sword and shield technology, when it made sense to group together in straight linear fashion. This method became devastatingly obsolete, however, when rifles arrived. Again, the old technique was used with new technology.

The same type of problem occurs as new innovations in computer technology are developed. Consider automatic teller machines (ATMs). The first ATMs were located inside the bank. Why? An ATM was just a teller window without the teller. Many commentators had reservations about ATMs, arguing that people would rather have personal customer service. But the banks persisted, placing them in bank lobbies. The real added value came, however, when ATMs were placed *outside* the bank, where they were available to customers 24 hours a day. Taking cash and leaving it in a machine in malls was not an easy innovation for most bankers to embrace. To many of them, it was a *joke*.

In fact, the nature of most innovations in the first stage of perception is a *joke*, the second stage is *denial* (i.e., "there is no way we would do that"), and the third stage is when the innovation becomes *accepted practice*. The real art to strategic innovation is to recognize when a joke is really an innovation, and to do so before the competition does.

Historically, industry leaders have left innovation experimentation to new, upstart companies. If an idea worked, then others would quickly follow by adopting the innovation. Increasingly, being just a fast follower is not a good strategy. Customers find out very quickly about a new competitive advantage and they can make a quick shift. For example, Visa's alliance with airlines allowing customers to receive frequent flyer points had an adverse effect on American Express, which had previously enjoyed an advantage in terms of preference among upscale business travelers. American Express took a couple of years to develop a comparable system. In the meantime, thousands of customers were lost and many of them never came back to American Express.

Organizations need to align their techniques with the technologies that are available for information gathering. In our discussion of information gathering methods, we included methods that would have been unthinkable only 10 years ago, such as electronic eavesdropping and data mining. Using today's technologies can increase the speed and the scopes of information gathered, as well as provide better understanding of the information, giving companies an advantage in anticipating consumer preferences.

▪ *Future Perfect*

Stan Davis, in his book *Future Perfect* (1987), illustrates a direct and powerful means to establish a vision of the future. His basic assumption is that technology is going to get *better* and *better* and *better*. If we accept this premise, it follows that employing technology will improve any business. When "better and better and better" is taken to its logical conclusion, it becomes perfect.

So, the trick is to determine what perfect will look like in the future. A company's continuous information gathering should put it on a journey toward perfection, and at least put it closer to perfection than the competition.

What does perfect look like? It is when customers are given what they want:

- Any time
- Any place
- Any way

If customers are required to go to their bank during banking hours in the city in which they live, there is a huge gap between perfect and actually receiving money. If the bank puts ATMs outside the bank and customers can withdraw money in $20 increments, however, that is closer to perfect than before. If ATMs are placed around the city, that is even closer to perfection. If those ATMs are located around the country, it is even better. If customers can withdraw money in increments other than $20, that is, exact change, the situation is even closer to perfect.

As a different example, consider the process of renting a car. Historically, most car rental companies required customers to wait in line, fill out forms, and then assigned a car of their choosing in a size requested. If a customer did not like the car assigned, however, an unpleasant situation was created, particularly if there was a long line. National Car Rental was the first rental company to innovate in this area with its Emerald Card. National stores customer information digitally on the Emerald Card so forms are not needed for every rental. The Emerald Card is scanned, and the customer selects the car of his choice from those available. This process not only allows customers to have it his way, it also reduces the time required for the rental process, and is closer to perfect. An added benefit for National is reduced clerical costs.

A classic example of limited inventory availability is sheet music. It is highly unlikely to find a particular piece of music in stock, and ordering may take weeks. Sadly, most music stores have inventory that rarely moves, often sitting on shelves for years. Several years ago, technology was developed that allowed customers to choose from thousands of pieces and print the desired music on a laser printer—in the preferred key—in the music store. Stores that purchased that technology had moved closer to perfect. Today, people can print music from the Internet while sitting at their home computer, which is very close to perfection.

In addition to any time, any place, and any way, the one remaining important factor is appropriate price. That is, people are willing to pay different prices depending on how well their time, place, and way preferences are addressed. For example, at golf tournaments worldwide, it is common to see vendors selling low-quality umbrellas for $20. Why would anyone pay $20 for a low-quality umbrella? If someone has paid $100 to watch the golf tournament, it has started to rain, and he did not bring an umbrella, it is worth it to him to pay an extra $20 so he can continue to watch the golf tournament with some degree of enjoyment. When eating an upscale restaurant, people regularly pay five to ten times as much for a glass of wine as they would if they bought the same wine in a supermarket or liquor store. Again, the time and place has an impact on what people are willing to pay for a product.

The perfect product or service is one that meets customer preferences on time, place, and way. Understanding these preferences is critical to differentiating products and finding market niches.

: Conclusion

Building sustainable competitive advantage (and products and services that approach perfection) in the future requires that organizations discover the functionality users require and desire. To do this successfully, organizations will have to harness information technology to help gather user requirements in new and novel ways. In this chapter, we have discussed many of the ways in which information can be gathered, and have underscored the challenges that await organizations in the years ahead.

: References

Browne, G. J., & J. C. Wetherbe. (2002) *Technical Report #0119-02*. Institute for Internet Buyer Behavior, Texas Tech University, Lubbock, TX.

Davis, S. (1987) *Future Perfect*. Reading, MA: Addison-Wesley Publishing.

"E-Biz: Down But Hardly Out." (2001) *Business Week*, March 26, 126–130.

"Fix It and They Will Come." (2001) *The Wall Street Journal*, February 12, R4.

"Friendly Spies on the Net." (2001) *Business Week*, July 9, EB26–EB28.

Ives, B., & G. Learmouth. (1984) "The Information System as a Competitive Weapon," *Communications of the ACM*, 27(12), 1193–1201.

"Making the Sale." (2001) *The Wall Street Journal*, September 24, R6.

"Opening the Spigot" (2001) *Business Week*, June 4, EB 17–20.

Porter, M. E. (1980) *Competitive Strategy*. New York: Free Press.

"Testing, Testing, Testing." (2001) *The Wall Street Journal*, December 10, R8.

Wetherbe, J. C., & N. P. Vitalari. (1994) *Systems Analysis and Design: Best Practices*. 4th ed. St. Paul, MN: West Publishing.

III

Competency/Value Measurement

Too many IT organizations cannot demonstrate their value to the business in terms that the business understands. Frequently, business and IT metrics of value differ. A balanced "dashboard" that demonstrates the value of IT in terms of contribution to the business is needed.

Frequently, organizations devote significant resources to measuring performance factors. They spend much less of their resources, however, on taking ac-

COMPETENCY/VALUE MEASUREMENTS
- IT Metrics
- Business Metrics
- Balanced Metrics
- Service Level Agreements
- Benchmarking
- Formal Assessment/ Reviews
- Continuous Improvement

COMMUNICATIONS
- Understanding of Business by IT
- Understanding of IT by Business
- Inter/Intra organizational Learning/Education
- Protocol Rigidity
- Knowledge Sharing
- Liaison(s) effectiveness

GOVERNANCE
- Business Strategic Planning
- IT Strategic Planning
- Organization Structure Reporting
- Budgetary Control
- IT Investment Management
- Steering Committee(s)
- Prioritization Process

IT BUSINESS ALIGNMENT MATURITY CRITERIA

PARTNERSHIP
- Business Perception of IT Value
- Role of IT in Strategic Business Shared Goals, Risk, Rewards/Penalties
- IT Program Management
- Relationship/Trust Style
- Business Sponsor/ Champion

SCOPE AND ARCHITECTURE
- Traditional, Enabler/ Driver, External
- Standards Articulate
- Architecture Integration:
  - Functional Organization
  - Enterprise
  - Inter-enterprise
- Architectural Transparency, Agility, Flexibility
- Manage Emerging Technology

SKILLS
- Innovation, Entrepreneurship
- Culture Locus of Power
- Management Style
- Change Readiness
- Career Crossover Training
- Social, Political, Trusting Interpersonal Environment
- Hiring and Retaining

tion based on these measurements. For example, an organization that requires an ROI before a project begins, but that does not review how well objectives were met after the project was deployed provides little to the organization. It is important to assess these criteria to understand (1) the factors that lead to missing the criteria and (2) what can be learned to improve the environment continuously.

4

Jerry Luftman and C. Timothy Koeller

Assessing the Value of IT

∶ *Chapter Summary*

1. Setting priorities for IT projects and effectively allocating resources to align IT and business strategies have become fundamental aspects of an organization's success. Both IT and other business managers should share in the evaluation of the portfolio of the organizations projects. It is important to recognize that the ultimate value of the project(s) will not come from the technology alone. The real value comes from how the business applies the technology to change the respective business process(es).
2. Changes to a business process should not be "owned" by the IT project team. It ought to be "owned" by a business sponsor and champion(s). The roles played by the business sponsor and champion(s) are critical to the success of the project and to the attainment of its benefits.
3. Ask 10 different business and IT leaders how best to measure the value of IT investments, and you will likely get at least ten different approaches. Traditional financial techniques (e.g., Return on Investment, Discounted Cash Flows, Net Present Value) have shortcomings that need to be recognized. It is the combination of getting IT and business to work together using portfolio management, real options analysis, and a value management approach that is most effective.
4. The value management approach provides organizations seeking an IT-leveraged path to competitiveness with a model that can help to identify improvements in customer-focused processes. It starts by understanding the business objectives and value. Second, the business process changes necessary to obtain the business value are reviewed. Last, the information technologies necessary to change the business process that will bring the business value are defined. IT and business management must work together to identify these organizational benefits, which represent a Total Value of Ownership.

∶ *Introduction*

Organizations are investing millions of dollars annually in information technology (IT). Setting priorities for IT projects and effectively allocating resources to align IT and business strategies have become fundamental aspects of an organization's success. The well-documented pace of investment in information technology (IT) during the past two decades has led many IT managers, consultants, and academics to identify useful methods for assessing and justifying the business value of these investments. Ask 10 different business and IT leaders how best to measure the value of IT investments, and you will likely get at least 10 different approaches. One difficulty of their search is increased by the recognition that traditional financial valuation methods typically look at each investment opportunity individually as an independent project. Focusing on individual projects limits the firm's ability to ensure that overall IT resources are being leveraged appropriately; hence, not aligned with business strategies.

Additionally, too frequently, the attainment of the benefits from these projects is based solely on the information technology. Naturally, the value brought to the business should be the focus of any measurement; it has long been recognized, however, that if the organization applies the latest and greatest information technology to inefficient, ineffective business processes, there will be little if any value added by the technology. The benefits come from how the business modifies its processes based on the new information technology. IT alone brings little value.

This chapter will provide an overview of several traditional valuation methods while introducing a combination of several new approaches. These approaches are summarized in table 4.1. This chapter also will elaborate on some of the IT governance concepts presented in chapter 7 concerning how IT and business executives share the responsibility for identifying project benefits, ensure that benefits are achieved, and effectively prioritize the allocation of IT resources.

▪ IT-Business Sharing of the Responsibility for Value Achievement

IT and business managers are required to evaluate and manage a collection, or portfolio, of projects, where each project is defined by its relative value to the business and by its relative risk.[1] These two dimensions reflect central elements of the firm's strategic management of its IT resources within the context of the firm's business goals.[2]

Another consideration that needs to be addressed, and that is implied in what has been described to this point, is that both IT and other business managers share in the evaluation of the portfolio of projects. It is important to recognize that the ultimate value of the project(s) will not come from the technology alone. The real value comes from how the business applies the technology to change the respective business process(es). Changes to a business process cannot be "owned" by the IT project team. It must be "owned" by a business sponsor and champion(s). The roles played by the business sponsor and champion(s) are critical to the success of the project and to the

Table 4.1
Summary of Value Processes

	Methodology	Strengths	Weaknesses
Return on investment (ROI), economic value added (EVA)	Analysis of financial statement data	Simple Numerical Result	Easy to manipulate. ROI can lead to contradictory or misleading results.
Real options	Conversion of IT investments into a financial concept similar to a call option.	Provides a straight forward analysis of strategic investment proposals allowing effective comparisons among both long term and short term projects. Reduces risks by permitting deferral of final commitment of funds until long term projects have reduced their uncertainty.	Requires effective skills in mapping investment opportunities into options categories while carefully defining their characteristics. Requires good judgment in risk analysis.
Portfolio valuation	Builds a framework in which investment planning, control measures that monitor project performance and incentive schemes, should all be tied to maximizing the firm's value. It is assumed that the firm will recognize the strategic mix of interdependent IT projects in evaluating them.	Assesses the interdependence of IT projects and seeks to ensure that the projects are aligned with business strategies. Ensures that the risks associated with IT investments are in line with the business view of acceptable risk.	Continuous monitoring of IT projects must be done and re-evaluations require active management of all IT investments. Needs committed and active business and IT management.
Information economics	Evaluates intangible costs, benefits and risks as complements to financial valuation results.	Improves IT investment decisions by explicitly addressing intangibles. Helps build consensus among IT stakeholders concerning investment strategies.	Relies upon subjective methods of weighting intangibles vs. financial investment criteria.

attainment of its benefits. The project executives should first identify the business objectives and benefits, and then identify the business processes that will be changed. Finally, the IT that will be deployed will be approved.

Process changes will be enabled or driven by the information technology. These process changes will be sponsored and championed by the appropriate business executives performing the appropriate roles. It is the changes to the business process, enabled/driven by IT that will bring the benefits. This value management framework is addressed in this chapter.

Another concern with traditional approaches is that, far too frequently, organizations that apply them at the beginning of a project rarely, if ever, apply them at the end of the project to assess the attainment of their goals. Additionally, these organizations fail to leverage the knowledge available at the end of the implementation to improve the process applied to select and prioritize projects at the beginning. Greater resources should be allocated to assess and learn from the measurements at the end of the process than are used to create and review the metrics created at the start of a project. It must be clear to all stakeholders that the objective of the post review is not so much to find blame but, rather, to better prepare for the future. The lessons learned could affect all aspects of project practices (e.g., prioritization, selection, resource allocation). A major opportunity to learn is too often missed.

In this chapter, we describe and critically evaluate established methods for assessing and managing the value of investment projects.[3] In addition to providing a financial basis for the investment selection decision, an important criterion in the evaluation of each method is its alignment with the strategic goals of the firm. In addition, an analysis of these methods will begin with the evaluation of an individual project, followed by methods that can be used to evaluate a portfolio of IT projects under consideration by a firm operating in an uncertain and dynamic environment.

⁞ Traditional Financial Approaches

ROI, Residual Income, and Economic Value Added of an Individual Investment

The measurement method known as Return on Investment (ROI) is widely cited as a technique for assessing the value of IT investments (see, e.g., Lewis & Koller, 2001; Violino, 1997). The ROI method was developed in the early twentieth century at DuPont Powder Co. as an effective way of allocating investment funds within a manufacturing firm comprising a number of functional activities (e.g., manufacturing, selling, purchasing), each of which is viewed as an investment center. ROI is generally calculated as net earnings from operations (earnings after deducting the depreciation expense but before deducting interest expense) divided by net assets (defined as total assets less goodwill, other intangible assets, and current liabilities).

In those early years, the ROI method was used at DuPont and other firms (e.g., General Motors) to complement extensive top-management insight concerning the technological and market conditions within which the firm's operating divisions conducted their business. After World War II, with the rise of diversified corporations and ever more decentralized decision making, the ROI measure became a popular metric used by top management to evaluate the performance of divisions and their managers. A well-known limitation of the ROI method is its potential manipulation by managers attempting to show enhanced short-term results. For example, a division manager can increase the ROI ratio by increasing its numerator (operating income) or by decreasing its denominator (the division's investment base). This manipulation could occur if management avoids profitable opportunities capable of earning ROIs in excess of the corporation's cost of financial capital, but that fail to exceed the current average ROI of the division. Actions that are taken solely to increase the short-term ROI can thus substantially compromise the evaluation, and achievement, of the corporation's strategic initiatives. For example, Lewis and Koller cite a recent survey in which 59 percent of a set of ROI analyses of Internet technology projects resulted in positive returns. This unrealistically high percentage is attributed in part to the firms' efforts to justify *expected* profits from investments in the developing technology. Assessing the results after the implementation might show a very different result. What was the lesson learned?

The limitations of the ROI method led to the development of the residual income and economic value added (EVA) techniques. The EVA method is noteworthy because it attempts to remove distortions to the investment decision created by the generally accepted accounting practices (GAAP) required for external financial reporting. Consider expenditures that, viewed from an economic value perspective, should be capitalized and amortized over time, but that must be expensed under GAAP. This distortion of economic value is especially evident for intangibles such as research and development, customer and market development, and enhancement of worker productivity. Kaplan and Atkinson (1998) have shown that long-term EVA and ROI will be overstated under GAAP as compared with the true economic value of the investment.[4] The GAAP overstates operating income and understates the investment base relative to an economic treatment of the investment activity, in which investments in intangibles would be capitalized in the early years of the investment and amortized in subsequent years.

This inconsistency between firms' treatment of investment projects from an internal economic value perspective and from the external reporting perspective of financial accounting is one reason for the lukewarm reception of the EVA method.[5] This unfortunate result has been observed despite increased pressures on firms from external financial markets to more effectively manage their portfolios of capital investments to the benefit of stockholders.

As Kaplan and Atkinson (1998) have suggested, managers' difficulties in effectively addressing these pressures may result from limited abilities to consider, and incorporate, the risks accompanying investment projects, including investments in IT. Too frequently, the projects that are funded are simply those that have the loudest proponents. The issue of risk will be covered in some depth in the balance of the chapter.

⁞ Discounted Cash Flow Analysis of an Individual Investment

The ROI and residual income (or EVA) methods, although relatively easy to implement, share the limitation that they do not explicitly reflect the economic circumstances of an investment project over its lifetime. For example, none of the previous methods can readily accommodate subsequent investment outlays, or uneven cash flows, that may arise during the project's economic life. Capital budgeting methods, including the net present value (NPV) technique, permit the firm to choose between alternative investment opportunities to advance the market value of the firm under these types of conditions. The NPV method of capital budgeting is described in appendix 1. By allocating its resources among such opportunities on a long-term basis, discounted cash flow methods avoid some of the short-term myopia of ROI calculations. They are not, however, without their own limitations.

A potentially difficult problem faces the standard NPV method when new information about the investment project is acquired during its economic lifetime, and uncertainty about its cash flows is reduced. The NPV technique developed as a method for evaluating projects based on their measurable cash flows, but not on their intangible strategic benefits to a firm's competitive position. To be fair, discounted cash flow techniques were originally designed to value investments in financial securities, reflecting the relatively passive nature of a firm's creditors and stockholders. In contrast to this static perspective, the strategic management of investments, including IT investments, has necessarily concerned itself with the dynamics of competitive position. New information provided to management as a project unfolds affords managers the flexibility to alter original strategies concerning the project and to exploit newly developing opportunities, or avoid developing losses. The flexibility afforded by these evolving options creates what Trigeorgis (1996) calls a "strategic investment criterion" reflecting both the passive NPV result and the value of options to alter decisions that may be exercised under flexible operations.

Extended forms of the NPV method, including sensitivity analysis, simulation, and decision tree analysis have been suggested to deal with the kind of sequential investment decisions that may occur as new information is expected to unfold during an investment project's uncertain lifespan. Sensitivity, or "what if," analysis examines the effects on the NPV of changing each of the key variables of the analysis (e.g., sales, cost of capital), holding the other key variables constant. The changes typically reflect optimistic and pessimistic estimates relative to a base-case scenario. This technique helps to identify the factors that contribute most significantly to the risk of the investment project. Unfortunately, it is not easily adapted to consider variations from the base-case scenario of many variables simultaneously, or when the key variables are interdependent. Trigeorgis suggests that mathematical simulation (or Monte Carlo) analysis may be useful in such cases. This analysis uses repeated random sampling from the probability distribution functions of each of the critical variables determining cash flows in order to devise a probability distribution function (or risk profile) of the NPV. It requires a carefully specified mathematical representation of the relationships existing among the variables, which may be complex.[6] Also, it is not clear how a manager would utilize the many NPVs possible under a probability distribution function. Of particular concern, however, is that Monte Carlo simulation incorporates a given operating strategy within its mathematical framework, and thus cannot easily accommodate the flexibility (and asymmetric probability distribution) resulting from management's ability to review and revise its operations in the light of emerging information.

Trigeorgis suggests that decision tree analysis (DTA) is a technique capable of accounting for a firm's revisions of its strategies and operations under uncertainty. Briefly, management is considering a sequence of decisions, each of which depends on uncertain future events that can be described probabilistically, in which probabilities are derived from past information or on future information that can be obtained at some cost. Management will choose the alternative that maximizes its risk-adjusted NPV. Examples of DTA are provided in appendix 2.

▪ Newly Developing Evaluation Methods

Real Options

Luehrman (1994) has provided a simple way to contrast the general class of discounted cash flow analysis (including DTA) with an options approach to newly developing information about an investment project. As shown in figure 4.1 (left), a DTA of discounted cash flows is based on the assumption that managers will make an investment decision and then wait to observe its results. In many important instances, however, managers can wait until some uncertainty is resolved before the investment decision must be made, as shown in figure 4.1 (right). The case shown in figure 4.1 (left) is not an option, while the case shown in figure 4.1 (right) is an option, and efficient capital markets will value the two cases differently.

As noted earlier in this chapter, discounted cash flow analysis was originally developed to determine the value of a static financial security, such as

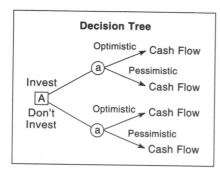
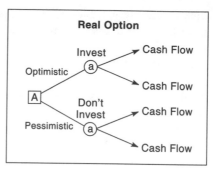

Figure 4.1. Decision tree analysis versus real option analysis

a bond or equity instrument. The discussion to this point, however, has suggested the inadequacies of this method when valuing investment proposals (including those for IT projects) having dynamic, strategic characteristics. What follows is a description of why the theory and analysis of real options is a more appropriate method for valuing such investments.

Many IT managers are aware of the future strategic options (e.g., cost savings, new products/services and markets) that may evolve from current investment projects even if they are uncertain about the eventual dollar amounts resulting from these options. Lacking a clear grasp of the fundamentals of real options valuation (a field normally mastered by financial specialists), however, these managers are generally unable to exploit the power of this method, and to more appropriately align their IT investments with the financial valuation of their firm. Fortunately, Luehrman (1998a) has provided an excellent explanation of this somewhat esoteric topic. The balance of this section will summarize a number of the key elements of his explanation. Following his example, it is assumed that the decision to pursue an investment project can be deferred for a period of time.

An opportunity to create an IT investment at some future time is similar to the financial concept of a call option. This is an option (but not an obligation) for the decision maker to buy an asset (e.g., financial security) by paying a given amount on or before a certain point in time. If a financial call option could be identified that is very similar to the IT investment being considered, then the market value of that financial call option, determined in a well-defined and efficient security market, would provide a good approximation of the value of the opportunities expected from the IT investment. As finding such a similar financial security is unlikely, real options analysis attempts to build one.

This is done by mapping five characteristics of the investment opportunity onto five corresponding characteristics of a financial call option, as shown in figure 4.2. The call option that is being described is a "European" call: an option that can be exercised only at the date of expiration.[7] The present value of the investment's assets to be acquired or developed corresponds to the stock price of the call option. The investment expenditure corresponds to the exercise price of the call option. The length of time before the investment decision must be made corresponds to the option's time to expiration. The risk concerning the investment project's cash flows corresponds to the standard deviation of the return to the security. The cost of capital is the risk-free rate of interest.

The value of the option to defer the investment derives in large part from the reduction in uncertainty that will occur by deferring the decision. That is, up to the time when the investment must be made, the decision maker is able to acquire evolving information about the wisdom of making the investment, primarily as expected future cash flows become known with greater certainty, but also as intangible benefits of the investment are brought into clearer view and measurement. Thus, the static NPV method and the flexible options approach to this situation will yield equivalent results only when the investment decision cannot be deferred. A discussion of the two sources of value derived from a real option is included in appendix 3.

Real Option Valuation of an Individual Investment

As described in appendix 3, the expressions for the real option's modified NPV and cumulative volatility (risk) permit the valuation of a European call option using the Black-Scholes model for options valuation. This model provides a dollar value for the option, based on the five factors shown in figure 4.2. As a simple example, consider an IT investment project that requires an investment of $3 million, in return for which the firm expects to receive assets with a present value of $2.7 million. The assets are risky, with a standard deviation of their value of 40 percent per year. The firm is able to defer the investment decision for three years, and the risk-free interest rate is 5 percent. According to the traditional NPV calculation, this project's

IT Investment	Options model variable	Call option
PV of IT project's assets to be acquired	PV (assets to be acquired)	Stock Price
IT expenditure needed to acquire the assets	PV (expenditure)	Exercise Price
Decision deferral period	t	Time to expiration
Time value of money	r_f	Risk free interest rate
Risk of IT project's assets	σ^2	Variance of return or stock

Figure 4.2 Mapping IT investment characteristics to financial call option characteristics. Adapted from Luehrman (1994)

NPV is −$300,000. The option to defer the investment is a three-year European call option with an exercise price of $3 million on underlying assets worth $2.7 million. For this option, the modified NPV is $2.7 million/[$3 million/(1.05)³], or 1.042. Cumulative volatility is (.40)($\sqrt{3}$) or .693. Using the Black-Scholes formula, this deferred option is worth about 28 percent of the value of the underlying assets of $2.7 million, or about $756,000.[8] This value exceeds the traditional negative NPV amount and suggests that the IT investment is expected to be worth pursuing if the firm defers its investment decision.

Luehrman (1994, 1998b) has shown that the two elements of value afforded by a real option can be effectively represented in a graphical "tomato garden" format. This format is provided in figure 4.3. The vertical axis of this diagram represents a project's cumulative volatility ($\sigma\sqrt{t}$) and the horizontal axis represents its modified NPV. As shown in figure 4.3, the space occupied by this "garden" can be segmented into distinct regions according to a project's standard NPV, modified NPV, and cumulative volatility. For each region, it is possible to characterize the appropriate investment strategy in a fairly simple, intuitive manner.

This framework also can be used to examine dynamic changes in appropriate investment strategies. For example, as time passes, the term *t* used to calculate both the modified NPV and cumulative volatility will become smaller, because the deferral period of the project has decreased. A lower value for *t* should result in a smaller cumulative volatility and a smaller modified NPV, assuming that none of the other four key variables have

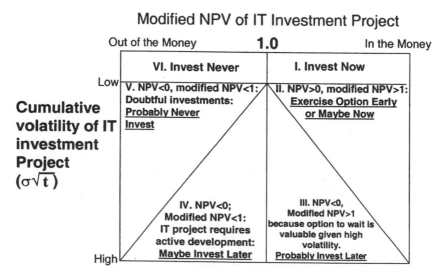

Figure 4.3. "Tomato garden" of IT investment project. Adapted from Luehrman (1994, 1998b)

changed. Within figure 4.3, this investment project will move up and to the left. Thus, a project formerly located, say, in region III, suggesting that the investment should probably be deferred, could now find itself in region IV, where it has become somewhat less promising.

Other uses for the Luehrman framework include the evaluation of investment projects with more complex real options. The key feature of his approach is unchanged, however. Options analysis of real investments forces the decision maker to realistically consider their decisions in line with the financial valuation of the firm. This evaluation of investment projects requires an understanding of the strategic options available to the firm, and managers who will incorporate the value of these options in their analyses.

The example of real options analysis described earlier is, of course, fairly simplistic, and potential problems with the real options approach can arise. For example, real options analysis uses much of the same data, present in spreadsheet form, that are used to conduct NPV analyses. The explicit incorporation of the uncertainty associated with real options, however, as reflected in cumulative volatility, theoretically adds a new element to the capital budgeting problem. This element could be addressed if methods such as sensitivity analysis were added to consider alternative "what if" scenarios concerning the value of the cumulative volatility. In addition, many corporate investment decisions are complex, especially if they require the analyst to consider expected interdependencies and synergies among investment projects and related options.

This "portfolio" aspect of the investments is addressed later in this chapter. Furthermore, options are often nested, in which cases the firm's decision may depend on correctly valuing options on options, and so on. This problem can be reduced by focusing on key sources of uncertainty that may be reduced through an option, and by breaking complex decisions down into a series of individual options.

Techniques such as rapid application development (RAD) that break IT projects down into smaller (three- to six-month) deliverables, or chunks, employ elements of the real options approach. For example, the evaluation team might agree to go forward with a project. At the end of the first deliverable (three to six months), the team can assess the options of whether to deploy the first part, expand it to a second part, or abandon it. If it is deployed, the organization can immediately obtain the benefits of the function provided. If the option to expand the project is selected, the evaluation team should prioritize what function will be included. After the second part is deployed, the team can again assess whether to deploy, expand, or continue with additional function. This approach has an additional benefit in that it helps manage the demand to change requirements that occurs during development. If a requirement change occurs, it should be deferred to a subsequent release. Effective prioritization of function to include in a release will provide a faster payback as compared to the traditional approach that waits for an entire project to be completed before it is deployed. This approach also provides IT with the opportunity to provide and demonstrate wins that are fast, frequent, and meaningful.

Information Economics

Housel et al. (2001) have suggested that the real options approach, like the other financial methods previously discussed, suffers from the limitation that it is based on cash flow projections. As previously discussed, however, IT investments (e.g., in support of core corporate processes) often do not result in easily measured cash flows. That is, the evaluation of IT investments typically includes only those financial items that the firm systematically records and reports; for example, the tangible cost of the investment, increased revenues, and cost savings. Little or no account is taken of other, less easily measured, strategic objectives, including how the investment can improve less tangible outcomes such as business processes, marketing, customer service, or the firm's competitiveness.

Parker, Benson, and Trainor (1988), Farbey, Land, and Targett (1999), and others have shown that aspects of information economics, multicriteria methods, and success factor analysis can be brought to bear on this shortcoming of traditional financial analyses for investment projects.[9]Buss (1983) has suggested a framework in which investment projects are ranked (as a high, medium, or low priority) for each of four criteria: financial benefits, intangible benefits, technical importance, and fit with business objectives. Each of these criteria would, in turn, be comprised of relevant elements. Buss, as an example, suggests that intangible benefits could include such elements as improving client service, speeding up decision making, improving the quality of information, and standardizing manual processes. Each element would be scored for an IT investment project and the total score derived for "intangible benefits" would be added to the total score for "financial benefits" (based on its own relevant elements, e.g., ROI), for "technical importance"and for "fit with business objectives." The sum obtained across the four criteria would be used to compare the IT investment against competing projects.

As reported by Semich (1994), Oracle Corp. developed a similar decision model in which financial investment criteria are combined with an information economic analysis of the intangible benefits and risks associated with investments in IT. Briefly, their method consists of the following steps.

1. Create a committee of stakeholders affected by the IT investment, including IT managers and business unit managers.
2. Define intangible benefits of the IT investment that are agreed to by the committee; for example, more flexible and efficient budgeting, improved decision analysis, improved information request responsiveness.
3. Define intangible risks associated with the IT investment; for example,

slow response to system change, poor integration with existing systems, and staff resistance to a new system.

4. Establish weights to the relative importance of the tangible benefits (the financial result), the intangible benefits, and the intangible risks of the IT investment.
5. Estimate on a scale of zero to five the likelihood of each benefit and risk being observed.
6. Multiply each likelihood estimate by the weight established for that factor and add up the products. The investment alternative that results in the greatest sum is the preferred alternative.

While these methods obviously depend on a number of subjective evaluations, they complement financial methods, including real options analysis, to the extent: (1) that they build consensus among the participants in IT investment decisions, and (2) that they couple financial calculations with intangible benefits and risks, aspects of strategic concern. Thus, rather than propose the real options approach as *the* preferred means of evaluating IT investments, its use in combination with these methods of incorporating intangibles and of building consensus among the stakeholders within the organization is suggested.

Evaluating a Portfolio of IT Investment Projects

A SIM (Society of Information Management) International Working Group on "Managing the IT Investment Portfolio" (2001) emphasized the need for organizations to adopt a portfolio management process in assessing and managing their "IT landscapes." Many financial services firms have adopted portfolio management from their investment banking organizations. It has been discussed by academics since the 1980s, and is growing in attention and use. This process would ensure that IT investments:

1. Are understood from the onset in terms of expected business outcomes, the efforts needed to reach those outcomes, and the risks involved in achieving the outcomes.
2. Will advance the value of the firm.
3. Risks are in line with the business's acceptable risk profile.
4. Are aligned with business strategies.
5. Have an effective vehicle for continuous project monitoring.

Luehrman's "tomato garden" (1994, 1998b) is consistent with the concept of a portfolio of investment projects undertaken by a firm. The financial theory of portfolio selection indicates that the risk-return profile of a portfolio of securities can be improved by recognizing interdependencies among the individual elements of the portfolio, particularly statistical correlations between their returns.[10] Luehrman's simple diagram captures the value and uncertainty associated with a collection of real investment projects, where each project falls into a decision region defined by its relative value and uncertainty. It also permits the analyst to address potential interdependencies among projects.

Value Management

This "portfolio" aspect of the "tomato garden" has been addressed by Trigeorgis (1996) somewhat more formally. He provides a framework within which a firm may undertake the valuation of investment projects using the real options approach and recognize the strategic mix of the interdependent projects. Briefly, his framework requires that investment planning, control measures to monitor project performance, and incentive schemes should all be tied to the objective of maximizing the firm's value. A key element of this objective is the requirement that sources of strategic value such as real operating options, competitive interactions, interdependencies among investments, and growth opportunities should be incorporated. His framework is based on the following concepts.

1. The objective of value maximization refers to a broad measure of NPV: Strategic NPV = Traditional NPV of expected cash flows + Value of operating options from flexible management + Investment interaction effects
2. Strategic management of investments requires the management of a collection (or portfolio) of future investment opportunities and options.
3. Appropriate control targets are necessary for the effective implementation of a value-maximizing (strategic NPV) approach.

Figure 4.4 describes the three phases of Trigeorgis's (1996) framework. Phase I emphasizes the valuation and planning of strategic investments. During this phase possible interdependencies, synergies, and future opportunities

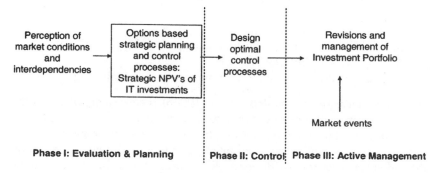

Figure 4.4. Strategic management of a portfolio of IT investments. Adapted from Trigeorgis (1996)

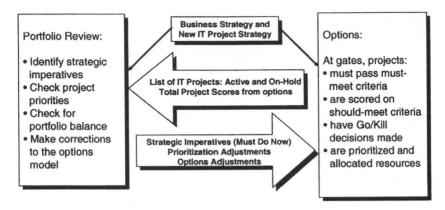

Figure 4.5. Overview of the portfolio-options management process

from projects should be considered, along with related operating options. During phase II, control targets are set that are consistent with continuous value maximization, and during phase III the firm engages in the active, flexible management of individual investment projects, including decisions about which operating options to exercise, or about what newly developing options should be considered. This last phase is developed more fully in figure 4.5. In keeping with Luehrman's "tomato garden" framework, the active management of a portfolio of IT investment projects will require periodic monitoring, and nurturing, of their changing position in the landscape of the "garden." That is, over time projects' modified NPVs and cumulative volatilities may change, as noted earlier. Consequently, the active management of IT investments indicated in phase III of Trigeorgis's strategic management framework will require reevaluations of options and of the strategic relevance of IT investments, as well as the development of promising projects. Figure 4.5 offers a simple representation of some of the elements of those reevaluations.

Trigeorgis's "strategic management framework" clearly offers an improvement to the methodologies used to conduct the evaluation of investment projects. Its acknowledgment that the firm is managing a portfolio of projects, among which may exist potentially significant interdependencies and synergies (e.g., cost reduction, existing market expansion, and the development of new markets), is much closer to the firm's goal of value maximization than are traditional, static financial calculations. Furthermore, this framework provides a fairly general context within which to consider the evaluation of real options, a realistic element of a firm's strategic management. Thus, the incompatibility between traditional NPV valuation methods and a firm's strategic planning activities can be overcome. Finally, implicit in Trigeorgis's framework is the well-known requirement that operating and investment decisions made by functional managers (e.g., IT managers) be

Table 4.2
Portfolio Assessment: A "Dashboard Approach"

Project name	"Must do"	Option value $M	Probability of technical success	Probability of business success	Option development cost $M
Project 1		30	0.80	0.50	3
Project 2		63.75	0.50	0.80	5
Project 3		8.62	0.75	0.75	2
Project 4	Government regulation		1.00	1.00	1.3
Project 5		50	0.06	0.75	5

aligned with the realities of the possible investment outcomes, real options, and organizational controls recognized by the firm's top management. Trigeorgis's framework is sufficiently general to incorporate, for example, the kinds of evaluation methods suggested by Buss and the Oracle Corp. as noted earlier, in which intangible benefits and risks are considered as part of the investment decision. These methods should help align the perceptions of IT managers and of business managers concerning the interdependencies and synergies of a proposed portfolio of IT projects. With this alignment in place the strategic value of the firm's collection of IT investments should be enhanced, along with the firm's value.

Table 4.2 provides a simple "dashboard" approach to capturing these elements of the IT portfolio. The expected benefit of each project is represented by its value, including benefits identified through information economic analyses and the potential value of the most likely strategic options associated with the project.

Critical IT projects are identified by the "Must do" column (e.g., government regulations, keep up with competitors, Y2K). Expected project risk is represented by the probabilities of the project's technical and business success. The cost of developing each project option is also a necessary element of this "dashboard" approach, and could be derived using TCO and information economic analyses.

It is important to note that this "dashboard" view of the firm's IT projects is not a static construct, but may exhibit changes over time as options are exercised, as intangible benefits and costs change, and as expected probabilities are revised in light of evolving technical and business knowledge. These changes should be considered as the firm manages its IT investment portfolio in alignment with the firm's strategic objectives. The review and prioritization of the portfolio should be done by a team of business and IT executives.

The discussions to this point have considered the financial evaluation of IT investments, the importance of pursuing investments that add value to the organization, and the relevance of the investment to the organization's strategic management objectives. In discussing the determination of the value derived from these investments the emphasis has been on financial value, or valuation. It is appropriate, however, to consider "value" more broadly. An expanded use of the term provides additional insight and detail concerning some of the issues addressed by the "information economics" approaches described earlier, in which intangible benefits and risks of IT investments are considered. It also sheds further light on the possible workings of Tri-georgis's strategic management framework.

The value management approach, and examples that follow, provide organizations seeking an IT-leveraged path to competitiveness with a total value of ownership model that can help to identify improvements in customer-focused processes. It is based on Cathy Curley's early research that was sponsored by IBM's Advanced Business Institute. The first two examples are shown in figure 4.6. Frito Lay had the business objective (e.g., increase profit, cost reduction, productivity or quality improvement, cultivating relationships, brand awareness) of increasing its market share of salty snacks. To meet this objective, managers recognized the need to change the processes (e.g., traditional business process enhancements, major business transformation, new business model experimentation) used for pricing and defining the mix of products for its delivery routes. The technologies that enabled these process changes were the use of a new handheld device, the network to transmit information, and an executive information system (EIS) to report sales status.

The second example is McGraw Hill's recognition of the need to provide college professors with the ability to customize textbooks for their courses. This required changes to the entire book producing process. The information technology necessary to support these changes included an on-

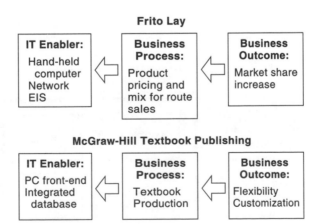

Figure 4.6. Examples of a value management framework

line repository of text that can be accessed by professors using an easy to use PC interface.

In these examples, the business objectives and value were initially defined. The business processes that would be affected were then identified. A business executive sponsor and business champions were committed to the success of these objectives and process changes. The information technology was selected to best enable the process changes, that is, to generate the greatest value to the business. Key to this approach is the understanding and acceptance that the total value comes from changes made to the business that were enabled (and perhaps driven) by changes to IT, not the technology unto itself. The total value should go beyond cost reduction to include revenue enhancement, improved product quality, higher levels of service, and organization satisfaction.

The preceding approach, when applied with the appropriate business stakeholders, also helps address the frequently discussed productivity paradox. Productivity growth comes from new technologies and new ways of doing business. The value management approach provides organizations seeking an IT-leveraged path to competitiveness with a total value of ownership model that can help to identify improvements in customer-focused processes. Also, the evaluation should take into account all potential stakeholders, including individual employees, departments and business units, the entire enterprise, and partners and customers. Considerations such as the quality and functionality of the project must be included. Adding these considerations to the previously discussed examples of figure 4.6, figure 4.7 illustrates an expanded value management framework used by C. R. England Trucking. This example once again begins with a definition of the business

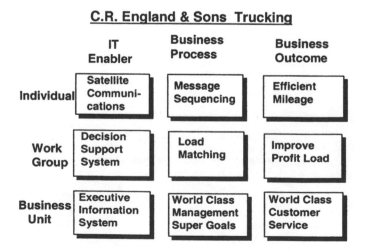

Figure 4.7. Expanded value management framework

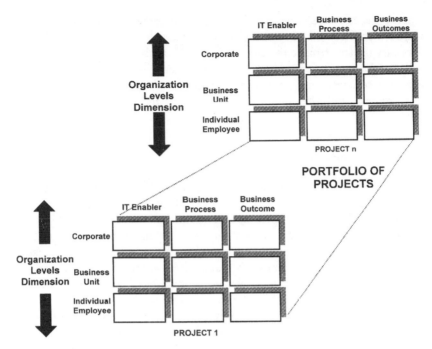

Figure 4.8. TVO framework: IT governance process that accesses a portfolio of IT projects

objectives and value. The business processes that would be affected were then identified. A business executive sponsor and business champions were committed to the success of these objectives and process changes. The information technology was selected to best enable the process changes, that is, that enabled process changes that added to the value of the business. The major difference in this example is that now the business value, business process changes, and information technology necessary to achieve the business outcome for the individual truck drivers, the group of truck drivers, and the firm as a whole is reviewed.

Figure 4.8 represents the governance processes, in combination with the application of portfolio management. The complete TVO process combines the use of portfolio management and the value management governance process. Each opportunity is identified, and compared against all opportunities from the perspective of the entire organization, business unit, and individual employee. Those that best meet the overall priorities of the firm are selected. Those projects that have been selected are broken down into manageable pieces and implemented using an options approach. Hence, table 4.2 is used to prioritize and select Project 1–Project 5 and figure 4.8 breaks down each project into corporate value, business unit value, and individual employee value; at the same time, business members of the governance process assess the overall business outcome and business changes, and IT members of the governance process assess the information technology necessary to drive/enable the changes. The IT and business governance team will use the completed table 4.2 during strategy formulation to select and allocate resources, during project execution to evaluate and monitor the projects progress, and after the project is deployed to assess the attainment of value.

Recommendations

As part of the IT governance process, discussed in chapter 7, a steering committee should be established to assess and prioritize projects. This steering committee should comprise senior representatives from IT and business units proposing projects. A combination of portfolio management, real options, and information economics approaches should be applied in evaluating project selection and resources allocation. These approaches are summarized in table 4.1. The resource allocation decisions should be based on the benefits that would be achieved by the firm as a whole.

The elements of table 4.3 can provide an effective vehicle for comparing the portfolio of projects while ensuring that the projects are reviewed after deployment. The critical success factors (CSF) represent those aspects of the business that will be affected. The success measures are the financial metrics chosen. The tracking frequency and adjustment columns address the governance aspects for assessing the deployment of projects. The sponsor and champions identify the business unit owners that will be responsible for the changes to the business process that are enabled by the information technology. The communication column describes the vehicles for ensuring that all stakeholders are aware of the state of the deployment.[11]

This approach enhances the allocation of resources by improving participants' understanding of the problems and opportunities that exist across

Table 4.3
Portfolio Matrix

CSF	Success measure(s)	Tracking method	Tracking frequency	Adjusting method	Adjusting frequency	Sponsor, champion, owner	Communica-tion

organizations. Another benefit is the opportunity for the participants to see how these projects can be leveraged across organizations, thus facilitating the integration of IT and the processes they enhance. The focus should be on leveraging return, not just a recovery of cost.

This steering committee also should have the responsibility to review projects after they have been implemented to assess how well they met the objectives set when projects were initially proposed. This review should be leveraged to apply to future projects the lessons learned regarding why objectives were met or not met. The application of these important lessons learned is likely to provide a significant return and an understanding of the total value of ownership. Developing the awareness and the successful implementation of this partnership will provide the foundation for improved communication, governance, and understanding that will lead to a more mature alignment of IT-business.

: Appendix 1: The Net Present Value Method of Evaluating Investment Projects

The traditional statement of the NPV method of capital budgeting is expressed as:

$$NPV = \sum_{t}^{T} E(c_t)/(1 + r_j)^t - I$$

where $E(c_t)$ is the cash inflow from the investment project expected to arrive at year t, I is the current investment outlay required to begin the project, T is the number of years of the project's economic life, and r_j is the risk-adjusted discount rate (cost of capital) appropriate to the project, which is the sum of a risk-free interest rate (usually on 3-month Treasury bills) and a risk premium compensating the firm's owners for the risk of the project. It is generally assumed that the firm's owners are adverse to risk. Investment projects that are within the same line of business as the firm and are no more or less risky than the firm's ongoing projects should be discounted at the firm's average cost of capital, calculated from the rates of return required to satisfy the debt and equity sources of the funding that supports the firm's activities. Investment projects with above-average risk (e.g., introduction of a new technology to increase market share) require a value for r_j in excess of the firm's average cost of capital. The capital asset pricing model of corporate finance has been suggested as a basis for determining the required rate of return for an investment project (r_j) as a function of its risk. The firm is assumed to optimize the expected returns from investment projects, given the risk of those projects.

Fama (1977) has shown that the present value of a future net cash inflow is its current expected value, as discounted at the rate r_j, where the discount rate is known and deterministic over time. Any uncertainty about the present value of cash inflows results from uncertainties about the cash flows through time.[12]

∶   *Appendix 2: Present Value Calculations of an IT Investment Using Decision Tree Analysis*

As a simple example of DTA, consider the case of an IT manager presented with an opportunity to develop a system at an initial pilot cost of $200,000.[13] This system is expected to enable the firm to generate useful information about customer preferences for some of the firm's products, and to use that information to create new products and markets. After a three-year pilot period, the firm will determine whether the new system is worth continuing, based on the solution of a number of technical and business problems. If so (there is a 30 percent probability that the effort will be continued), the firm will expand the system's development by making an additional investment of $6 million. It is estimated that the probability that the expanded system will be highly useful in enhancing operating performance is 20 percent, resulting in cash inflows of $16 million beginning in year 5. It is estimated that the probability that the expanded system will be moderately useful in enhancing operating performance is 60 percent, resulting in cash inflows of $8 million beginning in year 5. It is estimated that the probability that the expanded system will result in low usefulness in enhancing operating performance is 20 percent, resulting in cash inflows of −$200,000 beginning in year 5. The risk-adjusted cost of capital is 10 percent.

Figure 4A.1 describes the decision tree for this case. Squares represent decision nodes for management, and circles represent points in time when states of nature are revealed to management. Present value amounts are indicated in italics at decision nodes.

To determine the optimal decision at any point in time the analyst should start at the end of the decision tree and work backwards. Starting at year 5 the expected present value of cash inflows is:

$$E_5(PV) = .20(\$16M) + .60(\$8M) + .20(-\$200K) = \$7.96 \text{ million}$$

Discounting backward to year 4:

$$E_4(PV) = \$7.96M/(1.10) = \$7.2 \text{ million}$$

Discounting again to year 3 can obtain the NPV by subtracting out the $6 million investment required at that time:

$$E_3(NPV) = \$7.2M/(1.10) - \$6M = \$540,000$$

and to arrive at the decision point in year 0:

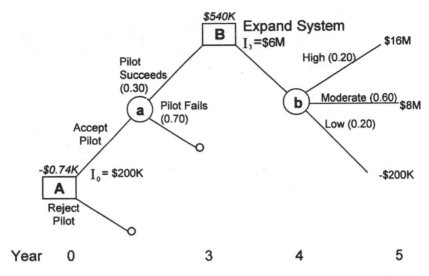

$540K
B Expand System
    $I_3 = \$6M$ $16M

Pilot   High (0.20)
Succeeds
(0.30)
                Pilot Fails   **b** Moderate (0.60)
    a   (0.70) $8M
Accept   Low (0.20)
Pilot

$-\$0.74K$ $I_0 = \$200K$ $-\$200K
A
Reject
Pilot

Year   0   3   4   5

Figure 4A.1. Decision tree of an IT investment. Adapted from Trigeorgis (1996)

$$E_0(NPV) = [(.30)(\$540K) + (.70)(0)]/(1.10)^3 - \$200K$$
$$= -\$74,000$$

Thus, the expected NPV of this project is $-\$74,000$, which would lead to its rejection by management. As Trigeorgis has noted, however, real-world managers who can exploit asymmetric outcomes of the DTA through flexible operations may find this project to be worthwhile. For example, flexibility can exist in the firm's ability to abandon the project at some point during the life of the project if its abandonment value exceeds the NPV of subsequent cash flows.

Following Trigeorgis, this simple case can be expanded to consider the option to abandon, and to consider expected cash flows in years 6 through 15 following the implementation of the fully-developed system. Figure 4A.2 shows the expanded decision tree.

The probabilities of market success in years 6–15 have been added on the right side of the tree. Management estimates that if the new system results in high market usefulness in year 5, then the probabilities of high, moderate, and low usefulness in years 6–15 are 60 percent, 30 percent, and 10 percent, respectively. If the new system results in moderate market usefulness in year 5, then the probabilities of high, moderate, and low usefulness in years 6–15 are 10 percent, 80 percent, and 10 percent, respectively. If the new system results in low market usefulness in year 5, then the probabilities of high, moderate, and low usefulness in years 6–15 are 10 percent, 30 percent, and 60 percent, respectively. In any of the years 6–15 manage-

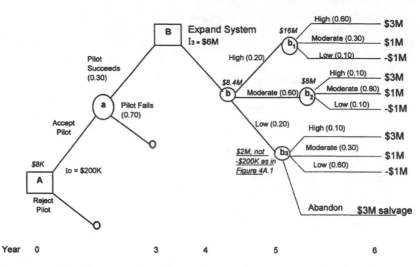

Figure 4A.2. Decision tree of an IT investment with an option to abandon the project. Adapted from Trigeorgis (1996)

ment expects net cash inflows of $3 million if the system results in high market usefulness, $1 million per year if the system results in moderate market usefulness, and −$1 million per year if the system results in low market usefulness. The firm has the option to abandon the investment at the end of year 15 for an expected salvage value of $2 million. The firm may also abandon the project at the end of year 5, at which time the salvage value is expected to be $3 million, derived in part from the proceeds of the sale of the customer information gathered up to that time. A detailed description of the cash flows associated with this investment project is provided later.

Based on the values discussed in the chapter, the expected annual cash flows in years 6–15, conditional on high, moderate, and low success in year 5, are:

$$E(\text{inflow; High success in year 5}) = (.6)(\$3M) + (.3)(\$1M) + (.1)(-\$1M) = \$2M$$
$$E(\text{inflow; Moderate success in year 5}) = (.1)(\$3M) + (.8)(\$1M) + (.1)(-\$1M) = \$1M$$
$$E(\text{inflow; Low success in year 5}) = (.1)(\$3M) + (.3)(\$1M) + (.6)(-\$1M) = \$0M$$

Thus, discounting back to year 5 and including the salvage value expected in year 15:

$$E_5(\text{year 6–15 flows; High success in year 5})$$
$$= \sum^{10} \$2M/(1,10)^t + \$2M/(1.10)^{10} = \$13 \text{ million}$$

E_5(year 6–15 floss; Moderate success in year 5)

$$= \sum_{}^{10} \$1M/(1.10)^t + \$2M/(1.10)^{10} = \$7 \text{ million}$$

E_5(year 6–15; Low success in year 5)

$$= \sum_{}^{10} \$0/(1.10)^t + \$2M/(1.10)^{10} = \$800,000$$

If the cash inflow is expected for year 5 with these expected values, the expected cash inflows can be derived beginning in year 5, conditional on high, moderate, or low success in year 5:

$$
\begin{aligned}
E_5(\text{years 5–15; High success in year 5}) &= \$3M + \$13M \\
&= \$16 \text{ million} \\
E_5(\text{years 5–15; Moderate success in year 5}) &= \$1M + \$7M \\
&= \$8 \text{ million} \\
E_5(\text{years 5–15; Low success in year 5}) &= -\$1M + \$800K \\
&= -\$200,000
\end{aligned}
$$

These values are consistent with the expected cash inflows at year 5 shown in figure 4A.1.

Trigeorgis notes that a simple NPV focus on the expected value of cash inflows as of the end of year 5, given information available at year 0 (= (.2)($13M) + (.6)($7M) + (.2)($800K) = $7M > 0) misses the point of flexible operations undertaken by this firm. The firm in this case has the flexibility (and option) to wait until the end of year 5 before it must decide whether to implement the system at that time. At time period 0, the *only* decision facing the firm is whether to undertake the pilot investment.

Information acquired up to the end of year 5, especially related to the probabilities of success in year 5, can be used to revise its IT investment decisions. For example, if at the end of year 5 it appears likely that the system will enjoy only low success, then the firm may decide to abandon the project since the expected value of continuing after year 5 is $800,000, as shown later, which is less than the $3 million disposal value available at year 5. The flexibility afforded to the firm in this case should be valued along with the static NPV calculation indicated in figure 4A.1. If abandonment is chosen in this case the value of the low branch in figure 4A.2 (b_3) emanating from node b changes from–$0.2M (as in figure 4A.1) to (−$1M + $3M) = $2M. The NPV calculation at year 5 would then be:

$$E_5(\text{NPV}) = (.2)(\$16M) + (.6)(\$8M) + (.2)(\$2M) = \$8.4 \text{ million}$$

instead of the value of $7.96 million obtained without considering the option to abandon the project in year 5. The present value of flexibility in this case is:

$$(.30)(\$8.4M - \$7.96M)/(1.10)^5 = \$82,000$$

Furthermore, the NPV of the project at year 0 would be the sum of the static NPV derived earlier (−$74,000) plus the present value of the option to abandon ($82,000), for an overall NPV of $8,000. That is, the project, which originally resulted in a negative NPV, now becomes desirable when the value of the abandonment option is incorporated into the analysis.

This simple example illustrates how decision tree analysis (DTA) can extend NPV analysis by explicitly considering the relationship between decisions made over time and conditional on previous decisions. It also permits the analyst to amend standard NPV calculations to incorporate the value of options to alter (e.g., abandon) subsequent decisions. Trigeorgis notes, however, that DTA suffers from a number of practical and conceptual limitations. First, the complexity of the decision tree can increase rapidly with increases in the number of managerial decisions, and with decisions that must be made more frequently than was suggested in the simple example above. Second, the use of a constant discount rate in NPV calculations is incorrect in problems involving a sequence of decisions and options concerning the use of assets. These options can, for example, reduce the risk of a project after a point in time, and should be reflected in a lower cost of capital. Finally, nothing in DTA requires the analyst to emphasize, or even consider, the options available to managers to amend their strategic plans as they unfold over time.

: *Appendix 3: Black-Scholes Values for a European Call Option*

Luehrman (1998a) has provided a simple way of representing the two sources of value derived from a real option. The first source is the interest income that can be earned on the investment funds during the deferral period. This value can be measured as the present value of the investment expenditure, or in financial terms as the present value of the option's exercise price, where the expenditure is discounted at the risk-free rate of interest (r_f):

$$PV(\text{expenditure}) = \text{Expenditure}/(1 + r_f)^t$$

where t is the number of time periods during which the investment expenditure can be deferred. To calculate a form of the NPV of the investment, Luehrman suggests using the ratio of the investment asset's value (in present value terms) to its cost (PV(expenditure above). Or,

$$\text{modified NPV} = PV(\text{assets to be acquired})/PV(\text{expenditure})$$

where the modified NPV may be greater than or less than one in value. This modified NPV will generally exceed the standard NPV result because it includes the interest income earned during the deferral period.[14]

The second source of value contributed by the real option results from the decision maker's ability to react to changing uncertain conditions during the deferral period by altering investment decisions to the firm's benefit. Uncertainty is measured in real options analysis as the cumulative volatility of the investment's future value, $\sigma\sqrt{t}$, where σ is the standard deviation of the investment's return per unit of time and t denotes the number of time periods in the deferral period. Note that the standard deviation is denominated in the same units (dollars) as the value of the future assets. Technically speaking, uncertainty is more properly measured as a variance per period, σ^2. The expression $\sigma^2 t$ would show the cumulative volatility of the asset's future value during the t periods in the deferral period, but this expression is difficult to interpret; that is, the meaning of dollars squared is not obvious. The square root of this expression, shown as $\sigma\sqrt{t}$, returns this metric to readily understood dollars.[15]

Sharpe et al. (1999) have reported that the Black-Scholes formula for estimating the value of a European call option V_c is:

$$V_c = N(d_1)\,PV(\text{assets to be acquired}) - N(d_2)(PV(\text{expenditure})/e_f^{rt})$$
$$\text{where } d_1 = [\ln(\text{modified NPV}) + (r_f + 0.5\sigma^2)t]/\sigma\sqrt{t}$$
$$d_2 = [\ln(\text{modified NPV}) + (r_f - 0.5\sigma^2)t]/\sigma\sqrt{t}$$

and where $N(d_1)$ and $N(d_2)$ are the probabilities that outcomes of less than d_1 and d_2, respectively, will occur in a normal distribution possessing a mean of zero and standard deviation of one. Table 4A.1, adapted from Luehrman (1998a), gives the Black-Scholes values expressed as a percentage of the investment's underlying asset value.

Table 4A.1
Black-Scholes Values for a European Call Option

Cumulative volatility	Modified NPV									
	0.90	0.92	0.94	0.96	0.98	1.00	1.02	1.04	1.06	1.08
0.05	0.0	0.1	0.3	0.6	1.2	2.0	3.1	4.5	6.0	7.5
0.10	0.8	1.2	1.7	2.3	3.1	4.0	5.0	6.1	7.3	8.6
0.15	2.2	2.8	3.5	4.2	5.1	6.0	7.0	8.0	9.1	10.2
0.20	4.0	4.7	5.4	6.2	7.1	8.0	8.9	9.9	10.9	11.9
0.25	5.9	6.6	7.4	8.2	9.1	9.9	10.9	11.8	12.8	13.7
0.30	7.8	8.6	9.4	10.2	11.1	11.9	12.8	13.7	14.6	15.6
0.35	9.8	10.6	11.4	12.2	13.0	13.9	14.8	15.6	16.5	17.4
0.40	11.7	12.5	13.4	14.2	15.0	15.9	16.7	17.5	18.4	19.2
0.45	13.7	14.5	15.3	16.2	17.0	17.8	18.6	19.4	20.3	21.1
0.50	15.7	16.5	17.3	18.1	18.0	19.7	20.5	21.3	22.1	22.9
0.55	17.7	18.5	19.3	20.1	20.9	21.7	22.4	23.2	24.0	24.8
0.60	19.7	20.5	21.3	22.0	22.8	23.6	24.3	25.1	25.8	26.6
0.65	21.7	22.5	23.2	24.0	24.7	25.3	26.2	27.0	27.7	28.4
0.70	23.6	24.4	25.2	25.9	26.6	27.4	28.1	28.8	29.5	30.2
0.75	25.6	26.3	27.1	27.8	28.5	29.2	29.9	30.6	31.3	32.0

⦂ *Notes*

1. This representation of the business effects of IT investments is simplified to provide emphasis on the concept of a portfolio of projects. A fuller representation of the characteristics of each of the projects comprising the portfolio would include business effects at the individual, work group, and business unit levels, as well as a more complete description of the processes by which the effects would be realized.

2. Ross and Beath (2002) recently offered a framework that analyzes an IT investment along two dimensions: technology scope and strategic objective. In this chapter we underscore the importance of the investment's strategic relevance to its valuation.

3. This chapter examines financial methods of evaluating investment projects, with some discussion of complementary techniques that address intangible aspects of these investments. We do not consider the extensive, and somewhat inconclusive, literature on the "productivity paradox" of IT investment. Thatcher and Oliver (2001) have provided an excellent synopsis of that literature as well as some economic explanations of its inconclusive results.

4. This distortion has been addressed to some extent in the recent use of the "Total Cost of Ownership" (TCO) model within an activity-based costing framework. TCO was developed to understand the true costs of owning and managing IT resources over their economic lifetimes, including the costs of the technology and the people who use and manage the technology. The selection of appropriate cost drivers within the TCO method can provide the firm with greater insight into, for example, IT cost behavior, the role of IT in the firm's operations, and opportunities for improved efficiencies in the delivery of IT services.

5. This inconsistency is also observed in the difference between a firm's reported accounting income and its residual income (or EVA).

6. Furthermore, the usefulness of the probability distribution function of the NPV result is questionable. Myers (1976) has shown that the discount rate used in the NPV calculation is already adjusted for the project's risk.

7. An "American" call option may be exercised at any time prior to expiration; the valuation of American call options is more complex than the case of the European call option, and is not discussed here.

8. Appendix 3 provides Black-Scholes values of a European call option.

9. The balanced scorecard approach is also valuable as a means of identifying key non-financial aspects of strategy. See, for example, Kaplan and Norton (1992).

10. See, for example, Sharpe et al. (1999).

11. The determination and assessment of consensus among stakeholders concerning financial and qualitative selection criteria may be conducted using well-known techniques such as the Delphi method and scenario planning as well as more sophisticated methods such as the analytical hierarchy process described by Saaty and Vargas (1991).

12. Myers and Turnbull (1977) have indicated that an investment project's true riskiness depends on factors such as the time pattern and growth rate of its expected cash flows and the methods by which investors revise their expectations about these cash flows. If a project's riskiness cannot be assumed constant in the periods of its economic life, then different costs of capital should be used in those time periods, not a single discount rate as suggested by the standard NPV calculation.

13. This case is similar to one presented by Trigeorgis.

14. This definition of modified NPV is somewhat similar to the profitability index

associated with the standard NPV model: profitability index $=$ PV(cash inflows)/ PV(investment).

15. As a practical matter a value for σ can be estimated in a number of ways. The firm could use the standard deviation of its stock price over the past few years as a rough approximation to σ. This approach assumes that past volatility of the firm's productive asset values have been reflected in it stock price. A second alternative would require some benchmarking of the volatility of returns to similar investments in the firm's past, or in other firms. A third approach would be to use Monte Carlo simulation applied to the project's expected cash flows to simulate a probability distribution function and σ.

▪ References

Buss, M. D. J. (1983) "How to Rank Computer Projects," *Harvard Business Review,* Jan.–Feb., 118–25.

Fama, E. (1977) "Risk-Adjusted Discount Rates and Capital Budgeting Under Uncertainty," *Journal of Financial Economics,* 5(1), 3–24.

Farbey, B., F. Land, & D. Targett. (1999) "Evaluating Investments in IT: Findings and a Framework," in L. P. Willcocks & S. Lester (Eds.), *Beyond the IT Productivity Paradox,* 183–216. New York: John Wiley & Sons.

Housel, T. J., O. El Sawy, J. J. Zhong, & W. Rodgers. (2001) "Measuring the Return on Knowledge Embedded in Information Technology," *Proceedings,* 22nd International Conference on Information Systems, 97–106: New Orleans, LA.

Kaplan, R. S., & A. A. Atkinson. (1998) *Advanced Management Accounting,* 3rd ed., Englewood Cliffs, NJ: Prentice Hall.

Kaplan, R. S., & D. P. Norton. (1992) "The Balanced Scorecard-Measures that Drive Performance," *Harvard Business Review,* 70, 71–80.

Luehrman, T. A. (1994) *Capital Projects as Real Options: An Introduction.* Harvard Business School Teaching Note. Boston, MA.

Luehrman, T. A. (1998a) "Investment Opportunities as Real Options: Getting Started on the Numbers," *Harvard Business Review,* 76, 51–63.

Luehrman, T. A. (1998b) "Strategy as a Portfolio of Real Options," *Harvard Business Review,* 76, 89–100.

Lewis, D., & M. Koller. (2001) "ROI: Little More Than Lip Service," *Internet Week,* Oct., 1.

Miller, J. A. *Implementing Activity-Based Management in Daily Operations,* 11–13. New York: John Wiley & Sons.

Myers, S. C. (1976) "Using Simulation for Risk Analysis," in S. C. Meyers (Ed.), *Modern Developments in Financial Analysis.* New York: Praeger.

Myers S. C., & S. Turnbull. (1977) "Capital Budgeting and the Capital Asset Pricing Model: Good News and Bad News," *Journal of Finance* 32(2), 321–33.

Parker, M. M., R. J. Benson, & H. E. Trainor. (1988) *Information Economics: Linking Business Performance to Information Technology.* Englewood Cliffs, NJ: Prentice Hall.

Ross, J. W., & C. M Beath. (2002) "Beyond the Business Case: New Approaches to IT Investment," *MIT Sloan Management Review,* 43, 51–9.

Saaty, T. L., & L. G. Vargas. (1991) *Prediction, Projection, and Forecasting: Applications of the Analytical Hierarchy Process in Economics, Finance, Politics, Games and Sports.* Boston, MA: Kluwer Academic Publishers.

Semich, J. W. (1994) "Here's How to Quantify IT Investment Benefits," *Datamation,* January 7, 45–48.

Sharpe, W. F., G. F. Alexander, & J. V. Bailey. (1999). *Investments,* 6th ed. Englewood Cliffs, NJ: Prentice Hall.

SIM International Working Group. (2001) *Managing the IT Investment Portfolio: Final Report,* www.simnet.org. San Diego, CA: SIM.

Thatcher, M. E., & J. R. Oliver. (2001) "The Impact of Technology Investments on a Firm's Production Efficiency, Product Quality, and Productivity," *Journal of Management Information Systems,* 18(2), 17–45.

Trigeorgis, L. (1996) *Real Options: Managerial Flexibility and Strategy in Resource Allocation.* Cambridge, MA: MIT Press.

Violino, B. (1997) "ROI: The Intangible Benefits of Technology are Emerging as the Most Important of All," *Information Week,* June, 36–44.

5

David Feeny, Blake Ives, and Gabriele Piccoli

Creating and Sustaining IT-Enabled Competitive Advantage

Chapter Summary

1. IT can create competitive advantage through efficiency improvements and other forms of cost reductions, through new channels or channel domination, or through differentiation of product or service.
2. Critics claim that IT alone cannot lead to sustainable competitive advantage because competitors can easily acquire IT and quickly replicate virtually any application. A useful framework must explicitly address the potential for using technology to prevent or delay competitive responses. Technology might, in theory, be easily copied, but it does not follow that strategies based on the use of IT cannot lead to sustainable competitive advantage
3. Competitive advantage generally does not stem from "visionary" initiatives, but from "evolutionary" ones that begin with an IT-based response to perceived environmental pressure or opportunities and a commitment to continuous learning. Often, organizational learning, a basis for sustainability, can only begin once the strategic initiative is enacted. This suggests that IT-enabled strategic initiatives can foster the development of capabilities that will evolve into strategies not readily envisioned at the start.
4. Their framework describes four barriers to obtain sustained value from IT. They are:
   1. IT Project
   2. IT Resources and Capabilities
   3. Complementary Resources
   4. Preemption

Introduction

Since the early 1980s, proponents have presented the strategic value of harnessing Information Technology (IT) to the creation of competitive advantage (Bharadwaj, 2000; Clemons & Row, 1991; Stratopoulos & Dehning, 2000) Frameworks for identifying such opportunities have been developed (Ives & Learmonth, 1984; Porter & Millar, 1985), as have measures for evaluating the extent to which IT can lead to competitive advantage (Sethi

& King, 1994). The widely accepted conclusion is that IT can create competitive advantage through efficiency improvements and other forms of cost reductions, through new channels or channel domination, or through differentiation of product or service.

The question of the sustainability of these IT-enabled strategic initiatives has attracted considerably less attention (Wade, 2001), and much of that attention has led to pessimistic conclusions (Mata, Fuerst, & Barney, 1995). The assumption usually underlying this pessimistic view is that "IT" per se cannot lead to sustainable competitive advantage because competitors can easily acquire "IT" and quickly replicate virtually any application (Powell & Dent-Micallef, 1995; Ross, Beath, & Goodhue, 1996). As a consequence, this view suggests that sustainable competitive advantage can only be achieved by using technology to leverage difficult to imitate complementary resources such as company culture or top management commitment (Henderson & Venkatraman, 1993; Powell & Dent-Micallef, 1995). We suggest instead that to focus solely on the complementary role of IT in the quest for sustainable competitive advantage is too narrow and risks oversimplifying the complexities and the potential contribution of the technology itself. Early work on the role of complementary resources, excluded other potential drivers of sustained competitive advantage from the discussion but cautioned that the "focus on differences among firms is not intended to suggest that other means of protecting an innovation are unimportant" (Clemons & Row, 1991).

The development of a comprehensive model of IT and sustainable competitive advantage must begin with the realization that IT is neither homogeneous nor undifferentiated. Rather, technologies differ with respect to their characteristics, and the context in which they are introduced and used (Orlikowski & Iacono, 2001). But, thus far, there has been little recognition of the characteristics of different technologies or the process by which these characteristics contribute to competitive advantage. For example, information technologies differ dramatically with respect to their complexity and the degree of organizational change that needs to occur during the implementation process (Feeny, 2001). While a website can easily be designed and deployed, large infrastructure projects (e.g., data warehouses, ERP implementations) are complex, lengthy and prone to failure (Wixom & Watson, 2001). Indeed, the publicity surrounding failures such as the SAP failure at Fox Meyer Drug that management claimed drove the company to bankruptcy (Davenport, 1998) can considerably curtail enthusiasm for the managers of other firms to follow a promising but too similar paths.

A framework for identifying or assessing sustainable competitive advantage must also reflect the dynamic nature of competitive strategy (Hidding, 2001). The ability to prevent or delay a competitive response is key to the sustainability of strategy (Chen & MacMillan, 1992; Porter, 1980). As IT increasingly underlies a wide range of strategic initiatives, a useful framework must explicitly address the potential for using technology to prevent or delay competitive responses. For example, the success of American Airlines' SABRE reservation system was largely guaranteed by the switching costs faced by the installed travel agents base (Copeland & McKenney, 1988).

Technology might, in theory, be easily copied, but it does not follow that strategies based on the use of IT cannot lead to sustainable competitive advantage.[1] In this chapter, we formulate a framework that identifies the determinants of sustainability and helps to explain the process by which they operate for particular IT-enabled strategic initiatives. IT-enabled strategic initiatives are strategic moves that rely heavily on IT and are intended to lead to sustainable improvements in the firm's competitive position (Ross et al.,1996). Typical examples of such initiatives include business process re-engineering, customer relationship management, organizational learning, knowledge management, electronic commerce, electronic business and infrastructure initiatives (Ross et al., 1996). This focus on IT-enabled strategic initiatives is consistent with the view that competition is carried out through an ongoing series of strategic moves (i.e., initiatives) and competitive responses (Chen & MacMillan, 1992).

In the following section we develop a framework for examining IT-enabled sustainable competitive advantage. It presents the potential drivers of sustainability of IT-enabled strategic initiatives. The model identifies potential sources of sustainability and explains how they operate. Our work is intended to enhance understanding of the network of factors linking the characteristics of the firm and of IT-enabled strategic initiatives to the achievement of sustainable competitive advantage. But in this chapter we also will focus, sometimes by example, on the framework's potential value in fashioning corporate strategy. The framework provides a means to evaluate the potential sustainability of IT-enabled strategic initiatives. We now introduce the concepts of sustainable competitive advantage and barriers to imitation and then present the sustainability framework.

∎ Sustainable Competitive Advantage

The concept of competitive advantage is rooted in the logic of value creation and distribution. A firm achieves competitive advantage when the value it creates in an economic exchange is greater than the value that could be created if the firm did not participate (Brandenburger & Stuart, 1996). In other words, the firm contributes something unique and valuable to its value system—the set of suppliers, distributors, customer in which the firm does business (Porter, 1991).

All firms perform discrete but interrelated activities intended to create value; these discrete activities represent "the basic unit of competitive advantage" (Porter, 1991, p. 102). Firms achieve competitive advantage by performing these activities either at a lower cost then the competition, or in a unique and valuable way (Reed & DeFillippi, 1990). IT can contribute to the creation of competitive advantage by enabling activities to be performed at a lower cost (Nault & Dexter, 1995), by changing activities so that they become unique and valuable (Nault & Dexter, 1995), or by improving the linkages among these activities so that, as a whole, they can be performed at lower cost or in unique ways (Porter & Millar, 1985). This perspective views strategy not as the making of a few large moves based on discrete "one-time" decisions, but as the configuration of interrelated and interlocking activities (Rivkin, 2000). Thus, IT-enabled strategic initiatives do not simply entail building a system that provides superior returns until it is successfully replicated. Rather, they consist in the configuration of an activity system, enabled by IT, designed to create and appropriate value. The chapter on IT Value (chapter 4) describes effective vehicles for selecting and measuring the contribution.

Competitive advantage is sustainable when the "firm's competitive advantage resists erosion by competitor behavior . . . [this] requires that a firm possesses some barriers that make imitation of the strategy difficult" (Porter, 1985, p. 20). The ability to sustain a position of competitive advantage therefore requires creating impediments, or barriers, to imitation (Reed & DeFillippi, 1990), which inhibit competitors from replicating the strategy. The height of these barriers determines the time and cost required for a competitive response and, therefore, the resistance of the advantage to erosion. IT investments, if carefully orchestrated, can help sustain competitive advantage by enabling strategic initiatives that erect and maintain high barriers to imitation over time.

Competitive imitation occurs in stages (MacMillan, 1988, 1989). Once they find themselves disadvantaged, rivals search for the source of the problem. This may involve considerable ambiguity, making it difficult for the imitator to mount a response (Nault & Dexter, 1995). As competitors identify the sources of the firm's competitive advantage they must decide, first, whether they are able and willing to respond, and if they are, what approach to take (Macmillan, McCaffery, & Wijk, 1985). Typically, competitors first seek to imitate the leader by attempting to modify their existing strategies (MacMillan, 1988), and then by directly attacking the source of the leader's competitive advantage (MacMillan, 1989; Sethi & King, 1994). *Response lag*, "the time it takes competitors to respond aggressively enough to erode the competitive advantage," represents the delay in competitive response (MacMillan, 1989, p. 24). The height of barriers to imitation is directly related to their ability to generate response lag and forestall imitation. *Response lag drivers* are the factors that determine the magnitude of barriers to imitation. Among these are characteristics of the technology, the firm, its competitors, or the value system in which it is embedded.

■ *IT-Enabled Strategic Initiatives and the Potential for Sustainable Competitive Advantage*

IT-enabled strategic initiatives can increase response lag, and by so doing sustain a competitive advantage. This can be accomplished by careful management of the characteristics of the development project, the firm's unique resources, and the characteristics of the value system in which the organization is embedded (Feeny & Ives, 1990). Four barriers to imitation (fig. 5.1) capture the determinants of sustainability in the context of IT-enabled strategies: *IT project barrier, IT resources and capabilities barrier, complementary resources barrier,* and *preemption barrier.* These four barriers contribute independently to the sustainability of competitive advantage by creating response lag and making it difficult, costly, or impossible for competitors to replicate the IT-enabled strategic initiative pioneered by the firm.

In the remainder of this chapter, we define the barriers to imitation, explain their relationship to sustainable competitive advantage, identify the

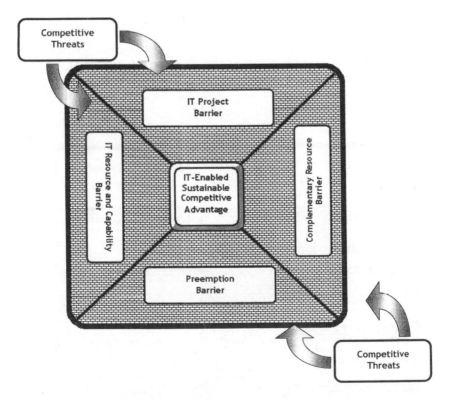

Figure 5.1. Sustainable competitive advantage and barriers to imitation

response lag drivers behind each barrier, and describe the process by which the barriers can be raised. The framework therefore allows for a preimplementation evaluation of IT-enabled strategic initiatives.

⦂ *IT Project Barrier*

The development and implementation of the IT project provides the first opportunity to raise barriers to imitation. The IT Project Barrier rises proportionally with the difficulty likely to be encountered by a competitor in designing, developing and introducing the IT necessary to copy the strategic initiative (fig. 5.2). Because IT-enabled strategic initiatives rely on an essential enabling IT core, they cannot be implemented until the necessary technology has been successfully introduced. The response lag drivers of the IT project barrier are driven by the characteristics of the technology and the implementation process.

IT Characteristics

Some have observed that IT cannot be considered a source of sustainable competitive advantage because it is easily copied (Mata et al., 1995; Ross et al., 1996). Instead, managers are advised to focus on developing complementary resources that can be leveraged through IT (Powell & Dent-

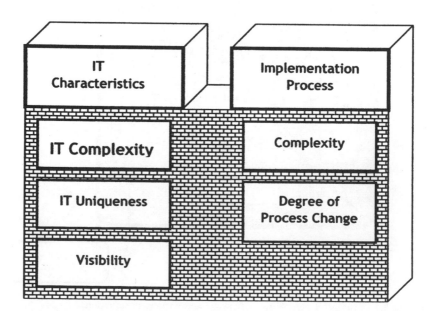

Figure 5.2. IT project barrier

Micallef, 1995). But this perspective discounts and obfuscates differences among technologies, treating all IT as homogeneous, at least in terms of how easy it is to replicate. This is an oversimplification, as different information technologies differ with respect to their complexity, uniqueness, visibility to competitors, and infrastructure requirements. Thus, they vary in their potential to produce response lag.

IT Complexity

IT complexity can be thought of as the bundle of knowledge and skills necessary to successfully assimilate and use new IT effectively (Fichman & Kemerer, 1997a). Technologies fall at different points on the complexity continuum (e.g., data warehouse vs. word processing software), and the same technology may present different challenges to different organizations (Downs & Mohr, 1976; McFarlan, 1981). For example, complex organizational technologies, such as ERP, impose knowledge barriers to effective assimilation (Attewell, 1992). But different organizations face knowledge barriers of different magnitude and are differently positioned to overcome them because of their learning-related scale, technology-related knowledge, and breath of technical knowledge (Fichman & Kemerer, 1999). Thus, one firm may be best positioned to introduce one technology, while a competitor has an advantage in another.

This applies to both process technologies (e.g., CASE tools, programming languages) used to design and develop systems, as well as packaged applications (e.g., SAP R/3). Technology complexity raises the IT project barrier by increasing development lead times for a competitive response. Moreover, when competitors face different challenges to the adoption of the same technology, the barrier's height will be affected as well.

IT Uniqueness

IT uniqueness, the next factor impacting the IT Project Barrier, also falls on a continuum. On one side are self-contained off-the-shelf IT products that need little integration or customization (e.g., a new electronic mail system). At the opposite end are custom developed applications or infrastructure subsystems that are unavailable in the open market. At various points along the continuum are applications requiring more or less integration and customization.

An example of the significant benefits to be achieved by customized integration comes from Amazon, the online bookseller. Amazon has made significant investments in technology in its warehouses, involving large package sorting devices fed by warehouse personnel equipped with handheld devices loaded with customized software. By fine-tuning the software and processes Amazon was able, with one third less staff, to process 30 percent more packages in peak days in December of 2001 than they had in peak

December days in 2000. The head of Amazon operations anticipates that with further fine-tuning they could eventually double their throughput of orders (Hansel, 2002).

Much of the benefits at Amazon came from tailoring the handheld devices carried by warehouse personnel—"the new software beams far more explicit instructions to workers about where they should go and what they should do" (Hansel, 2002). Such increases in IT uniqueness ratchet up the IT project barrier. To develop and introduce highly unique IT, the innovator must acquire the necessary know-how and technical knowledge (Attewell, 1992), expertise that will then serve as a barrier to replication. When the IT underling the innovator's strategy is not unique, consultants and outsourcing or service firms can be engaged by competitors to aid them in reducing knowledge barriers and, thereby, reduce the imitation response lag (Fichman & Kemerer, 1997b; Robertson & Gatignon, 1986).

Visibility

Visibility is the extent to which the characteristics of the IT underlying the activity system are observable to competitors. The visibility dimension can be conceptualized as a continuum spanning from custom developed internal systems (e.g., data warehouse) to inter-organizational or customer facing systems that require extensive education and selling to external users or customers (e.g., an online purchasing system).

Observability, a factor very similar to visibility, is the degree to which the characteristics and results of an innovation are discernible to others (Moore & Benbasat, 1991). Observability is generally linked to the rate of diffusion of an innovation (Fichman, 2000; Rogers, 1983). The visibility factor focuses more narrowly on the ability of competitors to gain in-depth knowledge about a firm's IT—the less the visibility, the higher the IT project barrier.

Implementation Process

Different information technologies are inherently dissimilar, as discussed earlier, and the processes by which they are implemented and become available to the organization differ as well. A measurement of barriers to imitation must explicitly address these differences because, depending on the implementation characteristics of the IT core of the strategic initiative in question, the strength of the barriers to imitation changes quite significantly.

Implementation Process Complexity

This response lag driver reflects the difficulty of implementing the technology. This is likely a function of the size and scope of the project, the number of functional units involved, the complexity of user requirements, possible political issues, and the likes.

IT infrastructure projects (Broadbent & Weill, 1997) represent a powerful example of complex systems that have substantial lead times, estimated to generally exceed five years. While each component of the infrastructure may be available for purchase by competitors, it is extremely difficult to integrate them into an effective system. For instance, HEB, the Texas-based grocery chain installed point-of-sale scanning systems in the 1980s and soon saw their potential for stock replenishment, but it was not until 1997 that the firm was able to achieve high enough precision to rely on the data for reordering. Problems were largely not associated with the devices, but with the firm's business processes and those of its suppliers.

Degree of Process Change

As both the Amazon and HEB examples illustrate, processes often need to change to fit a new system—particularly for large off-the-shelf systems such as ERPs. For IT-enabled strategic initiatives that rely on inter-organizational IT spanning the boundaries of multiple firms the challenges are magnified. The more departments involved and the more organizational boundaries crossed the harder and the riskier the change becomes (Markus, 2000). Yet, as complexity increases, so do the difficulties encountered by competitors.

: IT Resources and Capabilities Barrier

The role of IT resources and capabilities as sources of sustainable competitive advantage is now well known (fig. 5.3), with a number of such resources and capabilities identified (Bharadwaj, 2000; Feeny & Willcocks, 1998; Mata et al., 1995; Ross et al., 1996). IT-enabled strategic initiatives rely on IT to support a complex network of activities designed to create added value. IT can provide fundamental components of a strategy, supporting and enabling the activity system. Successful implementation of the strategic initiative is predicated on the ability to design, develop, implement, utilize and maintain the necessary IT.

IT-enabled strategic initiatives are dependent on access to the resources and capabilities necessary to produce and utilize the technology core. As the strategy becomes more reliant on preexisting IT resources—such as the IT infrastructure and data sources or repositories—and capabilities—such as IT development and management skills—it becomes increasingly difficult to copy. Two classes of response lag drivers contribute to the height of the IT resources barrier; these are IT resources and IT capabilities.

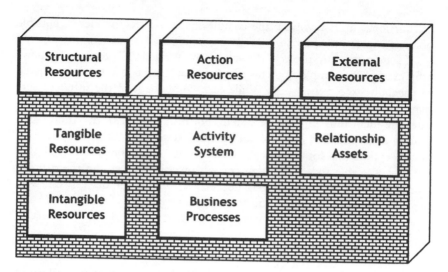

Figure 5.3. Complementary resource barrier

IT Resources

IT resources are physical technology assets available to the organization, including hardware components and platforms (e.g., a private network connecting globally distributed locations), software applications and environments (e.g., a proprietary revenue management system using custom developed models), and data repositories. These resources contribute to building response lag directly, by simplifying and speeding up the development and introduction of the initiative's IT core, or indirectly, by making it difficult for competitors who have no ready access to the needed IT resources to replicate the IT-enabled strategic initiative.

IT Infrastructure

An IT infrastructure is "the base foundation of the IT portfolio (including both technical and human assets), shared through the firm in the form of reliable services" (Broadbent, Weill, & Clair, 1999). Thus, an IT infrastructure is a set of IT components that are interconnected and managed by IT specialists with the objective of providing a set of standard services to the organization. Therefore, the IT infrastructure provides the foundation for the delivery of business applications (Broadbent & Weill, 1997). The IT infrastructure can be thought of in terms of both reach and range (Keen, 1991). Reach refers to the extent of the connectivity, within and outside of the firm. Range is the scope of services provided. As reach and range increase, the resources made available by the IT infrastructure and its ability to support a wide range of strategic initiatives increase as well (Broadbent et al., 1999).

The role of IT infrastructure as a source of sustainable competitive advantage is increasingly recognized (Bharadwaj, 2000; Ross et al.,1996). When underpinning the implementation of an IT-enabled strategic initiative, an IT infrastructure can contribute to the development of considerable response lag. An appropriate IT infrastructure enables strategic initiatives—such as cycle time improvement, business process redesign, cross-functional process, or cross-selling opportunities (Broadbent & Weill, 1997). As competitors move to replicate a successful strategic initiative, they not only must introduce the IT at its core but also must replicate the infrastructure services that underpin the strategy. With IT infrastructure development times estimated to generally exceed five years (Bharadwaj, 2000), the response lag and ensuing barrier to imitation is likely to be very substantial (Duncan, 1995). Recent empirical evidence lends support to this argument demonstrating that firms with an extensive IT infrastructure face fewer technological obstacles to the implementation of business process redesign initiatives than firms with a relatively less developed IT infrastructure (Broadbent et al., 1999). By contrast, a competitor's infrastructure, even if otherwise sophisticated, can serve as a barrier if it does not support a response to a particular strategic threat. Investments in enterprise resource planning software, for instance, may lock a firm into a limited set of business responses (Davenport, 1993).

Information Repositories

Information is now widely recognized as a fundamental organizational resource and firms are investing significantly to improve their ability to collect, store, manage, and distribute it (Wixom & Watson, 2001). Information repositories are often large data stores containing extensive information about customers, suppliers, products, or operations, organized in a structured form that is accessible and usable for decision-making purposes. But far more focused repositories also can play a strategic role. For instance, Lands' End's new custom-tailored trouser program keeps data on customer sizes that can be easily recalled, reused, and, if necessary, modified in subsequent orders (Ives & Piccoli, 2003).

As the Lands' End example illustrates, strategic initiatives can be built on superior or personalized information. Here, the information is tightly linked to the firm's unique offerings and its value is dissipated or greatly diminished unless the information is used with the firm's product or service. But information that can be kept secret, or is inherently noncodifyable and nontransferable (i.e., tacit), also offers a source of sustainable competitive advantage (Rumelt, 1987). A firm's information repositories can contribute to the development of substantial response lag by supporting strategic initiatives that use this idiosyncratic information. Competitors attempting to replicate the leader's strategic initiative must not only duplicate the IT at the core, but they also must accumulate a comparable information resource. Lands' End, for instance, follows up orders with customer satisfaction queries, containing specific questions about various elements of fit (legs too long or too short). This information can be used to fine-tune the tailoring algorithms as well as serving as predictors of future sales. Through the accumulation of such data, lag can be substantially increased and, if the customer is providing much of the information, there can be further opportunities for first mover advantages.

IT Capabilities

IT capabilities are derived from the skills and abilities of the firm's workforce (Bharadwaj, 2000; Ross et al., 1996). IT capabilities include technical skills and business understanding, IT management skills, IT usage skills, and relationship assets (Bharadwaj, 2000; Feeny & Willcocks, 1998; Ross et al., 1996). These capabilities directly influence the response lag associated with the introduction of IT at the core of IT-enabled strategies, because they facilitate and speed up the technology's design and development. They also play a fundamental role in enabling effective and timely implementation, maintenance, and utilization of the technology.

IT Technical Skills and Business Understanding

IT technical skills relate to the ability to design and develop effective systems. They include proficiency in system analysis and design, infrastructure design, programming, and so on (Bharadwaj, 2000). Another element is the depth of business understanding of IT specialists (Ross et al., 1996). Business understanding enables the IT specialists, charged with developing the technology supporting IT-enabled strategic initiatives, to envision a creative and feasible technical solution to business problems (Feeny & Willcocks, 1998). A high level of business understanding also contributes to the creation of response lag by mitigating the risks associated with the introduction of the strategic initiative and the relative investments in technology (Mata et al., 1995).

IT Management Skills

IT management skills refer to the ability to provide leadership for the IS function, manage IT projects, integrate different technical skills, evaluate technology options, select appropriate technology sourcing alternatives, and to the ability to manage change ensuing from the introduction of IT (Bharadwaj, 2000; Feeny & Willcocks, 1998). IT skills, because of their idiosyncratic nature, the learning curve associated with their development, and their socially complex and tacit nature, are a viable source of sustainable competitive advantage (Mata et al., 1995). Managerial IT skills can contribute to creating substantial response lag when techniques and routines developed over time can significantly reduce development costs and development lead times (Bharadwaj, 2000). These skills are likely to be generally applicable across a number of projects and technologies. Thus, when a new IT-enabled strategic initiative is introduced, managerial IT skills can be leveraged to deliver the necessary IT core in a timely and effective manner (Keen, 1991). Competitors who attempt to replicate the initiative but lack the same high level of managerial IT skills as the innovator face substantial obstacles to imitation.

Relationship Asset

An IT capability that has recently garnered research attention for its potential to lead to sustainable competitiveness is the relationship asset (Ross et al., 1996). This capability is accumulated over time and finds its roots in a mutual respect and trusting rapport between the IS function and business clients. When a firm has developed a significant relationship asset IS specialists and business clients are able to work together more effectively by coordinating and communicating extensively, they share a vision for the role of IT within the business, business clients share the risk and accept the responsibility for IT projects, and IS specialists are able to anticipate business IT needs and devise solutions that support these needs (Feeny & Willcocks, 1998; Ross et al., 1996).

The relationship asset's main contribution to response lag occurs in the early stages of design and development of IT-enabled strategic initiatives. As the business needs, or the opportunity, for the introduction of a strategic initiative is delineating, firms with strong relationship assets can involve the IS function and work together to jointly optimize the initiative and the IT core. The relationship asset has been identified as a driving force behind such success stories as American Airlines' SABRE and Wal-Mart purchasing and inventory initiatives (Copeland & McKenney, 1988; Stalk, Evans, & Shulman, 1992).

: Complementary Resources Barrier

Early scholars of economics and management strategy (Chamberlin, 1933; Penrose, 1958), suggested looking at firms as idiosyncratic bundles of resources. This perspective has been more recently formalized as the resource-based view of the firm (Barney, 1991; Wernerfelt, 1984). It advocates that sustainable competitive advantage is a function of the possession of valuable, rare, inimitable, and nontradable resources, and that firms that secure and leverage such resources can implement value adding strategies that competitors cannot copy (Barney, 1986, 1991). This perspective has inspired

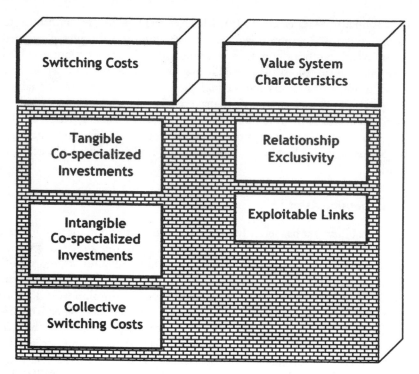

Figure 5.4. Preemption barrier

investigations into the role of IT in leveraging organizational resources (Clemons & Row, 1991; Jarvenpaa & Leidner, 1998; Kettinger, Grover, Guha, & Segars, 1994; Powell & Dent-Micallef, 1995). While IT is a fundamental component of the strategy, successful implementation of IT-enabled strategic initiatives requires that complementary organizational resources be mobilized as well. Thus, in order to implement an IT-enabled strategic initiative the firm must develop or acquire the necessary complementary resources.

As an IT-enabled strategic initiative becomes more reliant on distinctive complementary resources, the complementary resource barrier to imitation strengthens, and replication of the strategy becomes slower, costlier, and more difficult (fig. 5.4). That is, competitors will have to acquire or develop not only the IT at the core of the strategy but also the complementary resources that underpin the initiative. Response lag drivers contributing to the height of the complementary resources barrier are discussed here.

Structural Resources

Structural resources comprise non-IT related tangible and intangible internal assets used by the firm in the enactment of its IT-enabled strategic initiative.

These resources are important for the strategy and are cospecialized or complementary to the underlying IT (Clemons & Row, 1991).

Tangible Resources

In theory, any tangible resource available to the firm can underpin an IT-enabled strategic initiative. Among these are competitive scope (Clemons & Row, 1991; Feeny & Ives, 1990), physical assets (Feeny & Ives, 1990), scale of operations and market share (Clemons & Row, 1991; Kettinger et al., 1994), organizational structure, or governance (Feeny & Ives, 1990.), and slack resources (Kettinger et al., 1994). A classic example is Dell Corporation. Because the firm sold direct rather than through retail channels, it was much better positioned than its competitors (e.g., Compaq) to leverage the emergence of the commercial World Wide Web (Feeny, 2001).

Intangible Resources

A similar case can be developed for intangible resources. Examples of commonly cited intangible resources that can be leveraged to an IT-enabled strategic initiative include: corporate culture (Feeny & Ives, 1990; Kettinger et al., 1994.), top management commitment (Henderson & Venkatraman, 1993; Keen, 1991), and the ability to manage risk (Kettinger et al., 1994.). As with tangible IT resources, complementary intangible resources create response lag by making the strategy difficult to imitate unless competitors can garner the needed resources. These resources also can prove to be a source of rigidity. For instance, Levi Strauss's longstanding relationship with large retail chains, and perhaps fear of reprisal, has made it impossible for them to sell direct via the Internet. Thus, they can only attempt to replicate the Lands' End initiative by working with their retail partners.

Action Resources

A firm's action resources define how the firm carries out its productive activities. The action resources specify what activities are performed and what steps, or business processes, make up these activities. An IT-enabled strategic initiative relies on a collection of distinct activities, orchestrated to create added value, that are performed according to explicit or implicit business processes. For example, a customer relationship management (CRM) initiative calls for a concerted set of activities spanning marketing, procurement, staffing, operations, service, and enabled by IT. The activities that the firm performs, and the manner in which it performs them, can be leveraged to create response lag and sustain competitive advantage.

Activity System

The essence of IT-enabled strategic initiatives is a uniquely configured set of activities designed to create added value, in which IT play a central role (Ross et al., 1996). A performance maximizing activity system relies on a set of economic activities that are both interlocking and mutually reinforcing, expressly showing internal consistency—or internal fit—and that are appropriately configured given the firm's external environment—external fit (Siggelkow, 2001). While being one of the fundamental components of the strategy, IT must fit within the entire activity system. The concept of activity system and IT fit is parallel to that of strategic alignment (Luftman, 1996).

The process by which an established activity system contributes to generating response lag and to raise barriers to imitation is rooted in the interaction among activities. That is, when a firm has implemented a given configuration of activities and has developed the IT core supporting and mutually reinforcing the linked activities, replication of the technology alone is insufficient for successful imitation. Narrowly replicating one element of the activity systems (e.g., the IT core) leads to further decline of the imitator's current position, by wasting time, money, and management attention, rather than successful erosion of the leader's competitive advantage (Siggelkow, 2001). Imitation of the IT-enabled strategic initiative calls for reconfiguration of the linked activities, in addition to the introduction of comparable IT core. This approach rapidly becomes unmanageable as the number of activities to be replicated increases (Rivkin, 2000). Moreover, even successful imitation of complex activity systems may not prove successful as strong complementarities in the activity system are often thought to promote winner-take-all competition (Porter, 1996). A classic example of a firm that has an idiosyncratic activity system is Southwest Airlines. Because Southwest does not cater flights, does not offer seating assignments, has a standardized fleet of aircrafts, uses less crowded airports, and focuses on point-to-point travel by price sensitive customers, it is much more resilient to competitive imitation (Porter, 1996). The argument here suggests that when IT is introduced with careful attention as to how it complements and reinforces the firm's existing and unique activity system, considerable—and often insurmountable—response lag is generated and the strategic initiative is insulated from competitive imitation.

Business Processes

A business process is defined as the "specific ordering of work activities across time and place, with a beginning, and end, and clearly identified inputs and outputs: a structure for action" (Davenport, 1993, p. 5). Thus, a business process is mainly concerned with the manner in which work is performed, rather than with what work is performed (Davenport, 1993). The notion of business process is related to, but distinct from, that of economic activity introduced earlier. Economic activities describe what set of undertakings the firm performs while business processes describe how the firm performs them. Thus, two firms could perform the same economic activity (e.g., operating the customer service call center) yet perform them in widely different manner (e.g., "responds to calls within 40 seconds and, on average, complete calls in less than two minutes," as opposed to "segment inbound calls based on caller identification information, direct customers to agents assigned to the caller's lifetime value segment and handle the call accordingly").

The contribution business processes make to response lag and to the height of barriers to imitation depends on their uniqueness and strategic value. For instance, a spare parts manufacturer has chosen not to implement an industry standard enterprise system because its uniquely flexible customer fulfillment process is a source of positive differentiation in the marketplace (Davenport, 1998). When a firm is able to introduce an IT-enabled strategic initiative built around a business process with characteristics of uniqueness and differentiation, significant barriers to imitation are erected. Competitors pursuing a similar strategy will not only need to introduce similar IT but also redesign its processes to leverage the technology, a feat of considerable complexity and risk.

External Resources

As a firm performs the economic activities that form the fabric of its strategic initiatives and interacts with other organizations that belong to its value system, it accumulates external resources (Porter, 1991). External resources are assets that do not reside internally with the firm, like geographic location or the organizational culture, but accumulate with other firms and with consumers. External resources are generally intangible and developed over time (Porter, 1991).

When a firm's IT-enabled strategic initiative can leverage, or contribute to, the building of these external resources, it considerably improves response lag and barriers to imitation, forcing competitors to develop a comparable level of these resources before producing an effective response.

Interorganizational Relationship Asset

We discussed the value of IT relationship assets earlier in this chapter. When the relationship asset reaches across organizational boundaries, a similar dynamic emerges. This can be in the implementation of cross-organizational IT-enabled strategic initiatives such as EDI, supply chain management integration, or extranets (Hart & Saunders, 1997). An interorganizational relationship asset may not necessarily include the technology function of the firm's involved, but be limited to the business relationship between the parties—in the form of trust, commitment, or confidence. Interorganizational relationship assets contribute to reducing the perceived risk associated with participating in an economic exchange with the partnering firm (Crosby, Evans, & Cowles, 1990).

The interorganizational relationship asset contributes to the development of response lag directly by forcing the imitator to spend substantial money and time to develop the necessary relationship asset (Bharadwaj, Varadarajan, & Fahy, 1993). External resources, such as reputation or relationship assets, require substantial amount of time to be accumulated (Dierickx & Cool, 1989), IT-enabled strategic initiatives that leverage it can create significant barriers to imitation. A classic example of an IT-enabled strategic initiative that created substantial external resources is the Wal-Mart and Procter and Gamble partnership.

:   *Preemption Barrier*

A final barrier to imitation that can contribute to delaying or preventing the decay of sustainable competitive advantage stemming from IT-enabled strategic initiatives is the preemption barrier (fig. 5.5). Many of the classic examples of IT-enabled strategic initiatives discussed in the literature report on the introduction of innovative systems that provided the leading firm with early mover advantages and the ability to preempt retaliation from

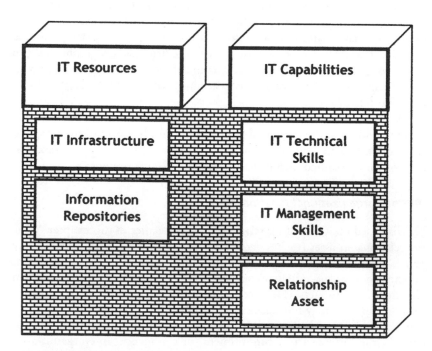

Figure 5.5. IT resources and capability barrier

imitators (Feeny & Ives, 1990). Initiatives such as Merrill Lynch's Cash Management Account, American Airlines' SABRE, American Hospital Supply Corporation's ASAP, and Pacific Pride System's Cardlock seem to owe much of their success to their ability to leverage their pioneering efforts (Copeland & McKenney, 1988; Feeny & Ives, 1990; Nault & Dexter, 1995). The IT-enabled strategic initiatives introduced by these pioneers led to preferential relationships with customers or other members of the value system and produced significant barriers to imitation, thereby helping to protect the leaders' competitive advantage.[2]

As an IT-enabled strategic initiative is introduced, it provides the potential for increasing response lag by establishing switching costs, particularly switching costs borne by customers joining the initiative. The structural characteristics of the value system in which the firm operates can magnify the effect of these switching costs on the preemption barrier to imitation. This effect is described in the following section along with the process by which switching costs operate.

Switching Costs

"Switching costs are the norm, not the exception, in the information economy" (Shapiro & Varian, 1998). IT-enabled strategic initiatives, heavily relying on the collection, storage, manipulation, and distribution of information, are particularly suited to the creation and exploitation of switching costs (Shapiro & Varian, 1998). We define switching costs as the total costs, including psychological, physical, and economic costs, borne by the parties of an exchange when one of them leaves the exchange. Switching costs stem from investments that are specific to the IT-enabled strategic initiative, where the term "specific" indicates that the value of these complementary investments is significantly lower in any alternative use. A classic example of switching costs is the total cost that computer users face when they decide to switch to a different platform (e.g., from the PC to the Mac). The decision entails costs due to investments in platform specific training, software, peripherals, data conversion costs, data loss, and the like.

Most agree that switching costs are a powerful weapon for defending a competitive position (Clemons, 1986; Feeny & Ives, 1990). Still, some have argued that switching costs may not represent valuable response lag drivers because customers can anticipate the risks of being locked-in, they have many IT sourcing options from which to choose, and suppliers leveraging switching costs may damage their reputations (Mata et al., 1995). Yet, customers often willingly agree to make the needed investments (i.e., absorb switching costs) when they perceive the firm's offerings to be of value. For instance, a customer of Lands' End's custom tailoring program is quite willing to provide extensive information on fit in exchange for getting well-fitted trousers. As we demonstrate later, switching costs are not only associated with the tangible and intangible investments needed to obtain and operate the necessary IT infrastructure; they also include opportunity costs associated with abandoning the initiative to adopt competitors' offers.

For example, companies that have used an electronic procurement marketplace—such as Avendra in the hospitality industry—for considerable time would be unwilling to switch to a competitor's because of the substantial value of the historical transaction data accumulated.

For switching costs to raise barriers to imitation, they do not need to severely lock-in customers. They simply need to create incentives for customers to remain in the relationship. When this happens, competing firms cannot simply match the leader's offering, but they need to either compensate the customer for the cost of switching (e.g., long distance telephone carriers paying customers to switch) or provide enough additional value to justify the customer's decision to incur the switching costs (Shapiro & Varian, 1998)—two potentially costly strategies. In other words, later entrants must be "that much better" (Feeny & Ives, 1990), where "that much" is measured by the magnitude of the switching costs. When substantial switching costs exists, significant barriers to imitation protect early movers.

Cospecialized Tangible Investments

When an IT-enabled strategic initiative is deployed it may require that the firm's customers acquire the physical assets necessary to participate in the initiative. We refer to the total capital outlay necessary to obtain these assets as *co-specialized tangible investments*. These cospecialized tangible investments range from computer hardware and telecommunication equipment to software applications and interfaces between the existing customer's systems and the firm's IT (e.g., hotel franchisees buy costly interfaces for the franchising brands' own reservation system, interfaces that become valueless if the property is rebranded). Whereas some of the classic examples are based on interorganizational systems, not all cospecialized tangible investments stem directly from the adoption of IT and dedicated computer equipment. Data and information repositories as well as maintenance and service contracts are examples of tangible investments cospecialized to the firm's IT-enabled strategic initiative. For example, the data accumulated by the customer may only be valuable as long as the customer maintains a relationship with the early mover. This situation arises when data is only compatible with the pioneer's systems and is impossible or costly to migrate to a competitor's systems. Another example is when the information collected is only valuable as long as the pioneer's products or services are being used (e.g., revenue management models and historical records that are brand specific and become valueless if the hotel is rebranded[3]).

The extent to which the IT-enabled strategic initiative requires customers' investments in cospecialized tangible investments, determines the potential for strong barriers to imitation associated with the initiative. But the contribution of this response lag driver may fluctuate over time because switching costs associated with tangible investments tend to decrease over time as the useful life of the investment grows shorter (Shapiro & Varian, 1998). Thus, the pattern of lock in may follow a reverse saw tooth pattern whereby switching costs are greatest on acquisition or upgrade of the assets (e.g., hardware and software) and degrades over time until the next investment is made. It follows that the firm's leadership position is most at risk as the customer faces the cyclical capital outlay.

Cospecialized Intangible Investments

When an IT-enabled strategic initiative is deployed it often necessitates that the firm's customers or channel partners make another type of investment to effectively take part in the initiative—cospecialized intangible investments (e.g., to benefit from customer relationship management initiatives customers often need to take the time to complete a profile). The costs associated with these investments may be financial, but often instead occur as investments in time. Cospecialized intangible investments may include "set-up" costs as well as ongoing costs (e.g., retraining of new travel associates using a reservation system). Common examples of cospecialized intangible investments include training specific to application and their interface (Feeny, 1988), proficiency that users have achieved with the current technology over time (Shapiro & Varian, 1998), transactions costs associated with searching for and contracting with other partners, and setting up new relationships (Makadok, 1998), the uncertainty surrounding switching decisions, and the available alternatives (Schmalensee, 1982)—likely to be high with complex IT-enabled strategic initiatives—and the costs associated with migrating existing databases to new providers or new platforms (Feeny & Ives, 1990).

Unlike their tangible counterparts, the switching costs associated with cospecialized intangible investments tend to rise over time (Shapiro & Varian, 1998). As a consequence, IT-enabled strategic initiatives that leverage cospecialized intangible investments have the potential to build self-reinforcing barriers to imitation. For example, individual proficiency with software programs tends to increase as a function of time and use. A proficient end user faces significantly higher switching costs as time goes on because adopting a competing software application would depress her productivity as new learning occurs. The same dynamic occurs when switching costs are subtler (Makadok, 1998). Some forward-looking banks are attempting to leverage ubiquitous network connections to reach a position of "trusted consolidator" of top clients' complex financial positions. This strategy entails the collection of significant amounts of information about customers banking profile and current services, insurance holdings, investment portfolio, mortgage, credit and loan positions, scheduled bills payment, and so on. The bank does not provide all of the above products, but it strives to offer a consolidated view of all financial positions by automatically retrieving and organizing the pertinent information. Assuming that customers find the service useful and continue to use it, the bank can leverage this preferential position to enhance and deepen its relationship with the customer. Once competitors begin to offer a similar service, customers face switching costs that extend well beyond their achieved proficiency with the bank's software. In order to change provider, they would have to research and evaluate competitors, compare feature/functionality, configure the competitor's application, migrate, if possible, historical data, open new accounts, close old accounts, and so on. Although a cursory examination may suggest that these costs are negligible, early research shows that even in markets with apparently negligible switching costs, like the money market mutual funds market, significant entry order effects, because of early mover lock in, does exist (Makadok, 1998). This result confirms that, "even when switching costs appear low, they can be critical for strategy" (Shapiro & Varian, 1998), and may be due to the relative magnitude of perceived switching costs to value differentials among competitors. A condition requiring later entrants to provide significantly higher value to "indemnify" customers of the switching costs they bear (Shapiro & Varian, 1998). As a bank executive we recently interviewed eloquently put it: "Do not underestimate the power of entanglement."

Finally, even though there may be more IT sourcing options than ever before, and customers can anticipate the risks of being locked-in, recent research suggests that customers will accept switching costs to benefit from the early mover's value proposition. Moreover, if the early mover delivers on its proposition, its reputation is more likely to be enhanced than damaged.

Collective Switching Costs

A unique form of switching costs is represented by collective switching costs. Collective switching costs occur when the market presents network externalities (Shapiro & Varian, 1998), and represent the combined switching cost of all entities in the network. Network externality refers to the disproportionate rise in a network or systems value as each new user adopts. The massive market share held by Microsoft is a classic example. Much of the value users obtain from the firm's operating system result from the large community of users who are trained and comfortable with the suite of tools it encompasses and supports. In the presence of network externalities, participation in the dominant network affords the most value to a prospective user who in turn, by joining, contributes to increasing the value of the network as whole. As a group, the participants face collective switching costs that exceed the simple sum of individual switching costs because unless a coordinated defection from the network occurs, any individual defector finds itself cut out of the network and its benefits (Shapiro & Varian, 1998). Only "wholesale defection makes sense" (Feeny & Ives, 1990, p. 40), but the coordination costs of wholesale defection are often daunting (Shapiro & Varian, 1998).

The emergence of a ubiquitous network infrastructure has created a number of strategic opportunities and has made possible the creation of communities to an unprecedented degree (Armstrong & Hagel, 1996). IT-enabled strategic initiatives that foster the development of communities, and create network effects, hold the potential to leverage substantial collective switching costs and raise strong barriers to imitation (Feeny & Ives, 1990). Examples of such initiatives include trading communities (e.g., eBay online auctions) or communities of interest (e.g., MCI Worldcom friends and family program, AOL bulletin boards).

Value System's Structure

A firm does not engage in economic activity in isolation but as a link in a larger value system including upstream and downstream members (Porter, 1985). The structure of this value system can provide significant opportunity for preemptive strategies and for the exploitation of the response lag drivers discussed earlier (MacMillan, 1983). Unlike response lag drivers, however, the structure of the value system does not directly impact the strength of the preemption barrier to imitation. It plays instead a facilitating or inhibiting role. As described later, when the value system display certain characteristics, the effect of early mover response lags, such as switching costs, are maximized and they can have dramatic impacts.

Relationship Exclusivity

A structural characteristic of the value system that magnifies the strength of the relationship between response lag drivers and the preemption barrier to imitation is the exclusivity of the relationship (Feeny & Ives, 1990). An exclusive relationship is said to exist when elements of the value system will elect to do business with one and only one organization providing the products or services offered by the focal firm (i.e., the firm introducing the IT-enabled strategic initiative). The firm's counterpart (e.g., customer, supplier) places a premium on dealing with either the firm or one of its competitors, but not both (Feeny & Ives, 1990). Relationship exclusivity is the norm with IT-enabled initiatives that provide integration services and that benefit from the accumulation of historical information. In the example, described earlier, of the banks attempting to consolidate all customers' financial information in order to become the trusted consolidator, the purpose of the initiative is defeated unless the customer makes the relationship exclusive.

Exclusivity strengthens the relationship between response lag drivers and the preemption barrier. When a business relationship benefits from exclusivity, the customer faces penalties for hedging behaviors and for sourcing the needed product or service from multiple firms. But, by relying on only one firm, the customer becomes highly dependent on the firm and the effect of existing switching costs is magnified. When competitors introduce competing offering, customers are already invested in their relationship with the incumbent.

Concentrated Value System Link

The various stages of the value system in which the firm is embedded can be characterized as links in a chain (e.g., raw material producers, suppliers, distributors, firm's customers, end consumers). The degree of concentration in the link is inversely proportional to the number of suitable business entities populating the link—where suitability depends on whether the firm would find the products or services offered by the entity populating the link acceptable. Thus, a highly concentrated value system link is one where there are relatively few organizations, or consumers, available for the firm to use or serve (MacMillan, 1983). In the case of airline reservation systems it is the total number of travel agents serving the market targeted by the airline sponsoring the system. In the case of fighter jets manufacturing, it is the pool of customers approved by the firm's national government. Note that, in theory, to be suitable for exploitation, a concentrated link needs not be directly preceding or following the firm's position in the value system—for example, the population of customers of the firm's customers.

The degree of concentration in the value system link strengthens the relationship between response lag drivers and the preemption barrier. A market of given size will only support a finite number of competitors (Makadok, 1998), and achieving a substantial penetration with the value system link is necessary to successfully preempt imitation (Feeny & Ives, 1990). As the degree of concentration increases, the time necessary to secure a relationship with a significant proportion of the link decreases, all else being equal. Previous research in consumer goods has demonstrated that longer time-in-market, the period of time during which the early mover has the only available offer in the market, is reflected in the sustainability of competitive advantage as measured by market share (Huff & Robinson, 1994). This time-in-market effect is attributed to the fact that, given more time, the leading firm has a better chance to successfully influence consumer learning, perceptions and preference (Brown & Lattin, 1994). While time-in-market effects have not been formally tested for IT-enabled strategic initiatives, similar dynamics may influence their penetration, particularly when interorganizational systems that perspective adopters must accept are at the core of the initiative. As the degree of concentration in the value system link increases, given the firm's resource constraints, the proportion of link members that can effectively be reached, educated, and influenced in a given amount of time increases. Consequently, the firm has a better chance of capturing a significant proportion of relationships and be able to leverage switching costs to "lock out" competitors, thereby maximizing its barriers to imitation. Conversely, when a link in the value system enumerates a large number of business entities, given the firm's resource constraints, the firm is unlikely to effectively reach a critical mass of entities and raise substantial barriers to imitation the same amount of time.

: *A Postscript: Dynamics Over Time*

In this chapter, we have conceptualized the process by which IT-enabled strategic initiatives produce sustainable competitive advantage as a static process by which firms analyze IT projects, their current portfolio of resources and capabilities, and the potential for preemption, and then use this information to formulate and deploy initiatives that maximize barriers to imitation. Yet, as with any other competitive move, IT-enabled strategic initiatives are subject to the decay of barriers to imitation and the erosion of competitive advantage over time (Porter, 1991). As a consequence, a complete view of the sustainability of competitive advantage must also address the dynamics of sustainability and the process by which erosion of competitive advantage can be prevented, delayed or limited. As a consequence, firms are urged to continually invest in the factors that underpin the initiatives' barriers to imitation (MacMillan, 1989; Reed & DeFillippi, 1990), or what we have termed response lag drivers. Although beyond our objectives for this chapter, we have elsewhere (Piccoli & Ives, 2002) presented a second framework for examining this dynamic aspect of sustainability of competitive advantage. The bottom line of that discussion is that sustainability requires considerable attention to the ongoing maintenance of the barriers to imitation identified here.

: *Conclusion*

This chapter has focused on the response lag drivers that strengthen the barriers to imitation of specific IT-enabled strategic initiatives and, in turn, the role these barriers play in fostering sustainable competitive advantage. From this analysis, we have found that this advantage generally does not stem from "visionary" initiatives, but from "evolutionary" ones that begin with an IT-based response to perceived environmental pressure or opportunities and a commitment to continuous learning (McKenney, Copeland, & Mason, 1995). Often organizational learning, a basis for sustainability, can only begin once the strategic initiative is enacted. For example, Wal-Mart's "cross-docking" logistic technique hinges on daily communication between its in store point-of-sales systems, its distribution centers, and its suppliers (Stalk et al., 1992). As its competitor did not develop similar IT-enabled strategic initiative, they did not have the "facilities" to begin the learning process. This suggests that IT-enabled strategic initiatives can foster the development of capabilities that will evolve into strategies not readily envisioned at the start. In investing in relationships, for instance, it may be confidence in the individual to make something happen that carries more weight than the anticipated payback from the initial spend. Similarly, the breadth of data a customer may be willing to give up in exchange for a particular service may, ultimately, provide more value than the sale of the service itself.

In this chapter, we have presented a framework for thinking about, envisioning, and evaluating IT-enabled strategies for achieving sustainable competitive advantage. Clearly, there is no easy path to sustainability, with considerable uncertainty surrounding investments and strategic directions. But the framework does provide a means for arguing against decisions that might otherwise seem straightforward. An obvious example is the decision to buy off-the-shelf systems that standardize valuable idiosyncratic business processes. By contrast, it provides fodder for defending investments in infrastructure or in core IT capabilities. Along with the approaches discussed in chapter 4, they provide an effective vehicle for assessing IT's contribution to the business. Most significantly it suggests means by which IT can be employed to help sustain competitive advantage by exploiting the characteristics of the technology, the characteristics of the firm, or the characteristics of the value system in which the firm operates.

⦂ Notes

1. Similarly, research examining sustainability of product innovations has repeatedly shown that products that a cursory evaluation would consider easily replicable by competitors often lead to sustained competitive advantage and large volumes of business (Macmillan et al., 1985; Makadok, 1998).

2. The preemption barrier to imitation emerges in the context of relationships between the firm and other organizations engaged in a business relationship with it. While these business relationships may occur with any entity in the firm's value system, for simplicity we refer to them henceforth as "the customer."

3. The software here is not proprietary or brand specific, and the data is not accessed over a network or hosted by the brand. Yet, the historic data and the models the hotel has developed assume that the hotel has a given brand (e.g., Four Seasons). If the hotel is rebranded, while the software, the data, and the models are retained, their value is much lower because the data and models are specific and assume the hotel sports the Four Season flag (i.e., has access to Four Season's brand equity, reservation systems, etc.)

⦂ References

Armstrong, A., & J. Hagel. (1996) "The Real Value of On-Line Communities," *Harvard Business Review*, 74(3), 134–41.

Attewell, P. (1992) "Technology Diffusion and Organizational Learning: The Case of Business Computing," *Organization Science,* 3(1), 1–19.

Barney, J. (1991) "Firm Resources and Sustained Competitive Advantage," *Journal of Management,* 17(1), 99–120.

Barney, J. B. (1986) "Strategic Factor Markets: Expectations, Luck, and Business Strategy," *Management Science,* 42, 1231–41.

Bharadwaj, A. S. (2000) "A Resource-Based Perspective on Information Technology Capability and Firm Performance: An Empirical Investigation," *MIS Quarterly,* 24(1), 169–96.

Bharadwaj, S., P. R. Varadarajan, & J. Fahy. (1993) "Sustainable Competitive Advantage in Service Industries: A Conceptual Model and Research Propositions," *Journal of Marketing,* 57(10), 83–99.

Brandenburger, A. M., & H. W. Stuart. (1996) "Value-based Business Strategy," *Journal of Economics and Management Strategy,* 5(1), 5–24.

Broadbent, M., & P. Weill. (1997) "Management by Maxim: How Business and IT Managers Can Create IT Infrastructures," *Sloan Management Review,* 38(3), 77–92.

Broadbent, M., P. Weill, & D. S. Clair. (1999) "The Implications of Information Technology Infrastructure for Business Process Redesign," *MIS Quarterly,* 23(2), 159–82.

Brown, C. L., & J. M. Lattin. (1994) "Investigating the Relationship between Time in Market and Pioneering Advantage," *Management Science,* 40(10), 1361–70.

Chamberlin, E. H. (1933) *The Theory of Monopolistic Competition.* Cambridge, MA: Harvard University Press.

Chen, M., & I. C. MacMillan. (1992) "Nonresponse and Delayed Response to Competitive Moves: The Roles of Competitor Dependence and Action Irreversibility," *Academy of Management Journal,* 35(3), 539–70.

Clemons, E. K. (1986) "Information Systems for Sustainable Competitive Advantage," *Information and Management,* 11(3), 131–7.

Clemons, E. K., & M. C. Row. (1991) "Sustaining IT Advantage: The Role of Structural Differences," *MIS Quarterly,* 15(3), 275–92.

Copeland, D., & J. McKenney. (1988) "Airline Reservation Systems: Lessons from History," *MIS Quarterly,* 12, 353–70.

Crosby, L. A., K. R. Evans, & D. Cowles. (1990) "Relationship Quality in Services Selling: An Interpersonal Influence Perspective," *Journal of Marketing,* 54(3), 68–82.

Davenport, T. H. (1993) *Process Innovation: Reengineering Work through Information Technology.* Boston, MA: Harvard Business School Press.

Davenport, T. H. (1998) "Putting the Enterprise into the Enterprise System," *Harvard Business Review,* 76(4), 121–31.

Dierickx, I., & K. Cool. (1989) "Asset Stock Accumulation and Sustainability of Competitive Advantage," *Management Science,* 35, 1504–11.

Downs, G. W., & L. B. Mohr. (1976) "Conceptual Issues in the Study of Innovation," *Administrative Science Quarterly,* 21(4), 700–714.

Duncan, N. B. (1995) "Capturing Flexibility of Information Technology Infrastructure: A Study of Resource Characteristics and Their Measures," *Journal of Management Information Systems,* 12(2), 37–57.

Feeny, D. F. (1988) "Creating and Sustaining Competitive Advantage," in M. Earl

(Ed.), *Information Management: The Strategic Dimension.* New York: Oxford University Press.

Feeny, D. F. (2001) "Making Business Sense of the E-Opportunity," *MIT Sloan Management Review,* 42(2), 41–51.

Feeny, D. F., & B. Ives. (1990) "In Search Of Sustainability: Reaping Long-Term Advantage from Investments in Information Technology," *Journal of Management Information Systems,* 7(1), 27–46.

Feeny, D. F., & L. P. Willcocks. (1998) "Core IS Capabilities for Exploiting Information Technology," *Sloan Management Review,* 39, 9–21.

Fichman, R. G. (2000) "The Diffusion and Assimilation of Information Technology Innovations," in R. W. Zmud (Ed.), *Framing the Domains of IT Management: Projecting the Future through the Past.* Cincinnati, OH: Pinnaflex.

Fichman, R. G., & C. F. Kemerer. (1997a) "The Assimilation of Software Process Innovations: An Organizational Learning Perspective," *Management Science,* 43(10), 1345–63.

Fichman, R. G., & C. F. Kemerer. (1997b) "Object Technology and Reuse: Lessons from Early Adopters," *IEEE Computer,* 30(10), 47–59.

Fichman, R. G., & C. F. Kemerer. (1999) "The Illusory Diffusion of Innovation: An Examination of Assimilation Gaps," *Information Systems Research,* 10(3), 255–275.

Hansel, S. (2002) "Amazon Ships to a Sorting Machines Beat," *New York Times.*

Hart, P., & C. Saunders. (1997) "Power and Trust: Critical Factors in the Adoption and Use of Electronic Data Interchange," *Organization Science,* 8(1), 23–43.

Henderson, J. C., & N. Venkatraman. (1993) "Strategic Alignment: Leveraging Information Technology for Transforming Organizations," *IBM Systems Journal,* 32(1), 4–17.

Hidding, G. J. (2001) "Sustaining Strategic IT Advantage in the Information Age: How Strategy Paradigms Differ By Speed," *Journal of Strategic Information Systems,* 10(2), 201–222.

Huff, L. C., & W. T. Robinson. (1994) "Note: The Impact of Leadtime and Years of Competitive Rivalry on Pioneer Market Share Advantages," *Management Science,* 40(10), 1370–1378.

Ives, B., & G. P. Learmonth. (1984) "The Information System as a Competitive Weapon," *Communications of the ACM,* 27(12), 1193–1201.

Ives, B., & G. Piccoli. (2003) "Custom Made Apparel and Individualized Service at Lands' End," *Communications of the AIS,* 11, 79–93.

Jarvenpaa, S. L., & D. E. Leidner. (1998) "An Infomation Company in Mexico: Extending the Resource-Based View of The Firm to a Developing Country Context," *Information Systems Research,* 9(4), 342–361.

Keen, P. G. (1991) *Shaping the Future: Business Design through Information Technology.* Boston, MA: Harvard Business School Press.

Kettinger, W., V. Grover, S. Guha, & A. Segars. (1994) "Strategic Information Systems Revisited: A Study in Sustainability and Performance," *MIS Quarterly,* 18), 31–58.

Luftman, J. (1996) *Competing in the Information Age: Strategic Alignment in Practice.* New York: Oxford University Press.

MacMillan, I. C. (1983) "Preemptive Strategies," *Journal of Business Strategy,* 3(2), 16–26.

MacMillan, I. C. (1988) "Controlling Competitive Dynamics by Taking Strategic Initiative," *The Academy of Management Executive,* 2(2), 111–118.

MacMillan, I. C. (1989) "How Long Can You Sustain a Competitive Advantage?" in L. Fahey (Ed.), *The Strategic Planning Management Reader.* Englewood Cliffs, NJ: Prentice Hall.

Macmillan, I. C., M. L. McCaffery, & G. V. Wijk. (1985) "Competitors' Responses to Easily Imitated New Products: Exploring Commercial Banking Product Introductions," *Strategic Management Journal,* 6(1), 75–87.

Makadok, R. (1998) "Can First-Mover And Early-Mover Advantages Be Sustained in an Industry with Low Barriers to Entry/Imitation?" *Strategic Management Journal,* 19(4), 683–696.

Markus, M. L. (2000) "Paradigm Shifts: E-Business and Business/Systems Integration," *Communications of the AIS,* 4(10). Available online at: http://cais.aisnet.org.

Mata, F. J., W. L. Fuerst, & J. B. Barney. (1995) "Information Technology and Sustained Competitive Advantage: A Resource-Based Analysis," *MIS Quarterly,* 19(4), 487–505.

McFarlan, F. W. (1981) "Portfolio Approach to Information Systems," *Harvard Business Review,* 59(5), 142–150.

McKenney, J. L., D. C. Copeland, & R. O. Mason. (1995) *Waves of Change: Business Evolution through Information Technology.* Boston, MA: Harvard Business School Press.

Moore, G. C., & I. Benbasat. (1991) "Development of an Instrument to Measure the Perception of Adopting an Information Technology Innovation," *Information Systems Research,* 2(3), 192–222.

Nault, B. R., & A. S. Dexter. (1995) "Added Value and Pricing with Information Technology," *MIS Quarterly,* 19(4), 449–465.

Orlikowski, W. J., & C. S. Iacono. (2001) "Research Commentary: Desperately Seeking 'IT' in IT Research—A Call to Theorizing the IT Artifact," *Information Systems Research,* 12(2), 121–134.

Penrose, E. T. (1958) *The Theory of the Growth of the Firm.* New York: Wiley.

Piccoli, G., & B. Ives. (2002) "IT-Dependent Strategic Initiatives: A Theory of Sustained Competitive Advantage," unpublished manuscript, Cornell University.

Porter, M. (1980) *Competitive Strategy: Techniques for Analyzing Industries and Competitors.* New York: Free Press.

Porter, M. (1985) *Competitive Advantage: Creating and Sustaining Superior Performance.* New York: Free Press.

Porter, M. (1991) "Towards a Dynamic Theory of Strategy," *Strategic Management Theory,* 12(1), 95–117.

Porter, M. (1996) "What Is Strategy?" *Harvard Business Review,* 74(6), 61–79.

Porter, M., & V. Millar. (1985) "How Information Gives You Competitive Advantage," *Harvard Business Review,* 63(4), 149–160.

Powell, T. C., & A. Dent-Micallef. (1997) "Information Technology as Competitive Advantage: The Role of Human, Business, and Technology Resources," *Strategic Management Journal,* 18(5), 375–405.

Reed, R., & R. J. DeFillippi. (1990) "Casual Ambiguity, Barriers to Imitation, and Sustainable Competitive Advantage," *The Academy of Management Review,* 15(1), 88–103.

Rivkin, J. W. (2000) "Imitation of Complex Strategies," *Management Science,* 46(6), 824–844.

Robertson, T. S., & H. Gatignon. (1986) "Competitive Effects on Technology Diffusion," *Journal of Marketing,* 50(3), 1–12.

Rogers, E. M. (1983) *Diffusion of Innovations.* New York: Free Press.

Ross, J. W., C. M., Beath, & D. L. Goodhue. (1996) "Develop Long-Term Competitiveness through IT Assets," *Sloan Management Review,* 37, 31–42.

Rumelt, R. P. (1987) "Theory, Strategy and Entrepreneurship," in D. J. Teece (Ed.), *The Competitive Challenge: Strategies for Industrial Innovation and Renewal.* Cambridge, MA: Ballinger.

Schmalensee, R. (1982) "Product Differentiation Advantages of Pioneering Brands," *American Economic Review,* 72, 349–365.

Sethi, V., & W. R. King. (1994) "Development of Measures to Assess the Extent to Which an Information Technology Application Provides Competitive Advantage," *Management Science,* 40(12), 1601–1628.

Shapiro, C., & H. R. Varian. (1998) *Information Rules: A Strategic Guide to the Network Economy.* Boston, MA: Harvard Business School Press.

Siggelkow, N. (2001) "Change in the Presence of Fit: The Rise, the Fall, and the Renaissance of Liz Claiborne," *Academy of Management Journal,* 44(4), 838–857.

Stalk, G., Evans, P., & L. E. Shulman. (1992) "Competing on Capabilities: The New Rules of Corporate Strategy," *Harvard Business Review,* 70(2), 57–70.

Stratopoulos, T., & B. Dehning. (2000) "Does Successful Investment in Information Technology Solve the Productivity Paradox?" *Information and Management,* 38(2), 103–117.

Wade, M. (2001) "Exploring the Role of Information Systems Resources in Dynamic Environments," Proceedings of the 22nd International Conference on Information Systems, New Orleans, LA.

Wernerfelt, B. (1984) "A Resource-Based View of the Firm," *Strategic Management Journal,* 5, 171–180.

Wixom, B. H., & H. J. Watson. (2001) "An Empirical Investigation of the Factors Affecting Data Warehousing Success," *MIS Quarterly,* 25(1), 17–41.

6

Sirkka Jarvenpaa and Kerem Tomak

Competing in Mobile Business

▪ *Chapter Summary*

1. A central question of this chapter is: What new business value does the convergence of Internet and wireless technologies, so called m-business (mobile business), create?
2. M-business, or Mobile Internet, extends Internet-related business developments into the wireless sphere where the access, reach, and possibly richness to information and knowledge are enhanced. M-business is defined as those transactions and communications that take place on wireless Internet infrastructures.
3. Despite a lot of hype about how m-business will enable transactions and business operations, firms have yet to realize many potential benefits.
4. To understand the new value added from mobile services (above the brick and mortar and e-business operations), one must focus on innovations in the mobile business models: transaction content, structures, and governance.
5. Business value is the sum of all values that can be appropriated by the firm together with its supplies and buyers in business transactions. The definition of business value takes into consideration the characteristics of the overall value chain—suppliers, firms, and buyers.
6. The Value Driver framework builds on the concept of business value and empirical research on e-business. The framework identifies four key value drivers: efficiency, complementaries, lock-in, and novelty. These value drivers are not limited to e-business but also apply to mobile transactions.
7. Examples are used to illustrate how different mobile services deliver value through the four value drivers: efficiency, complementarities, lock-in, and novelty in transactions.
8. Although one value driver at a time is discussed, the big payoff comes when firms integrate the drivers. Japan's NTT DoCoMo i-mode is a case in point.
9. Success in mobile business depends on how well firms can bundle the four value drivers.

▪ *Introduction*

Executives making decisions that aim to maximize the business value of their information technology investments receive guidance from scholarly work on strategic alignment. This chapter, in concert with chapter 4 provides important insights to assessing IT's contribution to the business. An increasing portion of their decisions involves investments in wireless technologies and coopting business resources. Wireless technologies extend a firm's transactions from a stationary virtual space to a mobile space. Mobility can be defined as both as an ability—to change a place, to move freely, and to lack fixity—and as a state—fluidity and instability. Mobility extends the (1) access, (2) reach, and (3) richness of transactions, processes, knowledge, and possibly relationships (see fig. 6.1) beyond those reached by wired information and communication technologies.

The most salient feature of mobility is the availability of ubiquitous access to information whenever and wherever it is needed, which reduces the constraints of desk-bound PCs. For instance, using a mobile device, an engineer can access an engine's repair history while inside the jet engine or while riding in a moving train. Wireless technologies offer a potential for greater communication reach by expanding the number of people reachable quickly and cheaply anywhere and anytime. In countries like Finland and Hong Kong, almost 80 percent of the population has at least one cell phone. Advances in wireless technologies promise to enrich digital information when ubiquity is coupled with location-specific and time-specific knowledge. With greater access, reach, and richness, mobility can open up new activity spaces—such as those parts of the day that people spend in commuting or in transit—that firms can exploit.

We define m-business as those transactions and communications that take place in the mobile space; that is, on wireless Internet infrastructures. M-business offers possibilities for new ways of enabling transactions and business operations. In this chapter, we illustrate how m-business services generate new business value. We first describe the value challenge that m-business faces and then introduce a value-driver framework that we use to examine how existing or soon to be released mobile services add value.

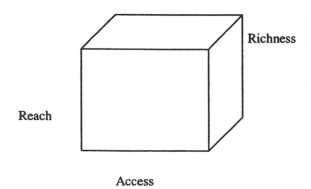

Figure 6.1. Defining mobility: access, reach, and richness

We conclude with a case study on Japan's NTT DoCoMo i-mode, which has introduced a new suite of multimedia services, new forms of connecting buyers and sellers to existing markets, and new incentives for customers to cocreate value.

: *The Value Challenge*

Citing the famous French historian Braudel, Keen and Macintosh note that "m-commerce is one of a comparatively small number of technologies that is capable of bringing about a transformation which changes the limits of what is possible in the structures of everyday life." They argue that m-business creates more choices and more knowledge about those choices for individuals and firms and, as a consequence, generates new value (Keen & Mackintosh, 1997, p. 46).

Like with e-business, many firms search for value in new business models. E-business brought changes in a firm's transaction content, structure, and governance rendering new classes of business models (Weill & Vitale, 2001). Firms expect mobile services to do the same. Given the greater access, reach, and richness, mobility should offer opportunities for new value creation and strategic positioning, either in the context of existing services or new offerings, businesses, customer and supplier relationships. For example, mobile services may introduce totally new categories of transaction services, because mobility opens up new activity spaces in a person's life (managing an office from a car) or change the expectations and demand of existing services. Mobile platforms also may change who participates in the transactions and who is linked with whom. The responsibility for a family's mobile grocery shopping may shift to the person who has the longest commute and the most time to kill while in transit. Buyer incentives may change. Customers may be more willing to pay for content on mobile Internet than on the wired Internet. For example, one CEO of a wireless portal remarked, "The free content model of the Internet is going to change in wireless. There is not the same resistance to paying for content among mobile phone users that there is on the web" (Ostergaard, 2002). M-business may change the locus of control in personalization. On the wired Internet, personalization is most of the time delegated to and triggered by the customer through own customized web sites and the content within. Mobile devices allow the firms to control the level of personalization and in a sense out-guess the customers' needs, taking personalization on a new level and providing additional value. This in turn makes each customer the center of competition and in essence, they become individual markets for which each mobile service provider competes. These types of innovations in the transaction content, transaction structure, and business governance may render new set of business models with new value added.

But value creation in m-business has so far proven difficult. One could blame slow, unreliable, nonstandard wireless technology, but perhaps the bigger culprit is a misconceptualization of how mobile innovations create value. Undoubtedly, a critical necessity for success is wide deployment of various mobile devices; but device penetration itself does not guarantee acceptance and growth of the mobile business. Interestingly, a better predictor of m-business success may be the lack of widespread PC and Internet penetration. Those parts of the world where PCs and wired Internet penetration is low may be the first areas to take off in m-business because mobility offers a greater added value. The higher the added value, the greater the vertical spread between customer willingness to pay and the opportunity cost to suppliers.

Economists have used willingness to pay, or customer value, as a measure of the new value created by a product or service. That is, the value that is appropriated determines the value created. In theory, if a firm can set prices tailored for each and every customer, then a perfect level of value extraction can be attained. Traditional economic price theory may not be suitable, however, in the context of mobile business because of the relationships among services, interfaces, and devices. For example, recent work in the IT literature (Bakos & Brynjolfsson, 2000) that considers bundling information goods is based on the assumption that the services and products offered in the bundle have no interrelationships and that the consumers value them, on the aggregate, equally. But mobile business differs from this scenario in that it inherits product and service characteristics: the consumer handset defines the type of application on the device; and the applications are determined by the content and service providers and sometimes by the mobile operators. Therefore, interrelationships are a key issue at all levels of interaction for customer value.

In business strategy, value discussions take on a broader perspective and consider both customer willingness to pay and the opportunity costs to suppliers. Value discussions center on drivers or sources that enhance the total value potential. Porter's value chain model argues that the configuration of the value chain can lead to differentiation, lower costs, or niche products and services, all contributing to value (Porter, 1980). Brandenburger and Stuart expand Porter's firm-specific value model to include a more external view (including the supply chains) in determining the value created (Brandenburger & Stuart, 1996). According to Brandenburger and Stuart, total value creation sets the upper limit for how much value a firm can capture. Business value is the sum of all values that can be appropriated by the firm together with its suppliers and buyers in business transactions.

The value created by the value chain is a customer's willingness to pay minus opportunity costs of suppliers. The customer's willingness to pay is measured as the monetary amount at which the customer is indifferent whether he or she has the product/service or the money. The opportunity cost of the suppliers is the monetary amount at which the supplier is indifferent whether the firm owns the resource (and deploys it) or sells it for money. Hence, the definition of business value treats buyers and suppliers symmetrically and stresses the point that meeting the needs of buyers is necessary but not sufficient for value creation. The definition of business value takes into consideration the characteristics of the overall value chain—suppliers, firms, and buyers.

According to Brandenburger and Stuart, added value of a firm can be thought of as "the difference between the value created by all the firms competing for the customer and the value created by all firms except the one in question" (Brandenburger & Stuart, 1996, p. 6). Whether a particular firm can expect a positive value depends on the asymmetries between it and other firms: its products or services need to be "different" from its competitors. Favorable asymmetries also can exist on the supplier side if the supplier firm for some reason is able to offer resources to one firm at lower cost than to other firms in the market.

A firm can influence customers' willingness to pay for m-business services by either creating asymmetries (i.e., increasing switching costs) or benefiting from the already existing asymmetries between it and its competitors. A good example is the major brokerage company that gives away RIM and Palm devices to its most valued customers in hopes of creating switching costs. Establishing a mobile channel for these consumers lowers their willingness to pay for other firms' products and services and hence generates business value to the firm in reference.

A firm can generate a similar impact on the supplier side. Trinity Development and Construction Services based in Columbus, Ohio, uses wireless handheld computers to extend its back-end billing system to its job sites. This allows the company to collect a payment from its customer weeks before it has to pay the supplier. By reducing the time to pay, Trinity reduces suppliers' opportunity cost of doing business, hence generating an immense switching cost (at least until Trinity's competitors do the same!). Another example is 2scoot.com. This company, based in Kingston, New York, provides cell phone faceplates that act like credit cards when near a 2Scoot network. The communications chip on the cell phone is supplied by Texas Instruments; faceplates are branded by Nokia to fit its 5100 phone series as well as Tricon, owner of fast food chains KFC, Taco Bell, and Pizza Hut. By establishing such value-managed partnerships, 2Scoot is able to reduce the opportunity cost to its suppliers (Drummond, 2001).

The combined interaction of consumer willingness to pay and the opportunity cost of suppliers provide a vertical relationship between a firm and its customers and suppliers. Next we introduce the value-driver framework that derives from this vertical relationship of customer-firm-supplier. The framework helps in the understanding of the business value created by mobile services.

: *Value-Driver Framework*

Building on the Brandenburger-Stuart business value concept, Amit and Zott (Amit & Zott, 2001) advanced four specific e-business drivers that they claim form the basis of value creation for Internet business models. These value drivers emerged from a study involving 50 e-business firms that derived at least 10 percent of their revenues from transactions on the Internet. The value drivers are listed here (and see also fig. 6.2):

- *Efficiency*: The greater the transaction efficiencies, the greater the value generated. Efficiencies of the Internet reduce transaction costs compared to offline business and thereby increase a buyer's willingness to pay or decrease a supplier's opportunity cost.
- *Complementarities*: The greater the difference between the value of bundled services and the sum of value each piece of service sold separately, the greater the value generated. Complementarities can exist on the buyer side (a firm's service is more valuable to a customer when

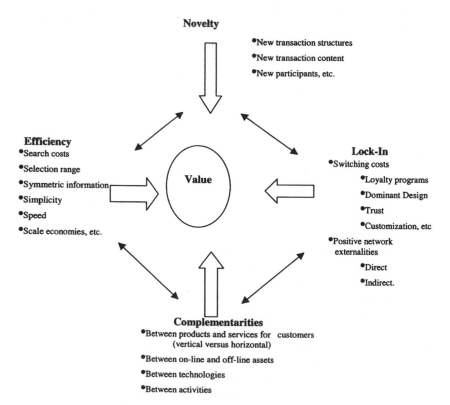

Figure 6.2. Sources of value creation in e-business (R. Amit & C. Zott, "Value Creation in E-Business," *Strategic Management Journal,* 2001 © John Wiley & Sons Limited. Reproduced with permission.)

accompanied by another firm's service) as well as on the supplier side (supply chain integration, infrastructure technologies).

- *Lock-in*: Increased switching costs prevent buyers and partners from migrating to competitors. Switching costs might be created through transaction costs or network externalities.
- *Novelty*: New structures and governance form through transactions that connect previously unconnected parties, deploy innovative transaction methods, and deploy protective property rights (e.g., Internet business method patents).

The strengths of Value-Driver Framework are fivefold. First, the framework offers an integrative view of value creation, taking into account a range of theories that each alone only offers a partial view of value creation. The framework integrates value drivers from the resource-based view of the firm (Barney, 1991) (complementary assets), transaction cost theory (Williamson, 1975) (efficiency, incentives), Schumpeterian innovation (Schumpeter, 1942) (novelty), and strategic network theory (Gulati, 1999) (network size and nature of links). Although value can arise from the presence of sources individually, the big payoffs come from linking them together.

Second, the framework recognizes that the network, not just the individual firm, is the locus of value creation. Although our reference point is a firm and its business model, a business model often expands to include multiple firms and covers a bundle of capabilities and resources of suppliers, customers and complementors. A particular firm's added value can only be understood in the context of the total value created in the network.

Third, the framework is built on the concept of business models. According to Amit and Zott, a business model "depicts the content, structure, and governance of transactions designed so as to create value through the exploitation of business opportunities" (Amit & Zott, 2001, p. 493). The total value created through a business model is "the sum of the values appropriated by all the participants in a business model, over all transactions that the business model enables." Building the framework on business models instead of value chains, highlights the fact that value is created from innovations (such as how transactions are enabled, and what exchange standards are used) rather than how goods are produced, marketed, and shipped.

Fourth, the Amit-Zott framework offers managerial guidance on how to target value-creating innovations, because, to many, e-business (as well as m-business) is about inventing new business models and reaping value from them. Innovations in business models call for fundamental change in one or more core components of a business model: transaction content, transaction structure, or transaction governance ("*Transaction content* refers to the goods or information that are being exchanged, and to the resources and capabilities that are required to enable the exchange. *Transaction structure* refers to the parties that participate in the exchange and the ways in which these are parties are linked . . . [or refers to] the order in which exchanges

Table 6.1
Value Matrix for eBusiness Models

Drivers Innovations	Efficiency	Complementaries	Lock-in	Novelty
Transaction Content				
Transaction Structure				
Transaction Governance				

take place (i.e., their sequencing), and the adopted exchange mechanism for enabling transactions. . . . Finally, *transaction governance* refers to the way in which flows of information, resources, and good are controlled by the relevant parties") (Amit & Zott, 2001, p. 494). Business model innovations may generate the necessary asymmetry in the firm's offering or position (vis a vis its competencies) and positively influence one of the value drivers, resulting in a 3×4 value matrix (see table 6.1).

Fifth, the Value-Driver Framework and Opportunity Matrix framework is not limited to e-business—stationary virtual spaces—but can apply to mobile transactions as illustrated in the remaining sections of this chapter. M-business is an evolution of e-business that provides increased levels of access, reach, and richness; and like e-business, m-business value is best conceptualized through business models that allow for the integration of value sources from innovations in transaction content, transaction structure, and business governance.

⋮ The Analysis of Mobile Services

Next, we discuss the underpinnings of the drivers and discuss how existing or soon-to-be-launched mobile services are taking advantage of each value driver. We will discuss each value driver sequentially, although much value arises from leveraging interdependencies of multiple value drivers in a mobile service.

Efficiency

A variety of organizational forms attempt to minimize the coordination and motivation costs embedded in every transaction, and thus increase efficiency. (Milgrom & Roberts, 1992). At the organizational level, coordination costs materialize in order to bring together buyers and sellers in a transaction. In addition, there is the cost of dissemination and sharing of information throughout the organizational hierarchy and the associated delay cost that impacts the timeliness of managerial decisions. Sellers incur costs as they determine buyers' tastes, convey product and service information using advertising and other means, and decide on pricing. From a buyers' perspective, search costs as well as the costs associated with an unsuccessful match to a seller become salient.

Constant access to information can increase efficiency and lower costs for critical decision making.

- Siemens is implementing a wireless extension to its SAP Business Warehouse back-end system in an attempt to give its sales and management personnel remote access through their PDAs. This will enable its employees to have up-to-date access to recent sales information and accounts receivable.
- UPS recently began using wireless devices to track shipments. The cost to UPS of each query to access CRM data via a wireless connection is reported to be 10¢, whereas the same inquiry by phone would cost $2.5.
- A firm that maintains medical lab machinery provides its technicians with Palm devices. With software provided by iMedeon, the devices are used to provide information about logistics, machine status, customer information, orders, and so forth.
- Office Depot truck drivers use a handheld unit produced by Symbol Technologies running an application designed by Aether Systems to communicate with inventory management and other supply chain systems. By disseminating necessary information about the distribution of products and other transaction-related data to the organization and its managers, coordination costs are decreased.

From the buyers' perspective, similar applications arise that target a significant decrease in coordination costs.

- CitiGroup customers in Poland receive daily bank balance updates via SMS messages if their accounts fall below a certain level.
- Major brokerage houses like E*Trade, Charles Schwab, and Merill Lynch provide wireless access to aggregated account information from multiple sources on one screen.
- Mysimon.com, which is an Internet-based shopping service that compares prices offered by online merchants, offers a wireless version of the service that enables customers who are walking down the aisles at a store to compare prices with those offered by online vendors.
- Dealfinder is a service offered by Mviva, a wireless portal, which operates on a WAP-enabled device, and allows customers to check price and product information by entering the products' UPC codes.

- GeePs.com is a location-based service provider that supplies real-time wireless advertisement to the visitors of any shop or mall. Customers can sign up for its services and receive SMS messages about product specials as they stroll through a shopping venue.

Motivation costs, which can be decomposed into informational incompleteness and asymmetry, lead to a situation in which "the parties to a potential or actual transaction do not have all the relevant information needed to determine whether the terms of an agreement are mutually acceptable and whether these terms are actually being met" (Milgrom & Roberts, 1992, pp. 29–30). Mobile technologies can remedy this situation and decrease motivation costs by providing access to information at the time when a negotiation or the signing of a contract is taking place. Negotiations can be automated further by the use of mobile intelligent agents that can be implemented on the mobile devices.

- A mobile platform provided by OneName creates business value by easily creating trusted business relationships. OneName's platform automatically negotiates legally binding digital privacy contracts between web agents for every single data exchange. This solution assures the identity of all parties in any transaction and lets a business customize permissions for the use of information specific to each type of customer, employee, partner and supplier relationship. The OneName Identity Server enables smart, self-service transactions including automated negotiation and updating of shared information.
- The payment systems provided by TeleVend and EverSystems extend payment capabilities to mobile phones. Users can dial a number linked to the vending machines, authorize the transaction, and choose from among various payment options. Since the transaction is charged to the mobile phone account, users do not need to enter any credit card or other personal information, which reduces the security and privacy concerns of using wireless devices in purchases.

Lock-In

Mobile business—like its fixed-wire counterpart and many other technology-related products—has ability to lock-in customers because the cost for those customers to switch vendors becomes too great. Shapiro and Varian note that "the great fortunes of the information age lie in the hands of companies that have successfully established proprietary architectures that are used by a large installed base of locked-in customers." (Shapiro & Varian, 1998, p. 135). It is important to successfully manage lock-in to achieve increased business value in mobile business.

The mobile channel provides a value-added extension to the wired Internet. Unique device ID numbers allow mobile service providers to track customer location and provide services based on their physical surroundings. The personalization level enabled by this capability gives the providers a better understanding of the customers' needs and allows them to create a certain level of lock-in that is difficult for rivals to eliminate. Examples abound:

- Travelers can track the traffic conditions in real time from mobile devices, which helps them better plan their travel length and find alternate routes.
- Vodafone provides a service that gives business information based on a user's location, such as the nearest restaurant. The wireless device—a phone or a PDA—can even provide directions to a business that has been selected by the customer.
- General Motors' OnStar delivers personalized services for the owners of GM vehicles. Together with vehicle-related services such as accident assistance, unlocking automobiles, roadside service, and directions, OnStar also provides the ability to make hotel reservations and find the nearest gas station or an ATM.
- NTT DoCoMo provides applications that find pets and children using a wireless device that transmits location information to the mobile service providers.
- Charles Schwab provides its customers with a mobile investing service, PocketBroker, available to users of Palm devices and mobile phones.
- Chase Manhattan Bank provides financial information in real time to its customers over a wide range of wireless equipment. Users have the option to customize the content and display format via a website.
- DBS Bank in Singapore provides a WAP service that supports service requests like checking balances, paying bills, and transacting foreign exchanges and provides financial news.
- In Finland, an online brokerage company, eQ Online allows its customer to see graphs of every stock listed on the Helsinki Exchange together with real time bid-ask prices.

Complementarities

The presence of complementarities in a service or product offering leads to additional benefits as the value of a bundled service tends to be more than the sum of the items in the bundle. If a bundle contains (seemingly) unrelated items such as the cable TV programming, the correlation among the individual components is at a minimum level as the bundle contains identical items. Tying is a common form of bundling in which firms offer product/service packages containing at least two different products (Shy, 2001). For example, a computer retailer may include various software packages with the sale of the computer hardware; or a wireless device, like a PDA, comes with a variety of services either embedded in the device or installable later. In mobile business, tying is a very important tool to increase the business value since as users involuntarily invest in complementary products, lock-in often results (Varian, 2001)

Standards, which are designed to allow for seamless interconnection of components, advance a form of complementarity as well, as consumers are more likely to purchase products that conform to their existing systems.

Together with the complementarity effect, it is possible to use mobile and wired Internet channels in conjunction to provide information that will lead to a finer customer segmentation (Zettelmeyer, 2000). Wired Internet provides a level of personalization that depends on the information the consumer transfers to the firm. Wireless devices provide a third dimension, which allows the firms to almost "feel" the customer through the unique device ID, and the location of the consumer. The information about the environment, which surrounds the consumer, can be gathered and analyzed together with the data collected over the wired domain.

As the service providers compete on multiple simultaneous channels, they can provide specific groups of customers with various amounts of information and impact consumers' valuations in a differential way.

- Web personalization company Yodlee recently announced Yodlee2Go which will give wireless phone customers a new window on the web, allowing them to access bank accounts, credit card information, brokerage accounts, e-mail, and other custom online services. Similarly, BroadVision, an e-business applications provider, announced its Mobile Solution, which is designed to deliver targeted information to mobile customers, partners, and employees. The system enables current BroadVision customers to add wireless capabilities to their existing business-to-business (B2B), business-to-consumer (B2C), and business-to-enterprise (B2E) applications.
- Through Chase, E*Trade and Charles Schwab, consumers can access the same information on the wired web as well as on the mobile device. But, since the mobile device is used continuously during the day whenever and wherever the consumer is, the financial services firms can offer a series of complementary services on the mobile device.
- Texas Instruments is using Radio Frequency Identification (RFID) to help businesses serve their customers by creating smart and secure RFID technology solutions for the B2C CRM and payment markets. The wireless technology that Texas Instruments RFID provides enables consumers to pay for gas, food, and other items at the check-out counter with a wave of their hand. Customers do not even need a wallet, because they can use their mobile phone or a special keychain to pay for their purchases. Through the use of wireless device, payment mechanism is complemented by the wireless technology.

Novelty

Schumpeter (1942) developed the creative destruction paradigm, which states that technological innovations can lead to new value creation until the innovations become commonplace. Porter's value chain analysis also encourages innovations in products and new methods in value chain activities. E-business popularized the notion of the business model and steered firms toward innovations in the transaction content, structure, and governance. Amit and Zott (2001) note that novelty in transactions is often linked to efficiency and complementarity. M-business can also leverage new sets of participants in transactions and enable them by adopting new exchange mechanisms.

- NTT DoCoMo ties in specific content and related application developers to push the content to the portal it provides. By contrast, Nokia supports open standards and generates a "plug-in" for all who want to deliver content on its handsets. The revenue models for these two approaches illustrate the value that can be created from providing content.
- Vodafone recently announced a $50 million user trial for m-payments in the United Kingdom, Germany, and Italy. Customers will be able to make credit or debit payments on a mobile platform, authorizing them with a PIN code. The payment system itself is an open standard—like Nokia's—and the cost of the call is the only fee charged by Vodafone (Giga Information Group, 2002).

The Vodafone example represents an important change in the financial payments industry that impacts the consumer and the merchant, the mobile operator, the content provider, and anybody else along the value chain. An even more disruptive change can soon follow: person-to-person payments. Such a concept could replace existing payment tools—primarily cash—and move us closer to the notion of a cashless society. Paybox (Germany) and PayPal (United States) have already instituted person-to-person payments. Although the current adoption rate is relatively low, we may soon wake up to the reality that cash is no longer a medium of exchange (see table 6.2)!

Total Value Generation

One of the revelations of studies on the value creation in e-business (wired Internet applications) has been that value is the total sum of the sources of value and their linkages. For example, e-businesses not only allowed for a more efficient use of customers as "cocreators of content," but the cocreator role also increased a user's lock-in with the site and increased opportunities for mass customization. In this example, the total value created is the sum of value from (1) novelty and (2) lock-in, and (3) their linkages.

Our studies in m-business suggest that firms are relying excessively on

Table 6.2
Value Sources of Mobile Services

	Efficiency	Complementarities	Lock-in
Business model structure	• Citigroup's Financial Transactions • Siemens back-end to wireless integration • Dealfinder • Mysimon.com To Go • OfficeDepot drivers	• Wireless financial service by Chase, E*Trade etc.	• Vodafone • GM's OnStar • Charles-Schwab's PocketBroker • DBS Bank • eQ Online
Business model content	• OneName • UPS	• Texas Instruments RFID • Vindigo	
Business model governance		• Ericsson/IBM alliance to support financial institutions on wireless devices	• Chase Manhattan Bank wireless services

one driver rather than a combination of drivers, and this may be a cause of their disappointment in m-business. A 2001 study examined 20 diverse companies across the globe that had launched mobile Internet services either internally or in their customer environments (Jarvenpaa, 2002). The firms represented a wide diversity of industries (content providers, service operators, intermediaries, and infrastructure firms) and geographic locations (firms headquartered in the United States, Hong Kong, Japan, Sweden, and Finland).

The study found that services that rode on the efficiency driver made mobile workers or mobile customers more independent of time and place and hence more efficient in their use of time, faster in their decisions, and more flexible with their immediate work groups. These mobile services also made the information flows more efficient at the work group level and hence reduced time lags in critical business processes, which often had indirect positive effects such as improved customer service. The initial impetus for many of these "efficiency-driven" services had been the push of "new mobile technology advantages" or the pull of their customers' "always on and connected mindset." As significant as these gains are, the analysis suggested that those services relying on multiple value drivers—for example, not just efficiency, but complementarities—generated much more value to the firm. Japan's highly successful and profitable i-mode service by NTT DoCoMo is an example how the leverage of multiple drivers can lead to significant value creation.

Caselette: NTT DoCoMo i-mode

The i-mode service was launched in February 1999 and, by the spring of 2001, NTT DoCoMo's i-mode was heralded as the world's most successful mobile data service for consumers. The i-mode was:

- The first packet switched "always on" (this means that users were connected to i-mode service continuously without having to wait to connect to a network). This is in contrast to the second-generation WAP phones that require the user to initiate a session by dialing into a WAP gateway, which can take 30 seconds.
- Unmatched in its user growth rates, the total number of users, and the number of i-mode compatible Internet sites.
- The most revenue-generating consumer mobile data service.
- The first mover in the third-generation mobile multimedia services.
- Aggressively pursuing a globalization strategy.

NTT DoCoMo is the wireless arm of Japan's largest and formerly state-run telecommunications services company, Nippon Telephone and Telegraph (NTT). NTT is a public-listed company, although its largest stakeholder is the minister of finance (53 percent). NTT DoCoMo is a public-listed subsidiary of NTT Corp., and NTT owns 67.1 percent of NTT DoCoMo.

In the early 1990s, NTT DoCoMo was formed to run NTT's cellular communication services. By the mid-1990s, NTT DoCoMO faced a saturated cellular market and sought ways to diversify its revenue sources.

A team of self-described mavericks who were brought in from outside—an innovation itself in a Japanese organization—conceived the idea of i-mode and brought it to market. It was marketed as a mobile entertainment and messaging service (e.g., "send messages to your friends") with no mention of the Internet and its 2.5-generation mobile technology; i- stood for information, not Internet. For most i-mode users, the phone was an introduction to the Internet. By 2001, NTT DoCoMO had become the largest Internet Service Provider (ISP) in Japan, surpassing its parent NTT's ISP business to PC users. The rapid subscriber growth and high usage levels caused network congestion and outages and led to quality of service complaints among users. But breadth of transaction content kept most users loyal to i-mode.

Growth in the number of i-mode subscribers was phenomenal bringing in not only revenue to NTT DoCoMO in terms of usage fees but also packet transmission charges and commissions for content subscriptions. More than five million people subscribed to i-mode in the first year and the number climbed to 11 million in 1.5 years. The user base exceeded 23 million after two years with the daily user increase of 40,000–50,000 and a monthly increase of over 1 million users. Although i-mode gained its initial reputation among teenagers and young adults, over time the customer base evolved to resemble the professional and mature user base of NTT Do-CoMo's cellular service. DoCoMo had partnered with 13 vendors to offer mobile intranet and groupware applications to organizations.

The high penetration was coupled with high usage rates. Over 90 percent of i-mode subscribers were active users, accessing an average of 11 sites per day. In December 2000, NTT DoCoMo claimed that the average i-mode user subscribed to 2.2 data services, with 48 percent of i-mode subscribers paying for fee-based sites; i-mode collected 9 percent commission for billed content subscription. Compared to its European counterparts, NTT DoCoMo had higher average monthly revenue per user. DoCoMo's culture thrived on consumer psychology and revenue focus: "If you cannot bill it, kill it."

For customers, i-mode was an affordable service. Prices were competitive in terms of other media. Internet access on phones was priced by packet, or volume or data downloaded, not per minute of airtime. Phones were less bulky than PCs in small Japanese homes. The lower and upper limits of the subscription fees for content were set by i-mode so that any content service could be within reach of most phone users of any age.

The business model of i-mode introduced fundamental changes in *transaction content, structure,* and *governance.* The i-mode provided new services to users: downloadable characters to decorate one's phone's screen, a virtual pen-pal service, or game in which users could live out a virtual life as a selected imaginary character. The quantity and diversity of content sites were unmatched by any mobile portal in the world; i-mode increased the chances that each customer found his or her "killer" application. All content creation was outsourced to third parties from the start of the service; i-mode was launched with 67 partner companies offering content sites off i-mode's menu. In spring 2001, i-mode had 985 alliance partner companies or 1,500 official I-menu websites and 42,224 voluntary i-mode Internet websites.

The way i-mode structured its relationships with content providers was as much of the innovation as the breadth and depth of content. NTT DoCoMo made it very clear from the start that it did not plan to share its data traffic revenue with the content sites that would be providing the traffic. An executive at NTT DoCoMo proudly said, "We do not pay content providers to be part of our service. They pay us." Yet, i-mode found a way to foster new content development by such well-known content brands—for example, Bandai, Sega. It attracted these affiliate partners by having a large installed base of mobile voice users and by setting up a billing infrastructure on the behalf of the content providers. A monthly fee, usually between 100 and 500 yen, appeared on the user's phone bill for subscriptions to specialized content. NTT DoCoMo garnered 9 percent of this fee in return for providing payment collection service.

Another structural innovation was the open content protocol. NTT Docomo was a member of the WAP forum; but decided to go with cHTML for its mark-up language. CHTML is architecturally similar to WAP, but much simpler for content providers to use. CHTML proved a blessing over WAP as it was protocol that HTML developers were already familiar and offered less cumbersome and expensive translation of normal HTML page. The cost to the developers was important because DoCoMO did not pay developers for content provisioning.

In terms of transaction governance, i-mode had both a closed and open model in its ecology. In terms of affiliate, or official, partners, NTT DoCoMo controlled their business models. DoCoMo dictated the terms by which affiliate sites could pursue an advertising-based revenue model. DoCoMo did not allow chatrooms and bulletin boards on affiliate sites. Affiliate sites were prohibited from carrying links to unofficial sites. Also, DoCoMo did not allow monetary incentives from partners to influence the i-menu placement, unlike many other carriers; i-mode created a dynamic system for i-menu placement whereby the most highly trafficked sites would go to the top of the menu list automatically.

Besides content aggregation with affiliate partners, NTT DoCoMo exercised vertical integration with its other suppliers. DoCoMo exerted strong influence on the mobile handset manufacturers. DoCoMo also used proprietary technology for the network gateways All this vertical integration created a closed model that contributed to a robust user experience but also faced criticism from competitors as well as government (For example, facing criticism that selection of official partners lack transparency and objectivity, NTT DoCoMo has announced plans to appoint an independent third party to oversee content providers' applications.)

But i-mode ecology also embedded an open flow of information, resources, and partners in the form of voluntary sites. Voluntary sites decentralized content production, pushing it *away* from official content providers and *toward* users themselves. Although estimates of total traffic to voluntary sites and official sites varied from 40/60 to 15/85, the traffic growth to voluntary sites was said to exceed the affiliate sites. The concept of voluntary sites was not part of i-mode's blueprint. The concept emerged serendipitously from i-mode's choice of open cHTML content standard. By the time i-mode launched, there were 10 individual and company homepages that were accessible by i-mode handsets that had no relation to DoCoMo and without its permission. DoCoMo made money from the traffic to the voluntary sites just as it does on traffic to the official sites. Contrary to affiliate sites, i-mode does not have any direct means to control the business models of voluntary sites.

Innovations in transaction content, structure, and governance in turn created efficiencies, complementarities, lock-in, and novelty. NTT DoCoMo's value sources included:

- **Efficiency**: i-mode allowed a customer reap efficiencies by having a single communication device for phone, a pager, and an Internet connection. An i-mode customer had access to over 50,000 websites (official and unofficial partner sites) allowing customers to benefit from a rich mix of free and fee-based online content. Consolidated monthly billing for the content services on a phone bill simplified the user transactions and perhaps reduced errors. The i-mode engendered quality and quality competition among a set of category sites (games, dating services, weather) within the directory on the handset's start-up menu (I-menu). The over 1,500 official i-mode affiliates that provided fee-based content benefited from being part of the i-mode menu and billing system—lowering marketing, selling, and personal costs.
- **Complementarities**: An i-mode user was exposed to a wide range of complementary products through the 1,500 affiliates. A large number of content providers allowed cross selling. The complementarities further expanded to both i-mode customers and partners when the unofficial sites were considered.
- **Lock-in**: The monthly subscription fees to the fee-based content sites encouraged repeat purchases. The personalized I-menu options similarly encouraged lock-in. Content providers (i.e., official affiliates) had high switching costs because i-mode demanded unique content and investment in its sites
- **Novelty**: The company was recognized as a pioneer in mobile transactions particularly in the way it had nurtured content creation by the voluntary community of individuals, interest groups, amateurs, and entrepreneurs who used its services.

The opportunity matrix in table 6.3 combines the innovations in transaction content, structure and governance, and the sources of value.

∶ Summary

Building on recent work in strategy management, our framework illustrates how mobile services can deliver value through the four key drivers of efficiency, complementarities, lock-in, and novelty in transactions. One of the revelations from studies on value creation in wired Internet applications (e-business) has been that value is the sum of the sources of value plus their interactions (Amit & Zott, 2001). In fact, the disappointing performance of m-business investments to date is due in part to the failure of firms to exploit more than one value driver. As firms exploit multiple drivers in their mobile services, the payoff from wireless investments will increase. Business value can be created through a careful and clever orchestration of features and services in ways that benefit from their cumulative added value. Japan's highly successful i-mode service by NTT DoCoMo is an example of value

Table 6.3
Value Matrix for i-mode

Drivers innovations	Efficiency	Complementarities	Lock-in	Novelty
Transaction content	Access to broad content Content aggregation Billing simplicity Costs for transaction processing	Multifunction device Cross-selling	Consistent user experience across content sites	New services such a virtual friend First to introduce many new services First to introduce the Business model
Transaction structure	Billing system for charging content fees		CHTML protocol–dominant design Customizable I-menu	Dynamic placement of sites on I-menu No revenue sharing with content providers
Transaction governance	Constraints on business models to ensure robust and common customer experience	Integration with hand-set manufacturers	Controls all gateway traffic Promotion of communities i-mode controls all user profiles–does not share with content providers	Decentralization of content creation to users

creation that leverages all four sources of value: efficiency, complementarity, lock-in, and novelty. This service is heralded as highly profitable suggesting successful value appropriation by NTT DoCoMo. Given the considerable uncertainty about the underlying wireless infrastructures, access protocols, and the glut of user devices, m-business offerings need to incorporate a bundle of value drivers in order for customers, the firm, and suppliers to create the necessary value to attract adoption and use.

⦂ Note

The Advanced Practices Council of Society for Information Management funded this study to the first author.

⦂ References

Amit, R., & C. Zott. (2001) "Value Creation in E-Business," *Strategic Management Journal,* 22, 493–520.

Bakos, Y., & E. Brynjolfsson. (2000) "Bundling and Competition on the Internet: Aggregation Strategies for Information Goods," *Marketing Science,* 19(1), 63–82.

Barney, J. B. (1991) "Firm Resources and Sustained Competitive Advantage," *Journal of Management,* 17, 99–120.

Brandenburger, A. M., & H. W. Stuart, Jr. (1996) "Value-Based Business Strategy," *Journal of Economics and Management Strategy,* 5(1), 5–24.

Drummond, M. (2001) "Wireless at Work: Forget Ordering Pizzas and Downloading Ring-tones for Now; U.S. Companies Are Leading the Real Business of m-commerce," Business 2.0, February, 65–67.

Gulati, R. (1999) "Network Location and Learning: The Influence of Network Resources and Firm Capabilities on Alliance Formation," *Strategic Management Journal,* 20(5), 397–420.

Jarvenpaa, S. L. (2002) "mBusiness: Search of Value in Information Mobility," Technical Report, SIM International Advanced Practices Council.

Keen, P., & R. Mackintosh, (1997) *The Freedom Economy: Gaining the mCommerce Edge in the Era of the Wireless Internet.* Boston, MA: Harvard Business School Press.

Milgrom, P., & J. Roberts. (1992) *Economics, Organization and Management.* Englewood Cliffs, NJ: Prentice Hall.

Ostergaard, B. (2002, January) "M-Payment Gets Real: Vodafone Launches 50 Million User Trial," Giga Information Group.

Porter, M. (1980) *Competitive Strategy: Techniques for Analyzing Industries and Competitors.* New York: Free Press.

Schumpeter, J. A. (1942) *Capitalism, Socialism, and Democracy.* New York: Harper.

Shapiro, C., & H. Varian. (1998) *Information Rules.* Boston, MA: Harvard Business School Press.

Shy, O. (2001) *Economics of Network Industries.* Cambridge: Cambridge University Press.

Varian, H. (2001) "Economics of Information Technology," Working Paper, University of California at Berkeley.

Weill, P., & M. R. Vitale. (2001) *Place to Space: Migrating to eBusiness Models.* Boston, MA: Harvard Business School Press.

Williamson, O. E. (1975) *Markets and Hierarchies: Analyses and Antitrust Implications.* New York: Free Press.

Zettelmeyer, F. (2000) "Expanding to the Internet: Pricing and Communications Strategies When Firms Compete on Multiple Channels," *Journal of Marketing Research,* 37(3), 292–308.

IV

IT Governance

The considerations for IT governance were defined briefly in figure 1.1. Ensuring that the appropriate business and IT participants formally discuss and review the priorities and allocation of IT resources is among the most important enablers/ inhibitors of alignment. This decision-making authority needs to be clearly defined.

COMMUNICATIONS
- Understanding of Business by IT
- Understanding of IT by Business
- Inter/Intra organizational Learning/Education
- Protocol Rigidity
- Knowledge Sharing
- Liaison(s) effectiveness

COMPETENCY/VALUE MEASUREMENTS
- IT Metrics
- Business Metrics
- Balanced Metrics
- Service Level Agreements
- Benchmarking
- Formal Assessment/ Reviews
- Continuous Improvement

GOVERNANCE
- Business Strategic Planning
- IT Strategic Planning
- Organization Structure Reporting
- Budgetary Control
- IT Investment Management
- Steering Committee(s)
- Prioritization Process

IT BUSINESS ALIGNMENT MATURITY CRITERIA

PARTNERSHIP
- Business Perception of IT Value
- Role of IT in Strategic Business Planning
- Shared Goals, Risk, Rewards/Penalties
- IT Program Management
- Relationship/Trust Style
- Business Sponsor/ Champion

SCOPE AND ARCHITECTURE
- Traditional, Enabler/ Driver, External
- Standards Articulate
- Architecture Integration:
  - Functional Organization
  - Enterprise
  - Inter-enterprise
- Architectural Transparency, Agility, Flexibility
- Manage Emerging Technology

SKILLS
- Innovation, Entrepreneurship
- Culture Locus of Power
- Management Style
- Change Readiness
- Career Crossover Training
- Social, Political, Trusting Interpersonal Environment
- Hiring and Retaining

7

Jerry Luftman

IT Governance

: Chapter Summary

1. Organizations need to ensure that the decisions about deploying IT are aligned with the firms' strategic business objectives.
2. Organizations also need to ensure that decisions about the strategic direction and deployment of IT are consistent across the firm and that they are in harmony with the organizational culture.
3. Successful organizations in today's information age integrate IT and business strategies, and leverage customers and partners in a web of relationships that share information and knowledge.
4. Important questions that need to be addressed include:
   - How should organizations make decisions about the deployment of IT?
   - Which projects should be funded? How much should be allocated?
   - Should organizations "make" or "buy" systems and software?
   - Who should make these decisions?
   - How should organizations make decisions about partners and alliances?
   - What processes should organizations use to make these critical decisions?

: Introduction

IT governance is the term used to describe how the processes and authority for resources, risk, conflict resolution, and responsibility for IT is shared among business partners, IT management, and service providers. Project selection and prioritization questions are included here. IT governance is about:

- *Who* make these decisions (Power)
- *Why* they make them (Alignment)
- *How* they make them (Decision Process)

Ideally, business and IT management jointly make these decisions. Underlying the principles of IT governance is the theme of effective and efficient communication among IT and business. This is critical for appropriate decision making regarding IT.

Business management's expectation of its investment in IT is that it will result in some improvement in the delivery of service to its customers/clients, reduce the cost to manufacture or deliver some product or service to its customers/clients, or shorten the cycle time required to develop and produce some new product or service. In short, business management's expectation is that its investments in IT will produce business value.

The gap between business's expectations of its return on its IT investment and IT management's tendency to overpromise and underdeliver are evidenced in many organizations as symptoms of misalignment:

- Poor business IT understanding and rapport
- Competitive decline
- Frequently fired IT manager(s)
- High turnover of IT professionals
- Inappropriate resources (HR,$$)
- Frequent IT reorganizations
- Lack of executive interest in IT (absent Champion/Sponsor)
- Lack of vision/strategy
- No communication between IT and users
- Ongoing conflicts between business and IT
- Outsourcing
- Productivity decrease
- Projects:
  - Not Used
  - Canceled
  - Late
- Redundancies in systems development
- Absent systemic competencies (key IT capabilities that create competitive advantage)
- Systems integration difficult (e.g., standards, politics)
- Unhappy users/complaints

For many business managers, the promises they hear from IT management versus the reality of delivery have led to a substantial credibility gap regarding the value of IT. These considerations are discussed in chapter 1, chapter 4, and chapter 18. Long lists of symptoms of IT-business alignment problems are a symptom of alignment problems!

Historically, IT management has focused on the promise of new technologies to address discrete business problems, but has failed to marry technology capabilities and resources to the overall needs of the business in an integrated fashion. Without having the commitment of business to actively participate and leverage the technology to change how they do things, IT has little chance of achieving, let alone demonstrating its contribution to value (see chapter 4). For example, when IT management of many organizations began to see the potential of the information age to transform business, business management often responded with one or more of the following rationales for not pursuing this important technology as part of the organization's business and IT strategy:

- We're doing too well financially (there is no sense of urgency)
- Change is too difficult, and no one has the appetite for this much change
- We have too many other priorities
- We're in the midst of a turnaround and can't focus on digital
- We don't know how to do it
- It's not in our current business plan
- It's not in our budget
- It's not part of our vision
- We don't want to alienate our existing customers
- We don't want to upset our sales and distribution channels
- Our customers aren't digital-ready
- Our employees aren't digital-ready
- We can't afford to spend money on the digital infrastructure
- Our management team isn't digital-savvy
- We're already too late

Given this perceived lack of interest on the part of executive business management to embrace the promise of the "information revolution," IT management often launched initiatives on its own to enable business processes, often selling the perceived benefits to middle managers or local project sponsors. The unfortunate result of many of these IT sponsored or "local" initiatives (substitute any technology you wish in this example: Web, CRM [Customer Relationship Management], document management systems, supply chain management, ERP [Enterprise Resource Planning], and so on—the result is the same) is that they collectively failed to generate the best possible return on the enterprise's overall investment in IT.

When decisions about IT investments are made either by business management without active involvement of IT management—or vice versa—the inevitable result is an investment that performs poorly or not at all. Worse yet, in many organizations the responsibility for setting the strategic direction of IT is not clear.

The common theme of these disconnects between business and IT is governance—or the lack of it—and how that lack of governance affects the organization's ability to make informed decisions about the direction and use of IT. In short, this type of organizational disconnect will exist when the organization's IT governance is not clearly defined, is "immature" (chapter 1) or under some form of political threat by internal constituencies.

The relationship that results among the team (business and IT) participating in the six-step process for defining the IT strategy (described in chapter 18) should be continued as the IT executive steering committee. The purpose of this group is to define and carry out the strategic IT governance direction for the organization. The process for establishing and maintaining IT–business alignment is ongoing. Typically, there will be other steering committees focusing on tactical and operational decisions.

In brief, IT governance addresses how to prioritize and select projects, and how to appropriately allocate IT resources (e.g., staff, budget). A list of some IT governance alternatives is provided later in this chapter. No one of the alternatives can assure effective business-IT alignment. It is the appropriate combination of most of them that can lead to sustained alignment. Frequently, it is the assessment of the governance alternatives that becomes the initial charge of the steering committee.

The executive steering committee will focus on strategic areas. Typically, there are separate committees that address tactical and operational activities. To have an effective steering committee comprising a group of IT and functional business executives at any of the three levels (strategic, tactical, operational) meeting on a regular basis is considered among the best practices for strategic alignment. Successful IT steering committees concentrate their attention on all of the governance alternatives. Gaining the commitment from these executives is difficult. Keeping their commitment is even harder. The critical success factors for effective steering committees, described later in this chapter, are important for all three levels of steering committees (strategic, tactical, and operational). How they are addressed and their relative importance may differ.

To ensure success, appropriate value measurements must be selected and continuously tracked. Stakeholders ought to be aware of the measurements and the actions that will be taken based on their results. IT's value should be demonstrated in terms of their contribution to the business. These measurements should affirm IT's role as an enabler or driver for providing the organization with an opportunity to do something new, or allow the organization to perform better, faster or cheaper. At a minimum, IT must understand the priorities of business value measurements and how the business perceives the contributions of IT. The value of IT was discussed in chapter 4.

: *Some Definitions of IT Governance*

IT governance is the operating model for how the organization will make decisions about the use of IT. IT governance addresses decisions about the allocation of resources, the evaluation of business initiatives and risk, prioritization of projects, performance measurements and tracking mechanisms, determinations of cost and their assignment (i.e., how IT costs are allocated), and the assessment of the value of an IT investment.

Also, just as business governance is concerned with make-buy decisions in business strategy, IT governance is also concerned with external relationships for obtaining IT resources. These relationships may embrace mechanisms such as strategic alliances, partnerships, outsourcing, spinoffs, joint ventures (for developing new IT capabilities), consortiums, and licensing activities.

IT governance involves authority, control, accountability, roles, and responsibilities among organizational units and their management for making decisions about the use of IT. The dynamics of these relationships are crucial to an organization's effective use of IT in an economic climate of increasing uncertainty and the need for ever-rapid strategic responses to the uncertainty of the external environment. A well-structured governance model is an important prerequisite in large, complex organizations to making effective and efficient decisions about the investment of scarce capital and human resources. In essence, IT governance involves important aspects of organizational power—*who has the authority* to make decisions about IT?

IT governance involves the organization's *processes and methods for making decisions* about IT investments or obtaining IT resources. These processes include the funding model for IT investments, the methods used to evaluate project cost and potential business value, project risk assessment methodologies, the procedures used to identify potential business initiatives, and the processes used to measure the value of IT.

Embedded within governance processes are also judgments about how well a decision about the use of IT enables or drives the strategic direction— the business objectives—of the organization. IT governance, then, addresses important aspects of alignment of IT and business—in other words, why a decision is made about the use of IT. As discussed in chapters 1 and 18, the alignment of IT with the business (and vice versa) is a critical component of overall business strategic effectiveness.

: Why Is IT Governance an Issue?

Despite the growing evidence that IT has become an integral part of business, IT governance is still an issue for many organizations. While the governance models for marketing or finance are rarely if ever discussed, the governance model for IT for many organizations is still not well understood, not well executed, and a topic of debate. Why is this?

Part of the reason is that the dominant business culture still does not value IT as an integral part of the business. In large measure, governance reflects the importance the executive management of the organization places on the component parts of the organization. Executive culture understands and values financial measures and treats employees as fungible assets rather than as investments to be nurtured (Schein, 1996). Based on its historically poor performance in delivering or demonstrating business value, and the tendency of the IT management culture to focus on itself (i.e., on the technology profession, and the hardware and software components of technology) and not on the business, executive business management too often tends to view IT as a "support" function rather than as a legitimate partner for generating business value.

Decisions about the use of "support" functions generally don't require executive business input or involvement, and the governance mechanisms for dealing with "support" or "commodity-like" functions are usually relegated to lower administrative levels of the organization's management structure. For example, it would be highly unlikely that the head of a strategic business unit or the CEO of a Global 2000 company would be involved in decisions about which cafeteria service company to use or which supplier of electric power should be used. The governance models for these types of decisions are straightforward and appropriately relegated to middle management or the heads of functional departments responsible for these supporting operations.

This devaluation of the importance of IT as a strategic asset by executive management is evident in many organizations: the absence (or minimal contribution) of the CIO on most executive management committees while the CFO, the head of marketing, product development, or the head of manufacturing sits on these very same committees. Yet, at the same time, the organization must make decisions about the use of IT that cut across many of these same organizational functions! Dysfunctional governance models are the inevitable result of organizational cultures that do not value IT.

The Business Case Issue

Should business cases be applied to ALL Information Technology projects? When is a business case not appropriate? Decades have passed. Billions of dollars have been invested. Applying IT in an appropriate and timely way, in harmony with business strategy, goals, and needs remains a key concern of business executives. Of the measurements presented in chapter 4, which should be considered? Is it more practical to just do the IT project or just do the financial analysis? Many managers realize that information is among their company's most important assets. Many, however, do not know how to leverage their investments in information technology.

Financial methods are important, but not to the exclusion of others. For an organization to perform well it must balance all of its measurements. It must balance its impact on customers/clients (e.g., profits, services, satisfaction, flexibility, differentiation), processes (e.g., time to market, productivity, quality), people (e.g., motivation, morale, job satisfaction, learning, social), and finance (e.g., Return on Investment (ROI), Activity Based Costing). For many applications a business case is not even considered. Organizations just do it! A case in point includes:

1. Maintenance, especially fixing application problems. Most of IT's people resource is dedicated to the preservation of the technical infrastructure. How many companies performed a financial analysis to decide to address Y2K? Albeit, some might have applied portfolio management to select which approach to employ.

2. Government legislation requirements to ensure compliance must be performed (e.g., tax laws and reporting demands).
3. CEO or senior executive has a "hot" idea. These projects receive top priority.
4. Competitor's innovative application of IT. This might be a matter of survival. The second, third, and nth bank considering automatic teller machines (ATMs) did not perform a financial justification.

Typically, important strategic applications do not require traditional financial assessments, especially if it is a matter of survival. Therefore, you might consider the request to prepare a business case on a project to be an indicator that additional marketing must be performed to senior management. Of course, when requested, IT must comply and prepare a business case. But that does not diminish the need to sell the strategic business implications of the project to the key stakeholders. Consider leveraging the five enablers and inhibitors described in chapter 1. Frequent requests to keep IT costs down and continuous treatment of IT as a cost center are other indicators for more effective marketing of the value of IT to the business. Focus on business measurements like profits, time to market, morale, new services, and quality.

Financial executives who are comfortable with accounting data and see project evaluation in traditional accounting and financial terms favor business cases. Traditional financial measurements should be rethought. Senior executives are beginning to reduce their emphasis on cost cutting. They are focusing their attention on business growth. Often, they see the opportunity to leverage IT as the enabler or driver to meet these objectives. IT should strive to be measured in terms of business value not just financial cost.

Often, the problem is that too much attention is placed on the technology itself rather than its links with other business operations, customer value, and management decision-making. Companies race to have state-of-the-art technology without considering their impact on the rest of the business. The benefit does *not* come from the technology. The benefit comes from the new products/services or the enhanced business processes made available from the innovative application of the technology. Chapter 4 describes a total value of ownership approach that combines portfolio management, options, and value management that has proven very effective. If traditional financial measurements are the primary vehicle applied to ensure that the project focus is on the business, you should rethink the business IT relationship and the measurements being applied.

Frequently, the long-term implications of technology on the business are difficult to assess. For example, retail banks invested heavily in automatic teller machines in the 1980s, believing them an essential aspect of customer service and critical to maintaining market share. As a result, ATMs rapidly ceased to be a competitive advantage and instead became an added cost of doing business.

Instead of reducing business costs and increasing market share as they hoped, the bankers were left with the expense of maintaining and continuing enhancements to the ATM systems in an environment of decreasing margins and profit pressures. These costs have been passed on to ATM users. The point here is not that any individual bank made an inappropriate decision. ROI alone does not always paint the entire picture, let alone an accurate one. Today the rush is on to create the "virtual bank." Remote banking using personal computers and Internet applications is today's competitive edge. Will it become a cost of doing business, too? It is a story that has parallels in many other industries (e.g., airline, brokerage, retail, petroleum).

The business area, because of their different perspective, may not see ROI the same way as IT. It is desirous to have the business see the project as a vehicle for competitive advantage, rather than financial advantage. In any case, how often does your organization conduct a postproject review to assess the achievement of the ROI? For example, frequently the ROI is defined in terms of reduced headcount. If all of the headcount committed by project plans were taken, there would be even more employees downsized.

While addressing the project value, another important consideration is the inability of IT to meet its project deadlines. This is a problem that has plagued businesses since the introduction of the modern computer three decades ago. Too often, IT is overwhelmed by all it has to do. Frequent requests changing the requirements of IT projects driven by changing business demands severely impacts the projects teams' ability to meet commitments. Business executives become increasingly upset that projects are late and over budget. Recent studies suggest 30 percent of IT projects are cancelled before completion; 50 to 100 percent are over budget, and 6 to 12 months late. The IT-business relationship that exists plays a major role in addressing this pervasive problem. Should IT be considered a credible business partner in light of its inability to meet its commitments?

How can IT achieve a harmonious relationship? This crucial question needs to be focused on to address many of the important issues raised regarding assessing the value of projects. There are known enablers and inhibitors that help and hinder business—IT alignment. IT executives experience them daily. This was presented in chapter 1.

IT and business must work together to define and implement the prioritized projects to meet the competitive demands of the firm. This requires a good relationship (all components of alignment maturity: communications, partnership, skills, value measurements, technology, governance) among the team members. The team needs to work together in business terms to assess a balanced set of measurements. ROI is only one available vehicle. IT must understand the business and be considered a valuable business partner. To do this effectively demands senior executive support. To earn this role, IT must do an effective job in marketing/communicating the business value available from leveraging information technology.

: *Why Have Governance?*

Organizations that cannot structure their IT governance model waste precious resources (capital, time and human) in an era where time is of the essence, capital is in short supply, and truly qualified IT people are still hard to find (despite the recent economic recession).

Why do organizations need an IT governance model? The very environment in which IT management must cope gives ample reasons:

- Insufficient resources to meet current and future commitments
- Unreliable delivery schedules resulting from insufficient staff and requirements changes
- Lack of focus on daily operations because of utilizing IT operations and maintenance staff on projects
- Reduced quality of delivered projects
- Potential for working on the wrong things
- Business functions begin to move in their own IT direction to satisfy their own requirements with minimal or no IT support
- Chaotic/nonstandard infrastructure, resulting in poor operational maintainability
- Poor communications and relationships between IT and business

For IT management to fulfill the promise of information technology to the business, it must:

1. Ensure that decisions about the use of IT are made jointly—by business and IT management
2. Develop mutual and agreed-upon expectations among business and IT
3. Help senior business management understand the costs and risks associated with IT investment and help them make the best possible decisions
4. Provide the IT capabilities required to implement the decisions made in (3)
5. Monitor and measure the value of the business' IT investments
6. Help senior business management understand that this is an ongoing process (Weill & Broadbent, 1998).

This is possible only with a suitably mature and robust IT governance model for the organization.

Governance Alternatives

There are several IT governance alternatives that must be considered, each with its strengths and drawbacks. Large organizations should employ more than one mechanism as part of an overall governance model:

Budget (the "how" and "why" of financial resources that are allocated to projects)—although this is the most basic governance mechanism, a flaw with this mechanism is that it tends to promote the perception of IT as a "cost" rather than an investment (see chapter 4).

Career crossover (IT staff working in the business unit; business unit staff working in IT)—this is an excellent alternative and is good for "seeding" business or IT organizations with people who have perspectives that can generate empathy and build relationships and understanding.

CIO-CEO (reporting structure having lead IT executive report to lead business executive)—having the CIO report directly to the CEO has the potential to dramatically energize the organization in its ability to leverage IT for strategic business advantage, if the CIO is a business visionary. Today, approximately 20 percent of CIO's report directly to the CEO. Over 50 percent of CIO's still report to the CFO. Reporting to the CFO makes it difficult for IT to be treated as anything other than a cost center.

Communicate/market/negotiate (IT staff must learn and continuously execute effectively)—continually "selling" and "marketing" IT's value to internal constituents will help to change perceptions as long as the ability to deliver value is present. This can degenerate, however, into a process of "deal-making" between IT management and business unit management to fund individual projects as a substitute for more formal decision processes regarding the use of IT as a generator of broader business value (see the discussion on portfolio management in chapter 4).

Competitive enabler/driver—demonstrating that IT initiatives can be a significant driver or enabler of competitive advantage can strongly influence business management's willingness to move IT away from being treated as a cost center and towards an investment center or profit center.

Education/cross-training (IT must understand the business; business must understand IT)—institutionalizing formal training for business executives in their roles and responsibilities regarding IT and, in turn, requiring formal training of IT management and key staff in the operational and management aspects of the business will enhance understanding, rapport and communication among the communities. This improved communication will result in improved communication of business needs to IT management and a better understanding by IT management of how these needs are aligned with the strategic objectives of the organization. This requires a substantial sustained investment of time and resources by the organization.

Liaison (primary point of contact for facilitating IT business relationship)—a person who facilitates the business and IT relationship. They understand and communicate well with both IT and business professionals. Their objective is to ensure effective communications among the communities. Too often the role defined may actually impede effective communication between business and IT by defining the liaison as the only person that can communicate between IT and business.

Location (physical placement of IT staff and business staff together)—co-locating the IT resources with the business resources they support is an underappreciated enabler of effective communication and understanding among IT and the business.

Organization—the degree of centralization/decentralization of the IT function and organizational lines of reporting (e.g., does the CIO report to the CEO or to the CFO?) is a substantial influencing factor in IT governance. The organizational alternatives will be discussed in chapter 8.

Partnership/Alliance Management—partnerships and alliances are becoming a fact of life in the business strategy and IT strategy of leading firms to gain new competencies, share the risk of developing new IT capabilities, move into new markets, or gain access to new resources (Hutt, Stafford, Walker, & Reingen, 2000). The management of these alliances and partnerships needs to take into account the formal and contractual aspects of governance as well as the interpersonal aspects of the relationship to ensure that goals are set and monitored, specific plans are made for joint activities, and that decision rights are clearly understood and communicated to all parties. The risk inherent in partnerships/alliances is that they, like internal partnerships, require formal and informal management of relationships to be effective, a task often overlooked.

Process (the team and approaches applied to define strategies, plans, priorities, and make IT decisions)—many organizations adopt some form of project approval process, which tends to be tied to the budget cycle. Other organizations have developed business systems planning processes that require business units to tie their IT initiatives to specific business plans. Still other organizations have instituted formal processes for making decisions about capital investments in IT. Clearly understood and well-communicated governance processes are a necessary prerequisite to a robust IT governance model, with the risk being that the processes, rather than the reasons behind the decisions, may become the focus of the governance model. Also, a formal process devoted to improving IT-business alignment maturity has been used effectively by many organizations.

Shared risks, responsibilities, rewards/penalties (strong partnership of business and IT leaders)—this approach drives the business and IT communities towards a more partnership oriented operating model in which the responsibility for IT decisions is jointly made by business and IT management and accountability for IT investment results is shared by the business and IT communities. This alternative requires a shared perception of value and trusts and is highly dependent on the prevailing organizational culture and its perception of contribution to business value.

Steering committees—This approach comprises three types of committee:

- *Strategic:* senior executives setting "long-term" direction
- *Tactical:* middle management planning
- *Operational:* day-to-day decisions

Steering committees are an approach that vests IT decision-making responsibility within a cross-functional body of executive management that typically comprises senior business executives and IT management. Generally considered a "best practice" in the management of IT decisions, the roles and membership of executive steering committees are usually a good indicator of how IT is valued in the organization. The role of an executive IT steering committee should include:

- Clearly stating the business role of IT in the organization
- Identifying the linkages (alignment) between the organization's strategic vision and IT's vision
- Establishing the principles for investing in IT and defining the methodologies and processes by which an IT investment may be made, for example, presentation of IT investment proposals before the steering committee, demonstrating that the benefits of an IT investment can clear corporate "hurdle rates"
- Establishing ethical guidelines and policies that guide the selection of IT alternatives and investments
- Establishing architectural principles and standards that will guide the selection and deployment of specific technologies
- Establishing goals and measurements for assessing the impact of IT investment decisions
- Effective communications among the different steering committees is important to ensure synergy across the firm

Steering committees will be discussed in more detail later in this chapter, given their wide implementation in many organizations.

Value measurement—Formal assessment and review of IT's contributions to business strategies and infrastructurethis was covered in chapter 4.

⫶ Forms of Governance and Leadership Roles in Cross-Functional Initiatives

One of the challenges faced by IT management is the transition from a local or proprietary infrastructure to more global standards that enable the organization to achieve strategic objectives that have worldwide reach. This inevitably places corporate IT management in conflict with local business units that have developed technologies that meet local (business) environmental needs.

Infrastructure transitions (e.g., the implementation of an ERP system with global reach, the implementation of a global management reporting system, or the replacement of proprietary technology standards with industry standards) have profound implications for effective IT governance. Infrastructure transitions are hard to justify on purely economic benefits and often require substantial cooperation and resources from organizations that are skeptical about the benefits of moving away from proprietary technologies. Exacerbating the problem is the fact that the existing local technology infrastructure must still operate while the new global infrastructure is being put in place and tested. Additional global governance considerations are described later in this chapter.

Merger and acquisitions place similar demands on IT—for example, how to effectively and efficiently consolidate the organizations. Naturally, this is also a daily activity confronting large multi business unit firms, whether their organizational structure is centralized, decentralized, or federal (see chapter 8). Many IT organizations "govern" these cross-functional initiatives by assembling a matrixed project team that is composed of individuals from the corporate IT organization and IT representatives from the affected business units. Corporate management runs it. This cross-functional team is typically responsible for establishing the architecture of the new IT infrastructure and designing the plan for its rollout. In this structure, the managers from the business units continue their reporting relationship to their business units. Corporate managers interpret the business and IT strategy and provide guidance to the business unit representatives who must then implement the new infrastructure according to corporate mandates. This form of IT governance ensures that the leadership role of corporate management is to determine the strategy and design of IT infrastructure for the organization. This form of governance also defines the role of business unit IT management as the implementers of the (mandated) corporate design (i.e., it is a very "top-down" style of management and governance). This form of governance also requires corporate management to evaluate the effectiveness of the business unit representatives with respect to their ability to implement the corporate objectives. The drawback to this form of governance—also called a "Thick Matrix" (Storck & Hill, 2000) is that the leadership roles almost always result in organizational conflict because of the competing interests of corporate management and representatives from the business units.

Another form of governance adopted by organizations to manage cross-functional initiatives is one in which corporate IT management acts in a role of providing guidance and assistance to the business units for adopting global infrastructure changes. In this form—called a "Thin Matrix" (Storck & Hill, 2000)—local business unit management has substantial flexibility with respect to interpreting corporate direction and making decisions about implementation approaches. Business unit management still, however, has the responsibility for making the appropriate level of investment to achieve the corporate objectives. The advantage to this form of governance is that it attains higher buy-in and cooperation on the part of business units, with the potential drawback that decisions may be delayed because of the need for consensus building. This form of governance works especially well in organizations whose cultures favor consensus building as a form of decision-making rather than the directive style of the "Thick Matrix."

A third form of governance for cross-functional initiatives is relatively new and recognizes the fact that organizations have to increasingly cope with geographically dispersed (and scarce) human resources and intellectual capital, but purposeful change to technology across the enterprise must still be effected for sound business reasons. The knowledge of these human resources (i.e., IT professionals) is the essential engine of innovation and organizational change. This third form—called a "Strategic Community" (Storck & Hill, 2000)—relies on the cultural and professional affinities of a community of IT professionals in the business and corporate organizations to manage the complexities of cross-functional initiatives in a collaborative fashion that emphasizes knowledge sharing among business unit managers. In this form of governance, the role of corporate IT management becomes one of defining strategy and facilitating and sponsoring (in some cases, providing funding and some level of infrastructure for communications) the community. Early experience with this form of governance has shown promising results, especially in the community's willingness to take a more prospective view of cross-functional issues rather than merely react to them in response to a corporate directive. This form of governance also appears to have a greater capacity to handle problems that are less well structured than the other forms of governance as the knowledge-sharing mechanisms lead to adaptive rather than reactive behaviors on the part of the individuals who constitute the community. It should be pointed out that the Alignment Maturity Assessment has been effectively applied to identify opportunities to improve the relationships among the central IT organizations (corporate headquarters) with the business unit IT organizations.

⦂ *Steering Committees*

As discussed earlier in this chapter, establishing steering committees is considered a "best practice" governance mechanism for making decisions regarding organizational investment and use of IT. Many large organizations have adopted executive steering committees at different organizational levels (e.g., "Global IT Steering Committees") to address investment in and use of IT for initiatives having enterprise-wide scope; divisional steering committees that address investment and use of IT at business unit level and so on) with varying degrees of success.

What makes some IT steering committees successful while others seem to merely muddle along in indecision? Let's first examine membership on the steering committee as an important critical success factor. Effective Strategic IT steering committees membership should include:

- The business executive committee (e.g., CEO, CFO, COO, VP of Marketing)
- The CIO
- The CTO (if the organization separates CIO and CTO roles)
- Divisional business heads

Membership in the Strategic IT steering committee is also an important indicator of the organizational value executive management places on IT. If the steering committee lacks significant membership from the business executive committee or the senior business unit management it will not have the organizational authority to make decisions regarding IT that are enforceable across the enterprise (e.g., cross-functional initiatives, common architectures, IT standards). The organizational credibility of the steering committee is highly dependent on having the right membership as well as the right members. Participants should possess relevant knowledge about what is happening internally and externally with regards to their organization and IT. They should be recognized as credible leaders with good connections throughout the organization. They should have formal authority and the managerial skills associated with planning, organizing, and controlling IT-business initiatives. Naturally, the tactical and operational steering committees should define their membership based on the decisions that they are to make.

Aside from membership, what other factors are critical to the success of an IT steering committee? IT managers should consider the following factors when proposing or establishing a steering committee:

Bureaucracy. Focus on the reduction/elimination of the "bureaucratic barriers" to expedite opportunities to leverage IT. This is essential to harness and utilize the IT advantage, since technologies are ever changing and traditionally—"bureaucracy" has been considered as an impediment rather than a facilitator for progress and an aid in the implementation of change.

Career Building. Opportunities for participants to learn and expand responsibilities. Since learning is a process in continuum and more responsibilities come with more knowledge, proper management, enhancement, and growth of careers should be focused upon. It goes a long way in not only helping participants to learn more but also to shoulder more responsibilities, take bold and educated decisions, calculated risks, and grow with the organization.

Communication. Primary vehicle for IT and business discussions and sharing knowledge across organizations. The importance of communication cannot be overemphasized or undermined in its importance, especially in the field of IT and business, where perceptions are usually off the mark more often than not, and expectations are unreal when it comes to the effect, utilization, and impact of IT in business. The members of the steering committee should be responsible for communicating the activities of the group to their respective organization. Effective communications among the different steering committees is important to ensure synergy across the firm.

Complex Decisions. Do not get involved in "mundane" areas. Decision making is a process in itself and complex decisions take time and analysis. But there is a tendency to get lost or too involved in the process of analyzing the pros and cons of a particular decision. These are "mundane" areas and are best avoided to enable swift decision making, which could make a huge difference to an organization and its business. Naturally, this is relative to the level/complexity of the decisions being made by the group (e.g., strategic, tactical, operational). For example, the strategic steering committee should make decisions that focus on cross-organizational uses of IT that require changes to organizational business processes. The operational steering committee would make day-to-day decisions regarding the distribution of a new version of software.

Influence/Empowerment. Authority to have decisions carried out. What good are decisions (which are made) that cannot be executed, acted on, or implemented? Who makes the decisions holds a lot of bearing on the direction the organization is going to take, and the extent to which it will utilize opportunities. Influence within the organization to make decisions and make others a part of it, so they will act on them, empowerment to take decisions, and empowerment to enforce authority results in the difference between success and failure of those decisions.

Low Hanging Fruit/Quick Hits. Immediate changes carried out when appropriate. Wisdom lies not just in effecting and implementing long-term change but also in recognizing opportunities for small, quick changes that could be effective and facilitate the realization of the organization's vision and objectives. Many decisions just do not demand "analysis-paralysis."

Marketing. Vehicle for "selling" the value of IT to the business. As with communication, marketing is another function that the steering committee has to adopt to "sell" the value of IT to the business organizations. Even if the value of IT is realized and understood, adoption of IT in traditional terms would probably not be possible until it is aggressively promoted across the organization.

Objectives, Measurements. Formal assessment and review of IT's business contributions. Although IT does have its inherent value—an assessment and review of the contributions of IT to the organization in business terms helps keep the objectives and goals in perspective. It aids in the process of marketing IT and contribution across the business, primarily to its business partners. Additionally, the steering committee should have clearly defined objectives that are regularly measured and assessed.

Ownership/Accountability. Responsible/answerable for the decisions made. The steering committee members should be capable of accepting responsibility and should know that they are accountable for the same. This acts as a reinforcement of faith in their ability and elevates them to high regard and respect in the organization. The steering committee, not an individual or business unit, owns the decisions made.

Priorities. Primary vehicle for selecting what is done, when, and how much resource to allocate (see the next section). Prioritizing is a key element of success. Knowing what, when, and how, and resource allocation to different projects—both big and small, is a critical component of effective decision making. Knowing the difference between "now" and "can wait" and to be able to prioritize accordingly is one of the most important success factors of a steering committee. Use of techniques such as scenario planning, described in chapter 18, can be helpful in making these decisions.

Relationships. Partnership of business and IT. In concert with communication and marketing, relationship building is critical for the success of a sound understanding and a sense of partnership among business and IT. Relationships also helps foster better understanding of each other's point of view and helps change wrong perceptions.

Right Participants. Cooperative, committed, respected team members with knowledge of the business and IT. The right team makes all the difference. It would be difficult to realize objectives if a team is in place but the right participants are missing. Commitment and mutual respect form an integral part of any team to succeed.

Share Risks. Equal accountability, recognition, responsibility, rewards, and uncertainty. Being committed also means that team members are willing to share the "good" and the "bad," which come along with making decisions. This approach dilutes risk and makes it more manageable and also enforces a strong sense of team spirit amongst the committee members.

Structure, Facilitator. Processes and leadership to ensure the right focus. There is a story about the hay cutters in the forests of Africa. They just blindly cut away, while the team leader climbs the tree and sees if they're going in the right direction. If they're not, they shout, "Wrong way, wrong way!" . . . Facilitators play this critical role to provide focus and help the team to adapt to a certain process that helps achieve set goals and objectives.

⁝ *Prioritizing Projects*

One of the most fundamental examples of IT governance is making decisions about project priorities. Which projects should be funded? How should risk be considered in making decisions about project priorities?

Some straightforward process guidelines are helpful in addressing these fundamental questions that expand the portfolio approach described in the chapter 4: Consider all projects; and group projects based on:

- *Necessity, Opportunity, Desirability*—one technique for performing this grouping is by evaluating the business issues the projects are supposed to address against two criteria (see figure 18.1):
  1. Impact on the Organization
  2. Likelihood of Occurrence
  Projects that address business issues with high organizational impact and are most likely to occur should receive initial attention from the steering committee.
- *Risk*—one technique for classifying and grouping projects according to risk uses classifications of "high," "medium," or "low" risk within categories of organizational impact, development effort, technology, and

organization capability (see fig. 7.1). For example, a project that was characterized by significant changes to business rules, employed emerging technology, was proposed to take over two years to implement within an organization that had a poor track record of implementing large complex projects would be classified as "high" risk.

Organizational capability is one of the most important categories of this risk classification technique, as it tends to make clear the organizational practices that enhance commitment by business to a project versus mere participation. IT management does not want to play the role of the pig in a breakfast of ham and eggs while the business plays the role of chicken. One is participating in the breakfast while the other party is committed! Priority should be given to those projects having characteristics of:

1. Highest impact on the firm
2. Highest likelihood of occurrence
3. Lowest combined attributes of risk (regardless of risk assessment method employed)

	Organizational Impact	Development Effort	Technology	Organizational Capability
High	· Significant change to business rules · Complex business processes · Multiple organizations involved	· Development/ system integration cost> $10 million · Over 2 years in development	· Emerging · Unproven · New for Firm	· Immature organization · Uses the ad-hoc processes · Organizational track record suggest inability to mitigate risk
Medium	· Moderate Changes to business rules · Medium complexity	· Up to 29 staff years · $2–$10 million · 1–2 years in development	· Proven in industry or at organizational level · New to organization	· Maturing organization · Reasonable level of success
Low	· Insignificant or no change in business rules · Low complexity	· Under 10 staff · Under $2 million · Under 1 year in development	· Standard Proven Organizational technology	· Mature organization · Strong track record · Stable organization

Figure 7.1 Risk level criteria. SIM, Seattle state government

4. Least resources demanded
5. Highest anticipated return

: *Global Considerations and IT Governance*

IT organizations in the twenty-first century must develop governance mechanisms that accommodate the global environment in which their companies will increasingly operate. Transnational strategies are a fact of life for major companies today. Drucker (1999) emphasizes the importance of globalization and its impact on every organization today in his statement that "no institution can survive, let alone succeed, unless it measures up to the standards set by the leaders in its field, anyplace in the world." IT has become the principal means by which organizations have implemented strategies for globalization, primarily because IT neutralizes the effect of geographical distance and time. Through its time/distance neutralizing effect, IT also has the power to shift labor markets in knowledge-intensive industries (e.g., the growing use of offshore application development companies, offshore customer call centers).

In addition to the obvious benefits of reducing the impact of time and distance, IT also allows organizations to share knowledge and information on a global scale and in a timely fashion. Twenty-first-century organizations are profoundly information and knowledge-based, with information being the "glue" that cements together the processes and people that make organizations run effectively (Davenport, 1997). True competitive advantage in the twenty-first century is increasingly dependent on an organization's ability to create and use new knowledge to develop new products or services, and not the products or services themselves. Business and IT management must be able to think and act globally (e.g., where to locate the next customer call center or distribution center), regionally (e.g., how the organization can exploit particular regional advantages in South America or Asia), and locally (e.g., what local distribution channels are available for the organization's products; to which local regulations must the organization adhere).

What IT governance mechanisms then, should be considered to support transnational strategies? Addressing that question first requires that IT management understand the types of global strategies and the special demands these strategies place on IT governance. One framework for categorizing international strategies describes them as falling into four basic types or business forms (Daniels & Daniels, 1996): Figure 7.2 summarizes the forms of global strategies.

Global Exporter. This form of international strategy characterizes organizations that typically expand overseas in search of new markets; usually employing agents or trading partners to market and distribute their products in different geographic markets. Country nationals of the home office typ-

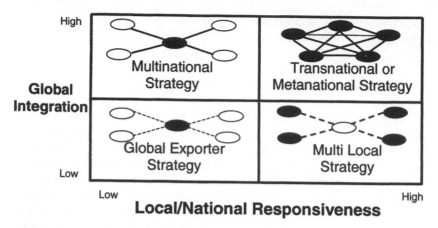

High

Multinational Strategy

Transnational or Metanational Strategy

Global Integration

Global Exporter Strategy

Multi Local Strategy

Low

Low   High

Local/National Responsiveness

Figure 7.2. Global characteristics of international (exporter), multinational, multilocal, and transnational or metanational companies

ically staff local offices and products are homogeneous—that is, there is typically no local manufacture of products. Most, if not all, corporate decision making as well as value chain activities such as R&D, sales, service and manufacturing is concentrated in the home office location. Customers of global exporters are treated the same whether they are global or local customers. High levels of integration and a sharing of common culture are strong characteristics of global exporters, with frequent communications between the local offices and headquarters being the norm. The principal basis of competition for the global exporter is taking advantage of production scale economies. IT, if used at all, is supported from the parent company.

Multinational. This form of international strategy tends to evolve from the global exporter form, with the organization typically moving sales and service functions and, ultimately, manufacturing functions to various country locations. The multinational organization usually retains tight control over the value chain activities that have been distributed. The home office tightly controls most functions, although some product development functions may be distributed to take advantage of local competencies. IT is controlled centrally from corporate headquarters, although some service might be supported locally. As with the global exporter, multinational products tend to be homogeneous, with allowance for some customization to meet the demands of local markets. Innovations generated by local offices are quickly harvested for incorporation into the headquarters' knowledge base, as the basis of competition for this strategy is sharing innovations that are generated by the headquarters organization. Headquarters typically plays a dominant role in governance by setting standards and policies, but local organizations have significant autonomy with regard to establishing processes to meet the demands of local customers. The multinational company services local customers via its national organizations, although their ability to service global customers is done only with difficulty.

Multilocal. These strategies focus on the need for responsiveness to local markets, with national organizations having a high degree of flexibility and decision-making autonomy to customize products and services for local needs. Value chain activities such as R&D, product development, manufacturing, sales, and services tend to be highly duplicated in each country, with the consequence that global customers find doing business with Multilocals to be high because of integration costs. Headquarters governance in this business form is weak, as the demands of local offices take precedence over headquarters' need for consistency in policies or procedures. Communications between different local offices is less likely than in either the global exporter strategy or the multinational strategy form, making the sharing and harvesting of knowledge for overall organizational benefit much more difficult than for the other international strategies. IT is typically decentralized.

Transnational or Metanational. Strategies that can be truly characterized as global leverage the benefits of the other international strategies with none of the attendant drawbacks. Global companies implement process and technology architectures that reap the benefits of mass customization—low cost and local responsiveness. These companies are highly networked so that they can "do business anyplace" while being able to share knowledge and information between headquarters and between national organizational units. Decision making in global organizations is based on centers of competence rather than on headquarters or local organizations; that is, decisions are based on expertise rather than on the basis of organization form or location. The global organization supports local as well as global customers equally well. IT is distributed and shared across the organization, typically organized in a federal or hybrid structure.

What IT governance mechanisms, then, are most applicable to each of these international business strategies? As IT governance is concerned with the locus of decision-making power regarding the use of IT and the processes for making these decisions, the mechanisms of IT governance for international strategies will tend to reflect the forms of decision-making authority for each of these strategies and the need for standardization of process and communication between headquarters and local organizational entities.

The IT governance mechanisms will also reflect the level of importance each international business strategy places on:

- The requirement for communication between the national ("local") offices and headquarters
- The requirement for communication between local offices
- The requirement for sharing information and knowledge between local offices
- The requirement for standardization of operations among local offices
- The need for local responsiveness

Based on the preceding discussion of each of the forms of international business strategy, the likely IT governance mechanisms by the forms of international strategy can be summarized in table 7.1.

▪ *IT Governance and Vendor Management*

Governance is fundamentally about the structure, form, and process of decision making regarding the organizational use of IT, so the forms of IT governance related to vendor management are typically centered around the management processes involved with identifying and selecting a vendor, contracting for services, monitoring vendor performance against the contract, and contract renegotiation (including contract termination and vendor deselection). These processes are very similar except for their scope and the level of decision making involved, regardless of whether the vendor is selling hardware, software, or services (this will be discussed in more detail later in this chapter, as well as in chapter 8).

Vendor Selection. Once the decision has been made by IT management to use the services or products of an external vendor, and these services or products have been identified, the next important decision that IT management must make is "to which vendor"? In large organizations, this decision may involve tens of millions of "hard dollar" costs associated with it over timeframes that extend five or more years (e.g., licensing an ERP package). In large organizations with sizeable IT organizational budgets, the governance mechanisms usually involved in vendor selection involve the engagement of a neutral "informed buyer" (Feeny, 1998). The informed buyer is usually a management consulting firm selected by senior IT management to identify qualified vendors based on experience in similar situations. The informed buyer will typically use a request for proposal (RFP) as a governance mechanism to solicit and compare contract bids from qualified vendors. Final vendor selection is typically done through the governance mechanism of a vendor selection committee which, for large contracts (e.g., the selection of an enterprise-wide ERP system) may include the CIO, CFO, a senior representative from the corporate legal organization, a senior representative from the purchasing organizations, and other key stakeholders, as appropriate. For vendor products or services that run into millions of dollars, the final decision as to the choice of vendor, however, should be shared among IT and business executives.

Contracting for Services. The contract between the organization and the vendor is the principal governance mechanism of vendor management. Depending on the scope of services being provided by the vendor, the size (dollar amount) of the contract and the number of organizations affected, typically the contract is developed by specialists in the IT organization with the active assistance of the legal department. Large IT organizations have established organizational functions that facilitate the development of IT

Table 7.1
IT Governance Mechanisms for International Strategy Types

International strategy type	IT governance mechanisms
Global exporter	• Centralized IT organization structure • Common architecture and applications established by headquarters • Technology standards and policies dictated and enforced by headquarters • Budgets established by headquarters for local organizations • Cost justification the basis for investment in IT
Multinational	• Mostly central with some federalized or hybrid IT organization structure • Corporate CIO and local office CIO/heads of IS • Common IT architecture for shared services and "common" functions such as e-mail, telecommunications network, etc. • Steering/architecture committees at corporate and local levels for decisions regarding IT investments • Business value justification for investment in IT
Multilocal	• Decentralized IT organization structure • Application investment decisions made by local offices to meet local market requirements • Minimal headquarters IT staf--focus on support of shared services (e.g., e-mail) • Minimal to low requirements for sharing information or applications between local offices • Local office CTO or CIO
Transnational/metanational	• Federal or hybrid IT organization structure • High requirement for integration and sharing of information and knowledge among all organizational units • Centers of Excellence (COEs) • Architecture committees with headquarters and local representation

vendor contracts for business units within the organization as well as for the IT organization itself. In general, the facilitation of vendor contracts is a governance function that improves coordination between the organization and the vendor. In developing a contract to license software from a vendor, IT management should consider the following as important elements to include in the contract:

- The right to assign the software license to a new corporate entity resulting from a merger, consolidation, acquisition, or divestiture
- The right to use the software for the benefits of a business unit formerly within your corporate organization that has been sold
- The right to assign the software license to or allow the software to be used by an outside entity if you outsource your data processing operations
- The right to make and own derivative works (i.e., code changes, translations, adaptations) based on the software
- The right to port the software to any platform supported by the vendor at no or minimum charge
- License that permit unlimited use within your corporate organization (i.e., "enterprise-wide" licenses)
- In situations other than enterprise-wide licenses, the right to transfer the software to other equipment and operating systems at no cost
- In situations other than enterprise-wide licenses, the right to use the software for the benefit of other entities (e.g., parent, subsidiary, division) within your corporate organization at no cost
- In situations other than enterprise-wide licenses, the right to transfer the software license to an existing entity (e.g., parent, subsidiary, division) within your corporate organization at no cost.
- Limited liability for breach of your obligations under the software license agreement.
- Prohibition against devices in the software that control your compliance with the software license The right to customize the duration of the software acceptance period
- The right to define software acceptance as occurring only on your written notice
- Specific remedies for vendor's nonperformance
- Incentives to licensors to reward the performance in providing services
- Remedies for consequential damages that you suffer
- Use of your own form in place of the licensor's form for licensing contracts
- Contractually defined differences between:
- Enhancements, releases, versions, and so on, that you receive by subscribing to software support
- Those the vendor insists are a new product requiring a new license
- Vendor's responsibility to meet the cost of procuring alternatives third-

party support if the vendor fails to provide adequate and timely service

- A cap on future maintenance prices
- Permissions to exempt individuals-employee, contractors from signing documents that acknowledge confidentiality of software or to bind them to terms of the license
- Avoidance of partial payments to vendors based on check points
- Contractual assurances regarding forward compatibility of software that changes in operating systems
- Contractual assurances regarding forward compatibility of software that changes in hardware
- Contractual assurances regarding forward compatibility of software that changes in other software from the same vendor

Contract Monitoring. This important IT governance mechanism, considered a core IT competency by some researchers (Feeny, 1998), is concerned with protecting the concerns of the business. It is needed to ensure that vendors—and the organization itself—fulfill their contracted obligations. This aspect of governance should also be concerned with monitoring the vendor's performance against accepted industry benchmarks of quality and service levels and preparing periodic reports to IT management on the performance of vendors against these metrics. Service level agreements (SLAs), along with incentives and penalties, provide an excellent vehicle for managing these criteria.

Contract Renegotiation. This governance mechanism is associated with the processes that are initiated as a result of an event in contract monitoring that signals either:

- Contract expiration
- A material breach in contract by the vendor (e.g., poor performance, security lapses, criminal activity)
- A major change in the organization's management or industry (e.g., bankruptcy or merger on the part of the organization or the vendor)
- A significant change in the price for the same vendor services
- New technology
- In any of these cases, this process addresses the requirement to continually realign the need for the vendor's services with the services provided by that particular vendor. In circumstances that are sufficient to warrant consideration to terminate the relationship with the vendor, IT management will need to repeat the process of vendor selection.

Vendor Relationship Development. An emerging form of IT governance for vendor management that looks beyond the formal contractual relationship between the organization and the vendor. The use of steering committees, previously discussed, is an effective vehicle to build and manage the relationship. These steering committees generally takes two forms:

• Periodic (at least annual) meetings between senior IT management and key vendor management to identify how to drive additional business value from the current relationship. This involves the sharing of strategic objectives and plans by both parties and a growing relationship of trust between the principals. The potential of tying increased vendor revenue to the realization of specific incremental business value and benefit is a powerful incentive to most vendors to share plans and ideas and add to the knowledge base of the vendor's client (the organization).

• "Vendor councils" comprising senior vendor representatives that convene periodically at the behest of senior IT management to address an issue of interest to the organization (e.g., an area of emerging technology). This is an opportunity for IT management to obtain insight on the issue of concern from a panel of experts from the vendor organizations in a noncompetitive fashion (i.e., free consultation). Moreover, the insights obtained will be in the context of the fact that the vendor already works with the IT organization—they know the issues of greatest concern to the business and to IT management. It also provides the vendors with the opportunity to gather insight and intelligence about the organization they are servicing and to strengthen the mutual perception of shared values and common understanding so essential to long-term viable relationships.

⦂ *Outsourcing Considerations*

Effective exploitation of IT in the twenty-first century requires IT managers to understand which IT competencies are core to their organization's ability to respond to environmental changes and to exploit IT for competitive advantage. Competition in the twenty-first century demands that IT management consciously identify and nurture "core" IT competencies that have strategic impact (enable or drive competitive advantage in an organization's products and services). Similarly, "noncore" IT competencies (e.g., applications development and support for "back office" processes, "help desk") are being identified that do not help an organization differentiate its core products and services. There is simply no longer any room in an IT organization for competencies that cannot be exploited for competitive advantage.

With outsourcing arrangements becoming a familiar operating model for IT organizations (currently 82 percent of U.S. companies practice some form of selective outsourcing (Lacity, 1997), what governance mechanisms need to be considered by IT management?

The governance mechanisms discussed earlier can apply to outsourcing arrangements as well, with a change in emphasis given to the scale and scope of outsourcing arrangements (many run into tens or hundreds of millions of dollars per year).

The first, and perhaps most important, aspect of governance, as it relates to outsourcing, is the decision itself to outsource (see fig. 7.3). Ideally, organizations should strongly consider an arrangement with a "transaction partner" to handle IT functions that are both "noncore" competencies (see earlier discussion) and not critical to the success of the organization. "Transaction partnering" describes relationships that embrace ERP vendors and ASPs as well as mainstream outsourcing arrangements.

Conversely, organizations should perform in-house the IT functions that are both "core" competencies and critical to the success of the organization. "Core competencies" and "critical success" factors/functions will differ among organizations but, in general, these "organizationally focused" IT functions will be those that are *critical* to the organization's:

- Day-to-day operation
- Ability to competitively differentiate itself
- Ability to deliver value to its partners and customers
- Ability to innovate

Organizations should consider a "strategic alliance" arrangement in situations in which the IT functions are not considered to be a "core competency" but are critical to the organization's success. The organization should consider either hiring or buying the resources and skills needed to meet the requirements expressed as critical success factors. An example of this arrangement might be a situation in which an organization contracts

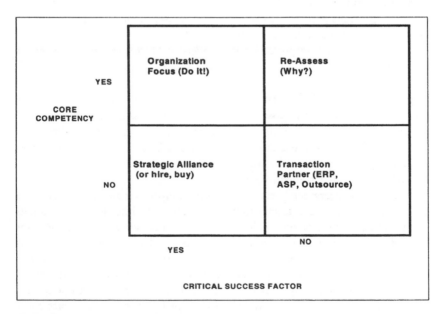

Figure 7.3. Insource or outsource?

for the creation and operation of a telecommunications network that is critical to the operation of its business but has determined that these competencies are not "core" to its business value proposition.

Finally, in situations in which the IT functions under consideration are a "core competency" but are not critical to an organization's success, the organization needs to reassess those functions' role in the organization and their contribution to the organization's value proposition. Even though they may be considered to be a "core competency," the organization may wish to consider other arrangements for IT functions that clearly have no critical role in contributing to the organization's success.

One last caution: organizations should be aware that a decision to outsource the IT function in total seems to be almost irreversible. Once the IT function has been outsourced, the overwhelming evidence is that it is almost impossible to insource these functions again.

Particular attention should be paid to the vendor selection process and to the RFP and its review given the potential scope and impact of an outsourcing arrangement on IT processes, infrastructure and staff, and the likely size of the outsourcing contract. Structuring an RFP for outsourcing services also becomes more critical than an RFP for other vendor arrangements, given the issues of staff transition and the number of employees potentially affected by the outsourcing arrangement.

To be effective, outsourcing relationships should be treated as partnerships or joint venture agreements instead of mere transactional relationships. The reason for approaching an outsourcing relationship as a form of partnership has much to do with the characteristics and desired outcomes of a partnership versus a transactional relationship (see table 7.2, adapted from Henderson & Venkataraman, 1990).

One of the most important early aspects of IT governance with regard to establishing an outsourcing relationship is the process known as due diligence, which is the process of examining the financial underpinnings of a corporation as one of the first steps in a large-scale IT purchase, with the goal of understanding risks associated with the relationship. Issues that could be reviewed include corporate capitalization, material agreements, litigation history, public filings, intellectual property and IT systems. Due diligence is also an important prerequisite for establishinga relationship of trust—one of the hallmarks of a partnership.

The use of "evergreen" clauses in vendor contracts is another governance considersation. Vendors know that information technology professionals don't manage contracts very well. Vendors are also aware that the turnover ratio of CIOs, CEOs, and account managers involved in originally negotiating the outsourcing contract tends to be fairly high. As a result, many contracts contain an "evergreen" clause. This clause provides for the automatic extension of the agreement if the vendor isn't notified by a certain date a few years down the road, when no one has seen the contract for a while, or when there are new people in charge of the project for which the

Table 7.2
Determinants of Partnership (Adapted from Henderson and Venkatraman, 1990)

	Partnerships	Transactional relationships
Mutual benefits	• Financial • Risk sharing • Innovation	• Financial (at best)
Commitment	• Shared goals • Incentives • Contracts	• Focused on completing the transaction
Predisposition	• Shared attitudes • Trust	• "What's in it for me?"

Shared knowledge	• Task
	• Domain
	• Culture
		• None required except
		  that required to com-
		  plete the transaction

Distinctive competencies and resources	• Physical assets • Skills • Specialized knowledge	• Skills • Specialized knowledge
Organizational linkage	• Information • Process • Social	• None
Duration	• Potentially long term	• Short term

deal was done. When challenged about the clause, the vendor usually responds by stating that it "just makes things easy." IT managers should, as a firm rule, never agree to "evergreen" clauses in outsourcing contracts. Similar to the evergreen clause are statements that inhibit the client from seeking bids from other vendors. These statements should be reviewed and removed.

IT management should include remedies for poor performance in outsourcing contracts as poor performance typically represents more than half of all reasons for terminating or renegotiating outsourcing contracts. IT management should incorporate governance mechanisms into outsourcing contracts that will address remedies for poor performance such as:

- Credits for performance shortfalls
- Two-party dispute resolution
- Third-party arbitration
- Termination remedies
- Litigation
- Prenuptial agreement describing how to "easily" end the relationship

⁞ Conclusions

IT governance is the organizational mechanism for making decisions about the use of information technology. It should be considered a required component for the effective use of IT as an agent of business transformation and an enabler of business value, and the IT steering committee should be seen as an IT governance "best practice," using approaches for prioritizing projects that are based on sound business principles. IT governance also needs to be viewed in light of the growing globalization of business and governance mechanisms that organizations need to manage vendor relationships.

▪ References

Daniels, J. L., & N. C. Daniels. (1996) "Building Global Competence," in J. Luftman (Ed.), *Competing in the Information Age*. New York: Oxford University Press.

Davenport, T. (1997) *Information Ecology*. New York: Oxford University Press.

Drucker, P. (1999) *Management Challenges for the 21st Century*. New York: Harper-Collins.

Feeny, D. (1998) "Core IS Capabilities for Exploiting Information Technology," *Sloan Management Review*, 98(3), 19.

Hartman, A., & J. Sifonis. (2000) *Net Ready—Strategies for Success in the E-conomy*. New York: McGraw-Hill.

Henderson, J. C., & N. Venkatraman. (1993) "Strategic Alignment: Leveraging Information Technology for Transforming Organizations," *IBM Systems Journal*, 41(2), 56.

Henderson, J., & N. Venkatraman. (1990) "Plugging into Strategic Partnerships: The Critical IS Connection," *Sloan Management Review*, 31(3), 7–18.

Hutt, M., E. Stafford, B. Walker, & P. Reingen (2000) "Defining the Social Network of a Strategic Alliance," *Sloan Management Review*, 41(2), 56.

Kaplan, R., & D. Norton. (2001) *The Strategy Focused Organization*. Boston, MA: Harvard Business School Press.

Keene, P. (1997) *The Process Edge*. Boston, MA: Harvard Business School Press.

Keil, M. (2000) "Cutting Your Losses: Extricating Your Organization When a Big Project Goes Awry," *Sloan Management Review*, 41(3), 55.

Lacity, M., L. Willcocks, & D. Feeny. (1997) "The Value of Selective IT Sourcing," *Sloan Management Review*, 37, 13–25.

Luftman, J. (2000) "Addressing Business-IT Alignment Maturity," Communications of the Association for Information Systems," Dec., 4, 1–50.

Rockart, J., M. Earl, & J. Ross. (1996) "Eight Imperatives for the New IT Organization," *Sloan Management Review*, 38(1), 46.

Schein, E. (1996) "Three Cultures of Management: The Key to Organizational Learning," *Sloan Management Review*, 38(1), 9–20.

Seattle State Government, SIM, www.wa.gov/dis/acadamy/presentations/portfolio/8.

Storck, J., & P. Hill. (2000) "Knowledge Diffusion Through Strategic Communities," *Sloan Management Review*, 41(3), 63.

Venkatraman, N. (2000) "Five Steps to a Dot-Com Strategy," *Sloan Management Review*, 41(3), 15.

Weill, P., & M. Broadbent. (1998) *Leveraging the New Infrastructure*. Boston, MA: Harvard Business School Press.

8

Carol V. Brown

The IT Organization of the Future

⁞ *Chapter Summary*

1. Three IT governance dimensions are discussed in this chapter: (1) decision rights for IT resources and tasks, (2) coordination mechanisms for coordinating decision making and work tasks across IT and business stakeholders, and (3) sourcing arrangements to manage external providers of IT products and services. IT organization design and governance are two important components of assessing alignment maturity.
2. The primary benefits for centralized and decentralized IT functions have remained somewhat stable, but the models for IT decision rights have expanded to include federal models and customized arrangements, for different business units.
3. IT decision rights should be closely aligned with business strategies and structures, which change over time. A current trend is toward more centralized IT decision rights because this model enables firms to implement packaged system solutions for integrated cross-functional processes across an enterprise.
4. Formal groups and integrator roles are structural mechanisms that help promote interpersonal collaboration across both business and IT stakeholders, as well as across centralized and decentralized IT managers. The use of groupware to supplement these more expensive interpersonal mechanisms is expected to become more common.
5. Both structural and nonstructural mechanisms are associated with three categories of coordination goals for IT organizations: strategic resource alignment, producer/consumer partnering on IT products and services, and knowledge integration.
6. Selective IT outsourcing, versus total outsourcing or total insourcing, is an increasingly important sourcing alternative.
7. Good outsourcing contracts include service delivery metrics and mechanisms for changing the contract, as business needs change. Contracts for application service providers (ASPs) require provisions to protect the customer from risks associated with the demise of not only the computer host, but also the vendors of the software being hosted.
8. Successful management of the outsourcing relationship requires an ongoing investment in IT personnel with account management skills.

: *Introduction*

IT governance has been recognized as a critical factor for achieving strategic IT alignment for more than two decades. In this chapter, I adopt a midrange definition of the term IT governance and discuss three dimensions: IT decision rights, IT coordination mechanisms, and IT sourcing arrangements. Each dimension is concerned with organizational design alternatives for achieving alignment across IT management, business partners, and IT service providers.

For each dimension, some design alternatives will be presented, based on a synthesis of prior research. A key assumption in this chapter, however, is that effective IT governance depends not only on knowing the alternatives and their potential benefits but also on having an understanding of some of their implementation challenges. Each section ends with some comments about current trends.

: *IT Decision Rights: The Sharing of Authority for IT Resources and IT Tasks Among Business and IT Management*

In its simplest form, decision rights for a given IT responsibility are either centralized or decentralized. Centralized IT decision rights reside in a central IT organization, which is typically a corporate IT unit within large, multidivisional firms. Decentralized IT decision rights reside in business units, which could be a business function or a business division in large, multidivisional firms.

Overall, the reasons for centralizing or decentralizing the decision rights for IT resources and tasks are relatively similar across organizations of different sizes. Centralized IT functions help an organization achieve three overall benefits at the enterprise level:

- Economies of scale and scope
- Standard IT architectures with platform connectivity
- Integrated systems

In contrast, decentralized IT functions help the business unit to which they report to achieve their own strategic benefits because they facilitate:

- Responsiveness to internal and external customers
- Local control of strategic application development and maintenance resources

: *Four Models for Decision Rights*

In practice, pure centralized or decentralized IT decision rights are not common, except perhaps for centralized decision rights in a small organization.

Highly centralized and highly decentralized forms are found in practice, however.

By the late 1980s, a new type of decision rights model had emerged: a *federal* form in which IT infrastructure responsibilities were highly centralized, but application planning, development and maintenance responsibilities were highly decentralized. Table 8.1 shows how the primary IT functions were typically split under the federal form.

Similar to the federated model for the overall organization espoused by management gurus, a federal model for IT decision rights was touted as the "best of both worlds" (Von Simson, 1990): it enabled business units to manage their own application development resources, while a central IT unit ensured platform connectivity and the delivery of cost-efficient IT infrastructure services across the enterprise.

Initially, organizations with federal forms of IT decision rights found that changing from a centralized to a federal form improved their IT-business alignment. As time passed, however, the federal model began to pose new alignment challenges. For example, the IT leaders who were moved from a central group to a business unit initially kept their "allegiance" to the infrastructure goals of the enterprise while servicing the needs of the business unit to which they now reported. Over time, however, they were faced with conflicting goals, and in the absence of rewards for dual allegiance, the goals of their business unit came first as IT investment decisions were made.

To recapture the dual allegiance necessary for achieving the benefits of both centralized and decentralized decision rights under a federal form, some CIOs gained buy-in to a matrix reporting structure for the decentralized IT heads. In some firms, decentralized IT heads added only a dotted-line report to the CIO, whereas in others, it became a true matrix (dual solid line) reporting structure.

Finally, a more customized approach to IT decision rights began to emerge in large organizations that had formally adopted a federal form. In particular, a hybrid model in which both centralized and federal forms of IT decision rights had been adopted for different business units or functions within the same organization. As shown in table 8.1, the customized form differs from the other three models in that it is *not* a monolithic approach to IT decision rights within an enterprise but instead is an enterprise-level response to differing needs of its business units. Sometimes it is also a temporary solution for an acquired business or a newly formed business unit that is granted more operational freedom in order to innovate.

⦂ *Aligning IT Decision Rights With the Business*

The emergence of the more customized approaches to IT decision rights in the past decade certainly begs the question: *under what conditions should*

Table 8.1
Four Models for IT Decision Rights

	Centralized	Decentralized	Federal	Customized
Management of IT infrastructure services				
Infrastructure planning	C	D	C	C
Computer operations	C	D	C	C or D
Telecom/network operations	C	D	C	C or D
Management of applications				
Application planning	C	D	D	C or D
Systems development and maintenance	C	D	D	C or D
End-user support	C	D	D	C or D

different IT decision rights models be implemented? Overall, the research findings that address this question can be summarized as follows.

First, highly centralized and highly decentralized forms typically reflect the authority structure within the overall firm. In other words, if there is little business unit autonomy, centralized IT decision rights are the best alignment choice, and vice versa.

Second the federal form for IT decision rights is also usually implemented to better align with the authority structure of the enterprise. As business environments became less stable—as "change" became the norm—top management teams gave more autonomy to business unit managers so that they could be more responsive to their customers and their environments in general. As IT began to play a more strategic role in the 1980s, business unit managers therefore began to also demand more autonomy over IT resources that could help them compete. Thus, the early examples of federal IT decision rights were in firms with growing business unit autonomy that had previously highly centralized IT functions—and this change to federal IT decision rights often occurred in conjunction with the decentralization of decision rights for the financial and human resource functions as well (Brown & Magill, 1994). As time passed and the dual benefits of a federal form for the IT function became more widely recognized in the field, federal decision rights became more widely adopted, and IT responsibilities and resources for application development activities in particular became decentralized to the business unit, function, or plant level.

In contrast, the customized form for IT decision rights was found to not only be a temporary form due to business acquisitions, but also to be a deliberate IT decision rights alternative *initiated by business unit leaders.* Two primary characteristics of a business unit are associated with a business unit

manager's decision to give up IT decision rights to a centralized IT organization when other business units in the same organization are operating
under a federal IT form:

- The lack of a strategic role for IT within a particular business unit. In
  other words, a federal model was adopted for other business units because business unit control over IT resources was viewed as critically
  important by some business unit heads within the enterprise, but not
  by all business unit heads.
- The lack of IT management expertise within the business unit. In this
  situation, a strategic role for IT does exist. One or more business unit
  leaders chooses to relinquish the business unit's IT decision rights to a
  central group, however, because of a lack of IT management knowledge at the business unit level or a lack of resources to buy the expertise that is needed, even though other (perhaps larger) business units
  in the firm choose to retain these decision rights.

In the second situation, it is likely that the business unit head will also
negotiate for some kind of "shared" decision-making role with the central
IT unit to help ensure that their strategic IT needs are met (Brown & Magill,
1998).

⦂ Current Trends: More Centralized and More Shared

Today there is a noticeable trend in the field away from pure federal IT
forms toward increased decision rights within a central IT organization. In
other words, business unit leaders in enterprises with highly decentralized or
federal IT forms are relinquishing some, or most, of their IT decision rights
to a central IT unit. Early business drivers for this recentralization trend can
be found in the writings of management gurus from the mid-1990s, who
argued for the pursuit of core competencies *across business units* for competitive advantage (e.g., Hamel & Prahalad, 1994).

For example, some large firms that had given a lot of autonomy to their
business units have implemented a "shared services" approach to delivering
not only IT services, but also other enterprise support services. As suggested
by its name, a shared services solution is a consolidated (centralized) service
approach at the enterprise, geographic region, or perhaps strategic business
unit group level. One of the primary benefits is cost savings, but shared
services arrangements also can provide access to scarce IT resources that
enable business units to develop strategic applications with new technologies.

In its purest form, the shared services alternative is an option for business
units or functions that *choose to* give up some of their IT decision rights to
gain benefits that can't be achieved when IT operations or applications development and maintenance are decentralized. IT assets and personnel are
pooled with those of other business units for an IT "insourcing" arrange-

ment. Sometimes a shared services approach for IT is implemented as part of a larger shared services organization that includes other enterprise support functions. The intent is to achieve cost savings and other infrastructure synergies across the enterprise.

Another driver toward more centralized IT decision rights is the emergence of enterprise resource planning (ERP) packages with suites of modules that provide integrated system solutions across back-office functions and across business units. Today, centralized IT organizations, or central project offices, are dedicating financial and human resources to implementing not only back-office ERP modules but also front-office customer relationship management (CRM) solutions, and e-commerce applications that link external customers and suppliers to internal systems.

Enterprise system projects typically entail multiyear IT project team assignments for not only IT professionals but also business managers, to effectively implement and leverage these cross-functional, and cross-business-unit, IT investments. Furthermore, moving to an ERP platform also typically includes a recentralization of previously decentralized IT resources and responsibilities. Over time, however, firms with enterprise system solutions are likely to once again seek a more balanced approach to IT decision rights.

What form will this take? Prior research suggests that the extent to which IT decision rights will be decentralized to the business unit heads will be driven by the extent to which the common solutions adopted for the integrated modules fulfill the strategic application needs of the business unit. In some firms this is likely to result in a federal form, but one with more "shared" decision rights for functions than shown in table 8.1. It is also likely, however, that not all firms will seek to rebalance their IT governance arrangements by diluting the decision rights of the central IT organization.

Another alternative to seeking more business unit input to a centralized IT governance model is described later. That is, CIOs may focus instead on effectively implementing suites of *IT coordination mechanisms* that are designed to increase the role of business unit leaders in the prioritization of the central IT organization's investments and monitoring of their deployment.

▪ *IT Coordination Mechanisms: Horizontal Structures and Nonstructural Mechanisms for Coordinating IT Decision Making and Tasks Across IT and Business Stakeholders*

Horizontal linking mechanisms that facilitate, or ensure, contacts between individuals in order to coordinate the work of multiple organizational units are design innovations that first appeared in the organization theory literature in the 1960s (Mintzberg, 1979). From the outset, these horizontal devices were viewed as supplemental designs to a firm's reporting arrangements to promote cross-unit collaboration. For example, Galbraith (1994) theorizes that both formal and informal types of interpersonal mechanisms will be used to create a *lateral organization capability* that helps to overcome the dysfunctional barriers created by a firm's reporting arrangements.

Two kinds of lateral organization capabilities are typically sought for IT coordination from an enterprise perspective (Brown & Ross, 1996):

- An *IT-business* lateral capability: mechanisms to link IT and business stakeholders
- A *central IT-divisional IT* lateral capability: mechanisms to link central IT and divisional IT stakeholders

Although the evidence from the field suggests that mechanisms for creating both of these kinds of capabilities are common, there is also evidence to support Galbraith's theory: IT leaders are likely to invest more heavily in a lateral capability that is designed to remove the barriers created by the organization's model for IT decision rights (Brown, 1999):

- CIOs with centralized IT decision rights are likely to invest heavily in mechanisms that link IT and business managers
- CIOs with federal IT decision rights are likely to invest heavily in mechanisms that link central IT and divisional IT managers

፧ *Four Types of Coordination Mechanisms*

Four types of mechanisms have been found to categorize well the coordination mechanisms that are implemented by IT leaders to create a lateral capability for IT governance (Brown & Sambamurthy, 1999, 2001). As shown in table 8.2, two of these mechanism types are what has been referred to in the management literature as structural overlays (formal groups, formal roles), while the other two types are mechanisms defined by Galbraith (1994) as part of an "informal organization." I will describe some ways that each of these four types of mechanisms have been utilized to help bring together an organization's key stakeholders for the benefit of the enterprise.

Formal Groups

The implementation of formal "standing" councils or teams (in contrast to a temporary project team or task force) has been a common IT governance mechanism. In particular, *steering committees* (see chapter 7) have been recognized for many years as an important structure for creating a lateral capability between a central IT unit and multiple business units for both strategic and tactical purposes. Favorable outcomes associated with this mechanism include strategic IT alignment, enterprise IT planning and budgeting, and the prioritization of large systems initiatives.

Nevertheless, there is also evidence to suggest that a steering committee

Table 8.2
Four Types of IT Coordination Mechanisms

Mechanism type	Description and examples
Formal groups	Formally established councils or teams with specific linking or oversight responsibilities for IT activities. *Examples:* steering committees, IT management council, other IT standing teams
Formal roles	Individual positions with formal responsibility for linking activities between a central IT unit and one or more business units. *Examples:* integrator roles such as divisional information officers, account managers
Informal networking practices	Intentional activities or practices to link managers in two or more organizational units who may engage in or impact cross-unit problem solving. *Examples:* physical co-location, interdepartmental events
Human resource practices	Human resource management initiatives to facilitate voluntary cross-unit problem solving. *Examples:* temporary job rotations, cross-unit input to performance reviews

mechanism is not a universally effective mechanism. For example, a steering committee of business executives for the CIO may be viewed as redundant in a firm with federal decision rights or a firm in which the CIO is an integral part of a top management team (Brown, 1999).

Another formal group overlay referred to as an *IT management council* is also commonly used to create a lateral capability between the central IT unit and decentralized IT heads in organizations with a federal model of IT decision rights. The committee members typically include the CIO, the decentralized IT heads, and also the CIO's solid-line reports within the central IT organization. Common group tasks include advising the CIO on strategic issues, devising policy, sharing best practices and solutions, and taking actions to develop IT leaders.

Another group overlay that has received some attention in the literature is the formation of standing teams to address specific IT issues on an ongoing basis. Common examples include teams created to develop recommendations on high-level infrastructure issues, and teams that form a competency center (center of excellence) for a valued IT skillset. For example, a center of excellence design was implemented within one large application development group of a large telecommunications firm in which all IT specialists were assigned to a skill center of their choice, which was a "virtual homeroom" rather than an actual physical site.

Integrator Roles

Although the formal group mechanism has received the most attention in the IT management literature, evidence from the field suggests that integrator role positions may be equally important or, even more important, for creating a lateral organization capability. Management theorists have distinguished between integrator roles and other liaison positions based on the degree to which they are full-time roles, which of course impacts the organizational cost for this type of mechanism. Effective use of liaisons is a major contributor to alignment maturity. Two types of IT integrators are the most prevalent:

- IT heads at the division level under a federal model
- Account managers under a centralized model

In firms with a federal IT form of decision rights, the decentralized IT heads are often asked to play a formal integration role with the central IT organization. As mentioned earlier, many CIOs have found that a formal group mechanism is necessary to collaborate effectively across the structural barriers that are created by the federal IT form. In large organizations in which IT is perceived to play a strategic role in the business, these integrator role positions are often held at an officer level, with a title such as *division information officer* (DIO). Sometimes the formal dual allegiance role that this creates is also signaled with a dotted-line reporting relationship to the CIO on the firm's organization chart for the integrator role position.

In its purest form, *account managers* have full-time responsibility for "managing the account" of an internal business unit, which includes developing IT plans, contracting for internal IT services, and monitoring progress on IT projects on behalf of the business unit customer. This type of integrator role has been found to be associated with achieving strategic alignment within firms with centralized IT decision rights.

Sometimes the account manager is physically colocated with the business account managers, in order to be perceived as part of the business unit's management team. Sometimes a dual reporting arrangement is established for the account manager to formalize their dual "allegiance" role, which can be a dotted line to the business unit or even a matrix (solid-line) relationship.

Two barriers to more widespread usage of this type of full-time integrator role have been identified. First, in periods of cost cutting, a lack of performance metrics for this full-time position, with no direct reports, make it a prime target for IT budget savings (Iacono, Subramani, & Henderson, 1995). Second, CIOs have reported a difficulty in growing internal managers and hiring former consultants with the needed mix of leadership, consultant, and business expertise. Similar to business consultants, there also is some evidence for high turnover rates for this type of integrator position.

Informal Networking and Human Resource Practices

The remaining two mechanisms in table 8.2 are not structural overlays but mechanisms designed to link IT and business stakeholders in a more *informal* way. The intent is to increase the likelihood that a given stakeholder will pick up the phone, send an e-mail to, or otherwise seek out an individual in another work unit in order to solve a problem or pursue a new opportunity. Stated differently, these mechanisms are intentional actions to foster the development of interpersonal networks that cross organizational boundaries.

Of the two informal networking examples listed in table 8.2, the most common mechanism is the usage of *physical co-location* to foster collaboration. Just as account managers are frequently colocated with their business clients, other business and IT employees could be temporarily (or permanently) co-located to facilitate cross-unit collaboration.

The final two examples are human resource practices that many organizations could easily implement, but are less common. The practice of *temporary job rotations* (another alignment maturity assessment component) to sensitize an individual about another work unit's business or IT challenges is a relatively inexpensive mechanism that deserves more attention. For example, one large IT organization that had difficulty creating strong interpersonal relationships across IT groups in other countries had avoided permanent people moves because of visa restrictions. When this type of mechanism was brought to their attention, they quickly recognized that personnel could be assigned to temporary job stints of a few months' duration at these sites and headquarters and could likely achieve some of the same long-term coordination benefits. Another example (a favorite of mine) is from a CIO in a smaller IT organization who reported that he had assigned his direct reports to periodic stints on the IT help desk to sensitize them to problems that business clients were facing. In both examples, walking-in-the-shoes of others was accomplished at little organizational expense but with anticipated long-term benefits.

∎ Mechanisms for Specific IT Capabilities

Three types of strategic IT capabilities capture the goals for all four types of IT coordination mechanisms, based on data collected from IT leaders in 38 organizations during the second half of the 1990s (Brown & Sambamurthy, 2001):

- *Strategic resource alignment*—fostering business "ownership" of IT initiatives and a shared understanding of business opportunities and threats
- *Producer/consumer partnering*—fostering IT-business communications and partnering on strategic IT initiatives

• *Knowledge integration*—leveraging IT and business application expertise dispersed across an organization

The most prominent mechanisms to achieve the most sought-after capability, strategic resource alignment, are formal groups and integrator roles. As mentioned earlier, these structural overlays are considered by organization theorists to be the most expensive mechanisms to implement due to the personnel commitment that they require. Furthermore, integrator roles are generally perceived to be more expensive than formal group mechanisms based on the definition that integrator positions are full-time roles. Multiple studies have suggested, however, that they both are important IT governance investments.

There is also some preliminary evidence that firms with federal IT forms are likely to invest most heavily in formal groups and integrator roles for all three strategic capabilities. This suggests that the "best of both worlds" benefit that has been associated with the federal form of IT decision rights is in fact difficult to achieve without significant additional investments in structural horizontal mechanisms as well.

: Current Trend: IT Networks as Coordination Mechanisms

Although the IT coordination mechanisms in table 8.2 rely heavily on face-to-face linkages, Galbraith's (1994) most recent taxonomy of horizontal mechanisms includes "IT networks" as an example of an informal organization capability (in the same grouping as the informal networking and human resource mechanisms discussed earlier). Other IT researchers have also pointed to the importance of groupware for removing barriers between individuals working in separate organizational units (e.g., DeSanctis & Jackson, 1994).

As collaborative applications and services continue to evolve, and workers who grew up with personal computers have entered managerial ranks, the likelihood of using electronic media rather than face-to-face contacts to communicate with others to problem-solve is certainly increasing. Although building "trust" via electronic communications channels may continue to be challenging, combining synchronous communications with groupware can yield dramatic problem-solving results (for example, see Malhotra, Majchrzak, Carman, & Lott, 2001).

: IT Sourcing Arrangements: IT Governance Arrangements for the Management of External Vendors Contracted to Provide IT Products and Services

Beginning with the landmark IT outsourcing decision at Kodak in 1988, sourcing practices began to be viewed as a major design alternative for data center operations, telecommunications management, and end-user PC support, as well as systems development and maintenance, systems integration, and portions of these IT functions. By the late 1990s, *selective* outsourcing for one or more IT functions was widespread, and the overall customer benefits included cost savings and access to both IT talent and advanced technologies.

The decision whether to outsource, or insource, a specific IT function is typically based on an internal analysis of the firm's *core* (and noncore) competencies and the role that IT plays (see chapter 7). Once a decision has been made as to which IT function(s) to outsource, the *owner of the decision rights* for the outsourced function should be included in the vendor selection process (Lacity & Hirschheim, 1995; Aalders, 2001) In some situations, an outsourcing decision is accompanied by a change in decision rights for that function(s), including decentralizing more decision rights to business units. A contributing factor to any decision rights change, however, should involve an assessment of who needs to be held accountable for effective management of both the outsourcing contract and the vendor. Although a senior IT manager is commonly given this responsibility, many organizations initially underestimate the management costs associated with managing an outsourcing contract (Lacity & Hirschheim, 1995).

The extent to which an organization outsources its IT functions, and whether multiple or single suppliers are involved, will of course impact the IT governance decisions. Nevertheless, a recent list of nine strategic IT capabilities sought by senior IT leaders included four core competencies related to external sourcing (Feeny & Willcocks, 1998).

Although high success rates (6.2 on 10-point scale) are being reported for outsourcing arrangements as a whole, a major barrier to success continues to be managing the customer/supplier relationship (Lacity & Willcocks, 2000). Two IT governance issues that appear to be critical success factors are sourcing contracts and managing the supplier relationship.

: *Sourcing Contracts*

The primary mechanism for managing the customer/supplier relationship is the negotiated contract. In contrast to the outsourcing contracts for Kodak and other early megadeals, today's long-term contracts are shorter (less than four years), are based on better due diligence and benchmarking processes, include service level agreements with metrics for baseline services, and provide mechanisms to negotiate contractual changes—including accommodations for new acquisitions and divestitures (Lacity & Willcocks, 1998).

As with other IT purchasing decisions, this requires an "informed buyer" who has the capability to develop and negotiate effective contracts. Whether this is an IT specialist or a purchasing specialist, the buyer needs to be well armed with detailed measures of internal IT provisioning costs, market benchmarking data for all relevant IT services, and good project cost estimates for new application initiatives. Some organizations require the use of an in-house intermediary for all vendor/user contracts (Willcocks & Fitzgerald, 1996).

One of the keys to success for the customer is the extent to which changing business needs are accounted for in the contract with the vendor— including the handling of business restructurings as well as increased or decreased service levels due to changing business conditions. A related challenge for the customer organization is communicating relevant contract details to the business users who will be directly affected. For example, business users may unwittingly request higher service levels from a vendor without the knowledge that a higher fee structure (excess fees) will be imposed for the increased service. This type of problem is less likely to occur if the business users have already had experience with an in-house process for developing and monitoring service level agreements for internal IT services.

Although research on managing outsourcing contracts over time is just beginning to appear, current views are that Service Level Agreements (SLAs) for outsourcing contracts should focus on a small number of critical business services, but that measures for these key services should be tightly measured (Aalders, 2001). Recent practitioner reports also suggest that contracts that impose financial penalties on the vendor for deficiencies in performance also have become mainstream.

: *Relationship Management*

In both total and selective outsourcing situations, some kind of IT management role is required. The stakeholders involved in an outsourcing arrangement may include central IT, business unit IT, and business managers of the customer organization, as well as senior managers, contract managers, and technical staff of the supplier organization. Some arrangements also require the vendor to partner with other vendors. For example, BP Exploration chose a total outsourcing solution that involved multiple vendors, and the contract stipulated partnering relationships with not only BP but with the other suppliers (Cross, Earl, & Sampler, 1998). Subcontractors of the outsourcer also may be involved with executing a given contract, which can also impact the customer/supplier relationship (Lacity & Willcocks, 2000).

A *supplier account manager* is typically responsible for maintaining customer satisfaction, as well as profitability for a given account or contract (Lacity & Willcocks, 2000). This type of role therefore requires an ability to carefully balance the competing objectives of cost-reduction practices to meet the supplier's goals and high quality delivery to meet the customer's goals. As with other strategic vendor alliance arrangements, most outsourcing arrangements give the customer the right to help select the account manager and the right to request a change in the assigned account manager after the contract has begun.

Within the purchasing firm, an account management responsibility is also typically needed. If the scope of the contract is short-term, an internal project manager or program manager could play the account management role. If the contract involves a long-term arrangement, however, an internal manager, team, or even a contract administration office, may be assigned the responsibility for managing the contract and relationship. In situations where the need for a high-level integrator has not been viewed as important, and the burden for the success of the relationship is placed in the hands of multiple business unit liaisons, a "bumpy ride" typically results.

For example, an IT organization that outsourced the entire operation and maintenance of about 200 legacy systems as it embarked on a global ERP implementation project initially placed the responsibility for communicating with the outsourcing vendor in the hands of IT account managers assigned to each of its business units. Although all of the IT account managers reported into the central IT organization, they were physically colocated with their business units and communications with the outsourcing vendor occurred in a piecemeal fashion. After problems were encountered, including cost overruns, the CIO created a new IT director position to manage the outsourcing relationship. This new director of sourcing and alliances became the leader of a virtual competency center for all of the IT account managers. He also was given a matrix report to the head of a central purchasing unit to ensure that the vendor contract was being well managed, including careful monitoring of any requests beyond the break/fix maintenance specified in the original contract (Brown, 2002).

Similar to account managers for managing business unit relationships, finding internal managers with the needed skillsets to manage relationships with vendors, and ways to retain them, appears to be a special challenge. In the example presented in the previous paragraph, the new director was an outside hire who already had a working relationship with the CIO.

: *Current Trend: Shared External Services*

In the earlier discussion on IT decision rights, the benefits of an internal "shared services" organization were presented. Today, some of these same benefits might be achieved via an external service provider. For example, shared services for commodity accounting functions have been offered at reduced rates to competing companies in the same industry by Big 5 accounting firms (Lacity & Willcocks, 2000).

A related trend has been the emergence of companies that offer an application service provider (ASP) role. An ASP provides remote web access to packaged applications and organizational data via its own (or subcontracted) host computers. The customer pays a monthly rental fee based on the number of users or number of transactions. This type of hosting service is currently provided by software vendors for their own packages, as well as by third-party intermediaries that own software licenses for packages from multiple software vendors to give customers access to sets of business applications that otherwise they might not purchase. Some ASP arrangements therefore require contracts that protect the customer from not only the usual operational risks of data center outsourcing but also risks associated with the reliability and survival of the software vendors with whom they have no direct relationship.

: *Conclusion*

To some observers, IT governance solutions appear to be *moving targets*. A business unit head in a large organization may have gained the decision rights and resources for application development and maintenance in the early 1990s, only to be asked to relinquish these decision rights to the central IT organization as part of a packaged ERP implementation. A CIO may have turned over "the keys" to major IT functions to an outsourcing vendor in the early 1990s, only to "backsource" these functions a decade later in order to develop an e-commerce capability. Today, capital investments in hardware and software also may be avoided in favor of an ASP contract.

Yet the types of IT governance alternatives presented in this chapter, and the primary business benefits associated with them, have in fact been quite stable. Rather, the moving target has been the business capabilities that can be achieved with the new technologies, *which in turn* require IT governance changes to effectively manage them.

Given this state of affairs, the least recognized IT governance dimension, IT coordination mechanisms, could be argued to be equally critical. For example, organizations faced with asking business units to relinquish IT decision rights can still maintain a strong IT-business lateral capability by implementing new structural overlays and informal mechanisms. Similarly, when IT functions are outsourced, a strong IT-business partnership can still be retained if coordination mechanisms are put in place to link the internal relationship managers for the outsourcer and the business unit. Today, these interpersonal networks can also be supplemented with media-rich technologies to communicate and collaborate across geographical boundaries.

All of these scenarios suggest that the ability to manage all three IT governance dimensions will be an important IT leadership capability in an information age.

: Note

I gratefully acknowledge the Advanced Practices Council of SIM International for their support of the IT coordination mechanisms research (with V. Sambamurthy).

: References

Aalders, R. (2001) *The IT Outsourcing Guide.* New York: Wiley.

Brown, C. V. (1999) "Horizontal Mechanisms under Differing IS Contexts," *MIS Quarterly,* 23(3), 421–54.

Brown, C. V. (2002) "Advantage 2000 at Owens Corning, Case Study IV-5," in E. W. Martin et al. *Managing Information Technology,* 4th ed., 653–669. Upper Saddle River, NJ: Prentice Hall.

Brown, C. V., & S. L. Magill. (1994) "Alignment of the IT Functions with the Enterprise: Toward a Model of Antecedents," *MIS Quarterly,* 18(4), 371–403

Brown, C. V., & S. L. Magill. (1998) "Reconceptualizing the Context-Design Issue for the Information Systems Function," *Organization Science,* 9(2), 176–94.

Brown, C. V., & J. W. Ross. (1996) "The Information Systems Balancing Act: Building Partnerships and Infrastructure," *Information Technology and People,* 9(1), 49–62.

Brown, C. V., & J. W. Ross. (1999) "The IT Organization of the 21st Century: Moving to a Process-Based Orientation." MIT Sloan School of Management, Center for Information Systems Research, CISR WP No. 306, July.

Brown, C. V., & V. Sambamurthy. (2001) *Coordination Theory in the Context of the IT Function: Linking the Logic of Governance and Coordination Mechanisms.* Unpublished working paper available from the authors.

Brown, C. V., & V. Sambamurthy. (1999) *Repositioning the IT Organization to Facilitate Business Transformations.* Cincinnati, OH: Pinnaflex.

Cross, J., M. Earl, & J. Sampler. (1998) "Transformation of the IT Function at British Petroleum," *MIS Quarterly,* 21(4), 401–24.

DeSanctis, G., & B. M. Jackson. (1994) "Coordination of Information Technology Management," *Journal of Management Information Systems,* 10(4), 85–111.

Feeny, D., & L. Willcocks. (1998) "Core IT Capabilities for Exploiting Information Technology," *Sloan Management Review,* 39(3), 9–21.

Galbraith, J. R. (1994) *Competing with Flexible Lateral Organizations.* Reading, MA: Addison-Wesley.

Hamel, G., & C. K. Prahalad. (1994) *Competing for the Future.* Boston, MA: Harvard Business School Press.

Iacono, C. S., M. Subramani, & J. C. Henderson. (1995) "Entrepreneur or Intermediary: The Nature of the Relationship Manager's Job," in J. I. DeGross, G. Ariav, C. Beath, R. Hoyer, & C. Kemeier (Eds.), *Proceedings of the Sixteenth International Conference of Information Systems,* 289–99. Amsterdam, December.

Lacity, M. C., & R. Hirschheim. (1995) *Beyond the Information Systems Outsourcing Bandwagon.* New York: Wiley.

Lacity, M., & L. Willcocks. (1998) "An Empirical Investigation of Information Technology Sourcing Practices: Lessons from Experience," *MIS Quarterly,* 22(3), 363–408.

Lacity, M. C., & L. Willcocks. (2000) "Relationships in IT Outsourcing: A Stake-holder Perspective," in R. W. Zmud (Ed.), *Framing the Domains of IT Management.* Cincinnati, OH: Pinnaflex.

Malhotra, A., A. Majchrzak, R. Carman, & V. Lott. (2001) "Radical Innovation Without Collocation: A Case Study at Boeing-Rocketdyne," *MIS Quarterly,* 25(2), 229–50.

Mintzberg, H. (1979) *The Structuring of Organizations.* Englewood Cliffs, NJ: Prentice Hall.

Von Simson, E. M (1990) "The Centrally Decentralized IS Organization," *Harvard Business Review,* Jul.–Aug., 158–62.

Willcocks, L., & G. Fitzgerald. (1996) "IT Outsourcing and the Changing Shape of the Information Systems Function," in M. J. Earl (Ed.), *Information Management: The Organizational Dimension.* New York: Oxford University Press.

V

Partnership

The relationship that exists between the business and IT organizations is another criterion that ranks high among the enablers and inhibitors. Giving the IT function the opportunity to have an equal role in defining business strategies is obviously important. How each organization perceives the contribution of the other, the trust that develops among the participants, ensuring appropriate business sponsors and champions of IT endeavors, and the sharing of risks and rewards, however, are all major contributors to mature alignment. This partnership should evolve to a point where IT both enables *and* drives changes to both business processes and strategies. Naturally, this demands having a good business design in which the CIO and CEO share a clearly defined vision.

COMMUNICATIONS
- Understanding of Business by IT
- Understanding of IT by Business
- Inter/Intra organizational Learning/Education
- Protocol Rigidity
- Knowledge Sharing
- Liaison(s) effectiveness

COMPETENCY/VALUE MEASUREMENTS
- IT Metrics
- Business Metrics
- Balanced Metrics
- Service Level Agreements
- Benchmarking
- Formal Assessment/ Reviews
- Continuous Improvement

GOVERNANCE
- Business Strategic Planning
- IT Strategic Planning
- Organization Structure Reporting
- Budgetary Control
- IT Investment Management
- Steering Committee(s)
- Prioritization Process

IT BUSINESS ALIGNMENT MATURITY CRITERIA

PARTNERSHIP
- Business Perception of IT Value
- Role of IT in Strategic Business
- Shared Goals, Risk, Rewards/Penalties
- IT Program Management
- Relationship/Trust Style
- Business Sponsor/ Champion

SCOPE AND ARCHITECTURE
- Traditional, Enabler/ Driver, External
- Standards Articulate
- Architecture Integration:
  - Functional Organization
  - Enterprise
  - Inter-enterprise
- Architectural Transparency, Agility, Flexibility
- Manage Emerging Technology

SKILLS
- Innovation, Entrepreneurship
- Culture Locus of Power
- Management Style
- Change Readiness
- Career Crossover Training
- Social, Political, Trusting Interpersonal Environment
- Hiring and Retaining

9

Sid L. Huff, Harvey G. Enns, and Scott L. Schneberger

Chief Information Officers: Strategic Roles and Peer Influence

: Chapter Summary

1. Effectively initiating and executing information technology (IT) strategy has become a critical core competence for many organizations. Chief Information Officers (CIOs) are the key to setting overall IT business strategy as well as initiating and implementing information systems projects.
2. It is not enough to have excellent IT strategies and implementation plans on paper. CIOs must be able to convince peer executives of the corporate value of the IT strategies as well as their contribution to the business. One critical element is the ability of the CIO to exert effective influence on peer executives.
3. Research suggests that CIO influence varies both in terms of how it is used and how effective it is.
4. CIOs in general showed a consistent pattern in bringing forward IT initiatives to their executive business partners. Peer executives would be approached independently first to discuss the initiative. Then, after informal approval, an IT initiative would be brought before the entire executive group for formal approval. The research showed that some influence behaviors are more effective than others.
5. CIOs are involved in shaping and supporting business strategy, thus exerting their influence in more areas than just IT projects. Consequently, it is important for CIOs to understand the nature and use of influence in organizations. Having power and effectively exercising influence are preconditions for accomplishing tasks in organizations. The CIO who exercises influence well can potentially be more effective in future IT strategy planning, IT implementation, and business strategy planning efforts.

: Introduction

Computer technologies and information systems have become critical components of modern organizations. They are widely used for establishing infrastructure services, lowering costs, and providing services that cross barriers of time and space. They are deeply ingrained in corporate processes, improving coordination, tying together internal corporate entities, and improving productivity. And they are connecting businesses with their external suppliers, customers, partners, and regulators. Once seen as simply cost-saving machines, today's information systems are sometimes the core of the business—such as with virtual, online businesses.

This is not to say they are always applied wisely to business needs; there are many ways to go wrong with IT. In seeking to avoid "going wrong with IT," CIOs strive to properly align IT strategies with business strategies. This has been so difficult in the past that the acronym CIO was jokingly said to stand for Career Is Over. Business executives may not have understood information technology and what it could do, seeing IT as only a cost-savings tool instead of a business enhancer. CIOs may have been invited to the executive table only *after* corporate strategies were identified, discussed, and chosen—if at all! And CIOs themselves, if they came from within the IT ranks and were technology-focused, may have found it difficult to operate at corporate executive levels.

But even when CIOs have identified or formed sensible IT strategies, they often find that it is not enough to have excellent strategies and implementation plans on paper—they must be able to convince other executives of the corporate value of the strategies and the soundness of the implementation plans. Moreover, the ubiquity of modern information systems only compounds these challenges to CIOs. And, while a clearly presented, rational argument is certainly one way to convince peer executives of the validity and appropriateness of IT strategies, there are a number of other possible, highly effective ways as well.

This chapter examines the ways in which CIOs influence peer executives within an organization regarding strategic IT objectives and plans. While considerable research has been conducted on individual influence behaviors in other domains, it is vital to corporate strategy to systematically examine CIO influence behaviors. At executive levels, a good idea is not enough; it must be communicated effectively and other executives must buy-in to it for it to be accepted and implemented. What influence behaviors do CIOs use? What can we learn about their use? What are the factors associated with their use? Are they effective, and if so, when and how?

To set the context of the study, this chapter begins with a brief discussion of the nature of influence, in particular, the difference between influence and authority, the strategic role and skills of the CIO, and discusses some of the key findings in previous research on influence behaviors. It then presents the results of the authors' own field study, based on in-depth interviews with 14 CIOs and their executive peers. It concludes with observations and a summary.

: *The Nature of Influence*

Broadly speaking, influence is the ability of an individual to produce effects on others; exerting influence is termed "influence behavior." A useful approach to conceptualizing influence is to contrast influence with authority. Authority is the recognized, legitimate exercise of decision making that affects the behavior of individuals in a firm. Subordinates often agree with decisions of a superior without question; they are willing to set aside personal judgments about the suitability of a superior's request—or at least behave as if they agree with the superior. By contrast, influence implies that subordinates do not automatically set aside their own opinions and intentions but must be convinced of the need to agree with someone else's position.

A similar view suggests that authority implies indiscriminate acceptance of superior directives, and that authority is embedded in or designated across hierarchical management positions. Some authors (Tannenbaum & Massarik, 1950), however, also recognize that a superior relies on advice or information from subordinates as well as their compliance. Thus, a person may exert some influence by offering information, providing advice, persuading, and making suggestions, while not exercising any authority when the final decision is made. Finally, authority is understood to flow "downward," whereas influence can flow in all directions. Individuals therefore have the capacity to influence superiors, subordinates, and peers.

This distinction between authority and influence is important in situations in which CIOs hold authority for IT and IT personnel but do not hold formal authority over superiors and peer executives—even in terms of their IT. They must, in executing corporate IT strategy, rely on influence to affect the acceptance and behavior of other individuals. While likely not startling to other types of business executives, it may not be intuitively obvious to some CIOs used to commanding—with total authority—the logic of computer software and the operations of the IT department. Computers and subordinates are one thing; strong executive peers with their own imperatives are quite another.

: *Chief Information Officers' Influence-Related Skills*

Skills refer to the competence to do things in an effective fashion. Yukl (1998) suggests the most widely established classification system of general (or high level) skills: technical, interpersonal, and conceptual skills. Interpersonal skills are particularly important for the exercise of influence in organizations. Interpersonal skills, which are primarily people focused, are evidently necessary when attempting to influence someone when formal authority is lacking. Adequate interpersonal skills also differentiate effective from ineffective managers.

The specific interpersonal skills that are relevant for influence include:

- Empathy and social sensitivity
- The ability to communicate effectively, clearly, and persuasively
- Tact
- Diplomacy
- Listening

Empathy and social sensitivity allow the manager to discern others' attitudes, feelings, and motivations. Knowing the attitudes and feelings of individuals allows a manager to choose more effective influence behaviors. Tact, diplomacy, and listening facilitate consultation and other behaviors. Good communication is important when articulating a position or proposal; it allows managers to more effectively use influence behaviors. A recent study of CIOs conducted by *CIO* magazine (Berkman, 2002) discovered that CIOs view effective communication as the skill most important for CIO success.

Similarly, highly self-monitoring executives (i.e., those who use cues from others to adjust their behavior) are more likely to effectively resolve differences with others. A related management skill is the ability to accurately "read" a situation and respond accordingly. This ability has been applied to situations such as the discretion to act. For example, managers who have developed this skill may be more inclined to act when organizational or personal benefits are likely to accrue. This skill is also useful in situations in which the manager has to successfully market ideas to others. A manager's ability to accurately assess the situation may lead to influence actions that are appropriate for the situation, enhancing the likelihood of others accepting a proposal.

Yet some CIOs have been criticized in the past for lacking the interpersonal skills to effectively influence their peers, since their focus is often on technology and technical skills. There is evidence that CIOs have been less well equipped than their executive counterparts in the fine art of proactively exerting peer-level influence. For example, Earl and Feeny (1994) have pointed out that CIOs often mistakenly attempt to use "hard" tactics such as edicts, which do not work as well as "soft" tactics such as persuasion and participation.

By contrast, evidence from Fiegener and Coakley (1995) and others suggests that CIOs are quite adept at using interpersonal skills and aware of the need to be sensitive to the preferences of others in their interactions with other executives. For instance, some suggest that successful CIOs know that formal authority and status are necessary but not sufficient to perform their job properly. Furthermore, successful CIOs know that in order to have good relationships with their peers, they must communicate with them in business terms and avoid technical language that can alienate them. These CIOs also have an intimate knowledge of the business and industry in which they are working, enhancing their credibility with peers. Effective CIOs tend to be aware of the types of influence behaviors required to influence specific individuals and they also make clear plans to obtain their support. This change in CIO awareness and capabilities in the influence area also has been enhanced by the fact that more executives recognize IT as critical for organizational success, placing CIOs and the IT agenda in a more favorable light.

⦂ Chief Information Officers' Strategic Roles and Influence

The debates between senior managers about what matters to a firm largely determines which initiatives are implemented. Within this give-and-take environment, a critical part of the CIO's strategic role is to provide thought leadership to other top executives, making them aware of the potential for information systems to support and enhance the strategy of the firm. One way CIOs can do this is to proactively convince other top managers to allocate attention and resources to information system projects. Indeed, CIOs not only have an inherent responsibility to influence others in the organization on IT issues but, if they do not, someone else (often with less technical knowledge) will.

Effective organizations recognize that having line managers take ownership of critical IT projects increases the likelihood of appropriate IT deployment and subsequent success. To get a strategic application proposal implemented, a CIO needs the commitment of other members of the top management team, without which the project would stand little chance of success. Thus, effective CIOs must skillfully apply their powers of influence to encourage other functional heads to become partners with them and embrace ownership of these initiatives. These persuasion skills are seen as important for CIOs as technical skills, general business knowledge, and other interpersonal skills such as listening and communicating.

In the past, when most CIOs were not part of the top management team, they often needed to apply different forms of *upward* influence to try to convince top management to support strategic IS projects (Lederer & Mendelow, 1988); CIOs often would count on top management to convince lower levels to support the projects. More recently, as CIOs have gained acceptance in top management teams, they need to be able to apply *lateral* influence to convince their peers in other functional areas to commit to the development of strategic IS initiatives.

There has been little systematic examination of CIO influence behavior, which influence behaviors CIOs use to convince their peers to commit to IT projects, or their effectiveness at doing so—despite the importance of this CIO skill. As further background to examining CIO influence behavior, we now focus on previous research on influence behavior in general.

⁚   *Previous Influence Behavior Research*

One of the first studies of managerial influence behaviors, conducted by Kipnis, Schmidt, and Wilkinson (1980), concluded that influence is exercised through many influence behaviors. The authors examined what they called influence tactics, by which the "agent" (or initiator) of an influence attempt tried to gain something from the "target" (or recipient of the influence behavior). In one study, participants were asked to describe, in an essay, how they used influence to get their way with a superior, subordinate, or co-worker. In-depth analysis identified 370 influence tactics, which the researchers categorized into 14 distinct groups.

In a second study, the 370 influence tactics were used to create a 58-item survey administered to 754 lower-level managers. Some of the managers responded with respect to their superiors, others with respect to their co-workers, and a third group responded with respect to subordinates. Statistical analysis revealed eight main types (dimensions) of influence. The researchers labeled these: *ingratiation, rationality, exchange, coalition, assertiveness, upward appeal, sanction,* and *blocking.*

In a third study, two of the same researchers (Schmidt & Kipnis, 1984) studied the upward influence of managers when pursuing organizational and individual goals. Over 110 managers completed a survey that identified, among other things, the frequency with which they attempted to influence their superiors for organizational and individual reasons. The study found that managers who exercised influence for *organizational* objectives held positions of power in their organizations and that line managers exercised upward influence to achieve *individual* goals less often than staff managers did.

The managers also commented on the strategies they used to influence their superiors. The influence strategies studied included ingratiation, exchange, reason, coalition, assertiveness, and upward appeal. One of the main findings was that influence strategies varied as a function of the goals (i.e., individual or organizational) being sought. For example, managers who sought personal benefits more often used exchange or coalition strategies. In contrast, those who were attempting to improve their superior's assessment of their job performance used ingratiation and assertiveness.

A fourth study by Yukl and Falbe (1990) proved important. They relabeled the sanction tactic "pressure" and added two tactics: *inspirational appeal* and *consultation,* based on their review of managerial leadership literature. They then obtained not only reports by the initiators of influence behavior but also feedback from the targets of influence, an extension of the earlier studies that only examined initiators.

The principal finding was that rational persuasion and consultation were the tactics used most frequently, regardless of the direction of influence. Based on all the data as well as other related studies, the researchers refined their list of influence tactics, or behaviors, to nine. The nine behaviors are defined in table 9.1.

Table 9.1
Influence Behaviors and Definitions (Yukl, 1998)

Influence behavior	Definition
1. Rational persuasion	The agent uses logical arguments and factual evidence to persuade the target that a proposal or request is viable and likely to result in the attainment of task objectives.
2. Inspirational appeals	The agent makes a request or proposal that arouses target enthusiasm by appealing to target values, ideals, and aspirations, or by increasing target self-confidence.
3. Consultation	The agent seeks target participation in planning a strategy, activity, or change for which target support and assistance are desired, or is willing to modify a proposal to deal with target concerns and suggestions.
4. Ingratiation	The agent uses praise, flattery, friendly behavior, or helpful behavior to get the target in a good mood or to think favorably of him or her when asking for something.
5. Personal appeals	The agent appeals to target feelings of loyalty and friendship toward him or her when asking for something.
6. Exchange	The agent offers an exchange of favors, indicates willingness to reciprocate at a later time, or promises a share of the benefits if the target helps accomplish a task.
7. Coalition tactics	The agent seeks the aid of others to persuade the target to do something, or uses the support of others as a reason for the target to agree also.
8. Legitimation	The agent seeks to establish the legitimacy of a request by claiming the authority or right to make it, or by verifying that it is consistent with organizational policies, rules, practices, or traditions.
9. Pressure	The agent uses demands, threats, frequent checking, or persistent reminders to influence the target to do what he or she wants.

Beyond confirming what most might expect—that managers use influence behaviors with superiors, subordinates, and peers—the studies provide a playbook of nine influence tactics managers can choose from. Rational persuasion and personal appeals not working?—try coalition tactics or exchange! But is there some guidance as to when to use which tactic on whom, especially within the top executive environment?

Most of what is known about senior management influence behavior is anecdotal, but what little research has been done confirms that some influence behaviors are more effective than others. For instance, heterogeneous top management teams often engender conflict; it is important, then, to gain their acceptance, commitment, involvement, endorsement, cooperation, or consent. The important factors in obtaining cooperation and commitment are social integration and consensus. Furthermore, it appears that persuasion and participation are more effective for easing implementation than edicts.

: *CIO Influence Behaviors*

What do CIOs do to successfully influence others? Are their methods appreciably different than those used by other executives? Does it make a difference that the subject matter is often technically focused?

The earliest research on top IT executives suggested they were not very influential—whatever tactics they were using. Some believe this was because the position of CIO was relatively new in the top echelons of management; the position has only been around for about 15 years and some still view this position (with some skepticism) as "the new kid on the block." In addition, senior management may have believed that CIOs had failed in the past to deliver IT projects on time or within budget—further weakening their ability to influence the organization. Finally, another proposed reason for this lack of CIO influence is that many CIOs may have been viewed as too technically oriented—and had trouble relating personally to executives with different backgrounds. From this perspective, CIOs were reluctant to engage in interpersonal interactions and did not vary their influence behaviors because they were simply awkward in their new, senior executive role.

By contrast, more recent views indicate that *some* CIOs have been quite influential in their organizations. A number of reasons appear to account for these successes. One is that some CIOs have an intimate knowledge of the business and the industry they are working in, thereby improving their ability to interact with other business executives. Another reason is that they have developed critical, personal relationships with other top executives in their firms, allowing better use of the first five influence tactics that depend on personal communications. The third reason is that they simply tend to use a wider range of influence behaviors; if at first they're not successful, they try, try again in a different way. The successful CIOs are willing to discard influence behaviors that are not effective; they learn from their experience with corporate executives and adapt. Effective CIOs also seem to be better at targeting specific individuals; they are aware of the types of influence behaviors that work and those that do not for specific individuals.

But which influence tactics do CIOs tend to use? While there is little evidence to answer this question, two tactics tend to stand out. *Coalition* tactics appear to be used to: convince executives of the potential strategic impact of IT, gain the acceptance of other executives, achieve a shared vision of IT's role in the organization, and create a positive impression of the IT department. The other tactic CIOs use to influence behavior is *rational persuasion*, used to identify new IT applications and create a positive view of IT (Luftman, 1996).

Strategy implementation research findings also contribute to our understanding of CIO motivation for engaging in interpersonal influence activities (Korsgaard, Schweiger, & Sapienza, 1995). First, a CIO can aid commitment and cooperation by being socially integrated with senior management members and by obtaining consensus—which is harder to do when executives are disparate. Second, if a CIO wants an important proposal implemented, the CIO needs commitment by others in the top management group. Finally, it is important for CIOs to use appropriate behaviors. "Hard tactics" such as edicts often do not seem to work as well as persuasion and participation.

There is also little information about the role of the CIO during implementation. Keen (1981) discusses the "fixer" role, which refers to the senior IT executive who has control over resources used to bargain with others, and is required for successful IT project implementation. In this situation, Keen suggests three tactics to overcome resistance by organizational participants: (1) bargain with IT department resources, (2) co-opt opposition, and (3) establish personal credibility.

Since no broad-based studies of CIO influence had been conducted, top executive interviews were conducted to study CIO influence, especially how a CIO influenced other executive members with respect to the *initiation and implementation of IT projects*, and to *overall business strategy*. The interviews provided initial insight into CIO influence behaviors, influence outcomes, and implementation success.

∶ A Field Study of CIO Influence Behavior

Two interviews were conducted in each of seven North American companies. The CIOs and all non-IT executives were part of their organizations' top management teams. The CIOs were initially contacted, and then they selected a non-IT executive who was a key business partner. The interviews were one to one and one-half hours long. The interview transcripts were sent to the executives to ensure that they accurately reflected their responses to the questions. Appropriate corrections were made to the transcripts as a result of the executives' feedback.

The data was categorized into appropriate clusters, reviewed for patterns, and summarized for presentation. The final analysis consisted of noting patterns and themes, and searching for contrasts and comparisons. The following sections describe the key findings from the field interviews.

Key Findings

Initiating IT Projects

CIOs used a variety of influence tactics to bring initiatives forward for organizational approval and implementation. Most commonly:

- CIOs presold their ideas to other managers on a one-to-one basis
- All explained initiatives in nontechnical terms
- All kept others well informed about project progress and changes
- Most listened carefully to their peers and other managers to understand different perspectives and overcome objections

The CIOs we interviewed rarely brought initiatives to the top management group unless they were preapproved. The CIO of a natural resources company suggested he always got others involved when contemplating a new IT initiative. He said, "In our company you do not surprise anyone, or create conflict. You never go forward with a recommendation to the top management group unless you know it will be accepted."

The targets of the CIO influence tactics, however, had some different perceptions. The more effective CIOs, in the judgment of the peer executives:

- Used consultation combined with rational persuasion
- Made specific plans to influence specific individuals
- Demonstrated the viability of a project through prototypes
- Relied less on external endorsement and active higher-level support
- Built relationships, partnerships, and networks with other executives, which were used to commit these executives and other key individuals to projects

A CIO from the financial services sector told us that when he started working for the company, "IT was considered a cost center. However, due to my relationships with others in the organization, and my track record of delivering on projects, IT is now considered an investment center." These findings were consistent with more recent anecdotal evidence concerning aspects of CIO influence and success in other situations. For example, CIOs elsewhere have been observed to enlist support from peer managers to indirectly present their views of IT to targets of influence.

Implementing IT Projects

Research has shown that individual commitment to change is a good predictor of IT project implementation success. To that end, CIOs educate others about the potential strategic impact of IT in formulating IT strategy and exhibit consultative behavior to communicate key IT issues to others. Our field interviews found these same tactics being used for successful IT project implementation.

In general, all the CIOs used interpersonal influence to gain commitment to IT project implementation. In the judgment of the peers, however, the more effective CIOs:

- Tailor the applied influence behavior to an individual target
- Vary their influence behaviors and styles to suit the situation
- Know when to stop trying to persuade someone

These findings contradict previous literature suggesting CIOs were generally reluctant to engage in interpersonal influence and did not vary their behaviors. Instead, we found that a complete range of influence behaviors were used, from little variation to proactive experimentation.

Forming Business Strategies

Every CIO studied clearly exerted an impact on their organization's strategic decision making. Some influenced the process throughout all stages of a new strategic initiative, and some became involved at the feasibility or analysis stage. In general, more effective CIOs brought forward strategic initiatives consistent with the current business strategy. Examples of these CIO activities included:

- Initiating and developing a new customer information system
- Introducing the World Wide Web component of a new range of products
- Introducing a new strategic planning methodology
- Providing opinions about the feasibility of new strategic initiatives
- Creating a new systems vision, which became a major shaper of the business plan

The CEO of a leasing company suggested that when the new information systems vision for the company was introduced, it had a major impact on the business strategy because "the only way to enhance our products is to find easier ways for our customers to do business with us. This tends to involve technological solutions represented in the systems vision because the easiest way to enhance our products is to do away with written contracts and do everything electronically." Previous research predicted that the number of CIOs in influential positions would grow; our findings supported this view.

፧ Conclusions

The historic rise of the IT executive from a relatively low technical manager—often in a financial or accounting department—to a senior executive management position as CIO says volumes about the increased importance of the CIO role in modern organizations. We see no evidence of that importance lessening. Indeed, we see it increasing even further as companies increase technological solutions for improving internal processes, solidifying links with external stakeholders, and adding virtual business lines. The CIO roles are likely to change as information technology becomes more mature and ubiquitous, and corporate users become more knowledgeable. The fundamental CIO role of being at the senior executive table involved in strategic decision making, however, will remain—and increase in intensity. This trend will only amplify the importance of CIOs using the right influence behaviors at the right time within the senior executive levels.

Yukl's (1998) nine influence behaviors or tactics are valid and provide an excellent "play book" for CIOs to use when planning to influence superiors, peers, and subordinates. These influence tactics can be taught, practiced, and adapted to business and personal situations. The preponderance of the tactics rely on strong interpersonal skills and business knowledge—key skill sets for CIOs beyond technical knowledge.

The findings of the study presented enhance the understanding of the relationship between CIO influence and IT project initiation, IT project implementation, and business strategy. For instance, CIOs in general exhibited a consistent approach to bringing forward IT initiatives to senior management—that each executive would be approached independently to discuss the initiative for informal approval before bringing the initiatives before the entire executive body for formal approval. The consistency of this pattern suggests that other CIOs should seriously consider this approach if and when the opportunity to initiate a strategic IT project presents itself.

Furthermore, it appears that successful CIOs possess a sophisticated understanding of the role of effective influence, and possess the skills necessary to execute influence properly. Specifically, the CIOs and their peer executives stated that some CIOs have a greater ability than others to vary their influence behavior to accommodate a situation. An exclusive reliance on rational persuasion (the most common CIO influence behavior) is not effective in all cases, especially in the context of strategic projects. As well, the respondents made it clear that some influence behaviors are more effective than others, in general. For example, rational persuasion combined with consultation appears to be more effective than persistence (a form of pressure).

There were some limitations to our study, and these should be understood. For example, the CIO chose the non-IT executive to be interviewed and this could have introduced bias in the responses and results. But care was taken to conduct the interviews separately and the CIO and non-IT executives only had access to their own transcripts of the interviews. Additionally, there was only one target in every organization that commented on the CIO's influence behavior; this also could have introduced bias in the responses and results, but obtaining responses from various companies tended to weaken this bias.

The key significance of this chapter is that CIOs today are involved in shaping and supporting business strategy, as well as exerting their influence in more areas than IT technical projects. Consequently, it is vitally important for CIOs to understand the nature and use of influence in organizations. Having power and effectively exercising influence are preconditions for accomplishing tasks in organizations. The CIO who exercises influence well can potentially be more effective in future IT strategy planning, IT implementation, and business strategy planning efforts.

■ References

Berkman, E. (2002) "The State of the CIO: Skills," *CIO,* 15 (Mar. 1), 78–82.

Earl, M.J., & D. F. Feeny. (1994) "Is Your CIO Adding Value?" *Sloan Management Review,* 35, 11–20.

Fiegener, M. K., & J. R. Coakley. (1995) "CIO Problems and Practices: 'Impression Management,' " *Journal of Systems Management,* 46 (Nov./Dec.), 56–61.

Keen, P. G. (1981) "Information Systems and Organizational Change," *Communications of the ACM,* 24, 24–33.

Kipnis, D., S. M. Schmidt, & I. Wilkinson. (1980) "Intraorganizational Influence Tactics: Exploration's In Getting One's Way," *Journal of Applied Psychology,* 65, 440–52.

Korsgaard, M. A., D. M. Schweiger, & H. J. Sapienza. (1995) "Building Commitment, Attachment, and Trust In Strategic Decision-Making Teams: The Role of Procedural Justice," *Academy of Management Journal,* 38, 60–84.

Lederer, A.L., & A. L. Mendelow. (1988) "Convincing Top Management of the Strategic Potential of Information Systems," *MIS Quarterly,* 12 (Dec.), 525–34.

Luftman, J. (1996) "Applying the Strategic Alignment Model," in J. Luftman (Ed.), *Competing in the Information Age: Strategic Alignment in Practice,* pp. 43–72. New York: Oxford University Press.

Schmidt, S. M., & D. Kipnis. (1984) "Managers' Pursuit of Individual and Organizational Goals," *Human Relations,* 37, 781–94.

Tannenbaum, R., & F. Massarik. (1950) "Participation by Subordinates in the Managerial Decision-Making Process," *Canadian Journal of Economics and Political Science,* 16, 408–18.

Yukl, G. (1998) *Leadership in Organizations,* 4th ed. Englewood Cliffs, NJ: Prentice Hall.

Yukl, G., & C. M. Falbe. (1990) "Influence Tactics and Objectives in Upward, Downward, and Lateral Influence Attempts," *Journal of Applied Psychology,* 75, 132–40.

VI

Scope and Architecture

This set of criteria tends to assess information technology maturity, the extent to which IT is able to:

- Go beyond the back office and the front office of the organization
- Assume a role supporting a flexible infrastructure that is transparent to all business partners and customers
- Evaluate and apply emerging technologies effectively
- Enable or drive business processes and strategies as a true standard
- Provide solutions customizable to customer needs

COMMUNICATIONS
- Understanding of Business by IT
- Understanding of IT by Business
- Inter/Intra-organizational Learning
- Protocol Rigidity
- Knowledge Sharing
- Liaison(s) effectiveness

COMPETENCY/VALUE MEASUREMENTS
- IT Metrics
- Business Metrics
- Balanced Metrics
- Service Level Agreements
- Benchmarking
- Formal Assessments/ Reviews
- Continuous Improvement

GOVERNANCE
- Business Strategic Planning
- IT Strategic Planning
- Reporting/Organization Structure
- Budgetary Control
- IT Investment Management
- Steering Committee(s)
- Prioritization Process

IT BUSINESS ALIGNMENT MATURITY CRITERIA

PARTNERSHIP
- Business Perception of IT Value
- Role of IT in Strategic Business
- Shared Goals, Risk, Rewards/Penalties
- IT Program Management
- Relationship/Trust Style
- Business Sponsor/ Champion

SCOPE AND ARCHITECTURE
- Traditional, Enabler/ Driver, External
- Standards Articulate
- Architecture Integration:
  - Functional Organization
  - Enterprise
  - Inter-enterprise
- Architectural Transparency, Agility, Flexibility
- Manage Emerging Technology

SKILLS
- Innovation, Entrepreneurship
- Culture Locus of Power
- Management Style
- Change Readiness
- Career Crossover Training
- Social, Political, Trusting Interpersonal Environment
- Hiring and Retaining

Chapters 10 to 16 provide excellent descriptions of current and emerging IT scope and architecture opportunities. Scope and Architecture is the only technical criteria included in the alignment maturity assessment. It is important to recognize that, just like the other criteria, executives must have an appropriate understanding and strategy that addresses how the business can leverage these technologies.

10

Edward A. Stohr and Jeffrey V. Nickerson

Intra Enterprise Integration
Methods and Direction

: *Chapter Summary*

1. Corporations grow, and as they grow the need for integration across the enterprise increases. Integration can be accomplished through various means.
2. Consistent with the theme of this book, the need for alignment—integration is really a business need, and the technology mechanisms won't help without the proper organizational structures, goals, and incentives. Both organizational and technological integration is necessary.
3. Business processes are the vital link between the technical and organizational infrastructures of the organization. Processes are also the mechanism through which most interorganizational interaction takes place and are therefore the foundation for increasingly electronic forms of commerce.
4. Enterprise integration doesn't happen naturally. It needs to be planned. Yet the planning cannot be precise, as business processes and facilitating technologies will change, creating different needs and different potential solutions.
5. New mechanisms for integration can be utilized to create a flexible, loosely coupled framework, within which special integration needs can be quickly fulfilled. These new technical mechanisms depend on standards that work both inside and outside the enterprise.

: *Introduction*

This chapter focuses on enterprise integration at two levels—the systems level and the organizational level. Integration at the systems level requires common standards and data definitions, and some means of synchronizing the communication between different software applications. This is usually what is meant by the recently coined term "enterprise application integration." As pointed out by Markus (2000) and others, however, systems integration in the software system sense is not, in itself, sufficient to ensure organizational efficiency and effectiveness. Organizations consist of individuals, departments, divisions and functions, which also must be integrated for the organization to be successful. Both integration and coordination have been discussed in the management literature going back to the 1930s (Gulick, 1937), and their definitions have changed over time. Today, coordination is the more general term, referring to people-oriented as well as systems-oriented dependencies. Integration is most often used in discussing the linkages between software systems. This chapter uses the two terms interchangeably when talking about the organizational aspects of integration.

We are not going to focus on a third level of integration, cross-enterprise integration and coordination, since this is the topic of the next chapter in this book. Any discussion of enterprise integration, however, must recognize that external needs, for example, customer requirements or supply chain efficiency, are increasingly important determinants of organizational effectiveness. Various points in the chapter discuss the boundaries between the systems owned by the organization and those owned by its trading partners and customers.

The chapter begins with a framework that encompasses both system and organizational integration. We then discuss the systems level of integration. We explain the major mechanisms and architecture choices. Finally, we provide a summary and some brief comments on future trends in enterprise integration.

⦂ *A Framework of Integration Requirements*

A useful definition, which applies equally well to both systems integration and organizational coordination is made by Malone and Crowston (1994), who define coordination as managing dependencies between activities. Figure 10.1 depicts the range of technical and organizational integration/coordination needs at a high level of granularity. A list of resource and activity dependencies is shown in the left column, common software and human coordination mechanisms in the middle column, and the supporting infrastructure elements in the right column. The resources, mechanisms, and infrastructure elements are roughly arranged horizontally according to their sphere of influence. The boundary between technical and organizational integration mechanisms is shown by the dashed lines in the cells in the center of the figure. Note that some of the mechanisms play a role at multiple levels in the figure.

It is argued that effective integration/coordination requires attention to elements at all levels on both the horizontal and vertical dimensions in the figure. The integrated architecture exists to support coordination in the use of the material, financial, and human resources of the firm.

The various levels in the figure at which integration is required are briefly described from bottom to top in the figure—from the most concrete to the most abstract. In so doing, it is pointed-out that integration is necessary not only *within* the various layers in figure 10.1 but also *between* the

	Resource/ integration need	Examples of integration mechanisms	Enabling environment/ infrastructure	
Organizational integration	Organizational units (func-(tions/de-partments)	E-mail, collaborative software, lateral teams — — — — — — — — — — Top management strategy, budgets, performance metrics	Organization policies/ structure	
	Decision makers	E-mail, collaborative software, knowledge management sys-tems — — — — — — — — — — Face-to-face meetings, job design, perfor-mance metrics		
Systems integration	Business processes (both internal & external to the firm)	Workflow, collabora-tive systems, SCM, CRM, Web ser-vices — — — — — — — — — — Process owners, teams, performance met-rics, service level agreements	Standards	Systems architecture
	Applications	Inter-process commu-nication, RPC, messaging, ERP, Web services	Networks	
	Data	Data dictionaries Databases, XML	Platforms	

Figure 10.1 Framework for business integration

layers. Also, integration in one layer depends on integration at lower levels in the hierarchy. For example, integration at the application level requires a common understanding of the data that is being interchanged, which in turn, implies integration at the data level. The discussion focuses on the role played by the mechanisms in the center of the figure. Where appropriate, there is also reference to the role of the infrastructure elements—standards, architecture, networks, and organization structure—in helping to achieve integration both within and between layers.

Data Integration

Definition

The *goal* of data integration is to allow organizations to combine, aggregate, and report on data from different sources. Data integration involves both syntactic and semantic considerations. At the syntactic level, software programs must be able to handle data stored on the same or different devices on different media in different formats. At the semantic level, the meaning of all data items must be understood and the same data item must have the same definition across multiple applications both within and outside the firm. To make the integration process worth the effort, the data must be of high quality—timely, accurate, and relevant.

Objectives

Data integration is desirable for several reasons:

- To provide timely and accurate information for analysis and decision making by both management (e.g., data warehousing applications) and customers (e.g., product catalogs).
- To provide a single authoritative source of information for use in performance measurement and the audit process.
- To facilitate interaction between software programs in order to achieve program and business process integration.

Mechanisms

Simple data integration mechanisms are found in most programming languages, ranging from Cobol to Java. File member libraries in COBOL allow programmers to share data definitions. Class definitions in Java fulfill the same function. At a higher level, data dictionaries also provide a systematic way of integrating information with an emphasis on semantics. None of these mechanisms scale well, however, when programs are written in different languages and query many different kinds of databases. As discussed later, the use of extensible mark-up language (XML) schemas is the currently favored solution for data integration. XML combines data and the description of the data in one place, which greatly simplifies integration (Ibbotson, 2001). In cross-enterprise integration, EDI has served a data integration role, providing a standard format for the exchange of common documents. Even here, the trend is toward XML.

Data Level—Application Level Integration

Definition

Integration across the data and application layers allows programs to access and understand data stored in heterogeneous files and different databases.

Mechanisms

Standards such as ODBC and JDBC allow databases from different vendors to be accessed by a single application.

Application Integration

Definition

When sets of applications are integrated, each can call on the functions of the others.

Objectives

The objectives of application integration are

- To break down complex processing needs into discrete steps performed by relatively independent programs (e.g., a program to perform a file update might be followed by an independent program that produces management reports).
- To minimize the number of manual steps. In particular, to ensure that data is entered only once.
- To support interactive processing (e.g., provide one-stop shopping for customers by linking diverse applications in a common front end.)
- To facilitate data and information integration.

Mechanisms

As discussed in more detail later, application integration is now supported by a wide range of middleware products. Initially, such integration was supported by RPC calls, and then by transaction managers, and now by application servers—each of these advances has incorporated the techniques of the previous mechanisms. IBM, BEA, Microsoft, and Tibco all provide many different variants of these mechanisms. These systems, however, do not interface with humans directly and so only indirectly support business processes (i.e., through the applications that they integrate).

At a higher level, ERP systems achieve application integration because ERP vendor-developed applications that perform common business functions are united through a common database (also providing data integration—one of the selling points of ERP systems). The integration of the functional applications implies also that integration at the next layer, business processes, is achieved. A major issue with ERP systems, however, is that they fail to bridge the gap between the application and process layers in a flexible fashion. This gives rise to the common complaint that it is easier to fit the organization to the ERP system than it is to adapt the ERP system to serve organizational requirements (Esteves & Pastor, 2001).

Application Level—Business Process Integration

Definition

Integration between the business process and application level occurs whenever an application is used in a business process. Almost all applications of computing in organizations fit this definition in a broad sense including traditional batch processing using legacy systems. The tightest integration between the layers occurs when a process calls an application automatically or when ERP, legacy, or client-server applications that are to be used by a human processor are automatically brought to the user's screen to be used as aids in decision making.

Mechanisms

Integration of applications and business processes is achieved to some extent by ERP systems as mentioned earlier, with the caveat that they are often perceived as costly and inflexible. Alternatively, workflow management systems (WFMS) are a form of middleware that provide integration between the application and process layers. Workflow is oriented toward processes, and hence it is discussed more fully in the next section.

Business Process Integration/Coordination

Definitions

A business process consists of related sets of activities that are performed by human and software actors according to business rules that may be more or less stringently applied. The connection between the software and human agents that perform a process is well integrated or coordinated when the process is efficient, accurate, and appropriate to the task at hand from a mechanistic, human, and organizational viewpoint. Moreover, the process goals must align with those of the organization as a whole. This is called *within-process integration.*

Processes often cross departmental boundaries and can therefore provide a coordination mechanism in the organization layer as discussed later. This is called *cross-functional coordination*. Processes must also be integrated/co-ordinated with each other. For example, the order entry process needs to be integrated with accounts receivable and with the back-end processes that produce the product or service desired by the customer. This form of integration is called *internal process-to-process integration*.

Finally, e-business demands that the internal processes of the firm be integrated with those of its trading partners and customers. *External process integration* means that the organization is able to connect its internal processes seamlessly with those of its suppliers, intermediaries, and customers. This is the basis of e-commerce. Automated and partially automated process integration is distinguished. Fully automated internal-external process integration has already been achieved to a remarkable extent for the purposes of security, when a firm links in real time to certificate authorities and credit-granting agencies, and in advertising, when an ad server company such as DoubleClick pushes advertisements to consumer web pages serving both the advertiser and the publishers in its network. As another example, there are two large, overlapping efforts in the financial services industry that seek to automate the entire range of trading-related business processes. One effort is called straight-through processing, emphasizing the goal of full automation. The second is called T+1, emphasizing the reduction in overall trade processing time. Both require that the internal processes of the financial services organization be closely synchronized with those of its customers and business partners.

At an even higher level of external process integration, processes must be coordinated between all the firms in the value chain to achieve improved performance and service. This form of external process integration, which is called *value chain coordination*, is the focus of modern supply chain management.

Objectives

Summarizing, the reasons why business process integration is desirable include:

- Coordination between individual human and software actors as they perform the work of the organization (integration within the process).
- Coordination between the efforts of organizational units such as departments and divisions that have different roles to play in the execution of shared processes (cross-functional coordination and internal process-to-process coordination).
- Connecting an organization with its suppliers and customers (external process integration).
- Optimizing the joint performance of all partners in the value added chain for a good or service (value chain coordination).

• Increasing the efficiency of the organization and its ability to compete in terms of its agility, cost, and service capabilities.

Mechanisms

Workflow management systems are explicitly designed to support business process automation by moving work between human and software actors according to rules (WFMC, 1995). These systems provide visual interfaces for process design, manage process instances, and interface readily with the organization's legacy, client-server, and ERP applications. They also contain simple organizational models (e.g. who reports to whom, who has approval authority for what, who can perform what roles, and who has access rights to what data and what applications.) And they perform a resource coordination function by managing, work assignments and load balancing between actors. In this sense, Workflow contributes to integration at all the levels in figure 10.1. Historically, workflow has been used mainly for process, cross-functional, and internal coordination. This is changing; the major trend in the workflow area now involves external and to some extent, value chain integration.

Business Process—Decision Making Integration

Definition

Integration between the decision-making and business process layers occurs whenever a human operator (or software agent) makes a decision that changes the flow of work through a process. For example, in a helpdesk process, a customer service representative may decide to escalate a problem case by referring it to an expert in another department within the organization.

Mechanisms

There are many ways in which this form of integration may be facilitated. One example is to use a workflow system that presents a user-friendly interface and automatically provides the decision maker with access to the tools needed to perform analyses and spot errors. *Informating* a process by providing decision-relevant information on an as-needed basis and feedback to the operators concerning their performance is another example. Embedding expert systems at decision points in the process is another. Finally, knowledge can be imbedded into the two-part process in which process data is collected and analyzed for patterns that are later used to modify the process or inform operators, a process best described as double-loop learning (Argyris, 1994). This level is really the level of the user interface, where the success of a company's systems will often hinge.

Integration Between Decision Makers

Definition

Integration/coordination of decision makers occurs when they are able to share their ideas and knowledge freely and when they coordinate their actions to the benefit of the enterprise. To achieve this integration, strategic decisions often have to be made by upper levels of management in the cooperating organizational units. Although the classical models of organizational hierarchies imply that leaders are isolated at the top, more current analyses of organizations show that decision makers are in constant contact with each other, and that their interactions are crucial to the success of a company. Whereas the concept of coordination in organizations originally stressed interaction between people, the current ways of thinking about it stress interaction between activities (Malone & Crowston, 1994). This more recent way of thinking has led to much significant work. It is at a cost, however— for the interactions between executives in a company are not simply around tasks. They are around friendships and families as well. The psychological side of integration in an organization should not be underestimated—large and costly projects can fail due to interpersonal friction. It is for this reason that decision makers choose less structured forms of communication—meetings, dinners, and e-mail—in dealing with their peers. And it is for this reason that companies encourage social interaction among their executives.

Mechanisms

The mechanisms of interaction include the simplest ones—face-to-face interactions and the telephone. But other, more asynchronous, methods are also important such as voice mail and email. Computer-based systems have generally provided lean rather than rich information to decision makers. Multimedia approaches can increase the richness and accessibility of information. To facilitate communication that is closer to human communication, richer forms of communication such as multimedia and interactive media are sometimes helpful. Collaborative systems are specifically designed to help human decision makers coordinate their activities, and build shared virtual spaces that allow teams to asynchronously communicate and share information and ideas.

Decision Maker—Organizational Integration

Definition

Decision makers are integrated into their organizational units to the extent that their actions are coordinated with each other to achieve departmental or divisional objectives.

Mechanisms

Classical organizational theory was very much concerned with this problem (Lawrence & Lorsch, 1967). Ideas such as span of control, delegation of authority, communication of goals from higher levels in the hierarchy, and budgeting were advocated. These mechanisms are still relevant today. The integration of decision makers into departments is also controlled through incentives. Decision makers are motivated very directly to meet the goals of the team they belong to. And they can be motivated to also contribute to the goals of other teams. There is a large literature on incentive schemes in economics (Jensen & Meckling, 1973), in management (Eisenhardt, 1989) and, currently, the Balanced Scorecard approach of Kaplan and Norton (Kaplan & Norton, 1992). An important development since the advent of tightly coupled value chains is the need to integrate decision making from one organization into that of another. For example, P&G manages its customers' inventory (McKenney & Clark, 1995).

Organizational: Functional/Departmental Integration

Definition

Through a process of differentiation, the organization is divided into multiple divisions or departments (Lawrence & Lorsch, 1967). Differentiation occurs because each unit of an organization needs to focus on a different set of conditions outside of the firm, and therefore needs to specialize. This specialization leads to differences in attitude of managers, along the four dimensions of goals, time orientation, interpersonal orientation, and structural formality (Eisenhardt, 1989), which increases the challenge of integration. Yet Lawrence and Lorsch point out that the best performing organizations are both highly differentiated and highly integrated (Lawrence & Lorsch, 1967).

Organizational integration requires first that communication is established so that cross-departmental processes are executed smoothly and that departments are informed of the activities of other departments, in connection with the resources they compete for and the processes that they share. Second, departmental integration requires that the goals of the various departments be aligned.

Objectives

Organizational integration is desired for the following reasons:

- Departments often depend on each other for inputs (sequential or reciprocal dependence (Thompson, 1967).
- Departments often need to cooperate to execute distinct parts of a process.

- Integration can mean more efficient sharing of resources and the development of organizational standards.
- Functional integration helps support process integration because the functional or departmental managers are better able to coordinate their decisions with respect to process execution.

Mechanisms

In the classical view of organizations, coordination and integration are achieved by the controlled delegation of authority and hierarchical command and control structures (Fayol, 1925; Urwick, 1938). Another reality of organizations, however, is that much of the work is performed through processes in which work is handed off between people that often belong to different departments or divisions. Advocates of the reengineering movement of the 1990s advanced the view that the process or horizontal view of organizations was required to overcome the inefficiencies of the vertical organization with its stove pipe mentality and often problematic handoffs of work between departments. To enable horizontal coordination, reengineering proponents and organizational theorists (Galbraith, 1995) advocate the use of process owners, or, at least, process teams with members from each of the functional departments involved in the process. Taking this further, reengineering and other organizational theorists have proposed process-oriented organizational structures in which the functional disciplines are subordinated to the process view (Galbraith, 1995). Adding process owners and cross-functional teams to the organization helps horizontal coordination but requires some kind of matrix management since the team members must balance the demands of their functional (vertical) as well as process (horizontal) coordination. What seems most important is that there are boundary spanners who, like diplomats, speak the specialized languages of all the departments to be integrated (Lawrence & Lorsch, 1967).

A major issue in achieving departmental coordination is that vertical chain-of-command; authority must be reconciled with the horizontal process needs of the organization. To address this problem, Rummler and Brache (1990) recommend that the share of resources and the goals of each department be derived from the department's contributions to the processes that cross its boundaries. Similarly, the goals of each job should be derived from both the process and functional requirements. This approach is markedly different from the usual practice in which functional goals and performance measures are set by the functions in conjunction with top level management without much consideration of horizontal coordination needs and job performance measures are determined by the functions with at most a parochial view of process needs.

Increasingly, organizations need to integrate not only their own internal departments, but also with other organizations. Supply Chain Management (SCM) software such as that provided by I2 seeks to optimize the logistics within the value added chain. CRM software such as that supplied by Siebel, seeks to integrate the firm with its customers. Finally, electronic exchanges such as Covisint, operated by the major auto suppliers, integrate the buy and sell transactions of many suppliers and buyers.

Summary

This section constructed a framework of integration that includes technical as well as organizational factors. The literature on enterprise integration focuses on the data and application layers in the framework together with the standards, architecture, and networking infrastructure alternatives that can integrate these technical elements. By contrast, the organizational design literature focuses primarily on the decision making and departmental integration layers along with the supporting organizational structure, policies, and strategy. Only recently have reengineering and organizational theorists focused on the middle layer, business processes. Business processes are the vital link between the technical and organizational infrastructures of the organization. Processes are also the mechanism through which most inter-organizational interaction takes place and are therefore the foundation for increasingly electronic forms of commerce.

Proper integration of the elements in figure 10.1 should help achieve an agile and efficient organization. This is only half the story, however. A man-machine system is described as if it existed without any purpose and without the resources that are needed to achieve this purpose. To complete the story, we assert first, that the organization must have a winning strategy, and second, that in pursuit of this strategy, the integrated technical and organizational components that have been discussed must coordinate and integrate the organization's material, financial, and human resources in pursuit of the organization's goals. The vast literature of business strategy, management science, finance, and organizational behavior all can be brought to bear on the organizational aspects of enterprise integration. This section of the chapter provided only a brief outline of the requirements for an integrated technical and organizational system through which the organization can achieve its ends.

⠒ *Technology Mechanisms of Enterprise Integration*

Introduction

It has been established that enterprise integration needs to occur at many technical and organizational levels. Some of the methods that can be used at each level have been introduced. This section takes a closer look at the facilitating technologies that can be used to attack the overall problem.

An organization, convinced it needs an architecture that supports integration across the enterprise, can easily state its ideal. The integrated enterprise of the future will tie together all existing applications, so that data from one application can be easily used in another. Business Processes, which may stretch across different applications, will be combinable, so the output from one will be input to another. The integration mechanisms will not create performance bottlenecks. And the integrated enterprise will be easy to change.

This ideal hasn't changed throughout the history of information systems. It is proving hard to achieve, but progress is being made. Four current trends in the quest for the ideal integrated enterprise system are looked at first.

Overall Frameworks Are Preferred to Point Solutions

Enterprises are seeking to solve the integration problem overall, instead of one connection at a time. This is leading enterprises into overall system-designing activities, looking across all major application system. The hope is that, with an overall platform in place, individual integration projects can be accomplished more quickly.

Loose Coupling Is More Popular Than Tight Coupling

Mechanisms for integration are trending toward the loosely coupled. In a tightly coupled environment, a change to one system needs to be coordinated with changes to all connecting systems. In a loosely coupled environment, a change to one system can often be made independently of the connecting systems.

XML Is Driving Out Customized File Formats

The use of the data description language XML is becoming a de facto standard within the enterprise. This is important because XML can describe all of the data flowing between systems in a uniform way, greatly reducing the myriad file formats enterprises support.

Industry-wide Efforts Are Driving Internal Efforts

The outside is driving the inside—industry standardization efforts are being adopted inside the enterprise. So, for example, a set of data definitions used by financial services companies to communicate with each other can also be used internally to integrate enterprise systems. Once done, internal and external communication can use the same standard set of messages. Both the RosettaNet standards, focused on the manufacturing industry, and the new

ISO standard focused on the financial industry are examples of industry models that are finding their way into the enterprise (ISO, 1999; RosettaNet, 2002; Johannesson & Perjons, 2001).

General Approaches

This section looks first at the three approaches to the problem that have evolved over time. It then discusses the actual mechanisms in use today, both the traditional and the trendy. Finally, it discusses the more systematic approaches to integration that have been proposed in both industry and academia.

Approach 1: Sequential Integration

The first instances of systems integration involved the movement of a deck of output cards to the input tray of the next program (fig. 10.2). This kind of sequential integration between programs became more sophisticated with the advent of IBM's Job Control Language. Using this language, a whole series of computer programs could be linked together. And batch jobs based on this language, involving complex runs of many applications, still do the majority of work in large-scale insurance systems. Sequential integration won't apply to certain problems. An airline reservation system calls for synchronization of many programs running at the same time, and cannot be serialized into a set of batch jobs. More modern approaches to sequential integration, such as the shell system of UNIX, provide a cleaner interface, but work the same way, and share the same limitations.

Approach 2: Databases

Two distinct applications can share information by alternately reading and writing to the same database server (fig. 10.3). The applications don't need to know about each other—they just need to share a common understanding of the data and what the data means.

This approach can handle problems sequential integration can't—any transactional system, such as a reservation system, can be implemented with database technology. In an airline system, many application programs will be interested in whether a particular seat is full—all these programs can be

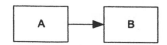

Figure 10.2. Sequential integration

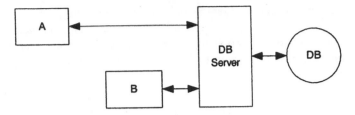

Figure 10.3. Databases

coordinated through access to a common database that updates the crucial link between a passenger and a seat.

Approach 3: Messages

Modern systems are defined in terms of their messages—every part of a system is thought of as a separate entity that can either originate or receive a message (fig. 10.4) (Rumbaugh, Jacobson, & Booch, 1999). The appeal of this approach is that it works on any scale—from the signals being sent between chip components to the files being interchanged between large computer systems. Sequential integration as well as database integration are described as specialized variants of message passing systems. More important, message-oriented middleware can be used as a way of building loosely coupled systems, in which each component does not need to understand everything that the other components are doing.

The De Facto Mechanisms of Integration

With these approaches in mind, the commonly used technical mechanisms of integration across an enterprise can be described.

Integration Using Files

Most companies don't integrate two technology systems until they absolutely need to. For example, if a company creates a new telemarketing sales force,

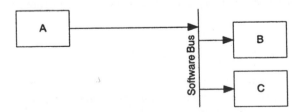

Figure 10.4. Messages

a new order management system associated with them might need to communicate with an existing sales commission system. The simplest way to integrate is to establish a point-to-point interface. The order management system can generate a file every night that is read the next morning by the commission system.

The disadvantage of this mechanism becomes apparent as the number of systems in the enterprise grows. If 15 systems need connections to each other, over 100 files need to be generated. An IT organization can be overwhelmed by the need to update and maintain file interfaces. The incremental cost of each new interface is low, but the combined ongoing cost to the organization is high. And by the time the organization realizes this, the replacement cost of the interfaces may be substantial.

Remote Procedure Calls

Remote procedure calls (RPCs) are the underlying mechanism of client-server computing. The client calls the server, requesting a response, and waits for the result. The server responds to multiple clients, and provides the responses as fast as it can—sometimes in turn requesting a response from another server, and relaying the answers. RPCs are behind many different integration frameworks, most notably CORBA and COM (Orfali, Harkey, & Edwards, 1996). RPCs require tight coupling. The client process needs to know exactly where the server is, and what the server expects. Neither the client nor server can change independently of the other.

ERP Integration

As discussed earlier, a company can integrate much of their operation by replacing financial, HR, and manufacturing systems with an ERP system provided by one of several large software vendors. All applications will share the same data model, the same databases, and the same interfaces. Reporting across functions or divisions becomes possible. This approach has worked for many companies. It also has failed for others. But ERP is more an approach than a technology, and there are signs that the next generation of ERP systems will take advantage of the new technology mechanisms such as standard application servers. These new ERP systems will be more loosely coupled, and therefore, more amenable to change, and more likely to succeed.

Integration Using Consolidated Databases

In its simplest form, a database is shared across a set of applications. The database serves as a shared memory for the entire universe of applications accessing it. Although attractive from the logical perspective, many organizations run into problems when they physically implement such systems, for it is easy to optimize a database for a single application, but difficult to optimize for several. And software designers do not like to forfeit performance control to another part of the organization. A single complex transaction from one application can lock up several tables and force a different application to back off, possibly for minutes.

To allow local control of data but still provide integration of information, sophisticated IT organizations use local databases for each application, and then use some other asynchronous technology to update a consolidated database that can be queried by applications that require more global sets of information. If the applications are only querying the database for decision support purposes, rather than operation purposes, then the consolidated stores are called data warehouses or datamarts.

The transaction to the local database is not slowed down, yet the information is integrated. (See fig. 10.5.)

For this to work, a universal data model needs to be modeled, agreed upon, and enforced. In the past, such efforts have proven expensive and time-consuming. It is a difficult exercise—and, once accomplished, it takes a great deal of attention to maintain the model in the face of changing

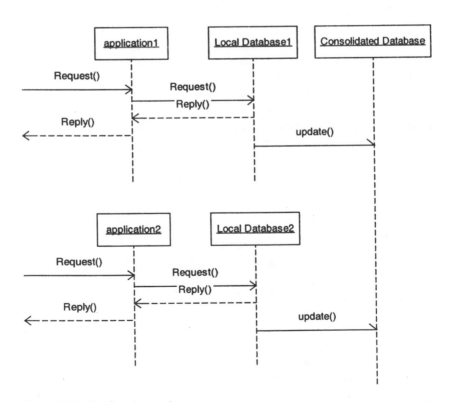

Figure 10.5. Database integration

business conditions. The current trend is toward pooling the effort of creating a model at the industry level. The industry model also can be used internally.

The Newer Mechanisms

Publish/Subscribe

The problem with most integration mechanisms is that they force one-to-one communications between senders and receivers—each needs to know about the other. The publish/subscribe mechanism decouples the communication, so that the publisher may not even know who is receiving—and is not affected by an increase in the number of receivers. And the receiver doesn't need to know the source of the information sought—the receiver simply subscribes to events of interest. (See fig. 10.6.)

This scheme is attractive as a mechanism for enterprise integration. Each major application system publishes events out on a bus. A new account opening, a sale, a supplier shipment notice—all of these would be sent. Then the systems that need particular types of information subscribe. For example, a risk management system might want to see all major sales transactions, as well as stock market quotes. The risk management system could be built without changing the sales or quote systems, which may not even know the risk management system exists (Eugster, Guerraoui, & Damm, 2001; Eugster, Guerraoui, & Sventek, 2000; Eugster, Felber, Guerraoui, & Kermarrec, 2001; Oki, Pfluegl, Siegel, & Skeen, 1993).

The publish/subscribe mechanism can solve many enterprise integration problems. It is also a complex technology, and it takes skill to integrate it into existing applications. There are many commercial vendors who offer this capability, and there is an emerging standard, Java Messaging Services,

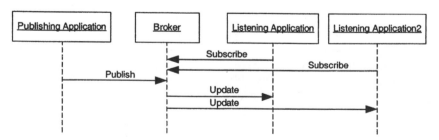

Figure 10.6. An application using a publish/subscribe mechanism publishes an event once. Listeners in other applications are always waiting for the event so that they can pull it into the application. In implementations, a broker often operates between the publisher and the listener, handling subscription changes and broadcasting resends if a listener misses an event.

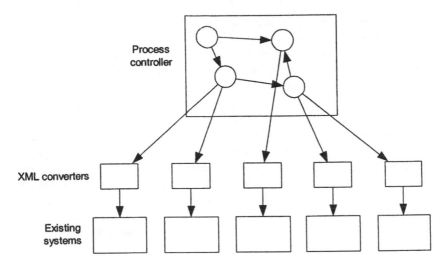

Figure 10.7. Enterprise application integration systems architecture

that will eventually create an environment for interoperability among most vendor solutions.

Enterprise Application Integration

A new infrastructure referred to as *enterprise application integration* ties together processes that reach across large numbers of systems. These systems usually ship with universal data models, mapping all common packaged systems database fields into one format. (See fig. 10.7.)

Unlike the other mechanisms discussed, EAI systems feature a process, rather than a message, broker. The broker pulls process information into a central control. By working at a process level, it becomes possible to link together disparate systems, specifying the data to be moved, and the compensating transactions to be fired in the event of a failure. Once created, using either a diagram format or a high-level language, the broker will handle the sequential integration and data integration between legacy systems (Johannesson & Perjons, 2001). There are many different ways this is accomplished, but a common method is to send XML messages to converters that will invoke the legacy systems in their preferred data format.

Web Services

A new set of standards seeks to create a way for programs to automatically discover other services on the Internet, and then use those services. While the model is oriented toward integration outside the enterprise, it will end up being used inside also, as it provides many of the integration mechanisms that are necessary in a large company.

The standard has three parts. The first is the Simple Object Access Protocol (Mitra, 2001), which defines an RPC call. The second is the Web Service Description Language, which defines how a service works—in a way that a computer can understand. The third is the Universal Description, Discovery, and Integration standard (McKee, Ehnebuske, & Rogers, 2002), which allows a program to automatically discover a service application.

The standards allow for programs to get the services they need—without being tied to a particular server. In the ideal scenario, a program is written that depends on a particular service. At the time the program is run, it queries a directory to find out who supplies the service. The program reads in detail the format of the messages needed, and converts its data into what is expected by the server. The server is called, and an answer is returned.

Agent-Based Methods

The more web services there are, the more likely it is that agents will flourish. Agents allow us to delegate a difficult transactional task. The agent can take an instruction from a program, and autonomously locate services, run them, and return results.

Once agents can handle simple transactions, they will be invoked to handle complex negotiating strategies involving price. In an integration environment, an agent can be used to tie together different systems through the accomplishment of a preset goal. Agents are tireless and patient, two necessary prerequisites to true integration of activities.

The design of automated agents is a rapidly expanding area of research, not yet commercialized (Riha, Pechoucek, Krautwurmova, Charvat, & Koumpis, 2001; Ottaway & Willis, 1997; Kwon & Lee, 2001; Klein and Dellarocas, 1999; Cost et al., 1999; Huang, Houng, & Mak, 2000; Shrivastava et al., 2000; Yan, Maamar, & Shen, 2001).

Workflow

The preceding approaches to integration focus on the systems aspects—the integration of data and applications. With the exception of ERP systems, they do not involve human interaction. In contrast to the preceding approaches, workflow management systems have the potential to integrate both the systems and organizational aspects of organizations, as discussed earlier. (See fig. 10.8.)

Systematic Approaches

In contrast to the methods described here, academic researchers have suggested systematic technical approaches to performing enterprise integration.

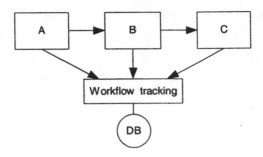

Figure 10.8. Workflow

From the standpoint of a software architect, integration has little to do with the specifics of a business. Instead, it is an issue of how to link things. First, Mary Shaw at Carnegie Mellon University pointed out that connectors between systems were often an afterthought—but to do integration properly give the connectors first-class status (Shaw, 1996). Then Chris Dellarocas at MIT pointed out that perhaps there is a need to give first-class status to component interdependencies, as interdependency is a higher-level concept than connection (Dellarocas, 1996).

Both these observations reflect the technical perspective that it is too difficult, and probably fruitless, to try to anticipate all the potential interconnections between business functions—that instead, it makes more sense to accept that functioning software components will be combined in ways that cannot be predicted. The problem becomes one of making assumptions about a component as explicit as possible so that compatible functions can be combined without further investigation and testing.

Earlier in this chapter the coordination science work done at MIT was discussed (Malone & Crowston, 1994) This work seeks to systematically map business problems to a set of coordination mechanisms.

As this applies to software systems, resources are broadly described to include CPU time, data, operating systems resources, and other hardware. Activities are either resource producers or resource consumers. Figure 10.9 shows all six permutations of producers and consumer interaction. The top row shows three common forms of coordination—in *sharing*, two processes might need to coordinate use of a finite resource such as a printer. In *flow*, one process waits for another to produce a result. In *fit*, two processes must combine their outputs into a common whole, as when software developers integrate their work into a final application. In the bottom row, the left diagram shows the circumstance in which a task reads from multiple resources. The right diagram shows a task producing multiple resources. And, in the center, a task reads from one resource and produces another. When this diagram is joined with the one above it, the combination suggests sequential flow across an unlimited number of tasks.

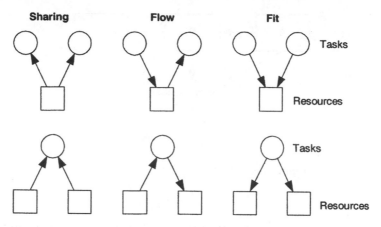

Figure 10.9. Combined from Crowston and Malone, showing all the permutations of tasks and resources. The middle top diagram shows a task producing a resource that is consumed by another task.

Malone and others in the MIT Center for Coordination Studies have codified dependencies and their associated coordination techniques in a process handbook (Malone et al., 1999). It is a bottom-up approach—by cataloging a set of business processes and their associated coordination mechanisms, the hope is that the practices of an organization continually can be refined. In contrast, there is a top-down effort to create an international integration standard called the Generalized Enterprise Reference Architecture and Methodology (GERAM) (Chalmeta, Campos, & Grangel, 2001).

It is far from clear that any single generalized architecture can work. It is also not clear if a process handbook can ever be complete. To date, neither the academic theory nor the industry architectures has had as much direct impact on enterprises as vendor products and internal IT teams have had. Yet ideas on architecture, no matter what the source, have a way of appearing in software products. It is expected that integration frameworks may grow to encompass many different technical and organizational mechanisms, applied according to the nature of the specific integration problem.

⦂ The Process of Integrating Across the Enterprise

Enterprise integration doesn't happen naturally. It needs to be planned. Yet the planning cannot be precise, as business processes and facilitating technologies will change, creating different needs and different potential solutions.

The reference architecture efforts mentioned define methodologies for building integrated architectures. There are few surprises in the sequences advocated—all the methods consist of a sequence of discovery, analysis, design, implementation, and maintenance, as in the development of an individual application.

Enterprise integration is similar to city planning. In city planning, it is important to develop the street plan, but not to focus on the individual buildings. The size of the block is important; so is the diameter of the pipes supplying water. But a city planner who tries to specify the size of each building's windows will not be serving the community. City planners try to anticipate, but not over fit. They know there are many alternative futures for a city.

An enterprise integration plan will have a similar structure, putting in place a framework that encourages integration by defining the standard mechanisms for connection between processes and applications. Once the standards are set, and the processes are defined, the planning activity has fulfilled its function. Individual systems can be built imaginatively within the defined framework.

City planning, and enterprise integration, is easier if nothing has been built yet. But in the case of enterprise integration, there is almost always a large and complex infrastructure in place. Those who have engaged in retrofitting an existing environment have often found there is resistance to the integration efforts. As discussed, the resistance is due to human issues such as compensation and recognition.

Enterprise integration will not work unless all layers of figure 10.1, both organizational and technical, are considered. On the organizational side, the problem of integration is exacerbated by the limits of human cognition, by behavioral issues, by the difficulty of aligning the goals of individuals with organizational units, and by the relentless need for faster change. There is a long history of research in organization design and many approaches have been advocated. But distributed, networked organizations act and interact in a world that moves much faster than before. Exploding information availability presents new challenges to managers as well as to systems architects.

Facilitating technologies can help both groups. New mechanisms for integration can be utilized to create a flexible, loosely coupled framework, within which special integration needs can be quickly fulfilled. These new technical mechanisms depend on standards that work both inside and outside the enterprise. Which presents interesting opportunities for those engaged in cross-enterprise integration, the subject of chapter 11.

⦂ References

Argyris, C. (1994) "Good Communication That Blocks Learning," *Harvard Business Review*, 72(4), 77–85.

Chalmeta, R., C. Campos, & R. Grangel. (2001) "References Architectures for Enterprise Integration," *Journal of Systems and Software*, 57(3), 175–91.

Cost, R. S., T. Finin, Y. Labrou, X. Luan, Y. Peng, I. Soboroff, J. Mayfield, & A. Boughannam. (1999) "An Agent-Based Infrastructure for Enterprise Integration," in *First International Symposium on Agent Systems and Applications/Third International Symposium on Mobile Agents*. Los Alamitos, CA: IEEE Computer Society.

Crowston, K. (1994) A Taxonomy of Organizational Dependencies and Coordination Mechanisms, http://ccs.mit.edu/papers/CCSWP174.html

Dellarocas, C. (1996) *A Coordination Perspective on Software Architecture: Towards a Design Handbook for Integrating Software Components*. Doctoral dissertation, MIT, Cambridge, MA.

Eisenhardt, K. M. (1989) "Agency Theory: An Assessment and Review Academy of Management Review," *Academy of Management Review*, 14(1), 57–74.

Esteves, J., & J. Pastor. (2001) "Enterprise Resource Planning Systems Research: An Annotated Bibliography," *Communications of the Association for Information Systems*, 7.

Eugster, P. T., R. Guerraoui, & C. Damm. (2001) "On Objects and Events," in *Proceedings of the 2001 ACM SIGPLAN Conference on Object-Oriented Programming Systems, Languages and Applications*, 254–69.

Eugster, P. T., R. Guerraoui, & J. Sventek. (2000) "Distributed Asynchronous Collections: Abstractions for Publish/Subscribe Interaction," in *14th European Conference on Object-Oriented Programming*, 252–76.

Eugster, P., P. Felber, R. Guerraoui, & A.-M. Kermarrec. (2001) *The Many Faces of Publish/Subscribe*. Swiss Federal Institute of Technology, DSC10: 2000104.

Fayol, H. (1925) *Industrial and General Administration*. Paris: Dunod.

Galbraith, J. R. (1995) *Designing Organizations: An Executive Briefing on Strategy, Structure, and Process*. San Francisco: Jossey-Bass.

Gulick, L. (1937) "Notes on the Theory of Organization," in L. Gulick and L. Urwick (Eds.), *Papers on the Science of Administration*, 3–13. New York: Institute of Public Administration.

Huang, G. Q., J. Houng, & K. L. Mak (2000) "Agent-based Workflow Management in Collaborative Product Development on the Internet," *Computer Aided Design*, 32(2), 133–44.

Ibbotson, J. (Ed.) (2001) *XML Protocol Usage Scenarios*. World Wide Web Consortium, W3C. www.w3.org/TR/2001/WD-xmlp-scenarios-20011217/

ISO. (1999) International Organization of Standards, ISO-15022.

Jensen, M. C., & W. H. Meckling (1973) "Theory of the Firm: Managerial Behavior, Agency Costs, and Ownership Structure," *Journal of Financial Economics*, 3(3), 305–60.

Johannesson, P., & E. Perjons. (2001) "Design Principles for Process Modelling in Enterprise Application Integration," *Information Systems*, 26(3), 165–84.

Kaplan, R. S., & D. P. Norton. (1992) "The Balanced Scorecard: Measures That Drive Performance," *Harvard Business Review*, 70.

Klein, M., & C. Dellarocas. (1999) "Exception Handling in Agent Systems," in *Proceedings of the International Conference on Autonomous Agents*. New York: ACM.

Kwon, O. B., & J. J. Lee. (2001) "A Multi-Agent Intelligent System for Efficient ERP Maintenance," *Expert Systems with Applications*, 21(4), 191–202.

Lawrence, P. R., & J. W. Lorsch. (1967) *Organization and Environment: Managing Differentiation and Integration*. Cambridge, MA: Division of Research Graduate School of Business Administration Harvard University.

Malone, T. W., & K. Crowston. (1994) "Interdisciplinary Study of Coordination," *ACM Computing Surveys,* 26(1), 87–119.

Malone, T. W., K. Crowston, J. Lee, B. Pentland, C. Dellarocas, G. Wyner, et al. (1999) "Tools for Inventing Organizations: Toward a Handbook of Organizational Processes," *Management Science,* 45(3), 425–43.

Markus, M. L. (2000) "Paradigm Shifts: E-Business and Business/Systems Integration," *Communications of AIS,* 4(10)

McKenney, J. L., & T. H. Clark. (1995) *Procter & Gamble: Improving Consumer Value Through Process Redesign.* Harvard Business School Case 195126.

McKee, B., D. Ehnebuske, & D. Rogers (Eds.). (2001) UDDI Version 2.0 API Specification, http://www.uddi.org/pubs/ProgrammersAPI-V2.00-Open-20010608.pdf

Mitra, N., Ed. (2001) *SOAP Version 1.2.* World Wide Web Consortium, W3C.

Oki, B., M. Pfluegl, A. Siegel, & D. Skeen. (1993) "The Information Bus—An Architecture for Exensible Distributed Systems," in *Proceedings of the Fourteenth ACM Symposium on Operating Systems Principles.* New York: ACM.

Orfali, R., D. Harkey, & J. Edwards. (1996) *The Essential Distributed Objects Survival Guide.* New York: J. Wiley.

Ottaway, T., & G. Willis. (1997) "An Adaptive Workflow Management System Utilizing Agent Technology," in *Proceedings of National Annual Meeting to the Decision Sciences.* Atlanta, GA: Decision Science Institute.

Riha, A., M. Pechoucek, K. Krautwurmova, P. Charvat, & A. Koumpis. (2001) "Adoption of an Agent-Based Production Planning Technology in the Manufacturing Industry," in *12th International Workshop on Database and Expert Systems Applications.* Los Alamitos, CA: IEEE Computer Society.

RosettaNet. (2002) http://www.rosettanet.org/

Rumbaugh, J., I. Jacobson, & G. Booch. (1999) *The Unified Modeling Language Reference Manual.* Addison-Wesley object technology series. Reading, MA: Addison-Wesley.

Rummler, G. A., & A. P. Brache. (1990) *Improving Performance: How to Manage the White Space on the Organization Chart.* Jossey-Bass management series. San Francisco: Jossey-Bass.

Shaw, M. (1996) "Procedure Calls are the Assembly Language of Software Interconnection: Connectors Deserve First-Class Status," in D. A. Lamb (Ed), *Studies of Software Design, Proceedings of a 1993 Workshop, Lecture Notes in Computer Science No. 1078,* 17–32. New York: Springer.

Shrivastava, S. K., L. Bellissard, D. Feliot, M. Herrmann, N. de Palma & S. M. Wheater. (2000) "A Workflow and Agent Based Platform for Service Provisioning," in *Proceedings Fourth International Enterprise Distributed Object Computer Conference,* 38–47. EDOC 2000. Los Alamitos, CA: IEEE Computer Society.

Thompson, J. D. (1967) *Organizations in Action: Social Science Bases of Administrative Theory.* New York: McGraw-Hill.

Urwick, L. F. (1938) *Scientific Principles and Organization.* New York: American Management Association.

WFMC. (1995) The Workflow Reference Model, Version 1.1., http://www.wfmc.org/standards/docs/tc003v11.pdf

Yan, Y., Z. Maamar, & W. Shen. (2001) "Integration of Workflow and Agent Technology for Business Process Management," in *Proceedings of the Sixth International Conference on Computer Supported Cooperative Work in Design,* 420–26. Ottawa, Ontario, Canada: NRC Research Press.

11

M. Lynne Markus, Sheryl Axline, Dana Edberg, and David Petrie

Toward the Future of Enterprise Integration
Interenterprise Systems Integration

: **Chapter Summary**

1. External systems integration refers to IT-mediated transactions between in-dependent business entities, for example, between a company and its cus-tomers, suppliers, or other business partners, such as co-producers and banks, and it is important for both economic and strategic business reasons.
2. External systems integration involves many technologies and business ar-rangements with different pros and cons, but they can be grouped in two broad categories: one-to-one or one-to-many approaches that link an indi-vidual company with its business partners and hub-and-spoke approaches that provide the possibility of many-to-many connections.
4. One-to-one approaches are most prevalent, although hub-and-spoke ap-proaches may offer the greatest business value in terms of cost and fit with the dynamic business environment of mergers, acquisitions, and divestitures and multiparty business arrangements, such as business process outsourcing and supply chain facilitation.
5. Few companies today have a systematic strategy for dealing with external systems integration. Both business issues and technical issues should be ad-dressed in an external systems integration strategy.
6. Because a level 5 in Luftman's maturity assessment requires organizations to have their systems integrated and coordinated with external partners, IT and business executives need to understand the business and technical issues in system integration to make appropriate choices about external systems inte-gration in the years ahead.

: **Introduction**

In the past decade, companies have spent billions on enterprise systems—including ERP (Enterprise Resource Planning) systems, data warehousing, and electronic commerce applications—and on systems integration, through such technologies as EDI (Electronic Data Interchange), Middleware, EAI (enterprise application integration), and XML (eXtensible Mark-up Lan-guage). Naturally, executives want to know how to position their companies better with enterprise technology for the business challenges of the decade ahead.

The Advanced Practices Council (APC) of the Society for Information Management (SIM) International asked us to help them answer these questions. The APC is a research-based program sponsored by SIM for senior IT and digital commerce executives. In particular, the APC was interested not only in the current state of enterprise systems integration but also in the future state. Given the intense interest in business-to-business e-commerce at the time the study was chartered, this requirement naturally suggested that the study should focus on *external* systems integration, that is, the electronic connections between an organization's systems and those of its business partners, as well as on internal systems integration.

APC members did not want us to be limited by current practice, even best practice. They asked us to look forward, anticipating what were likely to be the key issues facing CIOs in the future and identifying strategies for addressing these issues. Accordingly, our research approach was eclectic, and it evolved as the study progressed. We conducted interviews with a wide range of industry sources, including academics, consultants, and business people. We built on our own research in the enterprise systems area by reading other academic and practitioner research literature, relevant press articles, and market research analyses. We identified and analyzed trends and attempted to assess their likely future evolution. In addition, we conducted four in-depth case studies and derived recommendations from our findings for CIOs and business executives. Our 18-month investigation of enterprise systems and systems integration focused both inside the enterprise and externally toward business partners. This chapter mainly draws on our interviews and literature survey and synthesizes our findings pertaining to *external* systems integration.

In the first section, we address the questions of what external systems integration is and why it is important. The second section examines alternative approaches to external integration from a technical and economic perspective. The third section looks at the same issue more from a business perspective. The final section sketches some of the issues involved in developing an external systems integration strategy, since establishing effective external systems is fundamental to achieving a level 5 in Luftman's maturity alignment assessment.

⦂ *External Integration in Focus*

At its simplest, external systems integration refers to IT-mediated transactions between independent business entities, for example, between a company and its customers, suppliers, or other business partners, such as co-producers[1] and banks. When a company employs electronic data interchange (EDI) with a supplier, sets up an extranet for customers' purchase orders, shares flight codes with a partner airline, or participates in online funds transfer with its bank, the company can be said to have achieved a measure of external systems integration.

This simple definition raises a number of complex issues. First, what is meant by *transaction*? The term transaction implies commercial activity (ordering, invoicing, etc.) in contrast to pure information and knowledge sharing, as would be the case when companies give customers access to documents about product specifications and repair. There are gray areas, however, as when companies share product drawings and bills of material with suppliers in collaboration around new product development or in preparation for procurement activities (e.g., contract negotiations or an auction).

Second, *IT-mediated* is also ambiguous. It is well known that EDI has never been widely adopted by small companies because of cost, technological complexity, and the existence of competing transaction format standards. Consequently, many EDI adopters have resorted to one-sided integration strategies. For example, small suppliers may print out orders from a large customer's EDI system and manually reenter them into an in-house order entry system (Iacovou, Benbasat, & Dexter, 1995). Or, a large supplier's EDI system may generate faxed invoices to customers (Salmi & Tuunainen, 2001). Similarly, using Internet technology, a company may set up a secure extranet that does not enable integration with business partners' in-house systems (Koch, 2000). These examples represent IT-mediation without true systems integration, defined as computer-to-computer communication without human intervention.

Furthermore, *IT-mediated* suggests that automation is the main factor in external integration. And it often is. In some cases, however, organizations participating in external systems integration plan, not just to automate existing processes, but also to streamline or reengineer business processes to achieve greater savings. An example is eliminating the invoice in the purchasing process by agreeing to pay the vendor when goods are received (Hammer, 1990). Another is vendor-managed inventory, where the supplier decides what goods are to be shipped by analyzing the customers' sales data (Clark & McKenney, 1995). These examples show that external systems integration often involves redesigning interorganizational business processes, which in turn has implications for both partners' internal processes and systems.

Third, *independent* is also a problematic concept. It is clear that Ford's electronic dealings with its suppliers fall under the rubric of external systems integration, but what about interconnections between different divisions within Ford? There are good reasons to include the electronic transactions among major business entities of large organizations in the definition of external systems integration. Establishing electronic relationships alone does not ensure an effective partnership. Additionally, because of organization size, technology limits (e.g., telecommunications cost), and management policy (e.g., decentralization of IT decision making), decisions about internal systems integration in large corporations are often made at the subunit level, rather than at the level of the parent. So, for example, in one company we studied, each plant in a single country unit within a single business unit of a large corporation installed an ERP system from a different vendor (Markus, Tanis, & Fenema, 2000). In another company, all subunits used the same ERP package, but each configured it independently. Subsequently, realizing that it had not achieved enterprise-wide integration, that company began looking to supply chain management software (usually thought of as an external systems integration approach) to help manage transactions between its business units. In a third company, each unit had its own manufacturing systems, but the parent company ran a centralized financial system with which the local manufacturing systems needed to interface.

Why do companies pursue external systems integration? Since the advent of EDI, companies have been tempted by the *efficiencies* to be gained through the automation of their relationships with other companies. The benefits include eliminating redundant activities, reduced errors, and lower labor costs. In the chemical industry, supply chain costs amount to $120 billion out of $600 billion annual merchant sales in North America and Europe. Of these costs, perhaps $15 to $20 billion could be saved annually through systems integration mediated by B2B electronic marketplaces (Petit, 2001). Similarly, the members of Converge, a B2B electronic marketplace for the electronics industry estimate that they will be able to reduce their $200 billion annual raw materials costs by 5 percent to 10 percent within three years through the use of the marketplace (Markus & Soh, 2001).

For other companies and industry groups, *competitive advantage* is the allure of external systems integration. They hope to attract customers by being easy to do business with, or they hope to lock in their customers through increased switching costs. In the automobile industry, for example, systems integration with suppliers and dealers is seen as a way to advance the vehicle manufacturers' goal of producing a custom-built car to a customer's order in just three days (Howard, Vidgen, Powell, & Graves, 2001).

Similarly, systems integration is seen as a way to provide an integrated travel experience in the airline industry, which uses strategic alliances among independent airlines as a way to achieve global reach. Because many airlines are government owned, complete integration of systems and operations is unattainable. And because airlines frequently enter and leave alliances, the adoption of common systems is unlikely to provide a good "final" solution. But customer service demands the virtual integration of reservations, ticketing, frequent flyer programs, and the like. To accomplish this objective, established industry intermediaries such as Sita are providing integration services involving "Middleware" (integration software) and providing some functionality on a shared services basis (Heath, 2001). Similarly, the Star alliance is developing Starhub to achieve virtual integration of partner airlines' applications (Voigt, 2001).

In short, although there is considerable ambiguity about the definition and boundaries of external systems integration, there is no doubt about its potential advantages in terms of business efficiency and competitive advantage. The next section discusses various technical and organizational approaches to external system integration.

⦂ External Integration Approaches

Approaches to external systems integration fall into two categories: approaches that connect a company one-to-one or one-to-many with business partners, and hub-and-spoke approaches, in which companies connect once to a central intermediary that enables connections to multiple other companies.

One-to-One and One-to-Many Approaches

Dyadic approaches to external integration are by far the most commonly used. The original approach was EDI,[2] which is still widely used, although never as widely as proponents expected, in part because the technology is very expensive to set up and to operate. A few particulars will help explain why. EDI formats pertain to business *documents* such as a purchase order: they define, for example, what data elements go into the purchase order, in what format (alphabetic, numeric, number of characters), and in what sequence. A complete business process usually consists of many documents (e.g., purchase order, order acknowledgement, backorder notification, etc.), and typical business relationships involve multiple processes. Furthermore, two large companies may have multiple business relationships when their business units are considered as separate entities.

In EDI, each pair of trading partners must agree on the format of *each* document exchanged. (This is called a trading partner agreement.) Once agreed, the formats must be maintained: Changes in business rules, legislation etc., may demand altered transaction formats. In the automobile industry, for example, suppliers complain about the frequency with which vehicle manufacturers change EDI formats (Howard et al., 2001). Industry standards efforts can ease the burden of setting up on EDI somewhat. But participants often variously interpret standards; standards may not address the needs of all industry players; and in any case compliance with standards is usually voluntary (Damsgaard & Truex, 2000). Consequently, key players have been observed to drop out of EDI standards initiatives, precipitating their collapse (van Baalen, van Oosterhout, Tan, & van Heck, 2000). Furthermore, some companies do business with partners in several industries. Thus, it is not uncommon for suppliers to be required to set up and *maintain* multiple EDI transaction formats for the same document. (Maintenance is a very important factor to consider since it comprises a large portion of the total IT ownership cost.)

Add to startup and maintenance costs the high cost of EDI technology, telecommunications services, and service transaction fees. (Transmitting EDI documents over the Internet can lower these costs.) Add also the fact that EDI operates in the batch mode, which is not up to the real time information needs of many businesses.[3] Add finally the limited resources and technical skills of small companies, and it is easy to see why many do not adopt. Their nonadoption in turn imposes costs on the larger companies that do use EDI. Although companies can benefit from using EDI with only some of their partners, they have to maintain duplicate processes for trading with partners that do not use EDI.

In comparison to EDI, the Internet offers the possibility of substantially reduced startup and operating costs for external integration. Using the Web to access a business partner is substantially less expensive than using dial-up lines or leased lines and paying charges to EDI intermediaries (called value added networks, or VANs). Therefore, some companies build extranets for transacting with their partners (sometimes even replacing their EDI facilities altogether). Because the extranets do not allow for easy integration with *partners'* in-house systems, however, this solution imposes costs on partners who would prefer two-way integration (Koch, 2000).

One of the most hyped approaches to external integration is XML (eXtensible Mark-up Language), which enables automatic translations of data from the format of one company's internal systems into the format used by a partner's systems. This approach works well for clean, well-structured data (Plumtree Software, 2000). But, even within a single company, data may be inconsistently defined and of poor quality (Bashein & Markus, 2000)— problems that are compounded when multiple organizations are involved. A second problem is the need to develop XML "grammars" for the translations (Rapoza, 2000). There are many industry initiatives, creating uncertainty about which one to use (Stackpole, 2000). And some companies just develop their own unique translators. Consequently, XML can involve the same kinds of maintenance problems that plague EDI—updating multiple XML translators for the same business process. In addition, even when XML successfully integrates *data*, it does not always integrate the business *processes* of partner companies, which is necessary for the benefits of streamlining or reengineering.

The relationship between *data integration* and *process integration* is complex (Markus, 2000). Process integration *requires* data integration, but data integration does not always *support* process integration, because the latter requires source system standardization or modification, while the latter does not. While process integration is sometimes considered "better," it can be more difficult and costlier to achieve. Understandably, few companies are willing to undertake process integration efforts from scratch. Two approaches to easing the demands of process integration are industry-wide process standardization efforts and the "adapter" technologies of enterprise software vendors.

The best-known industry-wide process standards effort is the RosettaNet consortium in the computer and electronics industry.[4] RosettaNet is publishing standards in seven clusters, including ones such as order management, inventory management, and manufacturing. For example, the order management cluster contains the processes of quote and order entry, transportation and distribution, returns and finance, and product configuration. The standards include both data definitions and a prescribed process flow, allowing for process streamlining. Again, pairs of companies must decide whether and how to implement these standards, one process at a time (RosettaNet, 2001).

In a similar approach, companies that are already using enterprise resource planning software from the same vendor[5] can achieve process integration by using the "adaptors" built into the software. For example, Millennium implemented one proprietary ERP-ERP link with a business partner (PolyOne), but found it very costly (Mullin, 2001).[6]

> Millennium has already completed one direct ERP-to-ERP link with PolyOne. That project, completed last year, opened Millennium's internal IT system to an outside company for the first time and tested the efficiency of its SAP R/3 ERP system and its internal work processes.
>
> The connection totally automates transactions. PolyOne's system, working on a purchasing forecast, triggers order placements on Millennium's system, which checks product availability and sends a notice to the warehouse. A message is sent back to PolyOne to notify it that the shipment has been sent. "The only manual process is when someone at PolyOne keys in the receipt of the shipment. . . . It's pretty much 24–7, lights out."
>
> That one link, however, had a "six figure" price tag. . . . It would be much cheaper to link to every customer and supplier through one connection. (Mullin, 2001)

Again, as with EDI, extranets, XML translations, and industry process standards, direct ERP system-ERP system connections must be set up and maintained with each partner. To minimize the costs of this solution, experts have recommended that companies develop a private trading exchange, also called an integration hub, which allows them to connect once with many business partners. For example, the Dow Chemical Company created MyAccount@Dow—"a customizable private exchange through which Dow's customers can order products and obtain account-related services" (Brooks & Dik, 2001). Private trading exchanges can support deep integration with the partners' in-house systems.

One key advantage of private trading exchanges is that they can help overcome lack of *internal* system integration (Bermudez, 2001). As mentioned before, many large enterprises that have implemented enterprise systems at a subunit level (or companies that have not fully integrated their internal systems environment through a combination of technologies) have great difficulties when they try to interact electronically with customers and suppliers. They may not have enough internal integration to achieve, for example, worldwide inventory visibility, or to consolidate their product offerings into "one face to the customer" (Markus, 2000). By connecting up their disparate internal systems to the private trading exchange, they may be able to accomplish the needed internal integration as well as a one-to-many interface for external connections. For example, "a large high-tech company is planning to use [private trading exchange] technology to consolidate 150 separate supplier-facing portals within the company on a single platform" (Fontanella, 2001).

A further advantage of private trading exchanges is that they can support integration with partners from several phases of the supply system (e.g., suppliers' suppliers and customers' customers) (Radjou, 2001). By contrast, one-to-one linkages are frequently criticized for their inability to support a view of the entire supply chain.

Key to the success of private trading exchanges will be the evolution of standardized interconnection technologies from third-party vendors (Bermudez, 2001). Whereas private trading exchanges represent a big advance from one-to-one approaches like extranets and direct ERP system linkages, they are not true hub-and-spoke arrangements (discussed later in this chapter), because they do not support many-to-many connections.

In short, each of the one-to-one and one-to-many external integration approaches discussed in this section has pros and cons, summarized in table 11.1. As a class, the main advantages of these approaches are that they are relatively easy to start up, because they require the agreement of only two parties at a time, and they allow for highly tailored arrangements. The disadvantage is that it is very costly to set up and maintain different one-to-one connections with many partners.

Hub-and-Spoke Approaches

Hub-and-spoke arrangements employ a single intermediary, often a specialized industry consortium, to create many-to-many connections between companies and their business partners. In contrast to the one-to-many private trading exchange approach, hub-and-spoke arrangements often include actual or potential business competitors in the same infrastructure. The ability of a company's customers to access that company's competitors through the same system causes some companies to be concerned about the business implications of hub-and-spoke arrangements. The business implications are discussed in a later section; the discussion to follow focuses largely on the technical and economic issues of the hub-and-spoke approach to external systems integration.

Hub-and-spoke intermediaries often provide a range of services, including data and process standards, in addition to technical connectivity, setting them apart from the VANs employed to facilitate dyadic EDI transactions.

Table 11.1
The Pros And Cons Of One-to-One And One-to-Many Approaches To External Systems Integration

Approach	Pros	Cons
EDI	• "Standard" data and document formats • Good for high transaction volumes • Well entrenched among older, large companies	• Very expensive, particularly for smaller businesses (Stackpole, 2000) • Requires a separate trading partner agreement for each partner (Dan et al., 2001) • Small players often do not do back-end systems integration, losing the possibility of efficiency benefits • Batch processing does not allow for instantaneous data updating • May involve different solutions with different partners
Extranets	• Lower technology and access costs than EDI (Koch, 2000) • Good solution for small partners (Koch, 2000)	• Often do not enable integration with one partner's back-end systems leading to duplicate data entry costs and errors (Koch, 2000)
Custom XML data conversions	• Allow for higher level of integration and associated efficiencies than extranets • Quick and relatively inexpensive to set up, operate, and change (Stackpole, 2000) • No need to change existing legacy systems, just run translations (Chen, 2000) • No need to wait for agreement on industry standards (Dobrin, 2000)	• Offer few advantages when EDI is already in place (Chen, 2000) • Do not work well with poorly integrated and structured legacy systems where data are not readily available (Howard et al., 2001) • May lead to a nonrobust, ad hoc system architecture (Mayor, 2001) • Competing XML standards and lack of common vocabularies limit benefits (Stackpole, 2000) (Berinato, 2001a)

Process integration using industry data and process standards (e.g., RosettaNet's PIPS)	• Data and process integration standards for an entire industry group, promoting reusability in integration efforts (Koch, 2000) • Allows for tracking and managing an entire process or set of transactions even in the face of transaction failures (Dobrin, 2000) • Hedge against uncertainties associated with consortia (Bermudez, 2001)	• Requires industry-wide cooperation on standards, leading to delays (for instance, the RosettaNet has only implemented 10 PIPs to date (Koch, 2000) • Many large firms operate in multiple industries, so a single set of standards will not suffice (Pender, 2000) • Standards may not meet some companies' unique requirements (Damsgaard and Truex, 2000) • Still quite expensive and time consuming to implement (Grygo, 2000)
Direct ERP-ERP system linkages using adaptors	• Tight, customized integrations possible (Davenport et al., 2001) • Good for strategic business partners (Davenport et al., 2001) • No need to wait for agreement on industry standards (Dobrin, 2000) • Hedge against uncertainties associated with consortia (Bermudez, 2001)	• Can be expensive, at least at present while collective experience is low (Mullin, 2001) • Integrations may be unique to the business partner, not easily reusable (Davenport et al., 2001)
Private trading exchange	• Can support deep collaboration and process integration with existing business partners (Brooks and Dik, 2001) • Necessary to deal with the profusion of external connections a company has, including multiple e-marketplaces (Brooks and Dik, 2001) • Can enable internal systems integration, where this is lacking	• Do not enable companies to connect with business partners they do not already know (Brooks and Dik, 2001)
One-to-one integration approaches overall	• Highly customized to the specialized needs of the interacting business partners • Benefits generally require the agreement or participation of only two companies	• Integration solution may be unique to each pair of companies • With many partners, the development and maintenance costs are high

Hub-and-spoke approaches come in two flavors—those that facilitate data integration only and those intended to support process as well as data integration.

Data Integration Approaches

Data integration approaches focus on translating data and business documents from the formats used by one company into the formats used by another. The primary advantage of data integration approaches is that they automate interorganizational business transactions without requiring replacement of or major changes to companies' existing source systems, thus avoiding an expensive and time-consuming activity. The primary disadvantage is that they do not generally reengineer partner companies' internal business processes—a major opportunity for additional business benefits.

An example of the "data integration only" hub-and-spoke approach is the Australian Pharmaceutical Extranet Gateway (PEG) project (McGrath & More, 2001; More & McGrath, 2000). PEG was designed to automate passing of common order transactions along the supply chain via the Internet. Key to the project is a common product numbering scheme (based on European Article Number EAN standards) and the bar coding of every consumable. Consumable ordering is streamlined through use of common order "forms" and electronic ordering and acknowledgement. Use of the Internet, instead of expensive EDI VANs, makes project participation more viable for small suppliers.

The architecture of PEG is said "to have much in common with data warehouses" (McGrath & More, 2001). Each partner is permitted to use whatever internal systems they want. Participants communicate with central PEG databases using common EDI transaction formats. Transactions must conform to the PEG Catalog based on EAN standards. Custom-built interfaces convert partners' internal data into the PEG standard form—and back again. PEG rejects transactions that do not conform to its standards and returns them to the initiating company for correction. This "open systems" approach was intended to allow the partners great flexibility in choice of enabling technology and to avoid forcing partners to undertake expensive technology conversions. Member companies can upgrade their own internal systems without affecting PEG or other partners, although their interfaces to PEG must be maintained.

Full implementation of PEG is expected to reduce the cost of processing an order to AU$2–5 per order versus the estimated AU$50–70 for manual ordering. At current volumes, annual savings of AU$200M are estimated. Despite these clear benefits, however, PEG's integration approach has some major limitations (McGrath & More, 2001). These include:

- Some transactions (those with data in non-PEG formats) cannot be "matched" by the interface software. Partners *should* reconcile their source systems and databases with the repository when transactions are rejected, but "experience shows" they seldom *do*. Thus, the quality of the data resource declines over time. And the costs of rework and error correction can be high.

- Some small suppliers find the cost of developing and maintaining interfaces to the PEG system to be prohibitive, even though this cost is much lower than would be the case if they had to interface directly with each wholesaler. These suppliers can still interact with PEG over the Internet, but they have to rekey orders into their own systems, losing the advantages of integration—a situation that also was common with EDI.
- The approach does not improve internal systems integration or business process integration in the partner organizations.

An interesting question yet to be resolved is whether partners should be given access to data, other than their own transaction data, that resides in the PEG databases. If so, the potential exists for companies with greater IT know-how to gain competitive advantage from data mining at the risk of potential changes in industry market power (McGrath & More, 2001).

Another example of the "data integration only" form of the hub-and-spoke approach is the Autolinkki system for spare automobile parts ordering (Salmi & Tuunainen, 2001). The system was an initiative of the eight big Finnish wholesalers of nonbranded car parts, intended to address competition from the branded car parts sector. The Autolinkki parts ordering system is integrated into a parts inventory package used by approximately one thousand local Finnish car parts dealers, who in turn resell the parts to garages.

The system started as an EDI-based ordering service with faxed-back order confirmation.[7] The system also handles account balance inquiries and online product updates, but the latter feature is not much used because of telecommunications bandwidth limitations. A web-based ordering system (not integrated with the dealers' in-house systems) was recently added.

Like PEG, the Autolinkki system provides translation tables (resident in the dealers' client software, however, instead of in a central server as in the case of PEG) to keep track of the different parts numbering schemes and product data formats used by different wholesalers. The system has been well accepted by dealers, with the vast majority of orders initiated from the dealers' inventory systems instead of the standalone web-based ordering systems.

A third example of the data integration only type of hub-and-spoke approach is an e-Business Laboratory project of the Boeing Company sponsored under Taiwan's Industrial Automation and e-Business Development Plan (Gulledge, 2001). Taiwan is trying to position itself as a design and engineering hub for a complex web of international relationships in which the primary customers are in the United States and Europe, manufacturing occurs offshore in China, assembly may be done in yet another location, and logistics and financing arrangements may be both direct and indirect.

Many of the Taiwanese participants are small companies that cannot afford to maintain one-to-one electronic linkages with every business partner.

The hub-and-spoke arrangement proposed for the e-Business Laboratory involves a large Taiwanese tier-one supplier to the aerospace industry acting as the hub for electronic communications between small second- and third-tier suppliers and the large customers. The following scenario illustrates how the proposed arrangements will work:

1. Large Company releases PO to hub in any format (e.g., X12, EDI-FACT, or any flavor of XML).
2. Hub translates PO into XML flavor that is required for each of the three service provider solutions at each supplier location.
3. Suppliers respond to PO with a quote and settlement account number, using their flavor of XML.
4. Hub translates each quote into the format required by the large company and forwards all three quotes to big company.
5. Company evaluates quotes and sends award notification to the hub.
6. Hub contacts Cash Settlement Company and requests credit approval.
   a. If request is denied, hub notifies large company.
   b. If request is approved, hub notifies large company.
7. Hubs send award notification to supplier. (Gulledge, 2001)

A final example is TradeCard, an online payment service for large-dollar cross-border transactions (Farhoomand & McCauley, 2001). By integrating security mechanisms, credit insurance, electronic funds transfer, and document workflow, TradeCard hopes to replace the costly letter-of-credit and the risky unsecured open-account approaches to international trade financing. TradeCard is an Internet-based service that allows partners to continue using their technology of choice:

> All types of business documents are stored internally in the TradeCard system as XML, although TradeCard customers are not required to have XML compliant interfaces on their systems. For example, a seller can upload an invoice from an automated supply chain system directly into the TradeCard system, the buyer can view the invoice in HTML via a Web browser, and a freight forwarder can send the advance shipping notice in EDI format. (Farhoomand & McCauley, 2001, p. 20)

Process Integration Approaches

Whereas data integration approaches translate or standardize product data names and transaction formats, process integration approaches also standardize the sequences of transactions and activities that make up a business process. By allowing for the monitoring and management of related transactions, they adapt better to breakdowns and permit higher levels of automation (sometimes called "lights-out" processing, because human intervention is not required). Because process integration requires standardization or modification of source systems or the creation of a supportive IT infrastructure (RosettaNet, 2001), process integration is costlier to set up than data integration, but it also provides opportunities for companies to reengineer business processes to achieve additional business benefits.

An example of the process (and data) integration hub-and-spoke approach can be seen in the services offered by electronic marketplaces Elemica and Envera in the chemicals industry (Christiaanse, Sinnecker, & Mossinkoff, 2001; Markus, 2001). Most early discussions of electronic marketplaces focused on support for buying and selling via the aggregation of different suppliers' products in combined catalogues and matching of supply and demand through auctions. Elemica and Envera represent a new generation of electronic marketplaces designed to support efficient transactions *before and after* the sale is made, with less emphasis on the buying and selling process.[8] Formed as consortia of companies in the chemicals industry, where mutual buying and selling is common, Elemica and Envera also include important third parties such as chemical transportation companies.

Member companies make a single electronic integration between their in-house ERP systems[9] and these electronic marketplaces, and the marketplaces enable connections to any other marketplace member without heavy system integration efforts. Thus, these electronic marketplaces enable many-to-many connections instead of the one-to-one connections of direct ERP system-ERP system integration or the one-to-many approaches of private trading exchanges. Elemica and Envera are able to support ERP-ERP connections, not by requiring all members to adopt a common ERP system, but by relying on Chem eStandards, an XML-based set of data and process standards, derived from the RosettaNet initiative in the computer and electronics industry (Markus, 2001). CIDX, the chemical industry standards body, adopted RosettaNet's approach, believing it likely to play some role in the eventual consolidation of XML technology. CIDX could not use RosettaNet's approach intact, however, because RosettaNet had not then produced a complete set of standard "partner interface processes" (PIPs), and because the chemical industry has unique requirements associated with the transportation of hazardous materials.

The new electronic marketplaces also provide members with aggregated and detailed data about all transactions made through the system with any or all partners. Furthermore, Elemica, for one, planned to provide ERP hosting services, allowing member companies to avoid installing and operating their own in-house ERP systems. In addition, these electronic marketplaces perform a function similar to that of a private trading exchange in enabling the integration of member companies' unintegrated internal systems. A company can link each of its subunits' enterprise systems to Elemica and thereby achieve "one face to the customer" (see fig. 11.1 for a diagram of Elemica's "Solution Set"). Together, these services promise significant po-

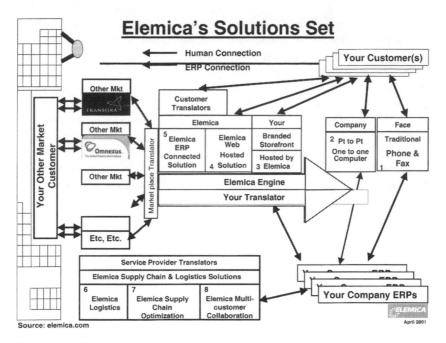

Figure 11.1. Elemica's solutions set

tential savings over traditional in-house systems operation (Harreld, 2001; Kern, Lacity, Willcocks, & Zuiderwijk, 2001), with their duplicated system integration and maintenance efforts.

Although Elemica *enables* connections between one member and any other, member companies remain in control of decisions about their business partners. (By contrast, some public e-marketplaces have open membership.) Furthermore, it is still possible within Elemica to develop customized linkages with particular partners. Full benefits from reduced connection costs require a standardized approach.

Another example of a process integration hub-and-spoke approach is Covisint. This consortium of automobile manufacturers and their suppliers provides a number of capabilities, including product development collaboration and post-sale product fulfillment. Covisint's IT-mediated process for direct material ordering is diagrammed in figure 11.2.

In summary, hub-and-spoke approaches to external integration represent an important alternative to one-to-one and one-to-many integration approaches. Hub-and-spoke approaches come in two flavors—data integration only and process (plus data) integration. Process integration is generally believed to offer greater potential benefits, but it may have higher costs, unless the capability is offered on a services basis. (This point is discussed more later in this chapter.) Compared to one-to-one integration approaches, hub-

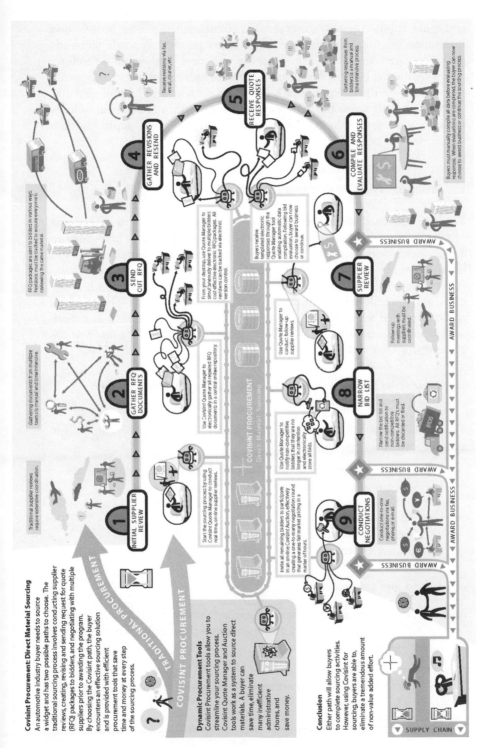

Figure 11.2. Covisint's direct material ordering process

267

and-spoke approaches have lower set up and maintenance costs, because one integration effort enables connections to many partners. A single hub-and-spoke arrangement is unlikely to suffice for most companies. Therefore, achieving the full benefits from participating in hub-and-spoke arrangements may depend on the emergence of hub-to-hub connections. Lack of data and process standards across the hubs may in turn delay the development of hub-to-hub connections. The pros and cons of hub-and-spoke approaches are summarized in table 11.2.

⁚ Business Issues in External Integration

We have indicated the existence of two competing paradigms of external systems integration: the private trading exchange as a portal for one-to-many arrangements with business partners and the shared infrastructure of the many-to-many hub-and-spoke arrangements such as electronic marketplaces. It is interesting and practically important which of these approaches is likely to be more prevalent in the future or how they might coexist. The previous section outlined many of the technical and economic arguments, but there are crucial business issues as well. This section summarizes the business arguments for each side.

Arguments Favoring Private Trading Exchanges Over Hub-and-Spoke Arrangements

The business arguments favoring private trading exchanges as a solution for external systems integration include:

- The need to do something now, coupled with uncertainty about the timing, performance, and winners among e-marketplaces.
- The desire for greater personalization of, and control over, particular business relationships.
- The likely need to interface with multiple e-marketplaces.
- Competitive concerns.

Timing and Uncertainty

Advocates of private trading exchanges argue that private exchanges provide "insulation" from the uncertainties surrounding future business practices and developing information technology:

Consider the unknowns:
- Will consortium exchanges survive? Which ones? Providing what services? How many will your company have to deal with?
- Which independent trading exchanges will survive?
- Which flavor of XML will win? What about RosettaNet?

Table 11.2
The Pros And Cons Of Hub-and-Spoke Approaches To External Systems Integration

Approach	Pros	Cons
Data integration approaches	· Substantially lower participation costs for smaller players (since initial development efforts are largely subsidized by government and/or large players) (McGrath and More, 2001) · Lower upfront participation costs because players may retain their legacy systems (McGrath and More, 2001) · Substantially lower transaction costs (e.g., cost of processing a purchase order) versus manual or EDI (McGrath and More, 2001) · May eventually involve all players in an industry supply chain (e.g., manufacturers, distributors, customers, end-users), magnifying benefits (McGrath and More, 2001) · May eventually lead to lower inventory carrying costs in the supply chain through information sharing and process improvements (e.g., just-in-time deliveries) (McGrath and More, 2001)	· Do not work well with poorly integrated and structured legacy systems where data are not readily available (Howard et al., 2001) · Therefore, small players may still not be able to afford system integration costs (McGrath and More, 2001) · Data integration efforts do not change the business processes and internal systems of participating companies; process improvements may not occur, and data integrity problems may arise (McGrath and More, 2001) · May raise concerns about the loss of control over proprietary data (McGrath and More, 2001)

(continued)

Table 11.2
The Pros And Cons Of Hub-and-Spoke Approaches To External Systems Integration (*continued*)

Approach	Pros	Cons
Process integration approaches	· Substantially lower participation costs for all companies, since many one-to-one connections are replaced with a one-to-many connection (Markus, 2001) · May substantially lower transaction costs (Christiaanse et al., 2001) · May introduce significant supply chain-wide process improvements (Christiaanse et al., 2001)	· Leading edge technology · May not meet some members' unique requirements (Davenport et al., 2001) · Member recruitment problems: may be resisted by larger players who fear loss of competitive advantage, those who fear loss of control over proprietary data, those who are generally slow to adopt · Benefits depend on the number and intensity of a company's partner relationships
Hub-and-spoke integration approaches overall	· Industry-wide standardization efforts and one-to-many connections lower costs compared to proprietary one-to-one solutions · Particularly beneficial to small players who lack IT expertise and financial resources for systems integration efforts · Possibly enable business network-wide efficiencies and supply chain restructuring	· Involve network externalities (e.g., critical mass) and associated startup problems (Damsgaard and Lyytinen, 1997) · Standards may address the least common denominator and not address some partners' specialized needs (Damsgaard and Truex, 2000) · May be perceived as injurious to the interests of industry participants (Damsgaard, 1998)

· When will most of your customers or suppliers be able to support XML transactions?
· What level of collaboration will be expected?
· What new applications will come along to transform B2B commerce in the next three years? (Bermudez, 2001)

Many analysts have argued that public e-marketplaces have been disappointing, because the technology is immature and their capabilities have been overhyped (Braunstein, 2001). Although this is not unusual for new technologies and business arrangements, it is unknown whether or when public e-marketplaces will prosper. In the absence of certainty about which consortia, independent trading exchanges, or technologies will succeed, companies are worried about backing the wrong approach. Developing a private trading exchange is argued to provide immediate benefits from internal integration and external integration with selected current business partners, while deferring difficult decisions involving hub-and-spoke unknowns.

Control

Another reason for using a private trading exchange is to control and customize the process of dealing with key customers and suppliers. The greater control of the private exchange approach also avoids the security and confidentiality concerns evoked by public, shared-services arrangements. For example:

> Companies that use private trading exchanges prefer them for the closer online relationships they can have with preferred customers and suppliers. They also think private exchanges are more secure, because data about their trades are at less risk of being exposed to competitors if there's a security breach. Companies use private exchanges to trade proprietary information like supplier performance metrics and sales forecasts in addition to orders and invoices. Companies also use private exchanges to establish central control over purchasing through contracts with established suppliers. (Varon, n.d.)

Similarly, "[The] Dow [Company] prefers that customers use the direct connections of *MyAccount@Dow* to buy from the company (since this gives it *greater control* over the relationship)" (Davenport, Cantrell, & Brooks, 2001). Dow realizes, however, that "some customers may want to maintain only one interface between themselves and various chemical companies," and therefore also "participates in the industry consortium eMarkets Omnexus and Envera" (Davenport et al., 2001). Dow, then, views private trading exchanges and e-marketplaces as complementary options (see also Varon, 2001).

Even the strongest advocates of private trading exchanges admit that the 80–20 rule applies: only the company's most important customers and suppliers are candidates for special one-to-one treatment through a private exchange; the rank and file should be served through more cost-effective connections such as a one-way integration website or a public e-marketplace (Deloitte, 2001).

: *Multiple Marketplaces*

The consensus in industry today seems to be that a fair number of e-marketplaces will survive, and that many industries will host more than one. Because large organizations often operate in more than one industry, chances are they will be expected to interface with several e-marketplaces, in addition to special one-to-one relationships with key customers or suppliers:

> Clearly, the marketplace has entered a period of rationalizing and select-
> ing business models that work, and eliminating those that do not. Ulti-
> mately, this is likely to result in approximately 200 major surviving in-
> dustry consortiums, 500 independent eMarkets, and 2,000 private
> exchanges. More and more, these eMarket types will complement each
> other rather than compete. Large organizations with multiple business
> units will eventually participate in a portfolio of eMarkets to meet their
> varied business needs. (Brooks & Dik, 2001)

> The study [by Booz Allen Hamilton and Giga Information Group] iden-
> tified three types of B2B exchanges: private exchanges, consortia public
> exchanges and independent public exchanges. Capers said companies
> should join multiple types to create a "portfolio of exchanges" in order to
> get the best results. "All those who thought they should go to one
> exchange have found they need a portfolio," he said. (Bartlett, 2001)

The need to maintain unique systems integrations with multiple e-marketplaces will put pressure on organizations to find ways to ease the burden. Many analysts see the private trading exchange as the company's single link with all external parties, whether e-marketplaces or individual partners.

Competitive Concerns

Companies also pursue private exchanges to avoid the competitive threats associated with e-marketplaces. "In some industries . . . suppliers have been reluctant to use public marketplaces because they fear buyers will aggregate their purchases and force prices too low, squeezing their profit margins" (Varon, n.d.). And there is evidence that these fears may not be unfounded. For example, use of the Autolinkki auto parts ordering system has had un-intended negative consequences for the wholesalers that supported its de-velopment (Salmi & Tuunainen, 2001). Formerly, dealers primarily purchased from one auto parts wholesaler. But ease of ordering from multiple wholesalers through Autolinkki led to an erosion of loyalty between dealers and wholesalers. Dealers now tend to order from several wholesalers. In addition, they tend to buy more frequently, in smaller lots, leading to logistics problems for wholesalers. Consequently, the wholesalers have not been willing to cooperate on the development of a new Internet-based ordering service that would be integrated with dealers' systems. And, indeed, some of the wholesalers are building their own private trading exchanges for customers (Salmi & Tuunainen, 2001).

Other competitive concerns may center on the (perceived or actual) unequal distribution of benefits from participation in electronic marketplaces. Many electronic marketplaces involve multiple participant types, each of which may realize different benefits from participation. Some participant types may realize (or appear to) greater benefits than others, either because the e-marketplace was set up from their perspective or because of their greater market power in the network. Perceptions of others' greater benefits may be a factor in decisions not to participate or withdrawals from an e-marketplace. For instance, the EDI-Land project (van Baalen et al., 2000) involved shipping lines, container terminals, road, rail, and barge transport companies, and empty container depots. Although the project was set up from a carrier haulage perspective, some participants perceived the powerful shipping lines to be receiving a disproportionate share of the benefits. Although unequal distribution of benefits was not cited as a primary reason for defection, several participants did drop out of the EDI-Land project, detracting from the benefits other participants received (van Baalen et al., 2000).

Differential *ability* to benefit also can lead companies to avoid participating in e-marketplaces. Some companies have already achieved considerable benefits from heavy investments in IT for internal and external integration and may view their proprietary systems as a competitive advantage (Varon, 2001). These companies may perceive public e-marketplaces as "leveling the playing field" for competitors they currently outperform. Because of "critical mass" dynamics, joining an exchange may help it succeed, and not joining may contribute to its failure. Thus, companies that are performing well and have an IT-based competitive advantage may refuse to join e-marketplaces as a competitive ploy to preserve their favorable position at the expense of their competitors.

In sum, for many large companies, private trading exchanges have considerable appeal. Even when they participate in public e-marketplaces, the two types of external integration options are not seen as either-or options. As what one analyst called "the most important systems project ever" (Bermudez, 2001), private trading exchanges may support both one-to-one connections with one's closest business partners and some of the advantages of hub-and-spoke arrangements.

Counterarguments

The benefits of the private trading solution come at a high price. The most significant drawback of the private exchange is great expense for in-house system integration and maintenance. Figures 11.3 and 11.4 illustrate the extent of the integration challenge. There are indications that public e-marketplaces can provide a very significant cost advantage over private exchanges. For example, public e-marketplaces can be thought of as an application service provider for private exchange capabilities. Research on application service provision has shown that customers have experienced sizable unanticipated cost savings (Kern et al., 2001). E-marketplaces' pricing offers are starting to tempt even companies that have invested heavily in private trading changes. Hewlett Packard is an example:

> Whether or not to take advantage of those emerging services is "one of the strategic decisions a CIO needs to make," says HP's Billington. "Let's think about the most private of private exchanges, a one-on-one. When I talk to the Converge [an e-marketplace in the electronic components industry] people, they say, whatever we pay [for that capability], they'll do it for 20 percent less. We'll have to think carefully about that." (Varon, 2001)

Another company in the same industry, Solectron, estimates that connecting with the company's 8,000 suppliers and 300 customers costs between $10,000 and $500,000 *each*. (This figure does not include maintenance costs.) Consequently, public exchanges are easier and less expensive.

> [The cost of one-to-one connections] is an expense we'd like to take out of the system, and one way is to have public exchanges reduce individual connection costs. (Varon, 2001)

Because some of Solectron's key customers and suppliers show no signs of wanting to use public exchanges, however, the company is also working on various private exchange projects (Varon, 2001).

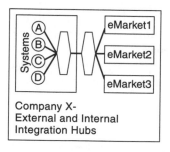

Figure 11.3. The private exchange or integration hub

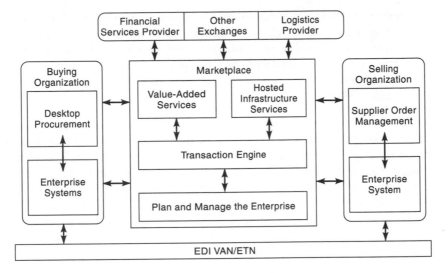

Figure 11.4. The integration points between companies

Although cost is a powerful argument in favor of public marketplaces, there are also supportive arguments based in the environment of business. The next section examines those arguments.

Arguments Favoring Hub-and-Spoke Arrangements Over Private Trading Exchanges

On the other side of the equation, the complexity and dynamism of many business relationships today weigh in for third-party hub-and-spoke arrangements as integration mechanisms. Consider, for example, two common business arrangements with important implications for system integration strategies:

- Mergers or acquisitions and divestitures.
- Multiparty business arrangements.

Mergers, Acquisitions, and Divestitures

For many companies, growth occurs primarily through mergers and acquisitions. An example is Delphi Automotive Systems, a multibillion-dollar spinoff of General Motors. Quickly integrating acquisitions and quickly divesting sold businesses is key to Delphi's strategy, and one important component of integration is IT support:

> When Delphi can quickly integrate a new unit, it doesn't have to buy temporary [IT] services from the divesting company. When Delphi can

> quickly divest a unit, it doesn't have to spend time providing IT services during the transition. Joint partnerships are also common [at Delphi]. For instance, Delphi might form a joint venture with the Chinese government to create a product for the Chinese auto market. In such cases [today], the controlling partner typically sets up a temporary IT system. (Scarlet, 2001)

Mergers and acquisitions have always been hard on systems integration efforts. Companies have been observed to spend much time and huge sums implementing ERP systems, only to abandon their investments after they merge (Larsen & Myers, 1997). A similar concern has been raised about proprietary enterprise application integration technology (Pender, 2000). If the companies to merge (or divest) had belonged to a third-party e-marketplace providing integration services prior to the merger (or divestiture), there would be no need to integrate (or dis-integrate) the partners' systems later. Thus, hub-and-spoke arrangements provide the flexibility to partner and disband quickly as business needs dictate.

Multiparty Business Arrangements

Mergers, acquisitions, and divestitures involve change in existing business relationships. Another source of dynamism in business today is the increase in multiparty business relationships. Examples of multiparty relationships include: business process outsourcing, extended supply chain relationships, and collaboration facilitation. Like mergers and divestitures, third-party relationships require systems integration, and companies find it difficult to integrate systems across multiple parties using one-to-one or one-to-many approaches.

In business process outsourcing, a company contracts with another to provide all tasks associated with a business process such as business expense processing, human resources benefits administration, manufacturing, or logistics. IT support for outsourced business processes can be handled in several ways. The contractors can use systems provided and maintained by the client companies, or the contractors can use their own systems. In the latter case, the clients usually require some degree of integration with contractors' systems.

Some business process outsourcing arrangements simplify a company's total information processing activities, for instance, outsourced manufacturing in which the marketing company purchases manufactured products from suppliers then resells them to customers in what is essentially a pair of two-way transactions. Other outsourcing arrangements markedly increase information processing complexity. For example, Cisco reportedly manufactures fewer than 40 percent of the products it sells. But Cisco never owns nor even touches many of the products it sells. Cisco takes orders and payment from customers then transmits orders and (a different) payment to suppliers, who ship the products directly to the customers. Thus, Cisco gains efficiencies by reengineering the pair of two-way transactions into an N-way transaction (see figure 11.5).

Restructuring the information flows among multiple parties in the supply chain can bring significant business benefits in terms of time or cost, but it also can create information processing nightmares.[10] Wouters, Sharman, & Wortmann (1999) noted that conventional ERP system software does not support N-way transactions without extensive customization. Software vendors have developed advanced planning and forecasting systems that massage data from parties throughout a supply chain, but these technologies do not make for seamless information processing for several reasons.

First, business partners must be willing to provide timely and accurate

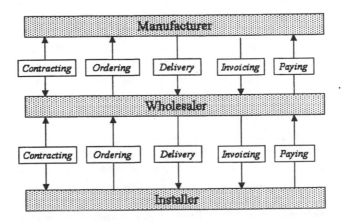

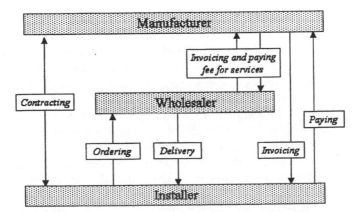

Figure 11.5. Restructuring two-way transactions as N-way transactions

information about such things as schedules, inventories, lead times, capacities, and demand, and they may not be willing to do so. For example, they may fear loss of negotiating power or loss of control over proprietary information. To overcome the reluctance to share information directly with business partners, some entrepreneurs have proposed supply chain collaboration services: business partners supply information to a trusted third party who provides the partners with an "optimized" solution, rather than the partners' raw data. Very similar to the value-added hub-and-spoke arrangements described earlier, these third parties are well positioned to provide (or coordinate) a full range of shared IT services to their participants.

A second problem with the conventional supply chain management software approach (where a company tries to collect and analyze data from its partners and partners' partners) is lack of some partners' technological readiness to provide timely and accurate information. Lacking the capabilities and expertise required for real-time data or process integration, these partners represent a weak link in any information supply chain. For instance, suppliers' inability to provide real-time product availability information was a factor in Hershey's ERP system disaster (Nelson & Ramstad, 1999). And even Cisco, vaunted for its "virtual [accounting] close," failed to anticipate the recent economic downturn, in part because the company lacked full information visibility throughout the supply chain:

> Cisco's supply chain was not quite as wired as was hyped. Cisco, Solectron and others do plenty of business with companies that still *fax* data. Some customers simply won't cater to the advanced infrastructure, making it harder to collect and aggregate information. "Cisco has hundreds of these huge customers who aren't going to do procurement the way Cisco wants them to. Things like end-to-end EDI, standards, they have to occur. Cisco's farther along, but there's a lot to do to make the infrastructure complete." (Berinato, 2001b)

In short, the business environment today is characterized by dynamism in the form of mergers and acquisition and multiparty business arrangements. It is very difficult to support these business changes quickly and inexpensively with traditional one-to-one or many-to-many systems integration strategies. By contrast, a third-party services hub would substantially reduce the time and cost associated with establishing and terminating business relationships. In addition, a third-party services hub would eliminate many of the problems created by distributing information processing activities across all parties to a multiparty business relationship.

The situation here is analogous to the problem that today's ERP systems were intended to solve. Companies embraced ERP systems because their legacy information systems, specialized in different functional areas, were unable to provide integrated information about business processes. Today, with the emphasis on supply chain management, the processes of interest cut across organizational lines. Could the solution to supply chain management problems be similar to the ERP solution in which a trusted third party processes information for the members of the chain? In addition to business benefits such as increased timeliness and reduced errors and redundancy, such a solution would significantly reduce information processing costs across the supply chain, making the chain more cost effective relative to competing chains.

Counterarguments

Despite their advantages, hub-and-spoke arrangements have a number of disadvantages that may prevent or delay their adoption. First, they have the disadvantage (shared with private trading exchanges) that they produce a common-denominator solution (Damsgaard & Truex, 2000). Companies with unique processes may find that a third-party "package" does not serve their interests well. This is not a new problem: many companies likewise found that ERP systems did not fit their unique business processes (Markus, Axline, Petrie, & Tanis, 2000). In some cases, these unique processes were legitimate requirements of business in a particular industry or true sources of competitive differentiation. In other cases, they were historical legacies that companies were unwilling to change. Similarly, participation in hub-and-spoke arrangements may require business process changes that companies are unable or unwilling to make.

Second, hub-and-spoke arrangements are more beneficial when many companies participate. The downside of this "critical mass" problem is that start-up problems are likely (Damsgaard & Lyytinen, 1997). By defecting or refusing to participate for competitive reasons, a key player may ensure that *others* do not succeed with a cooperative venture (Damsgaard, 1998), as was the case with some clusters in the EDI-Land case (van Baalen et al., 2000). With ERP systems also, change management proved to be a major challenge (Markus, Axline, et al., 2000). While managing change across organizational boundaries differs significantly from managing change inside an organization, some success stories suggest that it is possible to overcome a legacy of negative supply chain relationships (Corbett, Blackburn, & Wassenhove, 1999). For example, recognizing that the dominant firm in a supply chain had no interest in hosting a hub-and-spoke arrangement that its suppliers could use to communicate efficiently with its competitors, architects of the Taiwanese hub-and-spoke arrangement discussed earlier convinced a first-tier supplier to host the hub (Gulledge, 2001).

Despite their advantages, hub-and-spoke arrangements are immature, they suffer from critical mass problems, and they may well require new approaches to implementation and change management. Thus, their progress is likely to be slow at best, and they may entirely fail to gain acceptance. As a result, today, "private exchanges are evolving more rapidly [than hub-and-spoke arrangements] because that is taking baby steps instead of giant strides" (Varon, 2001). But if companies can overcome collective inertia and take giant strides, as they did with business process reengineering and ERP systems, the business rewards could be great. This suggests that companies need a strategy for whether and when to participate in hub-and-spoke versus private exchange or one-to-one external system integration arrangements.

: *Toward an External Systems Integration Strategy*

It may be an overstatement to assert, as others have done, that developing and implementing a strategy for external systems integration "will be the most important systems project ever" (Bermudez, 2001). There is little doubt, however, that external systems integration is an important corporate issue and that many companies do not yet have an explicit strategy for dealing with it. Few CIOs express confidence in their companies' integration strategies (Stiffler, 2001). Senior business leaders may lack the awareness that systems integration technology has important strategic implications. CIOs may "lack the power, mandate, or both necessary to take decision action" (Stiffler, 2001). Many companies appear to be approaching external systems integration as purely a technical issue; one-to-one connections are made on ad-hoc basis in response to current problems, business requests, or the desire to experiment with new technical approaches. With such an incremental approach, the likelihood of costly maintenance nightmare is great.

The alternative is to consider external systems integration as a whole and to develop a systematic approach to responding to requests for one-to-one connections. This section outlines some of the business and technical considerations involved in devising an external systems integration strategy.

Business Issues

An interesting paradox seems to be emerging in discussions of private exchanges versus public and consortium e-marketplaces. Companies tend to prefer private exchanges for dealing with their (key) customers, because this strategy gives them greatest control. But the same companies also tend to prefer e-marketplaces for dealing with their suppliers, because this strategy is more efficient and effective from an operational point of view. The conflict is clear: e-business preferences often differ on opposite sides of a transaction. As a result, glib pronouncements that following an independent e-business approach will give *us* competitive advantage may be at odds with customers' needs.

Furthermore, it is important to remember that e-marketplaces do *not* *all* aggregate and make publicly available their member companies' product catalogs and prices (Soh & Markus, 2002). Some, like Elemica, are created to facilitate transactions between pairs of partners already under contract with each other. Consequently, fears that joining an e-marketplace would result in lower prices for a company's products or other forms of competitive disadvantage may be unfounded. In addition, since hubs such as Elemica will support customizing business processes for special business partners, the hub-and-spoke arrangement may provide an umbrella under which one-to-one and one-to-many arrangements may be pursued in a cost-effective way, where they are most needed, while gaining the advantages of the hub-and-spoke arrangement with most business partners. All things considered, the hub-and-spoke arrangement deserves careful consideration in any external systems integration strategy.

The starting point for an external systems integration strategy must surely be careful analysis and segmentation of a company's customers and the technical options for serving them. For example, one consultant (Giesbers, 2001) proposed a version of the 80–20 rule: 10 percent of a company's customers make up 80 percent of a company's business and take about 20 percent of its total integration effort: these strategic customers are candidates for process sharing. Twenty-five percent of customers are repeat customers that account for 15 percent of business and consume 35 percent of integration costs. These partners are candidates for automatic information exchange (e.g., EDI over Internet). Sixty-five percent of customers are occasional customers who account for a mere 5 percent of the business; yet require 45 percent of the integration effort. For these customers, a web interface providing "self-service information access" should be sufficient (Giesbers, 2001). (Others, however, would argue for a hub-and-spoke solution for occasional customers.)

Another strategic approach segments customers into "innovative solution seekers" (in terms of a company's products), "hassle free" customers, and "lowest price buyers" (Fok, 2002). For each customer type, a "channel strategy" specifies whether each key process (marketing, sales, order entry, fulfill order, customer service) is best handled by a sales person, a customer service rep, an agent, a web site, or a customized "MyAccount@" private portal. This strategy takes into account both the attractiveness of a channel to the seller and the attractiveness of the channel to the buyer (Fok, 2002).

These recommendations suggest that several business factors should be taken into account when formulating an external systems integration strategy: the number and distribution of customers by size and profitability and customer IT readiness and preferences for type of electronic connection. They further suggest that for many companies, private exchanges, hub-and-spoke arrangements, and one-way integration approaches (e.g., self-service websites) may happily coexist, possibly all provided on a service basis by a hub operator.

Technical Issues

Despite the widespread adoption of ERP systems, few companies have achieved the degree of data and process standardization that would allow for easy external interconnection. Many companies still rely on nonstandard legacy systems for important business activities. In addition, many large companies have multiple instances of ERP systems without common data structures (e.g., product numbers, names, and descriptions) or a common process configuration. Lack of a well-integrated technology infrastructure (including important business decisions about standardized data) is a major barrier to achieving business benefits from B2B e-commerce (Meehan, 2002), and developing such an infrastructure in larger companies may be the number one priority after assessing the strategic situation.

A key consideration should be emerging data and process standards in a company's industry. Many industries (chemicals, computers and electronics, insurance, health care, etc.) have progressed far in standardization efforts, and most companies are well advised to migrate toward these standards. For example, Cardinal Health avoided difficult internal decisions about which of many different product-numbering schemes to use by adopting instead a format used by a third-party data provider (Bashein & Markus, 2000). The importance of common data standards in the retail industry is evidenced by a recent move by GlobalNetXchange and Worldwide Retail Exchange to push their catalog providers to use a common set of data standards (Meehan, 2001). In a few industries, it may be to a company's strategic advantage to maintain data formats and processes at odds with industry standard approaches, but the circumstances under which this is the best approach are likely to be special: dedicated supply chains, great market power, captive suppliers or customers, and so on. More frequently, being cost effective and easy to do business with will be more important success factors. A key implication of these observations is that a strategy for external systems integration should never be made without careful consideration of the technical and business developments *in a company's industry or industries.*

An additional technical issue is the emergence of the web services architecture (Hagel & Brown, 2001). While the web services architecture could support either one-to-one connections and private exchanges or hub-and-spoke arrangements, the web services architecture is likely to erode resistance to outsourced IT management and application services provision, thus making hub-and-spoke arrangements more attractive. To the extent that participation in hub-and-spoke arrangements is an element in a company's external systems integration plan, an important consideration is whether to customize a company's connection with particular business partners. Customization is an option within the framework provided by hubs such as Elemica, but experience shows that customization (and subsequently maintenance) is costly and may not be warranted (van Gastel, 2001). Finally, for smaller organizations, the costs involved in external (and internal) systems integration weigh heavily in favor of hub-and-spoke approaches, particularly those able to support enterprise systems capability on a hosted services basis.

: *Conclusions*

In short, companies today are spending heavily on external systems integration. Most efforts today are one-to-one in nature, in part because companies have immediate needs and in part because enabling technologies and hub-and-spoke initiatives are immature. But companies also may be pursuing dyadic interconnections because it is *the familiar thing* for technical professionals to do— it is a natural extension of today's internal systems integration paradigm and a natural extension of older EDI approaches. This observation suggests that decisions about external systems integration often may be made on the basis of technical and economic criteria with too little strategic business input, which was also the case with many companies' earlier investments in internal systems integration. In addition, the technical issues around external systems integration are abstruse and difficult for business people to grasp.

We conclude that there is considerable cause for concern about the state of external systems integration. We believe that technical issues need to be translated into business terms, combined with strategic business issues, and the whole discussion elevated to a senior executive level. In particular, decisions about external systems integration need to be made in the context of an industry-level analysis of strategic and technical trends as well as the company's own channel or supply chain strategy.

: *Notes*

We gratefully acknowledge the support of the Advanced Practices Council of SIM International, Bob Zmud, and Madeline Weiss.

1. Co-producers are similar companies that might be competitors in some areas but that occasionally work together to deliver some goods or services. Examples include aerospace companies that "subcontract" on each other's big programs and airlines in the same global service alliance.

2. Companies often use intermediaries called VANs to facilitate EDI connections with other companies, so that EDI superficially appears to be a hub-and-spoke arrangement. Separate trading partner agreements are needed for each transacting pair of companies, however, and one of the complaints about EDI by smaller companies is that they are forced to adopt different processes and transaction formats with different large partners. Therefore, EDI is better viewed as a dyadic arrangement than as a hub-and-spoke arrangement.

3. Suppliers who were still operating in a batch model caused great havoc when Hershey converted to a new integrated ERP system (Nelson & Ramstad, 1999).

4. Another interesting process integration effort is CIDX in the chemicals industry.

5. Adopting the same system is a form of de facto standardization. The approach may not work well, however, if one or both partners have heavily modified the "standard" software.

6. Others have noted similar costs. For example, RosettaNet partners have estimated

that each dyadic PIP requires one to two months to implement technically, *after* everyone agrees on the protocols and standards (Grygo, 2000).

7. The dealers' in-house systems are not configured to accept online order confirmations.

8. This distinction is important because suppliers sometimes resist participating in exchanges that are likely to result in lower prices for their products.

9. Assuming that their internal systems are integrated. If not, they may have to integrate the systems in each business unit to the electronic marketplace.

10. Information processing problems related to multiparty business relationships can occur inside large complex companies. We studied a subsidiary of a large corporation, in which the subsidiaries had independent information management regimes except for financial systems, which the parent managed for them. The subsidiary was having great difficulty integrating its sales and manufacturing systems with the financials of the parent, which was essentially providing a financial application hosting service.

▪ References

Bartlett, M. (2001) "B2B Exchanges Still Working Out Kinks-Study," *Newsbytes*, Nov. 20. Available online at: http://www.newsbytes.com.

Bashein, B. J., & M. L. Markus. (2000) *Data Warehouses: More Than Just Mining*. Morristown, NJ: Financial Executives Research Foundation.

Berinato, S. (2001a) "The Hype Stuff," *CIO Magazine*, May 15. Available online at: http://hwww.cio.com.

Berinato, S. (2001b) "What Went Wrong at Cisco," *CIO Magazine*, Aug. 1. Available online at: http://www.cio.com.

Bermudez, J. (2001) "Private Trading Exchanges: The Cornerstone for $5.7T in B2B Commerce," *AMR Research Central—Outlook*. Available online at: http://www.amrresearch.com/outlook/.

Braunstein, S. (2001) "Reconsider Online Marketplaces," *CIO Magazine*, Oct. 19. Available online at: http://www.cio.com.

Brooks, J., & R. Dik. (2001) B2B eMarkets: The Smart Path Forward. *Accenture Institute for Strategic Change,* Boston, MA.

Chen, A. (2000) "Getting to XML: The New B2B Lingua Franca Will Need to Live With EDI. Here's How to Mix the Two," *eWeek*, Aug. 7. Available online at: http://www.zdnet.com/eWeek/.

Christiaanse, E., R. Sinnecker, & M. Mossinkoff. (2001) "The Impacts of B2B Exchanges on Brick and Mortar Intermediaries: The Elemica Case," *Proceeding of The 9th European Conference on Information Systems,* 422–31. Bled, Slovenia.

Clark, T. H., & J. L. McKenney. (1995) *Procter & Gamble: Improving Consumer Value Through Process Redesign*. Boston, MA: Harvard Business School Press.

Corbett, C. J., J. D. Blackburn, & L.N.V. Wassenhove. (1999) "Case Study Partnerships To Improve Supply Chains," *Sloan Management Review*, Summer, 71–82.

Damsgaard, J. (1998) "Electronic Markets in Hong Kong's Air Cargo Community: Thanks, But No Thanks," *Electronic Markets*, 8(3), 46–7.

Damsgaard, J., & K. Lyytinen. (1997) "Hong Kong's EDI Bandwagon: Derailed or on the Right Track?" In T. McMaster, E. Mumford, B. Swanson, B. Warboys, & D.

Wastell (Eds.), *Facilitating Technology Transfer Through Partnership: Learning from Practice and Research*, 39–63. London: Chapman and Hall.

Damsgaard, J., & D. Truex. (2000) "Binary Trading Relations and the Limits of EDI Standards: The Procrustean Bed of Standards," *European Journal of Information Systems*, 9(3), 173–88.

Dan, A., D. M. Dias, R. Kearney, T. C. Lau, T. N. Nguyen, F. N. Parr, M. W. Sachs, & H. H. Shaikh. (2001) "Business-to-Business Integration With tpaML and a Business-to-Business Protocol Framework," *IBM Systems Journal*, 40(1), 68–90.

Davenport, T. H., S. Cantrell, & J. D. Brooks. (2001) "The Dynamics of eCommerce Networks," *Accenture Institute for Strategic Change*, Cambridge, MA. Available online at: http://www.line56.com/research/default.asp.

Deloitte, C. (2001) "Collaborative Commerce: Going Private To Get Results," *Deloitte Consulting*. Available online at: http://www.dc.com.

Dobrin, D. (2000) "The Collaborative Edge: B2B Fax and Other Tales of Global Gain," *CIO Magazine*, Nov. 1 Available online at: http://www.cio.com.

Farhoomand, A., & M. McCauley. (2001) "TradeCard: Building a Global Trading Electronic Payment System," *Communications of the AIS*, 7(Oct.), Article 18. Available online at: http://cais.aisnet.org.

Fok, J. (2002) "eBizz@DSM," Presentation given at the Elemica Global Conference, Brussels, Belgium.

Fontanella, J. (2001) "Building The Case For the Private Trading Exchange," *AMR Research*. Available online at: http://www.amrresearch.com/preview/010716alert186 .htm.

Giesbers, J. (2001) "Baan Experiences," Presentation at the 14th Bled Electronic Commerce Conference: e-Everything: e-Commerce, e-Government, e-Household, e-Democracy, Bled, Slovenia.

Grygo, E. (2000) "RosettaNet Marks Red-Letter Day," *InfoWorld*. Available online at: http://www.inforld.com.

Gulledge, T. (2001) "An Industry-Driven Approach to International e-Business Cooperation," *Proceedings of eBusiness and eWork 2001*, Venice, Italy, available on CD-ROM.

Hagel, J. I., & J. S. Brown. (2001) "Your Next IT Strategy," *Harvard Business Review*, (Oct.), 105–13.

Hammer, M. (1990) "Reengineering Work: Don't Automate, Obliterate," *Harvard Business Review*, 70(4), 104–12.

Harreld, H. (2001) "Companies Report Growing Demand For Hosted e-Biz Apps," *Computerworld*, Nov. 13. Available online at: http://www.computerworld.com.

Heath, P. (2001) "Serving All Parties in the Alliance," *Solutions@SITA*. Available online at: http://www.sita.int,

Howard, M., R. Vidgen, P. Powell, & A. Graves. (2001) "Planning for IS Related Industry Transformation: The Case of the 3DayCar," *Proceedings of the 9th European Conference on Information Systems*, 433–42. Bled, Slovenia.

Iacovou, C. L., I. Benbasat, & A. S. Dexter. (1995) "Electronic Data Interchange and Small Organizations: Adoption and Impact of Technology," *MIS Quarterly*, 19(4), 465–85.

Kern, T., M. Lacity, L. Willcocks, & R. Zuiderwijk. (2001) "ASP Market-Space Report 2001: Mastering the Customers' Expectations," *CMG Beneluz*.

Koch, C. (2000) "Four Strategies: The Options for Web-enabling Your Supply Chain

Are Beginning To Emerge. It's Time To Choose," *CIO Magazine*, Oct. 1. Available online at: http://www.cio.com.

Larsen, M. A., & M. D. Myers. (1997) "BPR Success or Failure? A Business Process Reengineering Model in the Financial Services Industry," *Proceedings of the International Conference on Information Systems*, 367–82. Atlanta, GA.

Markus, M. L. (2000) "Paradigm Shifts-E-Business and Business/Systems Integration. *Communications of the ACM*, 4(10). Available online at: http://cais.aisnet.org.

Markus, M. L. (2001) *Process Integration in the Chemical Industry*. Working paper, available from the author.

Markus, M. L., S. Axline, D. Petrie, & C. Tanis. (2000) "Learning From Adopters' Experiences With ERP—Successes and Problems," *Journal of Information Technology*, 15(4), 245–65.

Markus, M. L., & C. Soh. (2001) *A Strategic Vantage on B2B e-Marketplaces. City University of Hong Kong, Hong Kong*. Working paper, available from the first author.

Markus, M. L., C. Tanis, & P.C.V. Fenema. (2000) "Multisite ERP Implementations," *Communications of the ACM*, 43(3), 42–6.

Mayor, T. (2001) "Back to the Drawing Board," *CIO Magazine*, Aug. 1. Available online at: http://www.cio.com.

McGrath, G. M., & E. More. (2001) "Data Integration Along the Healthcare Supply Chain: The Pharmaceutical Extranet Gateway Project," *Proceedings of The 34th Annual Hawaii International Conference on Systems Sciences*. Maui, Hawaii, available on CD-ROM.

Meehan, M. (2001) "Rival Retail Exchanges Working On Common Standards," *Computerworld*, Nov. 21. Available online at: http://www.computerworld.com.

Meehan, M. (2002) "Users Say Lack of IT Integration Hurts B2B," *Computerworld*, Jan. 1. Available online at: http://www.computerworld.com.

More, E., & M. McGrath. (2000) "Health and Industry Collaboration: The PeCC Story," *Commonwealth of Australia*.

Mullin, R. (2001) "Exchanges Weigh In on ERP Link-Ups," *Chemical Week*, Jan. 31, 32.

Nelson, E., & E. Ramstad. (1999) "Hershey's Biggest Dud Is Its New Computer System," *The Wall Street Journal*, Oct. 29, 1.

Pender, L. (2000) "Enterprise Application Integration—Damned If You Do . . . ," *CIO Magazine*, Sept. 15. Available online at: http://www.cio.com.

Petit, B. (2001) Elemica. Presentation given in Amsterdam, The Netherlands.

Plumtree Software, I. (2000) XML and Corporate Portals—Technical White Paper.

Radjou, N. (2001) "SAP Leads Race to Build Adaptive Supply Nets," *Forrester Research, Inc.*, Cambridge, MA. Available online at: http://www.forrester.com.

Rapoza, J. (2000) "XML Schema," *eWeek*, Dec. 5. Available online at: http://www.zdnet.com/eWeek/.

RosettaNet (2001) "Case Study: Arrow and UTEX Replace EDI-Based Purchase Order Process With RosettaNet Standards," *RosettaNet*, Santa Ana, CA. Available online at: http://www.rosettanet.org.

Salmi, H., & V. K. Tuunainen. (2001) "Diffusion of Electronic Business in Networks—Case Autolinkki Teaching Case," *Proceedings of the Fourteenth Bled Electronic Commerce Conference*, Bled, Slovenia, on CD-ROM.

Scarlet, S. D. (2001) "More Than the Sum of Its Parts," *CIO Magazine*, Apr. 15. Available online at: http://www.cio.com.

Soh, C., & M. L. Markus. (2002) *A Strategic Vantage on B2B e-Marketplaces*. Working paper, available from the second author.

Stackpole, B. (2000) "Tag, You're It!," *CIO Magazine*, Mar. 15. Available online at: http://www.cio.com.

Stiffler, D. (2001) "Is Integration a Strategic Approach or Tactical Plan?" *AMR Outlook*. Available online at: http://www.amrresearch.com,

Van Baalen, P., M. van Oosterhout, Y.-H. Tan, & E. van Heck. (2000)*Dynamics in Setting Up an EDI Community*. Delft, Netherlands: Eburon Publishers.

Van Gastel, A. (2001) "Small e With a Big Impact—BASF Aktiengesellshaft. *Presentation at the Elemica Global Conference,* Brussels, Belgium. Available online at: http://www.elemica.com/home; shbrus—conf.jsp.

Varon, E. (2001) "What You Need to Know About Public and Private Exchanges," *CIO Magazine*, Sept. 1. Available online at: http://www.cio.com,

Varon, E. (n.d.) "The ABCs of B2B," *CIO Magazine*. Available online at: http://www.cio.com,

Voigt, B. (2001) "Using Information Technology to Build Global Alliance," *Presentation given at the Fourteenth Bled Electronic Commerce Conference,* Bled, Slovenia.

Wouters, M.J.F., G. J. Sharman, & H. C. Wortmann. (1999) "Reconstructing the Sales and Fulfillment Cycle to Create Supply Chain Differentiation," *International Journal of Logistics Management,* 10(2), 83–98.

Michael J. Earl

Learning and Earning From E-Commerce

: Chapter Summary

1. As the hype has receded, the first era of e-commerce can be seen to have been a period of rapid and dramatic learning.
2. Dot-coms quickly found out that a sound business model, a realistic business plan, reliable operations, and assiduous management were still necessary in the battle for survival and profitability.
3. Incumbent companies, by contrast, could not dismiss e-commerce as a mere dot-com bubble.
4. New business threats and opportunities were real and, while by 2001, venture capital might have more or less dried up for dot-com start-ups, corporate capital investment continued to be allocated to those e-business projects that made good defensive or offensive business sense.
5. Several IT departments that had been very active in building e-commerce projects were reflecting on their own learning experiences and realizing, perhaps, that four very worthwhile practices had emerged. These practices address four central and classical questions of IT management:
   1. strategic information systems planning
   2. IT architecture planning
   3. managing IT-user relationships
   4. systems development methodology
6. They not only made sense in the frenetic and exciting context of e-commerce, they also could be beneficial in the more mainstream and staid context of traditional IT activities.

: Problem

The discontinuity of e-commerce has left firms with the promise of four IT management practices that they should capture, retain, and develop—and certainly not dismiss as freak practices of a dizzy time. Indeed, they might elevate them to the level of principles. These practices address four central and classical questions of IT management:

1. strategic information systems planning
2. IT architecture planning

3. managing IT-user relationships
4. systems development methodology

All four are important components of Luftman's Strategic Alignment Maturity Assessment.

⦂ *Evidence?*

In 2000, Earl and Khan studied twenty-four companies in the United States and the United Kingdom to explore how IT departments were responding to the challenges of e-commerce. The sample included boutique e-commerce consultancies, dot-com start-ups, e-commerce spinoffs, and large incumbents. The unit of analysis was the IT unit, team, or department specifically and wholly engaged on e-commerce. Typically, interviews were conducted with the IT manager, the CEO or COO, and one other executive. Where they existed, documents on e-commerce practices were collected. In addition, deeper case study research was done in one dot-com, one spinoff, and one incumbent. Seven beliefs on how e-commerce was changing IT were discerned in these companies and seven new practices documented and explained. The authors proposed that four of these were significant not only in the context of e-commerce but also across IT activities more widely.

Subsequent discussions with companies suggest that two of these—three-tier architecture and use of multidisciplinary teams—are recognized as key learnings and are being adopted more widely. The other two—rolling IT plans and the new venture development life cycle—could offer equal promise.

⦂ *Genesis*

In the heady days of e-commerce, the pressure was on speed and flexibility. Getting new web-based products, services, and channels to market quickly seemed to be critical in the quest for first mover advantages, grabbing customer share and brand recognition, attracting further capital, and winning races to learn. Second, as learning occurred, adaptability and flexibility were key. "Launch and learn" were followed by "respond and revise." So time replaced cost as the currency of IT and entrepreneurialism and fun displaced formality and structure. In particular, conventional information systems planning processes were challenged. Rolling IT plans were one interesting response to this new context.

Then, as e-commerce became serious, another realization occurred; IT in many senses was the business. If the system went down, the channel was down and thus the product was unavailable and the customer may have switched to another provider. The operational mantra was 24-7. And, if business grew, the system and infrastructure had to be scalable, preferably in a seamless way. So speed and responsiveness had to coexist with robustness and scalability—two opposites seen by most IT professionals in the past as tradeoffs. Three-tier architecture was a response to these pressures.

At the same time, as systems development was becoming business development and as in such a fast changing, quick response world, it was absurd to allocate capital through conventional IT budgeting processes (whether annual budgets, IT project approvals, or IT steering committees), a new more holistic and entrepreneurial paradigm was required for systems development and acquisition. Earl and Khan (2001) detected a new approach emerging, one that planned, controlled, and organized system development more like new product development or, especially from a financing viewpoint, like venture capital. Earl and Khan "codified" and labeled this as the new venture development life cycle. In other words, IT projects were no longer just IT projects; they were how the business got built or developed.

For this reason, "business people" had to work with "IT people" (and vice versa!)—throughout the new venture development life cycle. Indeed, this union was happening and, often, whether by dress, task, location, language, or title, one could not detect who was "from the business" and who was "from IT." True multidisciplinary teams had formed; indeed, the new venture development life cycle depended on this.

So, two of our four principles addressed the issue of "speed versus robustness." Two also addressed the issue of "IT versus the business."

: Rolling IT Plans

The typical IT plan (in effect, a business development plan) in e-commerce operations comprises a portfolio of perhaps six projects with a time horizon of one to three months. In the archetypal case, the portfolio is reviewed weekly by the executive team and some projects fall off the list as they are completed or killed and others enter the list. Those in active phase are described and analysed in more detail in terms of goals, progress and problems. Those in scoping phase are described in outline and week by week take on more shape. Those that are "scaling up" or infrastructure projects may be handed over to the mainstream IT department or supplier. Typically, there are more candidate projects than those accepted onto the plan.

Accounting practitioners and scholars will see here similarities with rolling budgets. These are short-term; more detailed in the period ahead than in subsequent periods, and are continuously reviewed. Rolling budgets are a response to uncertain and volatile times. Likewise, rolling IT plans recognize the inherent uncertainty and volatility of e-commerce to date.

Most of our ideas and practices in IT strategic planning or IT strategy formulation were shaped by assumptions of environmental stability, careful and rational resource allocation, long and linear IT applications, and infrastructure development and acquisition processes, and a wider organizational context of long range or multiyear business strategic planning with occasional, probably annual, reviews. Management consultants and IT providers have developed "strategic information systems planning" methodologies, firms have evolved their own apparatus, and researchers have examined the character and outcomes of these different approaches (Segars & Grover, 1999; Earl, 1993). Rolling IT plans, however, are a departure from the traditions that evolved over the last twenty years.

There are several identifying characteristics of rolling IT planning. It is short-term, involves frequent reviews, and is executed by executive teams (including IT personnel) rather than by special procedures or committees. The outcome—or plan—is an active portfolio of timeboxed projects. It is not, however, chaotic. As one executive put it (in a research interview), "The vision is constant, but plans change and details drive tactics." An idealized rolling plan is depicted in table 12.1. In some ways, rolling IT planning is an entrepreneurial and strategy by doing operationalization of what I, in my study of conventional strategic IT planning (1993), labeled the organizational approach—or, more colloquially, "themes with teams." IT strategy may be framed by a business vision or business strategic analysis, but it becomes quite evolutionary and emergent over time. In particular, it is responsive to new ideas and signals from daily business operations and the marketplace. And it is a sort of middle ground approach to strategy in which strategic intent and business planning merge with project planning and control.

These qualities would seem to fit the "launch and learn" and entrepreneurial character of the first term of e-commerce. They also, however, are attractive properties of strategic IT planning more generically. After all, few businesses operate in certain and stable environments. Traditional IT time horizons have been rather lengthy, IT departments are generally not highly regarded for their responsiveness, many IT strategies do not get implemented, and too often IT planning is driven by and owned by the IT function, not the business.

There is much good and common sense in the concept of rolling IT planning. Significantly, it probably requires adoption of the principle of

Table 12.1
An Idealized Rolling Plan

Week 1	Weeks 2–4	Weeks 5–13
Completions, quick fixes, and scoping studies	Detailed project activity schedule	Rough cut schedules and candidate projects

three-tier architecture, fits well with the new venture development life cycle, and would benefit from the use of multidisciplinary teams.

⦂   *Three-Tier Architecture*

Architecture is the conceptual framework for IT infrastructure. Its main purpose is to strive for and satisfy the objectives of systems integration, technology interoperability, platform reliability, application maintainability, and IT cost management. Architecture therefore guides technical decisions and supplier choices on computing configurations, telecommunications topologies, data standards and schemas, and application interdependencies and interfaces.

Architecture planning is helped if overarching business principles can be agreed. Indeed, they are required not only to drive architecture, but also to justify and defend it. Weill and Broadbent (1998) advocate the crafting of maxims at the corporate or enterprise level to drive a more strategic and enabling architecture rather than doing deals and employing tactical sophistry, which tends to end up producing an architecture supportive of the business, but only in a short-term, business as usual fashion.

This grand view of architecture, however, which I also have espoused (1989), does face two recurring problems. The first is that it works better under conditions of business certainty, which in reality is rare. This is why the "maxims" versus "deals" school becomes expressed in organizational politics as "blue sky techies" versus "myopic business managers." The second is that it works better under conditions of technological certainty. Unfortunately, IT—for the last twenty years at least—has been far from certain; new technologies and techniques are emerging and being invented continuously. This is why most architecture plans end up being fine charts on the wall or bottom drawer pictures but only an approximation of reality.

In e-commerce to date, both business certainty and technological certainty have been conspicuously lacking. The combination of seeking early mover advantages, of discovering customer or user online attitudes and behaviors, of experimenting with products and services, and of exploring new business models means that website or user "front-end" design and building have to be rapid, adaptable, both live and experimental, and sometimes disposable. The fact that applications development, communications, data storage, and information processing technologies both emerge and change quickly means that technology platforms are far from constant as well. In 2000, for example, companies studied by Earl and Khan (2001) were developing and launching new e-commerce channels via mobile (cell) devices or interactive digital TV to complement PC-based propositions in three or four elapsed months.

By contrast, most e-businesses also have the need, as discussed earlier, for large-scale, robust, efficient, and scalable transaction processing systems, data warehouses, and networking. Furthermore, incumbent companies will have trusted legacy systems that they wish to build on and certainly not abandon.

The emerging approach to resolving the tension between quick-build and volatile front-end applications and robust and scalable back-end foundations is three-tier architecture (fig. 12.1). In essence, this is the pursuit of both speed and stability. Tier one of three-tier architecture comprises the front-end web-based/portal/user view of the product. Tier three comprises the back-end engines of IT and the middle tier comprises middleware and technical wrapping, which translates data messages between the two. Essentially, the middle layer stores processing logic, data objects (data handling routines), and translation rules.

The endowment from this e-commerce discovery of three-tier architecture is that it provides a more practical and sustainable praxis than our former ideas. All firms and all IT departments face some degree of business and technological uncertainty and architecture planners always were challenged by the speed and flexibility need versus the robust and efficiency need. The three-tier model has the potential to make IT architecture a practical reality. Furthermore, it is simple to understand and allows firms to capitalize on their legacy systems. It has promise for "old" IT as much as "new" IT.

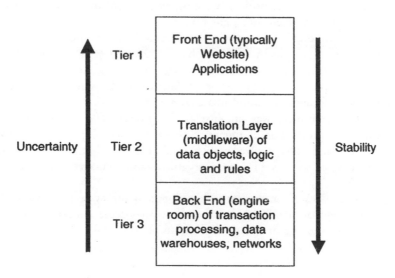

Figure 12.1. Three-tier architecture

⁝   *New Venture Development Life Cycle*

Students of IT, as well as trainee systems analysts, are brought up on the waterfall method of systems development, a sequential approach that begins with a feasibility study, moves through systems analysis, system design, programming, testing, conversion, and implementation, and concludes with ongoing maintenance. The method is formal and logical; it provides a rigorous structure and suggests review points for project planning and control. Both universal and proprietary versions of this systems development method exist and are widely used.

In the world of e-commerce, however, Earl and Khan found that it was perceived to be "too linear," "it doesn't appeal to creative designers," "it takes too long," and "it can't cope with continuous ideas and change." Even more iterative and evolutionary versions of the waterfall method were perceived to be too rigid.

What is emerging in several IT units devoted to e-commerce is quite a new, creative, yet also disciplined methodology. Earl and Khan codified it and labeled it the new venture development life cycle, because it is so akin to the venture capital industry's approach to business development. It has three distinguishing characteristics.

First, it uses aggressive "time-boxing." Many organizations reported that they would undertake e-commerce development projects only if they could complete them in three months or less. Some wanted to reduce the elapsed time of any stage to one month or less. In the spirit of time as currency, time to market was the project planning and control metric and a project was boxed or segmented into tight time periods.

Second, funding of e-commerce projects followed a three stage process: fund an idea development scoping phase, similar to seed corn in venture capital finance; if the idea was then judged attractive, fund a design and experimental phase, akin to first stage finance; if the signals are positive, fund the development or build phase, similar to second stage finance.

Third, the project was not just an IT project. The analogy is much more like new product development or new venture development. Therefore, all personnel and skills involved—such as advertising, fulfilment, and alliance management as well as IT—were organized and managed through these three stages.

So what does the new venture development life cycle really look like? Earl and Khan originally labeled the three phases the concept phase, the design phase, and the first-stage-application phase.

Concept Phase

In the concept phase, a team spends one or two days (or a week to a month for larger projects) brainstorming, storyboarding, and rapid prototyping. The idea is to develop a business or product idea and visualize it as a simple system. The team typically comprises business strategists, commercial managers, software developers, graphics and site-navigation designers, modelers, and storyboarders. Any or all may contribute to conceptual development.

Design Phase

The design phase typically lasts from one week to one month and produces a richer and more robust design. Graphics and navigation designers take centre stage here, along with modelers and software developers. Usability and customer-interaction tests are important in the design phase.

First-Stage-Application Phase

In this stage, which can last from one to three months, technology specialists attempt to make the application robust. They even may throw away the prototype from the design stage and start over.

Although the respondents did not cite a particular methodology for systems development, we inferred the basis of a framework to capture the new-venture approach (fig 12.2). Our ideal model adds a review point at the end of each stage and renames the stages brainstorming, designing, and building—or to borrow from organizational development "storming, forming, and norming."

In all sorts of applications development, there lurks a tension between formal methodology and the evolutionary approach. When customers or

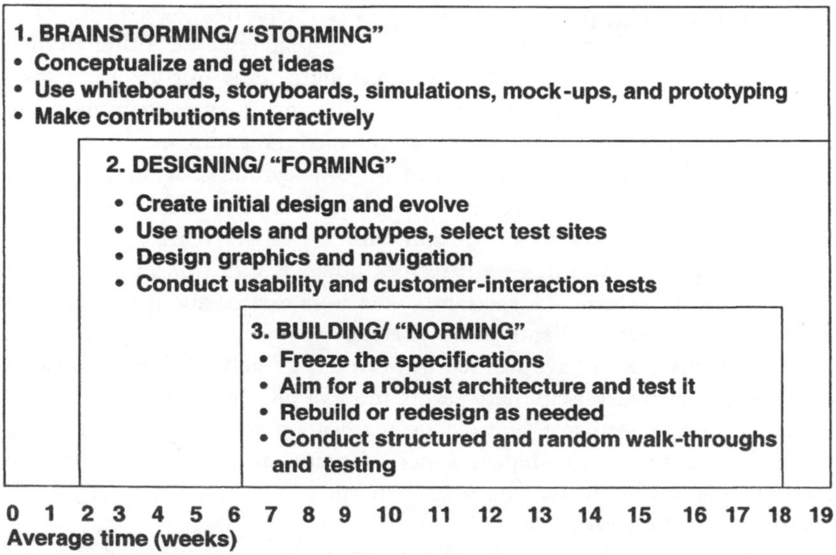

1. BRAINSTORMING/ "STORMING"
- Conceptualize and get ideas
- Use whiteboards, storyboards, simulations, mock-ups, and prototyping
- Make contributions interactively

   2. DESIGNING/ "FORMING"
- Create initial design and evolve
- Use models and prototypes, select test sites
- Design graphics and navigation
- Conduct usability and customer-interaction tests

      3. BUILDING/ "NORMING"
- Freeze the specifications
- Aim for a robust architecture and test it
- Rebuild or redesign as needed
- Conduct structured and random walk-throughs and testing

0 1 2 3 4 5 6 7 8 9 10 11 12 13 14 15 16 17 18 19
Average time (weeks)

Figure 12.2. The new-venture approach to IT development

users hear that a systems project will take one, two or three years they can't believe that IT can be such a brake on business change. When they are confronted by the rigorous discipline of the waterfall method, they fear that procedure and inflexibility will drive out learning and adaptation. Yet, quite often when offered a prototyping approach instead, they hesitate over trialing a rough and ready system live and "in the field." And IT professionals worry that prototypes become too embedded and the business becomes dependent upon a fragile foundation. Both users and IT professionals also know that sometimes a development project doesn't get killed when it should.

The new venture development life cycle thus has merit beyond e-commerce applications. It embraces timeboxing and reducing time to market. It provides more serious fund/stop funding decision points. It allows an evolution from loose exploration of an idea through iterative design to tight implementation. Above all, perhaps, it provides a framework more in tune with the idea of pursuing "business change" projects rather than "IT" projects (Earl, 1992).

: Multidisciplinary Teams

The traditional IT department is built around specialist jobs. A typical hierarchy consists of application programmers, systems programmers, systems analysts, and project leaders. Each role is clearly defined, and the demarcation between tasks is relatively unambiguous.

In IT units engaged in e-commerce, software developers, technology experts, graphics designers, business strategists, usability engineers, navigation designers, marketing specialists, modelers, and media designers work collaboratively—especially in the brainstorming and design phases. Although they bring their own expertise, they often contribute ideas outside their own speciality. Demarcation lines are porous, and anyone may contribute to the system's concept and design if the ideas enhance the endeavor.

Earl and Khan found one project in which television program producers worked alongside website developers, graphics designers, and legacy system developers. The CIO of an incumbent business observed that "even marketing managers are working with techies now." A CEO of an established dot-com aimed to recruit IT specialists who were excited about the business proposition and were evidently team players.

IT executives who have worked in both old IT and e-IT seem to value the principle of multidisciplinary teams most of all. To ensure that it continues as their e-commerce ventures grow, they are encouraging their peers in old IT departments to adopt it. Once advocated as a method to cross the user-versus-specialist divide, the team concept has emerged naturally from the dynamics of e-commerce.

The essence of the multidisciplinary principle is collaboration and colocation. In addition to having sound technical skills, IT professionals engaged in e-commerce must like the excitement of business development. Strategists, marketing executives, marketing and creative personnel, and technologists join forces. There is little concern over segregating IT skill sets. The linguistic apartheid of "business" versus "IT" becomes obsolete for several possible reasons. First, some of the new skills are not yet codified into specialist jobs. Second, the various personnel typically are co-located in a small space, and the frantic context of e-commerce deliberately encourages collaboration. And, finally, because systems development is business development, interdependence is logical. Once managers see the advantages of multidisciplinary teamwork, they are determined to preserve it and to transfer it into conventional IT units.

Co-location in IT projects was advocated by Bensaou and Earl (1998), drawing on their research in Japanese companies. Business-IT partnership often has been advocated (Henderson, 1989). Use of multidisciplinary teams is not a new idea either and was tentatively suggested for building "strategic information systems" (Ives & Vitale, 1996). Perhaps what e-commerce has taught us is that these three organizational goals are possible. If seeing or experiencing is believing, then multidisciplinary teams may prove to be the most important legacy of all.

⁞ *Pulling Four Ideas Together*

There is a thread or logic that runs across these four ideas (fig. 12.3). Not only do these principles address the "speed versus robustness" challenge and the eternal tension of "IT versus the business," they possibly are independent.

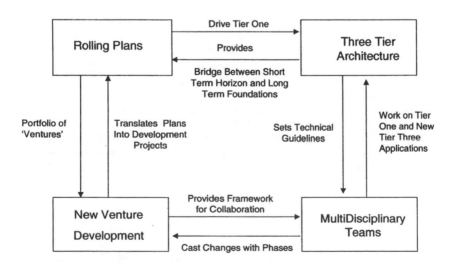

Figure 12.3. Four new principles for IT

Each, as figure 12.3 implies, works better because there are other consistent principles at work.

Rolling plans could conflict with most traditional ideas of IT architecture, but the three-tier concept makes them feasible. The new venture development cycle both responds to rolling plans and provides a structure to deliver systems in an appropriate timeframe. New venture development implies the use of multidisciplinary teams, but the cast can change with each phase. More technically specialist teams can work on the middle and legacy back end layers of three-tier architecture, but multidisciplinary teams work on tier one and new tier three applications—within a set of technical guidelines.

Of course, both research and development are required to advance and operationalize these ideas. It is timely, however, to reflect on IT lessons learned from e-commerce and these four principles are worth capturing for IT activity in general.

⫶ References

Bensaou, M., & M. J. Earl. (1998) "The Right Mindset for Managing IT," *Harvard Business Review,* 76(5), 118–28.

Earl, M. J. (1989) *Management Strategies for Information Technology.* Hemel Hempstead, UK: Prentice Hall.

Earl, M. J. (1992) "Putting IT in Its Place: A Polemic for the Nineties," *Journal of Information Technology,* 17 (July), 100–108.

Earl, M. J. (1993) "Experiences in Strategic Information Systems Planning," *MIS Quarterly,* 17(1), 1–24.

Earl, M. J., & B. Khan. (2001) "E-Commerce is Changing the Face of IT," *Sloan Management Review,* 43(1), 64–72.

Henderson. J. C. (1989) "Building and Sustaining Partnership Between Line and I/S Managers," *CISR Working Paper, No.195.* Center for Information Systems Research, Massachusetts Institute of Technology, Cambridge, MA.

Ives, B., & M. Vitale. (1996) "Strategic Information Systems: Some Organization Design Considerations," in M. J. Earl (Ed.), *Information Management: The Organizational Dimension,* 105–20. New York: Oxford University Press.

Segars, A., & V. Grover. (1999) "Profiles of Strategic Information Systems Planning," *Information Systems Research,* 10(3), 199–232.

Weill, P., & M. Broadbent. (1998) *Leveraging the New Infrastructure: How Market Leaders Capitalize on Information Technology.* Boston, MA: Harvard Business School Press.

Thomas H. Davenport

Information, Strategy, and Attention

: *Chapter Summary*

1. Any ambitious initiative in business needs substantial attention from substantial people over substantial periods of time. Whereas humanity's information base is growing by revolutionary leaps and bounds, the ability of individual humans to absorb that knowledge has changed little if at all. This situation leads to an obvious need for not more information but, rather, more human attention—with no obvious way to fill it!

2. Technology itself can absorb a huge amount of attention. In the vast majority of situations, however, it's what you do with information technology that brings productivity and competitive advantage, not the attributes of the technology itself. From an attention management standpoint, then, it's important to make technology as common and as generic as possible.

3. New technologies will continue to emerge, and they'll offer new features that promise to make our information environments better. But, if the past is any indication, they'll create an even greater need for attention.

4. In addition to searching, the progressive organization would educate its users in determining what information and knowledge they really need relative to their jobs. Education would also be provided on how to set up an effective information environment that encompasses e-mail, important information on the Internet and intranets, paper information, filing structures, and archiving techniques.

5. The management of attention in business is an entirely new subject. As the amount of information and knowledge that flows through organizations continues to grow, there is little doubt that creative new methods for allocating and even growing it will develop.

6. By devoting some attention to attention, organizations can begin to focus on the information and knowledge that really matters to their success. They won't overlook important information that can put them out of business. They won't waste organizational and individual attention on irrelevant topics that have no bearing on their work.

: *Introduction*

In the early years of the information age—that is, up until the development and widespread use of the Internet—most information strategies made an assumption of scarcity of information and difficulty of access to it. The aim was often to work at delivering as much information as possible to decision makers. Much emphasis was put on accumulating data, information, and later knowledge in online repositories and warehouses. Substantial resources were devoted to implementing applications that would produce more and better transaction data on how the business was performing. Information was viewed as so rare and valuable that companies were encouraged to capture and sell their "information exhaust" (Davis & Davidson, 1991).

But information scarcity is no longer the hallmark of today's business environment. Consider the 1.6 trillion pieces of paper that circulate through U.S. offices each year—up a third during the last decade (American Forest and Paper Association, 2001). If you are a contrarian who believes that paper is obsolete, think of the more than 200 messages the average U.S. white-collar worker sends and receives each day (Institute for the Future, 1998). Try viewing the over two billion web pages in the world, a large chunk of which can't even be found with the best search engine. Until recently, the amount of Internet traffic was doubling about every 100 days (U.S. Department of Commerce, 1998). Non-Internet online information comprised 11,339 distinct electronic databases on the market, up from 301 in 1975 (Outsell, 2000a). Within companies, the average firm will store 120 terabytes (each amounting to 38 miles of full file cabinets) by 2004, according to Gartner Group (2001).

Outside of the business world in the general society, the volume of information is similarly overwhelming. Think about all the text in those 60,000 new books that spew out of American presses every year, or the more than 300,000 worldwide. Think about the more than 18,000 magazines published in the United States alone in 1998—up almost 600 from the year before—with more than 225 billion pages of editorial content. There were more than 20 billion pages of magazine editorial content about food and nutrition alone! ("The Magazine Handbook," 1999). Try reading one of the 400,000 scholarly journals published around the world annually. If you prefer lighter reading, peruse some of the 15 billion catalogs delivered to U.S. homes in 1999, or the 87.2 billion pieces of direct mail that reached American mailboxes in 1998 (Elliott, 1999; Weinbach, 1999). If you prefer less textual entertainment, you have 80 percent more feature films to watch today than were released in 1990.

Of course, information doesn't only arrive in the form of words and pictures. Every new product or business offering is a form of information. In the grocery store during the 1990s, for example, there were over 15,000 new products introduced each year ("Decline in New Product Introductions," 1997). The average grocery store stocks about 40,000 different items or SKUs. How do they get purchased when the average household buys only 150 SKUs per year? How does a single brand of salsa get much mental focus from consumers when there are over 200 available?

: *The Need for Attention*

Obviously, we can't easily comprehend these quantities of information and stimuli of various sorts. Although humanity's information base is growing by revolutionary leaps and bounds, the ability of individual humans to absorb that knowledge has changed little if at all. This situation leads to an obvious need for not more information but, rather, more human attention—with no obvious way to fill it! From an organizational standpoint, the only way to get more attention is to hire more people, a step that many companies seem reluctant to take. Humans may be able to marginally increase their attentive capability, but few undertake such efforts. We are left with a radical imbalance of business and societal information over attention. Our information strategies must therefore reflect this imbalance.

At earlier stages of the information revolution, we could continue to point to the need for more and better technologies as the primary shortcoming in managing information effectively. "Access to information" was the rallying cry that justified the expenditure of trillions of dollars on hardware, software, and telecommunications. But we've won the technology war. New technologies will continue to emerge, and they'll offer nifty new features that promise to make our information environments better. But if the past is any indication, they'll create an even greater need for attention. Computer scientists have talked about "filters" and "agents" for decades now, but any progress in this direction has been woefully outstripped by progress at information distribution and access.

What business rationale is there for doing something about attention? It's difficult to measure, but how about the lost ability to focus on what's really important to your organization or your job? With 200 or so messages zinging by every day, it's undoubtedly difficult to catch everything that's important. To perceive a signal from the business and competitive environment, we must be attuned to it. If we believe that humans work best when they have some time to reflect before acting, we need to assess how much room there is for concerted attention and reflection. There can't be much reflecting going on in today's work environment. A Reuters study called "Dying for Information" found that 43 percent of managers in its sample believed that important decisions are delayed and the ability to make decisions affected as a result of having too much information (Vulliamy, 1996). In another Reuters study, "Glued to the Screen," about "information addiction," 55 percent of respondents worried about making poor decisions in spite of all the information at their disposal (Cunningham, 1997). Undoubtedly we could all think of occasions when we could have reacted earlier to information in our environments. Without so much information bombarding us every day, we could have headed countless problems off at the pass. Furthermore, it's unlikely that any project can get the concerted, long-term attention it needs if everyone is so busy responding to incoming e-mails and flashing voice mail lights. Any ambitious initiative in business needs substantial attention from substantial people over substantial periods of time.

These serious problems might be called "organizational Attention Deficit Disorder." Some of the symptoms are:

1. An increased likelihood of missing key information when making decisions.
2. Diminished time for anything but processing information.
3. More and more difficulty holding attention (for instance, having to increase the glitziness of presentations and the number of messages in order to get and keep attention).
4. Decreased ability to focus when necessary.

Failures of attention management are undoubtedly responsible for many business and societal catastrophes. As Richard Mason has pointed out, before many highly public disasters—the Bhopal chemical release, the Challenger space shuttle explosion, and the rise of domestic terrorism (not Mason's example, but my own)—there were information signals available to decision makers that were ignored (Mason, 2002). Perhaps if leaders had been focusing their attention on these signals, the incidents might have been avoided.

There are much more prosaic misdirections of attention. How many executive teams have been justifiably accused of being "asleep at the switch" while a major business or competitive trend was overtaking them? How many managers can claim that their attention has been focused laser-sharp on the truly important issues to their businesses and careers? All of us make the tacit—and we believe, correct—assumption that, when managers and professionals devote attention to a business problem or issue, it will usually be resolved or get better. But what if there simply isn't enough attention to go around? What if attention is going to the wrong topics?

The imbalance of information and knowledge is now everybody's problem. Every person in an organization is an information and knowledge provider, pushing out information and knowledge in both electronic and paper formats. Everybody sends e-mails, gives presentations, writes memos, contributes lessons learned, and chimes in on a discussion database. In addition, everyone's a consumer of all this content. Each and every person in a company or organization must figure out how to allocate his or her scarce attention amid a multitude of contenders. Of course, if you are a senior executive—charged with effectively utilizing the entire organization's resources—or an information or knowledge manager, this is particularly your problem to address.

Previously, the attention problem was not a major issue. If your company's business involved heating, beating, and bending metal or some other physical product, the production and consumption of information was an ancillary issue. Today, however, if you're in a high-tech or service business, or if your workers are mostly knowledge workers, processing information is what your people do for a living. The production of information and knowledge, and the effective allocation of attention, is all they've got to offer. If their attention isn't captured by important information, or if they are wasting their attention on things that don't matter to the business, you are in trouble.

⦂ *Attention-Conscious Information Strategies*

What can be done about the attention problem? Let me quickly address some strategies that may not work, and then I'll move onto what will. It may not always be feasible, for example, to try to increase the overall supply of attention. Doing so would entail adopting one of two different strategies. One would be simply to hire more people; with each new recruit comes a fresh supply of attention. This may be a good idea in certain circumstances. Indeed, managers might well begin to think of hiring new employees when there is not enough attention to go around for important topics among existing staff. This route to attention building, however, is probably only accessible to senior general managers, and it is rarely a popular idea with them to increase the headcount.

The other means of increasing the overall supply of attention would be to somehow expand the ability of individual brains to pay attention. I've heard claims that the average human uses only 10 percent of his or her brain, and perhaps this is true. But both common sense and research on the psychological dimensions of attention suggest that today there is no proven method available for expanding attention in the brain. Perhaps someday you'll be able to "learn to multitask in six easy lessons," but today we are all flying blind in that regard.

⦂ *Allocating Attention*

If attention can't be significantly increased, then organizations are left with the possibility of allocating it more effectively to the information and knowledge that matters. If you're either an organizational leader who cares about your organization's attention allocation, or an information or knowledge manager, what can you do about attention? There are several possibilities. Such a leader could assess where attention is going today, ensure that information distributed is attention-getting, limit the overall amount of information and knowledge through policy or technology, manage the flow of knowledge, and try to prevent distractions. Education also can be a powerful tool in allocating attention effectively.

Any attention-conscious information strategy would assess what information is truly important to the organization's success, and then ensure that it reached the right people's attention. Peter Drucker has argued for years that organizations would be well advised to pay more attention to external matters—market trends, customers, noncustomers, and so on—than internal. Yet what typically gets forwarded to us within companies is the easy-to-find internal financial and operational information. Without a conscious plan for where attention should be directed, it's unlikely that members of an organization would go to the trouble to find the information that truly matters.

Making a bit of information attention getting is difficult and expensive, as I will demonstrate. Not all information can or should be made equally worthy of attention. Therefore, a critical task for any information strategy is to assess what information really matters to different audiences within an organization. A CEO of a company that has just gone public, for example, might decide that it's critical for managers and employees to know the factors that drive quarterly financial performance, and to pay lots of attention to that information. Managers of a company entering a new market might need to pay special attention to customer needs and competitor initiatives in that market. It's important to remember the zero-sum nature of attention, however. If people begin paying attention to something new, it means that they must divert their attention from something else.

⦂ Assessing Where Attention Is Going

Perhaps the first step in better allocating attention is to know where it is going today. A colleague and I have developed a tool called the AttentionScape, which can aid in the process of understanding what information employees are attending to (Davenport & Beck, 2001). But there are several other less formal means of understanding where today's attention is going. For several of these steps, you may need the complicity of your technology managers:

- Analyze website traffic within your company to understand how much time is spent on nonwork related sites (in general, researchers have found that more than half of all visits to sports, personal finance, and even pornography sites are made from work during work hours; a Vault.com survey suggested that 90 percent of employees admit to viewing non-work-related sites during the average workday).
- Lurk around discussion-oriented intranet sites within your company to see what people are talking about.
- Employ programs that analyze the content of e-mail messages at an aggregate level (I do not recommend executives actually reading other people's e-mails).
- Ask some employees around the company whom you trust to tell you the truth what people are talking about and focusing their attention on.
- If you want to see whether a particular information channel is being

attended to, offer a prize to those who respond to a message embedded deeply within the channel (e.g., to anyone who reads page 96 of the Employee Procedure Manual).
· Hang around the coffee machine or water cooler yourself.

These methods will help to identify not only the work-oriented topics to which people in the organization are attending but also the attention problem areas for your company—attention sinks involving outside distractions, unproductive rumors and gossip, and information channels that are receiving no attention. You probably won't be able to resolve all of these problems, since it is effectively impossible to control what subjects people pay attention to. An assessment, however, will begin to suggest a plan for what other steps you might take regarding the effective allocation of attention.

Ensure That Information and Knowledge Are Attention-Getting

If we're going to bother with crafting a message to send to someone, we should also bother with getting the person's attention. But what works in bringing attention to a particular message? Based on what factors do we pay more attention to some bits of information than others?

Our exploratory research suggests that a few factors can play an important role in whether information gets attention or not (Davenport & Beck, 2001). The factor most related to the attention received by an informational message was personalization. When the recipients of information viewed it as having been created for them alone, they were likely to attend to it. Yet how often do we get messages that were created with a large group in mind?

The second most important factor in getting attention was whether the message provoked emotion in the recipient. We all know of circumstances in which we go first to messages that will make us happy—or even to those that will anger us. With regard to the source of the information, in order to get attention it was most important that the message came from a trustworthy or respected sender; this was more important than the sender being influential or charismatic. In terms of message content, the most important factor was that it was concise—more so than engaging to the senses or unique.

Limit Information Through Policy

One way to direct more attention to the information and knowledge that matter is to reduce the amount that doesn't matter. Few firms have yet attempted to limit the volume of information that circulates within them, although as the amount of information continues to grow, this will surely come to pass.

How would this be accomplished? Information policies might discourage employees from sending nonessential information—jokes, sports pool scores, and so on. One accounting firm, for example, tried to limit nonessential communications during tax season. Some organizations have half-hearted policies suggesting that large distribution lists for e-mails be minimized (good advice, perhaps, in view of the importance of personalization). Firms with extensive knowledge repositories are beginning to feel the need to cut back content to only the most valuable examples of lessons learned, sample proposals, and marketing presentations, because no one has enough time to sort through the bad ones.

In the future, firms are likely to need more institutionalized approaches to limit the amount of information and knowledge. A classical means of doing this is to charge information providers for the amount of content they send to consumers. Most media have done this from the beginning—what would television be like, for example, if advertisers weren't charged for access to viewers? Yet inside most companies and on the Internet in general, access to information recipients is free. If I want to send an e-mail to everyone in the company (thus absorbing a small fraction of a large group's attention), I can do so without charge or (probably) penalty. If I want to send spam e-mails to everyone on a large Internet mailing list, there is no economic reason not to do so. I believe that there will eventually be charges for using the online attention of employees, whether the information comes from internal or external sources. When organizations and the world at large begin to realize the value of attention, it is unlikely that noneconomic mechanisms will suffice to protect it.

That economic approach may need to be augmented by a controversial approach to differential information rights by position in the hierarchy. Under this type of policy, senior executives would have greater access to e-mail distribution lists or intranet discussion postings than would lower-level employees. To some degree this is already the case. It's not uncommon to find corporate policies that specify, for example, that only senior vice presidents and above are entitled to send broadcast e-mail messages to all employees. At Cisco Systems, for example, even though the organization is known for its flat organizational structure and widespread access to information, only certain groups of employees are allowed to post information on the company's intranet. The company cites both security and information overload as reasons (Petersen, 1999).

If business executives were going to play this role in earnest, however, they'd have to invest a lot more effort. They'd have to have meetings and create a strategy about what information really matters to the business. They'd have to develop policies about who was proficient to pontificate on what topics to whom. They'd have to create mechanisms for filtering out irrelevant or useless information. Of course, they'd have to be careful not to make people feel stifled and unable to accomplish essential communications. Today we simply don't know much about how employees would react to sparing their attention, because few organizations have made any effort to do so.

▪ *Limit Information Through Technology*

I've focused on policy as a means of filtering out unnecessary information, because people think it is the shortest and most pragmatic route to that objective. But technology is more often discussed as a means of filtering information and protecting attention. One key is to avoid technologies that cause attention problems. One guilty technology was "push" technology, which ensured a continuing stream of news items, stock prices, sports scores, and so on to users' screens. Many firms have abandoned this use of the technology, in part because of the attention it consumed. But it remains for another purpose: the automated distribution of work-related information. Backweb, a company formerly in the push technology business, now provides its customers with tools to attract attention to what is critical. It's "Polite Push" technology automates the delivery of critical information to personnel, even issuing alerts across an escalation hierarchy of technologies (first e-mail, then pager, then phone, for example) to say that an important piece of information has arrived. These tools, of course, place a premium on having a responsible manager determine what information is important.

The primary route to technology-based attention protection has always been the "filter" or "agent"—at least in principle, because these technologies rarely seem to make it out of the lab and into our daily information environments. There are filters in popular e-mail systems such as Microsoft's Outlook, but they are rudimentary and require that the user specify either senders or subjects that are to be deleted or dispatched without viewing to a particular folder. Most users don't have the ability—or at least the desire—to generalize about or predict such categories. And senders of useless messages and "spam" seem to refine their abilities to craft subject lines that resist easy deletion: "The information you said you wanted," or "Where were you at dinner last night?"

As a result, most of the technologies for attention protection and information filtering remain a vision. We've read about such tools for 20 years, but they have yet to affect our lives. In a recent *Wall Street Journal* supplement on information overload (Petersen, 1999) for example (an indicator of the growing prominence of the topic), academics and scientists spoke of computers as "little slaves," "kind, intuitive butlers," and "activist software" to understand and meet information needs. But it's likely that our information environments will grow more complex faster than the ability of software and hardware to manage them.

Perhaps a better approach to using technology is to display information in a manner that both attracts attention and requires less of it to comprehend. This is the focus of several existing products available in the marketplace. The Brain, for example, a software product for knowledge display, formats information as a graphic representation of relationships between different pieces of content. It allows a user to rapidly navigate through a complex web site or other complex online information environment. Inxight, a spinoff from the Xerox Palo Alto Research Center, offers another variation on the same information visualization theme. Such tools require an investment in formatting the information visually in the first place, but the investment is worth it for information that will be viewed often or by many people.

⦂ Managing the Flow of Knowledge

One of the few quantitative studies on how attention relates to information was done by Morten Hansen and Martine Haas of Harvard Business School (Hansen & Haas, 2000). They analyzed how much attention was given to a set of documents in a consulting firm's knowledge repository. It turns out that the flow of knowledge is one of the most important factors in how much attention a given piece of knowledge receives. Paradoxically, the researchers discovered that the less volume of knowledge a particular group produces, the more likely it is to receive attention. If the category of knowledge (indicated by the keywords used to categorize it) was crowded with many documents, each document was less likely to be viewed. The researchers also found that knowledge-producing groups that were very selective in what they released to the firm's repository got higher levels of attention in crowded topic areas. Furthermore, regular releases of a small number of documents yielded more attention than making them accessible in large batches. In other words, if your knowledge category has substantial competition, a "less is more" strategy works best. If the category is not crowded, releasing more documents makes sense.

This study, of course, was only in one firm. It would behoove any organization that is building a substantial capability to manage knowledge to begin to analyze what knowledge is attended to under what circumstances, and what isn't. To create a vast repository of documents that receive no attention is obviously a waste of time and money.

⦂ Protecting Against Attention Distractions

Information technology can be used to get and keep attention, or to protect against the distractions that technology can bring. As a member of an organization, I wouldn't want my attention controlled or my ability to use technology substantially limited. By contrast, if an organization is paying for its employees' attention—at least during work hours—it should have some say in where it goes.

There are three major distractions that absorb attention in contemporary organizations. One is, of course, the Internet and all it has wrought. One recent survey (Greenfield Online, 2000) found that 9 percent of employees believe that "their work performance has declined because they get distracted while using the Internet for business purposes and move off to investigate leisure time sites." Whereas most of its effects are beneficial, there is little doubt that the amount of non-work-related information to which employees (and managers, for that matter) are exposed is huge.

So what can be done about this? Many firms are beginning to filter out as much of the spam as possible before it hits employees' inboxes. Of course, it's really difficult to know whether an external message is legitimate without reading it (which would both violate privacy and defeat the purpose of filtering). Most of the actions in this regard are at the user end. We might suggest, for example, that employees be warned about opening e-mails from people they don't know (for security and attention protection reasons). Employees whose attention is particularly valuable should have help from secretaries or assistants in filtering the e-mail stream. Strict policies that forbid participation in listserves and "push" communications may not be appropriate, but I do think that employees should be told that only a modicum of such information is desirable.

The second great technological attention distraction of the age is producing (and consuming) presentations, mostly in PowerPoint. Lest you think this is a small matter, Microsoft estimates that more than 30 million PowerPoint presentations are made each day. In a few organizations this has become an important issue. At Sun Microsystems, Scott McNealy, the CEO, combined a concern for the attention issues around PowerPoint with his distaste for Microsoft and banned the use of the package within Sun. Now Sun offers its own presentation system, however, and there is no prohibition against using it. In the U.S. Army, high-ranking officers expressed concern that so-called PowerPoint Rangers were overly exploiting the capabilities of the package to produce attention-getting presentations. Several Army commanders suggested that basic text-and-bullet-point presentations were preferable to animated, clip-art festooned presentations that sucked up too much attention. When this situation was described in the *Wall Street Journal*, it appeared in the center column that is devoted to humorous matters (Jaffe, 2000). But what's really so funny about draining attention away from fighting wars or keeping the peace to advance an "arms race" of better and better presentations? If everyone's using colorful presentation formats and jazzy wipes and dissolves between slides, these attention-getting mechanisms cease to get attention anyway.

I recommend careful but definitive action in this regard. Employees should be told that they should save attention for what matters—for example, achieving better financial performance, or getting the attention of the customer. When the information being transmitted is relatively unimportant, or when the audience's attention is captive, it's a great waste of a scarce resource to use technology to get attention. I don't recommend banning the technology, however. Just as employees had to learn that extended personal conversations on the telephone were inappropriate at work, we need to learn how to use these new tools in a suitable way.

Finally, the third great distraction and absorber of organizational attention is departures from the routine. Any time we have to focus our attention on breakdowns in normal organizational processes and procedures, we don't have it to address something else. In order to free up attention for necessarily unstructured phenomena (e.g., responding to competitor initiatives or customer demands), it makes sense to automate routines and codify structured processes as much as possible. Standardize data, technologies, and ways of working where differences don't add real value. A broken or idiosyncratic internal budgeting process, for example, may suck significant attention out of minds that could be better focused on innovation and creative product or service development.

Technology itself can absorb a huge amount of attention. My philosophy is that in the vast majority of situations, it is what you do with IT that brings productivity and competitive advantage, not the attributes of the technology itself. From an attention management standpoint, then, it's important to make technology as common and as generic as possible. At Hewlett-Packard, for example, IT managers created a "common operating environment" that standardized many aspects of the desktop computing environment. According to Chuck Sieloff, an attention-oriented manager at HP:

> PCs are complex and time-consuming for individuals to manage; yet they deliver important capabilities. Rather than trying to get everyone to do a better job of managing their PC, a small group of specialists have created a fully automated environment for distributing, installing, and configuring PC software over a shared network infrastructure. This so-called Common Operating Environment has been voluntarily adopted by over 100,000 PC users as a way of dramatically reducing the amount of time and attention they have to devote to maintaining their PCs. For the most part, they are delighted to remain ignorant of the underlying expertise needed to create that environment. (Sieloff, 1999, p. 98)

: *Education*

Education about the proper use and management of information and knowledge is a powerful but underutilized tool in fostering good attention allocation. If employees and managers don't know how to use technologies effectively and how to manage their own information and knowledge environments well, they will be relatively unproductive as knowledge workers— relative, that is, to how productive they might be. Unfortunately, there are all too few role models in this regard. Few companies educate their workers on how to find, store, and use knowledge and information—yet what skills could be more useful in the current era?

Outsell, a research firm that studies information markets, published a quantitative study comparing the information-seeking habits and behaviors of information end users (Outsell, 2000b). The study found that respondents' information gathering skills did not come from any formalized training:

- Only 18 percent of all respondents had ever received more than eight hours of training in searching, gathering, and evaluating information and sources.
- Over half had never received any formal training.
- Sixty-six percent of the respondents who primarily use the web for research had never received any training, while 35 percent of the users of commercial desktop information products had received no training.

It's also clear that information users don't know what they don't know. Despite the low levels of training found in the Outsell survey, 96 percent of respondents considered themselves "skilled" or "very adept" at finding information. Yet I suspect that any information professional could find obvious flaws in their searching behaviors.

In addition to searching, the progressive organization would educate its users in determining what information and knowledge they really need relative to their jobs. Education would also be provided on how to set up an effective information environment that encompasses e-mail, important information on the Internet and intranets, paper information, filing structures, and archiving techniques. Otherwise, employees will devote too much attention to information and knowledge that don't matter to their own or their organization's success.

No Silver Bullet

In short, a multifaceted approach is necessary to keep information and knowledge from overwhelming the amount of attention available to comprehend it. No single technology, policy, or approach will suffice. Managers who care about managing their organization's scarcest resource must employ a variety of approaches to getting, keeping, and protecting attention. Of course, employing all these means is labor-intensive and expensive, which is why important information must be prioritized and only the most important information made truly attention getting. If I were building a new information portal for critical organizational information, for example, I'd employ some of the following techniques to ensure that the information was attended to.

- I would decide what information is most critical to my organization's strategy and success, and make only that information attention getting.
- I would not rely solely on the portal itself to communicate key information. If I had an important message to get across, I'd also employ e-mail, voice mail, paper mail, and any other channel that was feasible.
- The content within the portal should be personalized to the degree possible. If fully individualized content isn't possible, personalization based on role should be addressed.
- The material should be emotionally evocative to the degree possible. The use of stories is one means of involving the reader's emotions.
- There should be no more content on the site than is necessary to meet the business objective, and each item should be concise.
- If I were not a trustworthy source, I'd find someone who was and make that person the author.
- As much as possible of the site's content should be requested by the user, rather than "pushed." The act of searching, for example, implies an attentive reader.
- If information were to be pushed out, I'd do so in small quantities at regular intervals.
- The information should have some sensory appeal—if only to differentiate it from the vast amount of black-and-white text;
- There should be no technological barriers to the use of the information.
- Aggregate and individual use of information should be measured to see what information is actually being used.

▪ New Attention Frontiers

The management of attention in business is an entirely new subject. As the amount of information and knowledge that flows through organizations continues to grow, there is little doubt that creative new methods for allocating and even growing it will develop. These new methods will be both bottom-up—developed by individuals to deal with their own avalanche of information—and top-down—policies from executives who worry that their organization's attention is being squandered.

Once an approach to the internal allocation of attention to information has been developed, a likely next topic could be how customers devote their attention to the information and knowledge we produce. Customers are bombarded with information and don't necessarily attend to that from a particular supplier, or to the information the supplier feels is most important. How do we get customers' attention in the first place? Given their certain attention shortage, how do we get them to allocate their attention to the most important information about our products, services, and relationship? How can we help them to free up their attention so that more of it can be allocated to us? If we don't help them with their attention, chances are good that we'll suffer from the lack of it.

By devoting some attention to attention, organizations can begin to focus on the information and knowledge that really matters to their success. They won't overlook important information that can put them out of business. They won't waste organizational and individual attention on irrelevant topics that have no bearing on their work. Their most important resource—the attention of their knowledge workers—will be harnessed in the service of success.

⦂ References

American Forest and Paper Association. (2001) *The Annual Statistics of Paper, Paperboard, and Wood Pulp*. Washington, DC.

Cunningham, M. (1997) "Glued to the Screen," *Irish Times*, Dec. 18.

Davenport, T. H. & J. C. Beck. (2001) *The Attention Economy*. Boston, MA: Harvard Business School Press.

Davis, S., & B. Davidson. (1991) *2020 Vision*. New York: Simon & Schuster.

"Decline in New Product Introductions." (1997) *Frozen Foods Digest*, 13(1), 8.

Elliott, S. (1999) "You've Got Mail, Indeed," *The New York Times*, Oct. 25, C1.

Gartner Group. (2001) Quotation in "Lex" column, *Financial Times*, March 5.

Greenfield Online. (2000) "Cyberslacking at Work Continues to Threaten Productivity," "Quicktake" survey, March 6.

Hansen, M. T., & M. R. Haas. (2000) "Competing for Attention in Knowledge Markets: The Case of Electronic Document Dissemination in a Management Consulting Company," forthcoming in *Administrative Science Quarterly*; also available as a Harvard Business School Working Paper, 2000.

Institute for the Future. (1998) "Workplace Communications in the 21st Century Workplace," study conducted for Pitney Bowes.

Jaffe, G. (2000) "Pentagon Cracks Down on Powerpoint," *Wall Street Journal*, April 26, A1.

Mason, R. O. (2002, April 1) "Leadership, Ethics, and the Information Imperative," Verizon Lecture at Bentley College.

Outsell. (2000a) "e-brief," February 25.

Outsell, Inc. (2000b) "The End User Speaks: Attitudes and Behaviors Toward Commercial Desktop Services and the Open Web." June. Burlingame, CA.

Petersen, A. (1999) "A Fine Line," *Wall Street Journal*, suppl. on Information Overload, June 21, R8.

Sieloff, C. G. (1999) "Is Knowledge Draining Our Attention?" *Knowledge Management*, July 1999.

"The Magazine Handbook." (1999) New York: Magazine Publishers of America. Available online at: http://www.magazine.org.

U.S. Department of Commerce. (1998, April) "The Emerging Digital Economy." Available online at: http://www.ecommerce.gov/emerging.htm.

Vulliamy, E. (1996) "If You Don't Have Time to Take in All the Information in This Report, You Could Be Suffering from a Bout of Information Fatigue Syndrome," *Guardian*, Oct. 15.

Weinbach, J. B. (1999) "Mail Order Madness," *The Wall Street Journal*, Nov. 19, W1.

Eric K. Clemons

Information Technology Investments
Dealing Effectively With Strategic Uncertainty
Through Scenario Analysis

: ***Chapter Summary***

1. Information systems frequently require years to develop; that is, there will
   be several years between initial inception and complete and reliable installation.
2. How can strategic opportunities be more rapidly identified, how can they be
   assessed, and how can strategic investments in information technology be
   financially justified with greater speed and greater accuracy?
3. Some systems decisions are obvious; you need the systems, you need them
   now, and you are certain that you will need these systems under any foreseeable combination of future business conditions. You get them.
4. Other systems decisions are less obvious; you may need the systems under
   some sets of future environmental conditions, but you may not need them
   in other competitive environments. Worse yet, you may need them in some
   competitive situations, where they will be easy to justify in terms of strong
   financial returns, while you may find them counterproductive, even dangerous, in other situations, where they will have strongly negative financial implications. Moreover, other investments are even more obscure.
5. Combining scenario analysis and sequential decision analysis supports viewing IT infrastructure investments as strategic positioning investments or strategic options, and helps structure the decision on when to invest in these
   systems and when to deploy them.

: ***Introduction***

Information technology investment decisions are different from and in some
ways more difficult to make than many other forms of strategic investments,
because of the ways that strategic uncertainty and long lead times interact.
Information systems frequently require years to develop; that is, there will
be several years between initial inception and complete and reliable installation. In rapidly changing areas such as e-commerce, however, the time
between the initial perception of a potential opportunity or system require-

ment and the ultimate certainty that the system is needed now will frequently be significantly less than the time required for the system's development. How can systems development be accelerated? In particular, how can strategic opportunities be more rapidly identified, how can they be assessed, and how can strategic investments in information technology be financially justified with greater speed and greater accuracy? The material that follows is quite intuitive. It does, however, combine information technology, planning under uncertainty, and the use of scenarios in an innovative way that will be useful when considering potential investments in systems needed to support an e-commerce strategy.

Some systems decisions are obvious; you need the systems, you need them now, and you are certain that you will need these systems under any foreseeable combination of future business conditions. You get them. There may be tradeoffs between development cost and implementation speed, or between development cost and shared implementation with other industry participants, but if things are strategic necessities you find a way to get them, merge with competitors who can afford them, or exit the industry. Other systems decisions are less obvious; you may need the systems under some sets of future environmental conditions, but you may not need them in other competitive environments. Worse yet, you may need them in some competitive situations, in which they will be easy to justify in terms of strong financial returns. You may, however, find them counterproductive, even dangerous, in other situations, in which they will have strongly negative financial implications. Moreover, other investments are even more obscure; far from being obvious potential opportunities, you may not even perceive the possible future value of these investments until the need for them is actually upon you. Given the long lead times associated with implementation of many strategic systems, the best you can hope for is that most of your competitors have similarly been caught off guard; if not, if they have anticipated future conditions more accurately and proceeded with their implementations more promptly, you may need to contend with prolonged periods of strategic disadvantage.

There are many reasons for undertaking major, costly technology investments and for implementing information systems projects:

1. Some systems projects are intended to reduce costs. This class of technology project was widely undertaken in the 1950s and 1960s and is relatively well understood. These are traditional automation investments, and indeed they follow much the same pattern and have much the same rationale as investments in automation that date back to Henry Ford. These investment decisions have been studied for decades and can be treated through traditional discounted cash flow analysis.

2. Some projects are intended to increase capacity. This may entail putting systems in where none existed before, or improving the speed of existing hardware or software. These systems decisions are slightly more complicated to make than cost reduction products, as it is necessary to estimate the

increase in sales or other relevant volumes that will result, which in part will be determined by the ability to attract new customers, and in turn will be at least partly determined by the actions of competitors. These decisions are usually analyzed using discounted cashflow analysis as well, although it is important to perform some sensitivity analyses on volumes to capture the uncertainty related to growth.

3. Some systems projects are intended to improve the quality of management decisions. In one of the earliest papers on information economics written by information systems faculty to assess the value of information technology investments, James Emery (1974) wrote that the value of providing information could be assessed simply as the difference in the quality of the decisions made with and without the information. While these comparisons are not always possible to make with any certainty, there are contexts in which the investment decision clearly can be justified once it is framed this way. Air traffic control systems, military battlefield command and control systems, and trader workstations in financial markets are obvious examples. In the case of air traffic control and military command and control, split-second decisions must be made to protect lives and preserve expensive capital assets. Trader workstations entail equally rapid decisions to buy or sell financial assets—equities, government bonds, foreign exchange—and in this context it is possible to develop models based on the rate of change of the prices of financial assets, the speed with which information becomes available, and the speed with which competitors act. These models allow the calculation of the impact of information on the quality of traders' decisions and thus enable estimation of the value of systems that support those decisions.

4. Finally, some systems projects are intended to exploit strategic opportunities and to enable the firm to pursue strategies that were not possible before. Most e-commerce and online sales systems originally fell into the category; prior to the mid-1990s it was not possible to sell online in order to reach customers directly. Some online sales ventures behaved much like super-fast catalog sales (Amazon.com, CDNow, and The Golf Warehouse [TGW.com] were not very different from catalogs that allowed customers to order books, music, and golf equipment before the introduction of the net), facilitating evaluation, although the volatility of the stock prices of some online companies, and the outright failure of other dot-coms suggests that these analyses were not always easy. Other online sales ventures involved entirely new pricing strategies, such as Priceline.com (and its "name your own price" business model), or entirely new product categories, such as eBay (which created a new and previously nonexistent consumer-to-consumer market for used stuff).

It is the final category, systems to exploit strategic opportunities, or simply *strategic systems*, that I will consider in this chapter.

Scenario analysis is used to help manage strategic uncertainty by anticipating possible future competitive environments. Anticipating possible alternative future environments will assist in identifying possible alternative future systems requirements. As noted in a military context, however, "he who defends everything defends nothing"; similarly, he who attempts to prepare for everything, prepares for nothing. Thus, we need a mechanism for determining which contingencies to prepare for and, thus, which investments to make. As importantly, a discipline is needed that will enable us to determine, for those investments we have chosen to defer, when to proceed, and how to proceed rapidly and effectively when the time comes to act. This will at worst enable us to avoid strategic disadvantage, and may indeed confer competitive advantage relative to other industry participants. I describe such a mechanism later in this chapter. For the sake of concreteness, I will examine the decision to invest in systems for direct distribution and online sale to customers, and I will base my analysis on alternative scenarios for e-commerce.

⁞ *Scenario Analysis and Planning Under Uncertainty*

Scenario analysis is a powerful mechanism for improving the quality of planning in the presence of a high degree of strategic uncertainty.[1] It is useful, not for sensitivity analysis or the examination of incremental change (change in the values of significant parameters) but for discontinuous change (change in which parameters are indeed significant). That is, rather than examine a wide range of intermediate values for parameters that have been significant in the past, we deal with extreme uncertainty by asking which parameters may become significant in the future and conducting thought experiments, seeing what would happen if they took on extreme values.

I will now consider a firm—an airline—attempting to develop a channel strategy for e-commerce and attempting to justify investments in systems to support this strategy. The airline believes that the principal source of strategic uncertainty comes from its inability to predict consumer preferences, and it considers as its two strategic drivers the nature of consumer demand for e-commerce services:

1. What is the scope of goods and services that constitute a purchase or a transaction between buyer and seller? That is, does the consumer interact to purchase a single good or service, or does the consumer purchase a market basket assortment or a bundle of related goods and services? The former suggests that the consumer searches for the provider of the best individual goods and services, whereas the latter suggests that the consumer searches for the best provider of a collection of goods and services.

2. What is the duration of the relationship between buyer and seller? That is, does the buyer have an ongoing relationship with a favorite seller, in which they come to learn about each other, or does the buyer search for a different electronic vendor for each interaction? The former suggests an opportunity for tuning of offerings based on experience; the latter suggests

that consumers' desire for the best alternative at any time will prevent the formation of ongoing or stable relationships.

These drivers, and their extreme values, determine the following scenarios:[2]

1. *eSpot*—The eSpot scenario results from a combination of narrow scope and transactional interaction and represents in some sense the commoditization of everything. Each consumer selection of each product, good, or service, is one-off, with the consumer's selection made without consideration of other purchases to be made and largely independently of the consumer's previous purchasing history. In this scenario, competition is based largely on price charged to consumers, without relationships, bundle complexity, or difficulty in acquiring information available to soften competition among producers and intermediaries.

2. *eStore*—The eStore scenario results from a combination of wider scope and transactional interaction. It represents a world in which consumers continue to perceive cost, convenience, or service advantages associated with one-stop shopping for baskets of goods or services, but see limited benefit from ongoing relationships with the providers of these baskets. Here the complexity of bundles and market baskets softens competition among intermediaries, but intermediaries are able to increase their power and increase competition among producers.

3. *eLink*—The eLink scenario results from a combination of narrow scope and ongoing, relational interaction. Consumers are able to locate the best provider of each individual physical good or service to meet their needs and are willing to make a wide range of selections themselves, using different vendors and different service providers. Any assembly or bundling that is required can be arranged by consumers. Consumers do, however, see value in ongoing relationships, and are likely to use their preferred vendors and service providers for the same goods and services over time. In this scenario, producers are able to reduce the role of intermediaries, tighten their links with consumers, and soften competition among them. It is producers' most preferred scenario.

4. *eChain*—The eChain scenario results from a combination of wider scope and ongoing relational interaction. In this scenario, consumers rely on preferred providers to offer them integrated bundles of goods and services, selected to meet their needs. Relationship data allow both parties to improve the performance of their relationship. In particular, consumers can receive bundles of goods or services designed specifically to meet their needs, while providers can price accurately, based on expected cost to provide service and support. In this scenario, bundle complexity and the value of ongoing relationships softens competition among intermediaries; however, their strong relationships with consumers gives them considerable ability to direct consumer purchases of specific items within categories. This gives them tremendous power over producers, which enables them to demand overrides and price concessions, and thus to heighten price-based competition among producers.

: *Infrastructure Investments as Strategic Options*

Some things are clearly needed now, or are clearly needed in all scenarios, and you just do them if their expense can be justified. Insurance companies must comply with federal regulations concerning tracking potential Medicaid fraud and abuse; they must keep their costs under control to remain competitive; and they must monitor their geographic exposure to avoid excessive concentration of risk in any one location, and the potential of unsustainable losses from a single natural disaster. Systems for each of these are essential, and all insurance firms must acquire them now.

Some things may be needed in one scenario and unnecessary or even dangerous in another. That is, some strategies may work in some scenarios and be less effective in others; moreover, some strategies may be quite valuable in some scenarios while illegal in others. These contingent possibilities, those things that we can identify now as possibly useful at a later time, yield the most interesting investment decisions. For example, it may be useful for an insurance company that will be operating in some future fully deregulated environment to have detailed predictions of expected claims associated with individuals who have different family backgrounds, specific ethnic origins, and different individual genetic predisposition to expensive medical conditions. Even attempting to maintain such information today would be considered morally repugnant to most of society and would produce significant loss of brand image and customer loyalty, while attempting to use this information would be illegal and would result in expensive litigation. Thus, the development of systems for accurate predictive cost analysis may be considered a contingent possibility. We conclude that any systems innovations associated with contingent possibilities will have value and payback on investment, which will vary enormously depending on which scenario ultimately unfolds.

Strategic planners praise the use of scenarios to speed up recognition of which scenario has unfolded and to speed the development of strategic and tactical plans, when future events resolve our current strategic uncertainty; frequent practitioners of scenario analysis often call this "remembering the future" or "learning from the future." While this rapid recognition may be helpful in figuring out what is needed more quickly, the actual processes of systems development and implementation will still take several years; thus, scenario analysis may enable you to determine more quickly what you should have begun years earlier. That is, at least the scenario process enables you to experience "rapid regret"!

Increasingly, scenario analysis is used to predict the range of possible future environments, so that the range of systems they will require can be determined in advance. Unfortunately, with too many alternatives, and no certainty that any single one will be realized, it is still too expensive to build the full set of systems to support the full range of contingent possibilities. A first thought is to attempt to use scenario analysis not only to identify attractive possible systems development candidates but also to assign priorities. Investments associated with those scenarios deemed most likely, or most likely to be encountered in the near future, might be undertaken first. There are, however, still several problems associated with this.

1. It is often difficult, or even impossible, to assign probabilities to scenarios. The development process seeks to suspend disbelief by focusing on highly uncertain, highly significant trends, and is quite effective in highlighting critical possibilities for future competitive environments. As soon as skeptical probabilistic assessment is attempted, it is all too easy to discard the most important results of the scenario process and focus on the consensus view or the "official future."

2. After probability assessments, there may still be too many possible investments to undertake, each associated with a high payoff in a scenario that may occur but that is not certain to occur; at best implementing them all would be wasteful and at worst it would require more capital than can safely be committed.

3. Some contingent possibilities require strategic systems that must be unrolled rapidly in one scenario if they are indeed required, and must not even be attempted in other scenarios, where they may provoke either litigation or retaliation from affected parties. Electronic trading systems for online discount brokerage services should be implemented and marketed—even at traditional securities firms such as Merrill Lynch and Smith Barney—if customers demand them. These systems, however, should not be implemented or marketed if they are not necessary, as rolling them out will slash commission income for the firm and also risks offending the firm's best brokers and account executives. Perhaps the worst development plan entails (1) announcing such systems, resulting in the loss of the best brokers and AEs; (2) announcing them late, resulting in loss of those customers who actually did want them; and (3) announcing them before they are ready for customers' use, resulting in loss of AEs before systems are available to stem the loss of investors and trading customers. Proper planning would at least help assure that if speed were required, systems would not be announced until they could be rapidly delivered.

This third objection, the need for speed in completion of contingent investments when they are indeed required, initially appears to be the most difficult to resolve; however, this third case may provide the most valuable insight into the development of strategic systems. The need for rapid but deferred investment seems self-contradictory: don't begin work on a project until you are certain that you need it, and then provide it immediately despite the expected multiyear development cycle. In some situations, however, it may be possible to accommodate both the need for certainty and the need for rapid completion.

A financial option is the right to buy (call) or sell (put) a security at a predetermined price (the strike price) at a future time. Financial options can be viewed as investments in flexibility that increases in value along with price volatility and uncertainty. That is, an option to buy a security or sell a security at a future time will be more valuable as the historical volatility price, and the resulting uncertainty in the future price increase, since these are associated with greater likelihood that the future price will be significantly different from the strike price. This relationship was formally demonstrated by Fischer Black and Myron Scholes, and can be found in any text on derivatives (Cox & Rubinstein, 1985).

The use of *real options* is the managerial technique that comes closest to permitting both delay until certainty increases until a decision is clearer and speed when the decision to act can be justified. Real options are investments made to achieve flexibility. In their simplest form, they can be purchased options to buy a real or physical asset at or by a specified time; an airline can obtain an option to buy the latest Boeing or McDonnell Douglas wide-body aircraft at a future date, or a firm can obtain the right to buy a specific piece of real estate. If market conditions justify expansion, the airline can obtain aircraft at that date, rather than placing an order and waiting in queue for delivery, which might take years. If zoning regulations change, the firm can obtain the land it needs for its new plant at the specified price. If the future conditions do not justify expansion the airline has no obligation to purchase the aircraft, and if zoning does not permit building of the plant, the firm has no obligation to purchase the land. The cost of obtaining the option is simply the cost of maintaining managerial flexibility. This relationship was first developed by Stewart Myers (Myers, 1984). Other authors have expanded the treatment of real options to include not only options to obtain assets whose deployment may be critical to implement a strategy but *any* investments needed to prepare to implement a strategy (Kogut & Kulatilaka, 1997). Amram and Kulatilaka provide an excellent treatment of the general theme of options as investments made to preserve flexibility in the presence of uncertainty (Amram & Kulatilaka, 1999). The use of real options to value investments in information technology has been explored by a number of information systems researchers. Among the most recent is work by Benaroch and Kauffman (Benaroach & Kauffman, 1999), as well as chapter 4 of this book.

A similar theme—providing an estimate of the value of flexibility in the presence of uncertainty—has its origins in statistical decision theory (Pratt, Raiffa, & Schlaifer, 1965; Raiffa, 1970). Indeed, the concept of dividing a strategic decision into pieces, and the value of the flexibility that comes from waiting until more information is available before making the final decision was quantified by Raiffa. It is Raiffa's central idea—deferring decision, preparing for alternative strategies, and rapidly deploying the appropriate strategy when it is possible to choose—that I use in my own work.

⦂   *Strategic Chunkification*

Some systems investments can be divided into segments, tasks, or chunks that can implement sequentially. Development of the initial tasks can be undertaken early, perhaps immediately, and surely before there is certainty that the full project will be required. Later tasks can be undertaken when the state of the future (the emergent scenario) is clearer, or perhaps, even has been revealed with certainty. If the investment in the early tasks is limited, and if the investment in these tasks will result in a substantial reduction in time to complete the entire systems implementation process, these early tasks can be viewed as *strategic options* obtained to assure rapid completion if and when completion is required. The cost of implementation of the early tasks can be viewed as an *option premium;* the benefits from rapid completion of systems development, such as early market share gains resulting from early deployment, can be considered the benefits from *exercising an option that is in the money.*

For sake of simplicity, and to make this example concrete, let us assume that a development effort can be divided into two tasks, T1 and T2, of duration L1 and L2, with each requiring an investment, I1 and I2. In some cases, T1 may be significantly less expensive than T2, may take considerably longer to complete than T2, or may in some sense be much less dangerous than T2 if undertaken at the wrong time (under the wrong scenario).

It might appear that technically, an action that is dangerous would be analyzed only slightly differently from an action that is expensive. An action that is expensive has a high cost, which we can assume is known to be I2. An action that is dangerous under the wrong scenario will be punished, through litigation and assessed damages, lost reputation and lost sales, or lost channel power and lost sales. Thus, if implemented under the wrong scenario actions that are dangerous can be directly shown to be in some sense expensive. The difference is that software investments that are expensive are expensive with certainty, and generally would not be undertaken unless there were a high probability that they would be needed and would be deployed; software investments in systems to support actions that are dangerous may not, in themselves, be expensive, and thus we may be willing to invest in these systems in advance of their need and deploy them only when there is a high probability that they would be safe. Because investments for most Internet ventures are not extraordinarily high—indeed, this is one of the reasons that Internet startups were so prevalent and so easily launched—I will focus here principally on investments in which phase 2 investments are dangerous if launched at the wrong time.

1. A system to support individualized pricing of health insurance products (of the type described earlier in this chapter, would be necessary in a scenario that assumed full deregulation and would be illegal under any reg-

ulatory regime in the United States today. Implementation would require both a lengthy data gathering and data analysis phase, and a shorter phase addressed at rapid conversion of existing products. The first phase would be slow, as it would be necessary to gather data, formulate hypotheses, and test them, but it need not be expensive. The second stage, conversion of applications systems, might be relatively fast after the required analysis had been completed, but would be much more expensive. A multistaged approach would suggest initially investing in systems needed for data gathering and analysis so that accurate individual prices could be computed based on expected cost to serve individual applicants or policyholders. If the regulatory environment were not to change, then systems that exploited the information gained to support differential pricing would never be implemented and this initial investment would be wasted; if regulation were substantially reduced, then the second phase task—converting existing systems to exploit this pricing information—also could be performed, without substantial delay. When the actions of competitors are considered—the downside of being left with a risky portfolio because competitors have learned how to predict the risk of individual applications and thus to manage the risk of their portfolios—then rapid deployment becomes quite important.[3]

2. An electronic share trading system, as mentioned earlier, would be of little value until retail customers were interested in online investing and the lowest possible cost for their stock trades, while announcing such a system would be immediately damaging to the firm's relationship with its brokers and retail account executives. Under a scenario in which customers actually demanded discount, electronic trading, however, the risks of failing to provide these systems will be unacceptable; moreover, in these scenarios, brokers are of reduced importance, and the risks of offending them would be somewhat less as a result. A first phase—investment in development and testing of online trading systems—could be taken initially; the actual rollout, including going live with the website, training personnel within the firm, and announcing the new service to customers via a media blitz, could be performed only when necessary. With this two-phased implementation, there would be no damaging preannouncement of the firm's plans for online trading, and thus no lengthy period of vulnerability in which the loss of brokers and account executives occurred even before alternative trading systems were available.

The first example—differential pricing in insurance—uses two-staged investment to preposition the firm for rapid response to changing and uncertain future conditions, even though the first phase will be of little value if future conditions do not justify deploying the second phase. The second example—rapid rollout of systems to bypass the traditional distribution channel—is not aimed at avoiding an unnecessary expense but, rather, at avoiding punishment from the channel associated with premature attack.

┇   *An Example of Two-Stage Investment: Development of a Multi-Purpose Website*

In practice, it is not always necessary to be overly formal in the valuation of strategic systems options. Their value, like the value of a well-timed trick play or "stunt offense" in football, may be apparent.

Consider companies such as Nikon or Olympus, long engaged in "horizontal channel competition" with each other, which they believe that they understand well. This competition requires investment in research and development, to produce the best available cameras at the lowest cost, and in advertising to develop consumer awareness and loyalty and to create a brand premium. Competition between Olympus and Nikon also limits the prices that either can charge for their products. Increasingly, however, e-commerce increases the range of activities that can occur in "vertical channel competition" between camera manufacturers and camera retailers; neither Nikon nor Olympus fully understands the alternatives or the implications for their profitability.

As companies explore their e-commerce channel options we begin to gain necessary experience. The major airlines have capped commissions, retaining much of the revenue and profit that used to be captured by travel agencies. This has been noticed, and manufacturers of branded merchandise are trying to create their own websites to market directly to consumers; in direct conflict with them, major retailers also have created their own websites and some warn their suppliers not to attempt direct business-to-consumer e-commerce. In this environment, with its continued horizontal channel competition and increasing vertical channel competition, what should companies such as Nikon or Olympus attempt to do with their websites? Two alternatives suggest themselves immediately:

1. Direct distribution: The companies can begin to develop websites to support new vertical channel competition, by launching their own websites for direct distribution to consumers. Unfortunately, this runs the risk of offending the major camera shops, including giant retailers that already have a strong internet presence; these retailers will immediately perceive the camera manufacturers' websites for what they are, an attempt at channel bypass and disintermediation of the retailer network. While this might work if consumers' adoption of direct distribution were very fast, slower adoption might result in effective retribution from the retailers, who would be expected to show strong preference for selling the cameras of manufacturers who were supporting them rather than attempting to bypass them.

2. Web-based information exchange and branding: Alternatively, the camera manufacturers can view their websites as an extension of their traditional activities in horizontal channel competition. Websites would be seen as more powerful than print media, able to communicate more of the companies' product information and to do so more effectively, and able to

capture, with consumer consent, data on individuals who visited their sites.

A casual inspection of the websites created by Nikon and Olympus suggest that they are following the second alternative. Their sites provide detailed information on the full range of the companies' products, but have no facilities for taking orders from consumers. Indeed, at least one of the companies actively discourages orders from consumers who telephone after visiting the website, and will find the consumer a retailer with inventory in stock instead of accepting the order themselves. These websites have considerable value to their operators: after visiting a website and making an informed purchasing decision, the consumer then contacts the camera retailer looking for a specific camera from a specific manufacturer, rather than looking for some (any) digital camera. Without this, the camera store would be free to sell the consumer any product, more than likely the product that offered the retailer the highest margins.

However, a third alternative, sort of a trick play, suggests itself:

3. Assuming that at present consumers are behaving in a manner more consistent with the eStore scenario, they will be buying from retailers who can package together components from many individual manufacturers into an integrated working solution.

Even in the eStore scenario, however, websites can be used as more than extensions of traditional print advertising. Camera manufacturers' websites now provide new product information and reviews, of course. They also provide technical support, both through responses to FAQs (frequently asked questions) as well as rapid response to more difficult questions through e-mail. They can provide lists of compatible products, much as a camera store would do. And they provide additional services, not directly related to selling products, indeed not directly related to their products at all; customized picture postcards can be produced, either with their stock of digital images or by providing your own, and sent to recipients via e-mail. Gradually, with a low profile that is invisible to retailers, camera manufacturers create websites with strong relationships to consumers.

These websites, while not threatening to retailers, are superbly prepositioning manufacturers to exploit an eventual transition from the eStore to the eLink scenario. That is, while these websites' current functions are not inviting retaliation from retailers, they are developing the strong relationships with consumers that would be essential to any manufacturer's strategy for direct distribution and bypass of the retailers.

Thus, the Internet strategies of major camera manufacturers could be viewed as a two-staged investment in Internet capabilities. The first stage provides real value to consumers in the current strategic scenario, while safely building the relationships needed for a transition into an attack on retailers. This building of relationships, while not particularly expensive, is extremely time-consuming and could not safely be undertaken through a direct attack on retailers at this time. The value of the manufacturers' current investments in websites, however, can only be fully understood as strategic positioning to prepare for the rapid exploitation of future opportunities; that is, current websites have a considerable options value.

⦂ Staged Investments: Valuing Information Options Under Emerging Scenarios

Formulas such as Black-Scholes are not much help in the valuation of the type of systems investments described earlier. The assumption under which Black-Scholes was developed and, more important, the data needed (such as the volatility in the value of the underlying information system) is not available and indeed cannot even be defined. The value of these systems options is whatever the market value is of having a strategy in place, having the product offerings in place, and having the systems in place to support those offerings, and doing so earlier than would be possible without the initial investment in the phase 1 task.
We can be more specific.

- The options premium, or the cost of the option, can be estimated by estimating I1, the cost associated with the investment needed to complete the first task.
- The value of the option will be most difficult to estimate in a meaningful fashion. It is determined by the value of the sequence of investments I1 at T1, I2 at T2, compared to the value of both investments made beginning at T2. While this value cannot actually be determined, business simulation modeling can be most effective, when factors such as response time and adoption rate of customers, and the value of first mover advantages, can be incorporated.
- The reduction in time will frequently be close to L1, the time required to complete implementation of the first task and thus the duration of the first phase; only rarely will strategic uncertainty be reduced, and the state of the emergent scenario revealed, faster than this. (Assuming that both tasks would need be performed sequentially, the sequence {I1,I2} would be accelerated by L1 if the first task were performed in advance.)

The options value described here would have been calculated under the assumption that both investments I1 and I2 are actually needed; therefore, before this value can be used in practice it needs to be weighted in some sense by the (estimated or subjective) probability that the scenario under which they are required will actually be realized. As noted earlier, the necessary probability estimate is almost never available as a result of the scenario process and, given the nature of the scenarios examined, its value would be extremely difficult to determine. It may therefore be more useful to estimate the options cost and the unconditional options value, and then determine the probability that would be needed to justify making the investment I1 in the first task at time T1. If only a low probability of the associated scenario occurring is sufficient to justify the option, then we may conclude that the option is a good investment; if a much higher probability is required then perhaps the option may be considered too expensive, given its expected payoff.

: *A Specific Example of Options Valuation for e-commerce*

Understanding the Scenarios and the Context for Investment

I will now discuss a specific example, an airline (Bold Airline, or BA) considering alternative strategies for its entry into e-commerce; their competitor (Uncertain Airline, or UA) is more reluctant to consider an outright attack on the agency system. This was an actual decision being considered by British Airways and others in the early 1990s, long before widespread adoption of the Internet, and in what follows we will assume that the decision is being analyzed in this time frame. That is, the use of the present tense reflects a date of 1995.

Of course, the airline does not know how customers/passengers will respond to its online offerings. Perhaps its website will attract significant traffic, both *lookers* who gather information and *bookers* who actually make reservations and purchase tickets. Perhaps the website will attract a major form of retaliation from travel agencies, who view it as an attack on their entire business; depending on customer adoption, competitor responses, and other circumstances, this retaliation may have minor impact on the airline or it may be catastrophic for the airline's profits.

The airline has no historical data on the adoption of web-based distribution in the United States because, in the time frame of the analysis, there was virtually no web traffic and there were no successful web-based sales organizations. This precludes the use of historical return on IT investments as a mechanism for valuing development of software to support web-based distribution. Likewise, it precludes the use of formulas such as Black Scholes for valuing the software as an investment in support of an innovative sales strategy.

Of course, this does not mean that the airline is without information or is without some mechanism for structuring its decision analysis. It currently believes that the e-commerce marketplace for air travel will initially resemble the eStore scenario, in which customers will book though agencies, though agencies will not initially develop strong customer loyalty or the ability to perform value-added services based upon strong relationships. The airline believes that ultimately e-commerce for its marketplace will look either like eLink or eChain.

In eStore, since customers continue to rely on agencies, not much is required from BA to prepare for e-commerce, other than to invest in brand, which can be done through continued use of traditional media advertising, a web-based campaign, or both. Direct distribution through the web is unlikely to be effective, but it may invite retribution from agencies fearing attack and disintermediation.

In an eLink scenario, in which customers are willing to shop online and deal directly with suppliers such as airlines, there is more that BA can do via e-commerce. Direct distribution would be effective, especially if the airline had already succeeded in forging strong relationships with its most frequent travelers. If consumers do not move toward this scenario, and hence do not adopt the eDistribution alternatives offered by airlines, however, eDistribution will be ineffective. Agencies will of course feel threatened by airlines' attempts to bypass them and can be expected to retaliate, shifting customers' ticket purchases to airlines that continue to value traditional agency relationships. Moreover, understanding the timing of customer adoption is crucial. Even if consumers do ultimately accept eDistribution, an airline's premature launch of eDistribution will result in slow customer adoption, benefits to BA will be slow to materialize, and effective retribution from agencies becomes more likely.

In an eChain scenario there is a strong need for branding, and probably for web-based branding. Consumer adoption of individual airlines' eDistribution system is unlikely, slow, and uncertain, however, while retribution from agencies is immediate, certain, and effective.[4]

The Investment Decision

How should BA proceed?

At present, at the time represented by X in figure 14.1, BA can either make an investment in website technology or can defer this investment. Figure 14.2 shows base case profitability, if neither I1 nor I2 are developed or deployed by either airline.

Investments I1, for eBranding, and I2, for eDistribution, are both quite modest, and the firm could afford to invest in both. The deployment of full eDistribution may be dangerous, however, and the firm needs to determine how best to deploy its technology for competitive advantage, without inviting retribution from travel agencies. Figure 14.3 shows the profitability of an aggressive eBranding system, which can actually assist customers in making bookings, direct some incremental business to BA from customers without strong preferences for other travel options, but still allows customers to be ticketed through their current agencies and allows those agencies to continue to receive full commissions; figure 14.3 is clearly preferable to figure 14.2. Aggressive eBranding, at least, appears to be worth deploying.

The potential for disintermediation of travel agencies—is not being exploited with this strategy. BA also considers whether or not to deploy the full capability of its I2 investment, eliminating commissions to agencies for

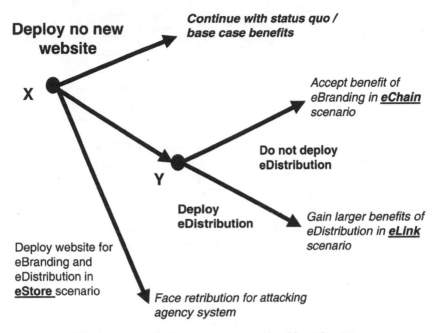

Figure 14.1. The investment decision sequence considered by airline BA

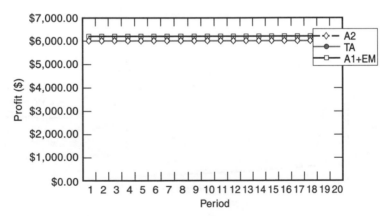

Figure 14.2. Base case profitability without BA's launch of e-commerce strategy. There is no contribution from the electronic market (EM), which has not yet been launched. Both airlines are profitable and have equal profitability.

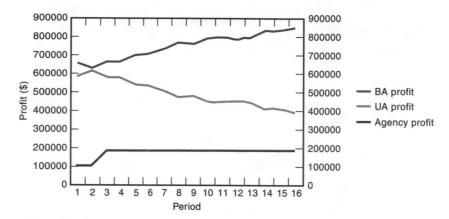

Figure 14.3. Profitability after BA's launch of aggressive eBranding strategy, without eDistribution. Note significant shift in wealth from UA to BA. Note also that the cost savings that result from eBookings also increase travel agent wealth.

all flights booked through its website and capping commissions at 5 percent or $50 for those flights that continue to be booked through traditional channels.

Figure 14.4 shows that if customers do not adopt or use these systems, and if the airline attempts to disintermediate agencies without first gaining customer support, the cost will be unacceptable; figure 14.4 also shows what will happen if traditional channels retain their power and the ability to punish attempts at disintermediation. If BA is not certain that it will have

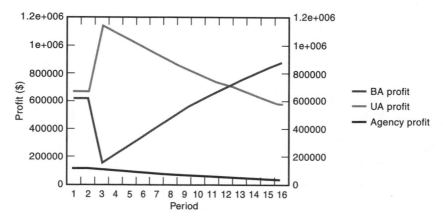

Figure 14.4. Premature attack. BA launches a powerful eDistribution system, attacking the agency channel, before customers are prepared to switch to direct electronic bookings. The agency system retaliates. Note strong initial shift of wealth from BA to UA and prolonged period of depressed profitability for BA.

rapid adoption, figure 14.4 suggests that it proceed with caution and the company decides not to launch eDistribution at this time.

At time Y, after successfully launching its eBranding website, the company can once again reconsider its decision of whether or not to deploy eDistribution. In contrast with the strategy based solely on eBranding, figure 14.5 depicts the situation in which customers have adopted BA's website for eBranding and eDistribution to a sufficient degree to embolden BA to launch a full eDistribution strategy, with expectation of success; in figure 14.5, BA eliminates commissions for travel booked through its website and caps commissions on all travel booked through the traditional channels.

Each of the strategic contexts and the figures that portray them (excluding fig. 14.1) can be described in more detail.

Figure 14.2 shows the base case. Both airlines are profitable, as is the agency system that supports them (not shown in the figure).

Figure 14.3 shows BA's introduction of an eBranding website, which performs traditional advertising and brand awareness functions, much as media advertising would. Unlike traditional print and broadcast advertising, however, the website allows customers to inquire about specific flights and book their reservations, although it requires the use of travel agents for ticketing and other forms of customer support. The website greatly increases customers' convenience and would be expected to increase BA's market share if competitors did not respond; of course, competitors did respond (this model was not included), so this form of website does not really improve the profitability of BA or its competitors. These systems were enormously popular with travel agents, however, because customers used them to perform some of the work that agents previously had to do for customers; although the agents' work was reduced, their commissions were not.

Figure 14.4 shows the results of BA's premature attack on the existing agency-based distribution system. BA begins to sell online, allowing customers to book flights and purchase tickets and e-tickets directly from the airline. BA is able to reduce its distribution costs, both by paying no commission on the tickets that it sells online and by reducing the commissions that it pays to agencies. Unfortunately, customer adoption is slow, so the savings are small. More important, the agency system is outraged, and retaliated by selling competitors' flights more aggressively. The resulting loss of market share slashes BA's profits and they remain depressed for three years (12 quarters on the graph).

Figure 14.5 represents BA's well-timed attack. BA enjoys the benefits of eBranding immediately. As described in the analysis of figure 14.3, agencies' profits increase during the initial period as well. Subsequently, when BA attacks the agency system, its profits increase still more; this is because it no longer pays commission on the business that it sells directly, and it pays only reduced commission on the remaining business. Agency profits, naturally, are reduced. The agency system attempts to retaliate against BA but cannot do so effectively; too many customers, and too many of the best customers,

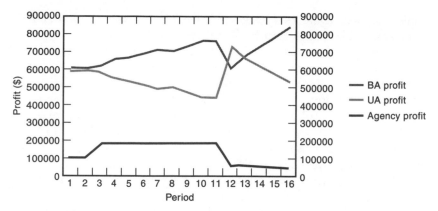

Figure 14.5. Well-timed attack. BA launches a powerful eDistribution system, attacking the agency channel, after it has established a powerful web presence. The agency system is now unable to retaliate effectively. Note strong initial shift of wealth from the agency system to the airlines, and from UA to BA.

have already begun to book online. The agency system is left with those customers who require a great deal of individual support, such as those planning complex vacations, who would be difficult to serve online and whom the airlines are all-to-willing to allow the book their flights through travel agents.

Figure 14.6 represents simultaneous attack, the strategic situation that eventually did unfold. BA launched an eBranding site, as did everyone else. BA and its less bold competitors all attacked the agency system at the same

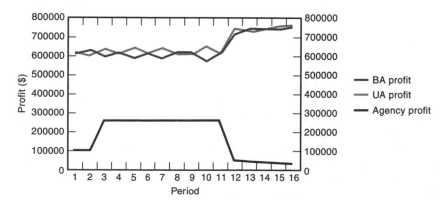

Figure 14.6. Attack on agencies, spontaneously joined by competitor. Note that while the benefits to BA are real, they are substantially less than in figure 14.5. This is because BA continues to enjoy reduced distribution cost, but does not achieve an increase in market share if its competitor matches its deployment of online systems.

time (for the historical record, Delta attacked first with *ticket capitation* and all U.S. carriers responded almost immediately[5]). There is no shift in market share resulting from systems that are undertaken by all competitors; however, it is impossible for an agency system to punish all competitors by refusing to sell any air tickets, and thus in this situation airlines were able to reduce commissions without any fear of retaliation from the agencies.

▪ The Decision—Creating a Strategic Option

How will BA proceed? At the present time, indicated by X in figure 14.1, it will invest in both I1 and I2, but will not fully deploy the eDistribution strategy that I2 enables. At a later time, indicated by Y in figure 14.1, it will reassess its decision concerning full deployment of I2 capabilities. Figure 14.4 clearly shows that as long as customers' adoption of its website is limited, a direct attack on the agencies would be dangerous. In contrast, figure 14.5 clearly demonstrates that when adoption is sufficiently large BA is safe from retribution by traditional agencies and will launch its attack.

Why might BA invest in I2 before it is ready to use it and, indeed, before it is certain that it will want to use it? It will make the investment for the following reasons:

- It is not expensive, and therefore it does not need certainty or near certainty to justify the investment
- It is safe to make the investment if it is not deployed, so there is no secondary expense—expected loss—associated merely with making the investment
- When I2 can safely be deployed, the payoff from the investment is very high, and there is a strong possibility of first mover advantages, as shown by the loss of profits experienced by UA relative to BA; to enable it to proceed with speed at a later time, BA is willing to make the investment I2 before it is required and before it is known if it will be required.

This example shows the value of a two-staged investment for "stealth," to avoid punishment by downstream channel participants. Other two-staged investments are motivated more for speed, to enable movement ahead of other horizontal competitors (companies in the same industry, more traditionally seen as competitors).

▪ Conclusions

Often rapidly changing conditions make it difficult to determine how to value investments in information infrastructure. This is particularly true when preparing for e-commerce, where some investments may be necessary in one scenario but not in another, while other investments may be necessary in one scenario but unacceptably dangerous in another. Combining scenario analysis and sequential decision analysis supports viewing these infrastructure investments as strategic positioning investments or strategic options, and helps structure the decision on when to invest in these systems and when to deploy them. In particular, an investment can be made that has little cost or downside risk, and that has a subsequent use in another scenario or at a later time when conditions may be different. Making the first investment can be viewed as investment in creating a strategic option. Subsequently, when conditions warrant it, making the second investment and completing implementation of the strategy enabled by the first investment can be viewed as exercising this option.

: *Appendix*

The simulation model on which the analyses in this chapter are based has been described elsewhere (Clemons & Row, 1998). The simulation models the behavior of a group of customers over time. Each customer can be described by the following attributes:

Brand loyalty (customer preferences for one airline over another)—the premium that each customer is willing to pay for one airline over another.

Channel loyalty (customer preferences for one channel over another)—analogous to brand loyalty, the premium that customers are willing to pay for one channel over another. Initially all customers use travel agents and may prefer travel agents, but some customers are more willing than others to consider online distribution. Channel loyalty changes over time, as the use of electronic reservations systems makes customers more willing to use it in the future.

Nature of travel (business or leisure)—business travelers are easier to serve, are more willing to book online, and are willing to pay higher prices.

The simulation model also has parameters like the in-play ratio, the rate at which customers consider alternative distribution channels.

Airlines can set their strategies, including how to use online systems for branding, for customer service, and for direct distribution. Agencies can set their own strategies, including how they may choose to retaliate against airlines that seek to bypass them.

The model was used to produce the simulations illustrated in this chapter:

Figure 14.2/Base Case: The simulation was run under baseline conditions, without e-commerce investments from either airline.

Figure 14.3/Aggressive eBranding: The simulation was run under conditions of slow adoption by consumers (low in play ratio), some limited ability to influence passengers' choice of airline through the website, no bypass of agency by airline, no reduction in commissions paid, and thus no retribution by the agency force against BA. The results of the simulation show some modest gain for BA, although in reality UA would probably match, reducing ability to influence choice of airline by either airline or agency.

Figure 14.4/Premature Attack on Agencies: The simulation run under conditions of slow customer adoption, limited ability of airlines to influence passengers' selection of an airline, full attempt at commission cuts and disintermediation, and in essence a full attack on the agencies by the airline BA. Although customer adoption is limited, the agency counter-attack is immediate and effective. Figure 14.4 clearly shows that the slight savings in commissions paid is not sufficient to compensate for retribution by the agencies.

Figure 14.5/Well-Timed Attack on Agencies: The simulation was run under conditions of high in play ratio and rapid customer adoption, leading to extensive customer use of the airline BA's website for direct distribution. BA pays no commission on flights it books through its website and it pays only limited commissions on flights booked through the agency system. Figure 14.5 clearly shows the benefits from this attack strategy, under conditions of rapid adoption and assuming that the attack is deferred until sufficient adoption has already occurred.

Figure 14.6/Simultaneous Attack: The simulation was run under conditions identical to those of figure 14.5, except that both airlines followed the same strategy. Clearly, with the same strategy pursued equally well by both players, it does not shift market share or profits between the two, but, because counterattack through punishment is not possible in this situation, both airlines are able to profit at the expense of the agency system.

: Notes

This work was supported by the Reginald H. Jones Center, Project on Information Strategy and Economics. Officers from Rosenbluth International, Marriott Hotels and Resorts, and Unilever North America provided valuable insights. Software for the analyses was provided by Michael C. Row and Bin Gu when they were doctoral students at the Wharton School.

1. Peter Schwartz provides perhaps the best general introduction to scenario planning in *The Art of the Long View* (1991). I appear to have been the first to use the technique to improve the quality of information systems designed to support business transformation in the presence of strategic uncertainty (1995).

2. These scenarios are developed in more detail elsewhere (Clemons & Row, 1998, 2000).

3. The power of differential pricing is explored in the credit card industry in the study of Capital One Financial (Clemons, 1997). Their enormous success, with revenues increasing more than 40 percent annually, and profits and share price increasing at better than 20 percent annually, since the company's inception, show the power of differential

pricing. The collapse of powerful competitors, especially of AT&T Universal, shows the danger of failing to implement this strategy if and when it becomes possible to do so. The power of this strategy and its generality to other industries has been described in this work as well.

4. Channel power and retribution are described elsewhere (Clemons & Row, 1998, 2000) and the use of software to model channel conflict situations has been published previously (Clemons & Row, 1998).

5. Ticket capitation is the capping of ticket commissions at some fixed dollar amount. Commissions were initially capped at $50, and subsequently they have been reduced.

▪ References

Amram, M., & N. Kulatilaka. (1999) *Real Options: Managing Strategic Investment in an Uncertain World.* Boston, MA: Harvard Business School Press.

Benaroch, M., & R. J. Kauffman. (1999) "A Case for Using Real Options Pricing Analysis to Evaluate Information Technology Project Investments," *Information Systems Research,* 10(1), 70–86.

Clemons, E. K. (1995) "Using Scenario Analysis to Manage the Strategic Risks of Reengineering," *Sloan Management Review,* 3(4), 61–71.

Clemons, E. K. (1997) "Technology-Driven Environmental Shifts and the Sustainable Competitive Advantage of Previously Dominant Service Companies," in G. Day and D. Reibstein (Eds.), *Wharton on Dynamic Competitive Strategies,* 99–121. New York: John Wiley.

Clemons, E. K., & M. C. Row. (1998) "Electronic Consumer Interaction, Technology-Enabled Encroachment, and Channel Power," *Proceedings, 31st Hawaii International Conference on System Sciences.*

Clemons, E. K., & M. C. Row. (2000) "Behavior is Key to Web Retailing Strategy [FT Survey on Mastering Management]," *Financial Times,* Nov. 13.

Cox, J. C., & M. Rubinstein. (1985) *Options Markets.* Englewood Cliffs, NJ: Prentice Hall.

Emery, J. C. (1974) "Cost / Benefit Analysis of Information Systems," in J. D. Couger and R. W. Knapp (Eds.), *Systems Analysis Techniques,* 395–425. New York: John Wiley.

Kogut, B., & N. Kulatilaka. (1997) "Capabilities as Real Options," *Proceedings of the Conference on Risk, Managers, and Options in Honor of Edward Bowman,* Reginald H. Jones Center, Wharton School of Business, University of Pennsylvania, Philadelphia.

Myers, S. (1984) "Finance Theory and Financial Strategy," *Interfaces,* 14, Jan., 126–27.

Pratt, J. W., H. Raiffa, & R. O. Schlaifer. (1965) *Introduction to Statistical Decision Theory.* McGraw Hill.

Raiffa, H. (1970) *Decision Analysis.* Reading, MA: Addison-Wesley.

Schwartz, P. (1991) *The Art of the Long View.* New York: Doubleday.

15

James A. Senn

The Influence of Wireless Networks on Information Technology Strategy

: *Chapter Summary*

1. The number of wireless devices in use, handheld and otherwise, and the networks that transport the data will continue growing throughout the world. The potential impact on business and society is dramatic.
2. Enterprises have not incorporated wireless networking into their information technology strategies nor have they considered its potential value for driving and enabling business strategy.
3. There are specific issues that business and information technology managers need to address to systematically capitalize on the potential benefits of deploying wireless networks.
4. Information technology managers must explicitly confront a set of key issues today or they will encounter difficult strategic challenges in the future.

: *Introduction*

The widespread global interest by people and businesses in connecting to communication networks wirelessly is evermore evident by the large and rapidly growing array of wireless devices in use. Moreover, the increasing sales of mobile phones, as well as wireless palm computers and personal digital assistants, and the expectations of use by employees, customers, and suppliers should be a signal to executives that their businesses may be affected permanently by wireless networks services and innovative information systems.

With few exceptions, however, the level of interest in these devices is not carrying over to systematic, well-conceived strategies for their use in business applications. A field investigation to explore this concern reveals that enterprises have not incorporated wireless networking into their information technology strategies, nor have they considered its potential value for driving and enabling business strategy.

The discussion that follows explores the role of wireless networking in business enterprises. In the first section, the rapid growth of wireless devices is explained and the current and emerging alternative technologies that underlie their use are examined. The next section describes the different categories of wireless networking applications that are emerging in practice.

The last section focuses on the specific issues that business and information technology managers need to address in order to systematically capitalize on the potential benefits of deploying wireless networks. As will be shown, information technology managers must explicitly confront a set of key issues today or they will encounter difficult strategic challenges in the future.

⁝ Growth of Wireless Networking

In the United States, innovations in networking systems have been influenced dramatically by the rapid evolution of the Internet. It is rare today to find a personal computer (PC) that does not connect to the Internet. Outside of the United States, the rate of PC installation has not been as rapid. Even so, the global PC installed base is approaching 400 million and will, without any doubt, continue to grow (fig. 15.1). Given both the functionality and powerful capabilities of PCs, it is understandable why corporations have focused so much attention on incorporating desktop—and, more recently, notebook—computers into information technology application strategies.

As computers have become more portable, their users have increasingly sought to interconnect them with their company's networks and to use online systems. While e-mail is often the most frequently desired application for notebook users, a growing number of people seek to link up to mission-critical enterprise applications (e.g., sales support and order entry, engineering and design, customer relationship systems).

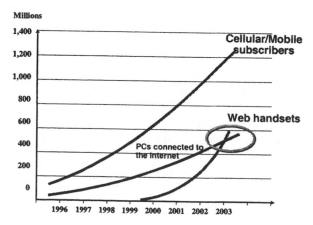

Figure 15.1. Growth of PC and technology wireless (Dataquest)

Table 15.1
Evolution of Digital Wireless Transmission Methods

1st	1980s	Analog voice transmission
2G	1990s	Digital voice and low bandwidth data transmission Transmission speeds of 9.6–19.2Kb/s
2.5G	2001	Packet-based Digital voice and data transmission Transmission speeds up to 115 Kb/s
3G	2002+	Digital multimedia Voice, text, photos, music & video Transmission speeds up to 384 Kb/s

Growth in Wireless Devices

As impressive as the growth of PCs is, wireless devices—mobile phones, wireless palm computers, and personal digital assistants—have demonstrated even more spectacular growth patterns. The first wireless telephone call was made in 1973 by Marty Cooper, of Motorola Corp., thereby kicking off the first generation of mobile phones (table 15.1). Although the large, bricklike wireless phone was awkward looking compared to today's sleek mobile phones, it was a clear signal of the future.

Today, the global installed base of wireless mobile phones is approaching one billion, with no slowing in the rate of growth foreseen over the next few years. In some regions, especially Scandinavia and Singapore, the penetration rate of mobile phones is in excess of 75 percent. It is not unusual to find in these areas that individuals use their mobile phone as their *primary* phone, replacing the conventional desk phone. Moreover, because they are small and portable—a sharp contrast to Cooper's first such phone—they carry them everywhere, always ready for use. Yet many mobile phone users do not own PCs. Advancing the capabilities of mobile phones, rather than PCs, is therefore understandably more important for them.

But there is another wireless area where rapid growth is occurring: wireless devices that can connect to the Internet's World Wide Web. *Web handsets*, as they are called, are equipped with wireless communication capabilities and a browser that facilitates downloading graphical information to appear on their display screen. The display screen itself is larger than those found on conventional mobile phone and features color and higher screen resolution. New model web handsets also incorporate touch screen capabilities for activating and controlling applications.

The installed base of web handsets is also growing very rapidly. Even more important, industry projections indicate that the number of web hand-

5(1) sets in use worldwide will soon *exceed* the entire installed base of personal computers.

The combination of so many mobile phones and web handsets in use, as well as an expected jump in notebook computers equipped with wireless communication capabilities, has focused attention on the potential importance of the wireless Internet. It is widely believed that just as traditional PCs and fixed-base communication links drove the rapid development of Internet applications for personal and business use, wireless communication devices similarly will be an unstoppable force behind the expanded use of the *wireless Internet.*

Improvements in Wireless Communication Bandwidth

Until recently, the transmission speed—the bandwidth—afforded wireless devices has been a limiting factor for anything other than voice conversations or the occasional sending and receiving of e-mail. Compared to the high speeds associated with PC communication (i.e., dedicated communication lines, broadband cable, and digital subscriber lines [DSL] lines, all with transmission speeds in excess of about 1 megab it per second [Mb/s]), the slow 9.6 *kilobits* per second speed available to wireless devices has until recently deterred their use in mainstream business applications.

Today, the speed barriers for wireless applications are falling rapidly. New generation wireless technologies are enabling the transmission of data at dramatically higher rates. Operators of the world's public cellular (i.e., mobile phone) systems are actively launching successors to the current second generation (or 2G) systems (see table 15.1). New 2.5-generation systems, the label given to Generalized Packet Radio Systems (GPRS), are providing users with transmission speeds of up to 115 Kb/s, while the network itself operates with the preferable packet transmission methods that characterize the Internet. Next generation (3G) systems promise even more, with speeds of from 384 kilobits per second to 2 Mb/s.

Other wireless advances are occurring independent of those in the public cellular systems. Wireless local area networks (i.e., WLANs) are being implemented in both private buildings and public concourses. WLANs following the IEEE 802.11b standard operate at 11 Mb/s. (An alternate 802.11a standard is also emerging, with expected transport rates up to 54 Mb/s.) Most new notebook computers are expected to be equipped with IEEE 802.11 LAN capabilities, making them a viable wireless device and thereby meriting these computers a place in an enterprise's information technology strategy.

In addition, a wireless personal area network (WPAN) standard, known as Bluetooth, is being rolled out. Devices equipped with the inexpensive Bluetooth technology can transmit wirelessly across distances up to 10 meters. Early indications are that Bluetooth will be used to synchronize information between, say, notebook computers in offices and conference rooms or via public access points in facilities such as airports, train stations, and sports arenas. Of course, as in all of these areas, vendors and user enterprises alike have probably not yet conceived the cleverest and most beneficial applications. They are yet to come.

: Application Framework

Any mention of wireless communications services in the context of enterprise IT strategy quickly brings to mind interest about the potential roles they may play in transaction services. Transaction services are only one of four principal categories identified during field investigations involving users and service providers. The following sections describe four categories of services: voice, transaction, content, and telemetry (table 15.2).

Voice Services

Voice services will continue to be an important application running on wireless networks. The many mobile phones already in use are of course one reason. Another technology, voice-over-Internet protocol networks, is also increasingly important, however. Internet protocol (IP) is a widely accepted standard for controlling the movement of data packets over communication channels and is also a principal factor in the Internet's success. The Internet protocol makes it possible for any device equipped with the protocol (including, but not limited to, computers and telephones) to connect and communicate over the Internet.

Recent progress in research seeking to apply the Internet protocol to voice communications has made it possible to transmit voice calls over data networks while achieving high quality and reliability. This was not feasible just a few years ago. As a result, it is now possible for organizations to

Table 15.2
Framework for Wireless Applications

	Passive Self-activating	Active User must activate
· Voice Services	—Voice calls —Voice over IP	—Voice calls —Voice over IP
· Transaction Services	—Toll collections —Automatic funds transfer	—Sale force automation —Shopping
· Content Services	—e-mail —Breaking news	—Information browsing —Directory services
· Telemetry Services	—Status monitoring —Interactive Marketing	—Stock quotations —Appliance management

develop voice services over their own private fixed and wireless networks. The capability merits consideration in enterprise IT strategies as it is highly likely that new voice services will emerge from this innovation.

Transaction Services

Some industry observers expect a large number of traditional business trans-actions to be conducted over wireless networks. To the extent this proves to be the case, companies will link these networks to front and back office business systems where transaction processing is carried out. Field services, sales force automation (including information retrieval *and* data capture), and tracking systems are already among the most frequently used transaction services. For instance, UPS enables its customers to use wireless devices in North America, Europe, and Asia to track package movement (in multiple languages and character sets) via a wide variety of wireless devices.

Moreover, the wireless Internet is reshaping conventional thinking about both business and consumer-oriented e-commerce applications. Online shopping, ticket booking, and payment transactions are expected to be among the principal transaction services conducted between wireless devices and corporate business systems or e-commerce intermediaries (e.g., electronic markets and electronic hubs operating on the Internet). Within the banking and financial services industry segments, it appears that wireless services sup-porting savings, payment, transfer of funds, as well as brokerage and invest-ment transactions will be rigorously promoted. For example, E*Trade, the online investment and banking firm, already offers many services that its customers can initiate from nearly any mobile phone, wireless PDA, or in-teractive text pager. Its wireless services are accessible by customers of the leading wireless carriers in the United States and elsewhere.

Because of the visibility and early successes of applications such as these, the use of wireless networks to initiate and pay for purchases and services in real-time is expected to increase as users gain the capability—and the comfort—to manage them. Likely to be of increasing importance (although not without concern over potential loss of personal privacy) is the role of wireless communications for conducting *micro transactions*—paying for small value purchases of, say, less than $10 (e.g., subway tickets or purchases from vending machines). Such purchases fall below the minimum value threshold needed to pay by credit card. These transactions are more suited for "digital cash," a name indicating that digital information rather than hard currency is exchanged to settle a transaction. In Scandinavia, banks and consumers are already experimenting with digital cash loaded into the memory of their mobile telephones. By pressing a few buttons on their phone, shoppers can pay for vending machine and even fast food purchases. The payment infor-mation—the digital cash—is transferred from the mobile phone to the vend-ing machine, cash register, or other such device. Although these applications are early in the prototype stage, they clearly indicate an interest in having micro transaction payments as a wireless service feature.

The fact that early innovators, such as shipping companies, brokerage houses, banks, and even booksellers (e.g., Amazon.com) have already created wireless transaction services to test their business potential is an important evolutionary step. The benefits of wireless transaction services *may not be comparable*, however, to those for traditional information systems applications. Rather, the payoffs will probably be realized in ways that have yet to be devised. Still, prudence suggests that IT managers must scrutinize wireless services, ensuring that they are evaluated for their potential business value (such as increased productivity, improved service and speed, lower transaction costs, and—where possible—a competitive edge) rather than clever technologies.

Content Services

Managers in a wide variety of companies from different industries are envisioning wireless channels as an important distribution resource for *digital content*. This category of services, which also includes remote e-mail and short messages (160 character text messages), may even overshadow transaction services.

On the consumer side, the early experiences of wireless service providers, such as Japan's NTT DoCoMo, have demonstrated that content services for some people will mean entertainment (e.g., games and music) playing on mobile phones. The CNN wireless news subscription service provides a different type of content and features "breaking news," whatever the recipient's location.

Network service operators have also established wireless portals. Their wireless Internet business model, paralleling business models used in "traditional" Internet companies, enables browsers to scan a broad set of healthcare, financial, travel, weather, and entertainment information directly from their handheld wireless device. Digital magazines, newsletters, and short stories also are being distributed over these channels. The portals' directory services include yellow pages and personal locators. Of course, consumer browsing will surely include checking transit schedules, market prices, sports scores, and information on ticket availability.

Businesses are exploring the possibilities for delivering products—digital products—and services over wireless channels. Both scheduled and spontaneous delivery systems are being implemented. The question is whether individuals who, perhaps for entertainment, regularly download stylish ring tones for their digital phones will begin transferring that interest to commercial activities, such as retrieving business software or business databases. Even the delivery of digital news has yet to be proven an economically viable content service on wireless platforms.

It is *likely* that enterprises will focus their efforts on providing product and service support to their customers. Early adopters are testing the benefits of high bandwidth networks by creating applications that permit on screen viewing of videos and animated demonstrations as a tool for "on-the-spot" troubleshooting, maintenance, and training.

It appears *unlikely*, however, that the highly touted use of wireless devices to view movies and lengthy entertainment videos will be realized in the near future. Even with higher bandwidths, there is still a limit to how much of the wireless hype, typified by these examples, can be turned into reality.

Telematic Services

The transmission and receipt of status, sensing, and measurement information—telemetry—forms the basis for still another large set of new applications involving wireless networks and mobile devices. These innovations make it possible for people to use wireless phones and the like to communicate with various appliances and machines from their homes, offices, or in the field. Telematic capabilities can be embedded in another system or may comprise a stand-alone system.

Embedded Self-Monitoring and Control Systems

Devices and machines in this category feature a built-in capability for self monitoring of their state or location and periodically transmitting the details to a control center. The systems also may be designed to transmit status information when an unacceptable or unexpected condition is detected. For example, the island city of Richmond, British Columbia, relies on a system of 180 pumping stations to work around the clock, pumping water from the island back into the surrounding river and thereby keeping the city from being flooded. The city recently implemented a local area network interconnecting the stations as an aide in monitoring for malfunctioning pumps. If a malfunction occurs, a message is transmitted from the pumping stations to a control center and in turn to wireless palm computers carried by city managers. Managers are now alerted instantly (i.e., any time, any place) to a pump failure by way of messages appearing on their handheld computers. (Dunne, 2002).

Remote Monitoring and Control Systems

Devices and machines in the remote monitoring category do not monitor themselves. Rather, the built-in control module receives and responds to incoming wireless signals asking for data on their status. They can also receive instructions for making performance adjustments. For instance, delivery truck drivers may "ping" intelligent dispensing machines or in-store computers to determine where their rolling inventory is needed most or which locations need service immediately. Similarly, users can transmit messages to activate remote recording devices or service systems. Coca-Cola has created prototype applications that remotely adjust the vending machine prices charged for soft drinks based on fluctuating demand or changing weather conditions.

As these examples illustrate, the combination of wireless devices and telematics has many potential applications. Some companies are seeking to use them in managing energy and security systems. Other uses are being developed in the fields of transportation (roadway, rail, and waterway traffic monitoring and control) and healthcare (patient monitoring, including clinical and field monitoring of drug tests).

⁞ *Initiation Alternatives*

Wireless networking applications can be designed for active or passive initiation. They are *active* if they perform their service only when manually invoked. When an individual initiates a purchase, transmits a payment, requests information, downloads requested content, transmits payments, or retrieves status information, the user actively initiates the transactions.

In *passive* applications, an information system program or control system provides a service automatically, without being told to do so. For example, the automatic collection of toll charges is becoming more frequent as wireless technology components (e.g., signaling chips and transponders) are installed in ordinary devices (even an automobile). If this capability is embedded in an automatic highway toll collection system, payments can be transferred and recorded automatically when a sensor in a wireless toll network detects an approaching vehicle's digital cash device.

Passive security, intrusion, and emergency telemetry services are advancing the capability for remote monitoring of facilities and individuals. Events or conditions that are deemed unusual or unacceptable, based on parameters entered during implementation of the system, cause the device to transmit a notification and even take action automatically. For instance, leading global airlines have implemented wireless systems that alert registered frequent travelers about airport security conditions, changes in flight schedules, or upgrades to their seat assignments. Some airlines are deploying wireless networks that do so only when a passenger enters the airport terminal or passes by a kiosk. Others are exploring wireless systems that can transmit over greater distances, thereby giving airlines the ability to notify passengers well before they arrive at the terminal.

⁝　*Wireless Networks and IT Strategy*

The mix of wireless applications implemented within enterprises will evolve unevenly, influenced by industry forces, the company's geographic location, and its business strategies. In some cases, those individuals living in Europe and Asia will, in the short term, be more attuned to the potential value of wireless networks than their North American counterparts, simply because they make more frequent use of them as vehicles for personal communication. For instance, those who routinely send and receive wireless short messages (160 character text messages—more common in Europe and Asia) may be quicker to recognize their potential value for commercial use.

Yet there is little doubt that enterprise IT strategies will be influenced by these innovations. Any planning for evolutionary strategies, and for the potential portfolio of applications, however, should be anchored by a set of key assumptions about expected technology developments. In addition, the strategy should address the all-important matters of device, platform, and application integration strategies.

Strategic Assumptions Regarding Wireless Networks

Even though the set of desirable wireless applications will vary by enterprise and industry, IT executives should consider the following four basic assumptions:

1. *Wireless Devices*: The variety and number of wireless devices suitable for interconnection with a firm's business systems will continue to grow. This assumption can be made as a direct result of continued innovations in the capabilities and characteristics of wireless devices of all types: mobile telephones, personal digital assistants, and products with embedded wireless capability. Moreover, because the installed base of devices will grow, more people and enterprises can be expected to want to use them as a tool of business and commerce. If firms are already facing a challenge in this area today, the challenge will not diminish. Wireless networks are not a temporary fad but a fundamental force influencing the business and technology platforms from which IT strategy must be constructed.

2. *Applications on Wireless Networks*: The implementation of enterprise wireless networks will become much more commonplace. Application demands within and between enterprises will increase in scope to include wireless networks. Such expansion will occur with as much force as that encountered when many businesses shifted to online access of enterprise systems over the last two decades.

3. *Multichannel Wireless Applications*: Wireless applications will span *multiple wireless* channels, in addition to fixed-base, wired lines. The more an enterprise uses its wireless technologies to interact with its employees,

customers, and firms outside of its own borders, the more it will be forced to support several heterogeneous wireless methods (e.g., WLAN, WPAN, and 3G voice services). Globally, no single public or private wireless channel will dominate in the near future.

4. *Multichannel Data Streams*: It will become common for single information systems applications to process and integrate data from multiple data streams. Some will originate within the enterprise and others will come from the external business environment. Developers of the architectures on which IT strategy is based can expect numerous and repeated challenges in the creation and management of a system of communication channels that push heterogeneous data streams into enterprise databases.

Each of these assumptions must be evaluated within the individual enterprise. As each assumption is accepted, its significance should be factored into an enterprise IT strategy and in turn to the integration of device, platform, and application strategies essential.

Wireless Device Strategy

Seasoned IT planners remember all too well the earliest challenges of legacy systems and the associated islands of automation—challenges stemming from stand alone information systems applications that could neither be connected to nor integrated with other business systems for data sharing. These characteristics are still present in many legacy systems. A different but equally important challenge is emerging as a result of the wide variety of wireless devices being adopted within companies. IT directors will need to decide whether, as part of a larger strategy, a single device strategy should be pursed for the enterprise (i.e., a solution calling for an application to support only one specific type of device). Alternatively, they may determine that strategic business applications should be constructed with the anticipation of connecting several useful types of wireless devices, each very useful but incompatible with the other.

For instance, IT directors already have to decide whether to provide wireless access to corporate and remote e-mail with a common point solution (e.g., a single brand of interactive pager) or to support a mix of wireless devices (e.g., pagers, PDAs and wireless notebook computers). Choosing solutions that call for just one type of wireless device (perhaps to ease support problems) may later be judged as too limiting if the enterprise decides to expand the mix of business applications having wireless features. Undoing earlier decisions may be difficult. (Moreover, the most popular text pagers often cannot be adapted to fit more than one type of application.) Dealing with a mix of devices, each unique to a single application, may or may not be necessary. In either case, this choice should be deliberate and not made by default. Even then, the rapid evolution of this technology will probably make it necessary to revisit the strategy annually.

Wireless Platform Strategy

IT directors are facing growing pressure to support heterogeneous operating and software platforms. It is highly unlikely that the wireless segment of the IT industry will enjoy the same widespread convergence to a single PC platform that occurred during the Internet's evolution. There is neither a single dominant wireless network provider nor is there a prevailing platform comparable to Microsoft and the Windows platform.

In contrast, competing but widely used stand-alone vendor platforms are the norm For instance, the Palm, Microsoft Windows CE, and RIM Blackberry operating system platforms are all widely used, but each is incompatible with the others. Manufacturers of mobile phones also use proprietary operating systems. Still other operating systems are under development as a result of alliances between vendors.[1]

Choosing to standardize on just one platform seems attractive in comparison to supporting multiple platforms and interfaces for each and every wireless application. Here, too, however, as in choosing wireless devices, failing to consider the firm's overall IT strategy or selecting one platform too early in this evolutionary process, may create unforeseen hazards and barriers for integrating future applications.

Wireless Integration Strategy

There also is a need to consider whether to construct high impact, but separate, applications that capitalize on the benefits afforded by wireless networks or to follow a policy calling for deliberate integration of information systems, whether they are wireless or not. Treating solutions separately risks the creation of an environment of stand-alone (i.e., stovepipe) wireless applications, each separate from the other company systems. IT directors are already finding that they must reconcile the current incompatible solutions offered by wireless device, network, and software vendors. Yet many are at the same time underestimating the strategic value of integrating wireless network applications with the many legacy systems and databases that hold the majority of company data.

The following six questions may guide IT directors in this area:

1. Which information systems applications are likely to be based *solely* on wireless communication channels in the future?
2. Which applications are likely to require data streams that originate from *both* traditional (i.e., fixed) and wireless network channels?
3. What are the benefits or drawbacks to avoiding diversity in the installed base of wireless devices, and which applications are likely to be affected the most by any decision?
4. What equipment, machines, and control systems now being used or

planned will utilize wireless networks for transmission or receipt of data?

5. What business strategies will exhibit the greatest influence on the enterprise application architecture and which applications will support those strategies?

6. From what sources and locations will the greatest amount of wireless traffic originate? How often are these profiles expected to change?

∷ Conclusion

It is clear that the number of wireless devices in use, handheld and otherwise, and the networks that transport the data will continue growing throughout the world. The potential impact on business and society is dramatic. For this reason, it is time for business and information technology planners to examine the ways in which their organization can take advantage of these developments, both to serve their customers and employees and to improve business processes and the enterprise's overall performance.

Some of the developments regarding wireless information systems applications that will occur in the future can be predicted based on current knowledge and experience. In other cases, neither the application nor the impact of using these innovations can be foreseen.

Therefore, it is essential that organization executives responsible take deliberate actions to consider the potential strategic value of wireless networking. Those responsible for formation of information technology strategies must do the same, aligning their strategies with those of the enterprise. It would be unfortunate for all if those responsible for these strategies assumed that the impact of wireless networks would be limited. All experiences to date seem to suggest the opposite. Innovations are emerging at an accelerating rate. Hence, failing to plan for their emergence means that the enterprise is not standing still but, rather, falling behind . . . at an accelerating rate.

∷ Note

1. For example, Symbian—a joint effort with participation from Ericsson, Nokia, Matsushita (Panasonic), Motorola, Psion, and Sony—is developing an advanced, open operating system (Symbian OS) for data-enabled mobile phones.

∷ Reference

Dunne, D. (2002) "Wireless That Works," *CIO Magazine,* 15(9, Feb. 15), 61.

16

Yolande Chan

Competing Through Information Privacy

⦂ *Chapter Summary*

1. Despite differing viewpoints, few would disagree that in the Information Age, astute information systems management is high on the list of priorities.
2. Information, whether corporate, personal, or financial; whether in individual pockets or massive databases, has become one of our most valuable commodities. How personal (as contrasted with publicly available) information is managed, with whose interests in mind, and how these issues fit into the already complex information management challenges are the subjects of this chapter.
3. Privacy represents a significant challenge for businesses that needs to be addressed in terms of firm strategy and alignment.
4. Privacy as a competitive advantage does require that customers value at a minimum, and are willing to pay for, at a maximum, the careful, ethical treatment of their information.

⦂ *Introduction*

Definitions of privacy are varied and myriad. Nonetheless, a viable definition can be provided from Roger Clarke, early privacy advocate, who said: "Privacy is often thought of as a moral right or a legal right. But it is often more useful to perceive privacy as the interest that individuals have in sustaining personal space, free from interference by other people and organizations" (Clarke, 1999, p. 60). There is nothing new about people wanting to have a bit of personal space. In terms of the space occupied by information, however, recent decades have witnessed an unprecedented transformation in information generation, storage, transfer, and retrieval. A global marketplace, "greased" by the Internet and electronic/mobile commerce, has created information management and privacy challenges that would have been viewed as science fiction even 10 years ago.

This chapter presents logical arguments concerning, and practical examples of, how privacy issues play out in the contemporary management of information and information systems. These issues, however, cannot be studied in a technological vacuum. As Behrman and Richards point out, "Privacy management not only concerns technology, but also business processes, management policy, and understanding customer needs. Several factors drive the privacy issue, such as cultural attitudes, politics and legislation, special and public interest groups, financial and technology industry organizations, globalization, and market forces" (Behrman & Richards, 2001, p. ii).

Privacy issues have permeated everything from private sector business decisions to popular culture. A recent *Ottawa Citizen* cartoon illustrates a cashier at a supermarket thanking a stunned customer as the cashier refers to the customer's full name, address, and eating preferences based on inferences drawn from her purchases, which were tracked using a buyer card and entered in a company database (*Ottawa Citizen*, 2001). Perhaps in this instance it is all in fun, but it is an example of how personal details have become part of the fabric of marketing and commerce. Paying by cash may now be the only way to maintain personal anonymity—and even this may be compromised if the area is under video surveillance which tracks and records people's movements. Furthermore, widespread use of information and information-gathering technologies has blurred the line between public and private information. According to Caudill and Murphy's "Consumers' Personal Information Model," the line between public information and private information has moved by increments over the past couple of decades as the space allotted to private information has gradually diminished (Caudill & Murphy, 2000).

Views on privacy differ widely, from the strictly pragmatic view held by Ontario's privacy commissioner Anne Cavoukian that privacy is "the next business imperative" to views that weave privacy together with elements of basic humanity, such that privacy is an essential component of a person's independence, dignity, and integrity (Culnan & Bies, 1999). How do these varying viewpoints affect IT strategy? They provide opportunities for firms to differentiate themselves based on their information privacy policies. To approach this issue from a different angle, consider that "[f]irms such as the Body Shop, Tom's of Maine, and Ben & Jerry's target the moral desires of potential customers by engaging in social-cause marketing. Such firms seek to identify with particular social causes, such as saving whales, as a means of attracting consumers who want to support those causes. Consumers may choose to do business with them solely on the basis of an assumed alignment of moral preferences" (Goldberg, Hill, & Shostack, 2001, pp. 414–15). In this case, the reference is to social causes, but privacy issues, like other value-based issues, can be conducive to targeting consumers on the basis of "values alignment" or "alignment with moral preferences." In this way, consumer values can be explicitly factored into the business strategy and alignment equation.

: *Privacy as an IT Alignment Issue*

Discussions of alignment often touch on the necessity of characteristics such as flexibility and balance (Burns, 1996). When privacy is introduced into the equation, as a factor to be considered when achieving information systems strategic alignment, privacy considerations have a bearing on everything from systems design to customer service, and include issues of employee and customer education, and matters of corporate and public policy. But it is not only internal strategies and functions that must mesh; there also must be a fit with external elements such as customer preferences, partner firm practices and legislation. Businesses that can best balance these often opposing issues may be on their way to developing a trusting customer base. In other words, firms that "best develop a cohesive customer relationship management strategy globally while remaining flexible enough to meet the privacy requirements of each local market will be the most likely to succeed" (Behrman & Richards, 2001, p. 13).

A company's IT is fundamental to any attempt to build a shrewd and successful business strategy. How systems are developed and the extent to which they embody privacy considerations are, for many, sources of concern. Clarke notes, "Marketing, technological and provider imperatives are creating tendencies for hitherto anonymous events to be converted into identified transactions, resulting in yet more data trails available to be trawled and mined" (Clarke, 1999, p. 61). Although privacy issues cannot undergo a lasting fix solely through the application of new software (Behrman & Richards, 2001), new technology can promote privacy and accountability if this is built into the design, rather than trying to retrofit privacy considerations into an existing system (Caudill & Murphy, 2000). Goldberg et al. are arguably most vehement on the issue of system design: "In creating a system, it is easy to move it towards verified identity, and hard to move away from it. Once the system relies on having identity verification, it is difficult to recreate the same system without that component of identity verification. Thus, the nymity graph, when applied to real systems, is a *slider* during the design phase. The implementation, however, transforms it into a nymity *ratchet*. Good system design should thus aim towards the anonymous end of the slider to preserve flexibility with respect to new system requirements" (Goldberg, Hill, & Shostack, 2001, p. 421).

That information—and how it is managed is so important to company decisions—goes far to support the claim made in an *Atlantic Monthly*'s recent cover story that privacy is "*the* true enabler of the information economy" (Lester, 2001, p. 28). It is also clear that, because government policies are so divided on the issue of appropriate privacy policy (ranging from the stringent European Data Protection Directive and Canada's similar Personal Information Protection and Electronic Documents Act to the widespread reliance of the United States on self-regulation), firms' responses must address privacy with more consideration than mere compliance with existing

regulations. Take, for instance, "Fair Information Practices," or FIP, originally heralded in the 1960s as the appropriate way to deal with expanding
data processing capabilities. No matter how strictly companies may adhere
to them today, these decades-old principles fall short of what is required in
the "dramatically more powerful, network-based IT of the 2000s" (Clarke,
1999, p. 65).

IT is profoundly important to businesses, then, not only on the level
of how customers feel about giving a company their personal information,
but also because it often drives key internal functions such as payroll, human
resources, and accounting. Since the advent of the Internet and e/m-
commerce, however, IT is often the only aspect of the company a consumer
sees, and therefore it reflects directly on and shapes a customer's first and
lasting impression of the company. As Van Der Heijden notes, "When IT
departments move beyond purely internal applications and incorporate electronic commerce (e-commerce) in their service portfolio the relationship
between business and IT becomes an even more important issue" (Van Der
Heijden, 2001, p. 13). IT and privacy issues come together when a company
decides, for example, if potential customers will be required to register at
their Internet site and, if so, how much information will be identifiable or
required. Once a customer decides if the potential services are worth relaying
the requested information, what a company decides to do with the information it gathers will have profound impacts on the business in everything
from its internal processes to its external profile.

Privacy scholar Phil Agre observes, "The idea that technology and privacy are intrinsically opposed is false." He goes on to note that the same
technology that is now used for surveillance made possible many benefits
that people are reluctant to surrender (Lester, 2001, p. 28). Primarily technological advances do not fuel surveillance but, paradoxically, surveillance is
fueled by the growing demand for privacy, as more "tokens of trust" are
required when private individuals interact (Lyon, 2001). In fact, historically,
technology, no matter at how rudimentary a level, has promoted privacy.
The invention of writing, for example, allowed for private communication
for the first time, as did single party telephones; modern roads and automobiles allow for private travel; and television and radio continue to bring
news and entertainment into private homes (Lester, 2001).

IT management, however, has begun to sway in the other direction, so
that IT's privacy infringing capabilities have become more publicized than
its privacy enhancing potential. Database manipulation allows for easy recovery, replication, and transmission of millions of pieces of data at once.
Also, the possibility—and reality—of function creep makes people legiti-
mately wary of passing on too much personal or identifiable information.
Function creep is the term that has come to describe what happens when
information is gathered for a specific and legitimate purpose, but then is
consequently re-used in a different situation, which is possibly unlawful and
nearly always unknown to the source of the information (Miyazaki & Fer-

nandez, 2000). Roger Clarke (1999) coins his own term "dataveillance" to refer to society's unbridled fascination with (other people's) information. He also uses the phrase "information privacy" to describe a subset of privacy that deals specifically with individuals' claims that "data about themselves should generally not be available to other individuals and organizations, and that, where data is possessed by another party, the individual must be able to exercise a substantial degree of control over that data and its use" (Clarke, 1999, p. 60).

Information technology and management have everything to do with the perception of information gathering practices. Hine and Eve (1998) use the term "benign technology" to describe the type of technology companies can consciously and purposively employ to benefit both their desire and need for information, and also their customers' privacy imperative. They point to subtle differences in design and application of technology such that the "collection and use of information may be construed as intrusive or nonintrusive, depending on the construction of the technology involved in the process and the extent to which the technology is visible. Representations of technology and what it can or cannot do combine with other factors, such as identity, control, and relationships with data-using organizations, to produce a situation that may be subsequently construed as invasive" (Hine & Eve, 1999, p. 254).

The issue of trust, alluded to only briefly previously, also has profound implications for a company's ability to align privacy concerns—whether they are their own or their customers' or their business partners'—with their design and implementation of information systems. Although technology is again at the root of company decisions, information management practices are also tightly intertwined with customers' ability or willingness to trust an organization. From a pragmatic perspective, which weds both the technological and management angles, organizations will have to encourage trust not only in their ability to do business, but also in the systems they use to gather data and how they will use it (Caudill & Murphy, 2000; Miyazaki & Fernandez, 2000). Culnan and Bies (1999, p. 156) define such trust as "the willingness of one party, here a customer, to be vulnerable to the actions of another party, here a firm, based on an expectation that the firm will perform a particular action of importance to the customer, independent of the customer's ability to monitor or control the firm." Part of what makes the trust discussion both so necessary and so fragile is that it diverges from other management issues that are more readily measured and altered. Trust, however, is an emotional, "heart and mind" issue. Many managers are reluctant to make investments with potentially delayed returns such as those involved in building trust; many customers are reluctant to trust technology, particularly in the hands of businesses (Lester, 2001). Companies who would like to unleash the latest e/m-commerce capabilities often encounter a roadblock in the form of consumer distrust in corporations (Clarke, 1999, p. 63). What is needed right now, according to Clarke (1999, p. 63), "is a solution to the crisis in public confidence in IT that is being brought to a head by the rapid growth and far-reaching impact of the Internet." He goes on to assert that the information economy "is dependent on trust. Trust *must* be earned, and intrusion-permissive and intrusion-enabling arrangements preclude trust."

Perhaps ironically, so much of the trust debate as it focuses on information technology and management ultimately moves back to human decisions of how to align strategy factors (such as judgments regarding the trustworthiness of partner firms and what information will be shared with these firms). There is no substitute for ethical and wise managerial decisions, which is what leads to the subsequent section of this chapter, on Information Privacy Strategy as an element of information strategy to be aligned with other company initiatives.

⦂ Information Privacy Strategy

In the past, it was generally held that good IT management practices led to improved business performance; however, today the view is that good *information management* practices, and even good *information behaviors and values* lead more clearly to improved business performance (Marchand, Kettinger, & Rollins, 2000a). In the Information Age, the focus has shifted from aligning specific systems and technology with the business strategy, to aligning far-reaching information practices and culture. The term "information orientation" has been introduced to describe firms' information capabilities and choices. It refers to IT practices, information practices, information behaviors and values (Marchand, Kettinger, & Rollins, 2000b). Information privacy is an important information orientation component. Just as a good CIO is able to discuss the firm's IT strategy, today's forward-thinking CIO is able to discuss the organization's information privacy strategy.

Business and IT managers have both an admittedly challenging and a potentially rewarding responsibility when it comes to shaping their company's information privacy strategy and aligning it to existing or evolving business directions. It is hard to dispute the argument that "IS professionals and managers should be aware of information privacy issues—especially the potential impact on existing IT and on future systems development. IT managers have the oversight responsibility for information liability as they have the most extensive knowledge of their organization's systems and programs and an intimate understanding of the data. To perform this oversight function effectively and to provide justification for increased information security to policy makers, however, IT managers and professionals must understand the driving forces surrounding individuals' concern about personal information privacy" (Henderson & Snyder, 1999, p. 215). Managers' privacy-related decisions can go far in aligning positive business impacts with necessary external directives, whether they come in the form of consumer demand, industry regulation, or even national and international legislation. External dimensions, however, are not the only driving forces behind managers' decisions with respect to information management. Depending on the firm's values, strategy, and information orientation, managers will be guided by an internal "information privacy orientation" (Greenaway, Cunningham, & Chan, 2002) that will determine whether they choose to use information to promote the joint interests of the business and of the customer, or to promote the interests of the business *at the expense* of the customer. Business policies and practices regarding information ownership, access, use, and distribution will vary, and tradeoffs will be made among the rights and benefits of the business and the customer.

Procedural fairness, and fair information practices (Culnan & Bies, 1999), are logical starting points for a company's information privacy strategy. Mere adherence to legislation and industry codes of conduct, however, amounts to a low privacy orientation—an avoidance of the negative (e.g., bad press and customer complaints). A high privacy orientation organization moves toward the positive—differentiation through ethical information management and the establishment of high trust customer relationships. To appeal to privacy conscious customers, the organization can voluntarily subscribe to established codes of conduct, trademarks, and audits such as those provided by TRUSTe, WebTrust and the Platform for Privacy Preferences (P3P) (Clarke, 1999).

The costs of a high privacy orientation need not be exorbitant. Organizations can begin to use the same technologies that allow them to gather information (for example, through online tracking) to request permission for, or inform customers about, the use of this information. Privacy can actually be cheaper than ever before because of communication technologies that allow for fast and easy permission asking and giving (Culnan & Bies, 1999). The costs of a low privacy orientation organization can be significant. Businesses can lose sales, customers, international opportunities, image, and investors, while incurring increased legal costs (Gellman, 2002).

Just as businesses with different strategies—for example, prospector, analyzer and defender firms (Miles & Snow, 1978)—tend to use IT differently in their search for competitive advantage (Gupta, Karimi, & Somers, 1997; Sabherwal & Chan, 2001), firms, while complying with legislative and regulatory requirements, will demonstrate a range of information privacy orientations. For instance, prospector firms seeking flexibility and the ability to exploit emerging market opportunities will be more likely to evidence moderate or average privacy orientations. Risk-averse analyzers are likely to evidence high privacy orientations, while we anticipate that cost-conscious defender firms will evidence low privacy orientations. A privacy strategy then is an important first step for firms to secure the competitive advantage that may accrue from respecting customers' privacy preferences.

: *Privacy as Competitive Advantage*

Businesses that choose to compete on privacy can reduce costs and increase revenues by setting themselves apart from their competitors. Examples abound of how businesses that have either respected or invaded their customers' privacy have either profited or suffered as a result. Lester argues that as privacy becomes scarce, and demand remains high, it will command a higher price (Lester, 2001). The reverse phenomenon was seen recently when customers' displeasure was signaled in the stock market when AOL's stock fell 4 percent when the company announced a plan to sell subscriber phone numbers to telemarketers (Caudill & Murphy, 2000). It subsequently backed away from the move, but the damage had been done. In fact, in 2000 alone, AOL received about 475 civil subpoenas and incurred significant—unnecessary—legal costs (Gellman, 2002). Other observers note that "for e-commerce to continue to grow, it is imperative that [Internet service] providers solve end-user concerns. . . . the end consumer is incredibly concerned with privacy (this is especially true for older customers) . . . and if consumers feel their ISP cares about privacy, it will make a huge difference competitively" (Carroll, 1999, p. 46).

Just as privacy issues have reached the realm of popular culture, so, too, have they made a mark on politics and political decisions. Allaert and Barber point out, "By definition, members of Parliament are not necessarily specialists in the legal domain or in any kind of specific technological field. Thus, their decision to vote in favor or against proposed legislation is motivated by political considerations even if they try to be as informed as possible on the eventual . . . consequences of their vote" (Allaert & Barber, 2000, p. 100). Politicians and other nonexperts are starting to pay attention to the fact that how they handle privacy issues will have both a domestic and international impact. Then-President of the United States Bill Clinton admitted, " 'Information is one of the nation's most critical economic resources. . . . In an era of global markets and global competition, the technologies to create, manipulate, manage and use information are of strategic importance to the United States.' . . . The EU data protection Directive threatens U.S. leadership in the information economy and is heightening U.S. concern over protecting that so-called dominance" (Cate, 1995, p. 440).

Part of interpreting privacy as a competitive advantage in the strategy equation can depend on the amount of responsibility given to each party, so that privacy takes on the characteristics of a social contract (Culnan, 2000; Milne, 1997; Phelps, Nowak, & Ferrell, 2000). By this reasoning, exchange relationships are established in which consumers give up a portion of their privacy (but still believing their trust is not misplaced) to obtain personalized services in exchange for personalized marketing. The implied contract is breached if marketers misuse the information, do not tell customers they are collecting information, do not give customers the opportunity to remove their name, or give the information to other parties. If this occurs, competitive advantage is lost and the contract is effectively nullified. At present, even companies that claim to respect privacy interests sometimes compromise standards in the name of competition (Caudill & Murphy, 2000). This may provide only a short-lived advantage.

Privacy as a competitive advantage does require that customers value at a minimum, and are willing to pay for, at a maximum, the careful, ethical treatment of their information. Recently, a number of businesses offering privacy protection services to online consumers marketed themselves primarily on the basis of their privacy practices and services. Anonymizer.com and Zero Knowledge, for example, were two companies that offered consumers the possibility of complete Internet anonymity. Zero Knowledge, in fact, boasted that even in the event of legal persuasion or subpoenas they were completely unable to trace or reveal who used their services. Interestingly enough, both Anonymizer.com and Zero Knowledge have been forced to close their doors due to lack of business, since, although the demand for their services exists, people do not seem willing to pay for them.

This would not surprise law professor Arthur Miller. In an interview for *CIO Magazine*, Miller says: "If you put the issue of privacy in terms of civil liberties or medical records, you get very strong pro-privacy reactions. But if you put it in terms of accessed goodies, then it becomes a tradeoff, which leads one to believe that Americans care less about privacy in the commercial context than they do in the medical or employment context" (Bass, 2001).

Perhaps customers do not expect to have to pay to maintain their privacy in commercial transactions and express this preference by simply voting with their feet and taking their wallets with them. As the AOL example showed, customers are prepared to take their business elsewhere if they are dissatisfied with a firm's privacy practices. So whereas an information privacy strategy appears not to be a viable stand-alone business strategy in North America, at this time, it is an important element of, and must be in alignment with, the overall business strategy. For instance, we must "walk the talk" of one-to-one marketing, and mass customization, when we say we regard customers as important *individuals*. Organizations need to be prepared to align customer information practices with its marketing and manufacturing practices. Information practices will influence perceptions of product and service quality, and ultimately company reputation.

A corporate practice that is on the rise involves hiring a visible and accessible executive who is the champion of information privacy within the organization. This executive must have the consumers' interests at heart, and cultivate what Culnan and Bies call a "culture of privacy" (Culnan & Bies, 1999) within the organization. To put it more bluntly, companies simply must "get ready to hire a chief privacy officer" (Fitz-James, 2001, p. 15) if they expect to be able to please the privacy-aware consumer and be socially responsible. Not only must privacy officers have the interests of the consumer at heart, they must energetically promote these interests. Since customers are increasingly paying attention to the privacy initiatives of the companies with which they do business, privacy must become part of the quality service equation, on equal footing with speed, courtesy, and good value. The question of the future regarding organizations, according to Lester, is "are they privacy-enabled?" (Lester, 2001, p. 32).

All the best efforts of a privacy officer, however, will be wasted unless companies also invest energy and time in creating privacy policies, fostering an appropriate privacy orientation, and educating employees in the issue of privacy as it relates to good business. Consumers will naturally educate themselves by their own means, but they are frequently willing to receive helpful—and nonintrusive—company communications. Companies can take advantage of this by taking the initiative to deliberately educate customers about their privacy options, thus creating the possibility that the customer— if dealt with ethically, respectfully, and honestly—will learn to trust one company above others.

Education, however, does not start and end with customers. As previously noted, it is imperative that employees also understand and follow privacy guidelines as adopted by the company as a whole. Potentially devastating misalignment of company strategy can be as simple and as destructive as one employee, either knowingly or otherwise, ignoring company mandates on how to deal with requests for information. In an example cited by Culnan and Bies (1999, p. 159), "an employee of a large database company allowed a television reporter using a personal credit card and posing under the name of a well-known pedophile to acquire a list of children living in a California suburb. The transaction violated company policies; nonetheless, it resulted in negative publicity for the firm." Employees have to be trained and retrained based on developments in the information systems and technology at the company's disposal, and also based on evolving information management practices.

As with many strategic alignment issues, the responsibility for dealing with privacy falls on managers' shoulders. As a consequence, managers "should establish adequate policies and ensure that they are properly promulgated to those workers who have responsibility for the protection of privacy" (Henderson & Snyder, 1999, p. 217). They need to address privacy issues proactively through "intellectual engagement . . . resource commitment, acculturation of staff, adaptation of business processes, the establishment and operation of complaints-handling processes, communications with the corporations' clientele, and control and audit mechanisms" (Clarke, 1999, p. 65). Marchand et al. draw the circle of management responsibility even wider: "If there is a starting point for improving how businesses use information, it's in a perception many senior managers share: Companies must do more than excel at investing in and deploying IT. They must combine those capabilities with excellence in collecting, organizing and maintaining information, and with getting their people to embrace the right behaviors and values for working with information" (Marchand, Kettinger,

& Rollins, 2000b, pp. 69–70). Culnan and Bies write: "Our vision of privacy for the [21st] century is that all firms will begin to compete on their privacy practices" (1999, p. 162).

▪ Note

I wish to thank Anna Dekker for her invaluable research and editorial assistance. Without her contributions, this chapter would not have been possible. I also wish to thank David Lyon, Peggy Cunningham, and Kathleen Greenaway, co-investigators in ongoing information privacy research funded by the Social Sciences and Humanities Research Council of Canada. Thanks go also to the Queen's Centre for Knowledge-Based Enterprises for their financial support of this project.

▪ References

Allaert, F. A., & B. Barber. (2000) "Law and Standards," *International Journal of Medical Informatics,* 60(2), 99–103.

Bass, A. (2001) "Miller's Privacy Warning," *CIO Magazine,* November 1, 2001. Available online at: http://www.cio . . . archive/110101/miller_content.html (accessed November 2, 2001).

Behrman, D., & T. Richards. (2001) "Privacy Management and Compliance: The Tip of the Iceberg," *Meridian Research,* 5(2), 1–29.

Burns, J. (1996) "IS Innovation and Organizational Alignment—A Professional Juggling Act," *Journal of Information Technology,* 11, 3–12.

Carroll, K. (1999) "E-commerce Success May Depend on Online Privacy," *Telephony,* October 25, 46.

Cate, F. (1995) "The EU Data Protection Directive, Information Privacy, and the Public Interest," *Iowa Law Review,* 80(3), 431–43.

Caudill, E. M., & P. E. Murphy. (2000) "Consumer Online Privacy: Legal and Ethical Issues," *Journal of Public Policy and Marketing,* 19(1), 7–19.

Clarke, R. (1999) "Internet Privacy Concerns Confirm the Case for Intervention," *Communications of the ACM,* 42(2), 60–67.

Culnan, M. J. (2000) "Protecting Privacy Online: Is Self-Regulation Working?" *Journal of Public Policy and Marketing,* 19(1), 20–26.

Culnan, M. J., & R. J. Bies. (1999) "Managing Privacy Concerns Strategically: the Implications of Fair Information Practices for Marketing in the Twenty-first Century," in C. J Bennett and R. Grant (Eds.), *Visions of Privacy: Policy Choices for the Digital Age.* Toronto: University of Toronto Press, 149–67.

Fitz-James, M. (2001) "Get Ready to Hire a Chief Privacy Officer," *Business Without Borders,* June, 15–17.

Gellman, R. (2002) "Privacy, Consumers, and Costs: How the Lack of Privacy Costs Consumers and Why Business Studies of Privacy Costs are Biased and Incomplete." Available online at: http://www.epic.org/reports/dmfprivacy.html (accessed March 28, 2002).

Goldberg, I., A. Hill, & A. Shostack. (2001) "Trust, Ethics, and Privacy," *Boston University Law Review*, 81(2), 407–22.

Greenaway, K., P. Cunningham, & Y. E. Chan. (2002, May 17) "Privacy Orientation: A Competing Values Explanation of Why Organizations Vary in Their Treatment of Customer Information." Marketing and Public Policy Conference, Atlanta, Georgia.

Gupta, Y. P., J. Karimi, & T. M. Somers. (1997) "Alignment of a Firm's Competitive Strategy and Information Technology Management Sophistication: The Missing Link," *IEEE Transactions on Engineering Management*, 44(4), 399–413.

Henderson, S. C., & C. A. Snyder. (1999) "Personal Information Privacy: Implications for MIS Managers," *Information & Management*, 36(4), 213–20.

Hine, C., & J. Eve. (1998) "Privacy in the Marketplace," *The Information Society*, 14(4), 253–62.

Lester, T. (2001) "The Reinvention of Privacy," *The Atlantic Monthly*, March, 27–29.

Lyon, D. (2001) *Surveillance Society: Monitoring Everyday Life*. Buckingham, UK: Open University Press.

Marchand, D. A., W. J. Kettinger, & J. D. Rollins. (2000a) "Company Performance and IM: The View from the Top," in D. A. Marchand, T. H. Davenport, & T. Dickson (Eds.), *Mastering Information Management*, 10–16. Harlow, UK: Pearson Education Limited.

Marchand, D. A., W. J. Kettinger, & J. D. Rollins. (2000b) "Information Orientation: People, Technology and the Bottom Line," *Sloan Management Review*, Summer, 69–80.

Miles, R. E., & C. C. Snow. (1978). *Organizational Strategy, Structure, and Process*. New York: McGraw-Hill.

Milne, G. R. (1997) "Consumer Participation in Mailing Lists: A Field Experiment." *Journal of Public Policy and Marketing*, 16(2), 298–309.

Miyazaki, A. D., & A. Fernandez. (2000) "Internet Privacy and Security: An Examination of Online Retailer Disclosures," *Journal of Public Policy and Marketing*, 19(1), 54–61.

Ottawa Citizen. (2001, November 18), "Betty."

Phelps, J., G. Nowak, & E. Ferrell. (2000) "Privacy Concerns and Consumer Willingness to Provide Personal Information," *Journal of Public Policy and Marketing*, 19(1), 27–41.

Sabherwal, R., & Y. E. Chan. (2001) "Alignment Between Business and IS Strategies: A Study of Prospectors, Analyzers, and Defenders," *Information Systems Research*, 12(1), 11–33.

Van Der Heijden, H. (2001) "Measuring IT Core Capabilities for Electronic Commerce," *Journal of Information Technology*, 16(1), 13–22.

VII

Skills

Skills were defined in figure 1.1. They include all of the human resource considerations for the organization. Above and beyond the traditional considerations—such as training, salary, performance feedback, and career opportunities—are factors that include the organization's cultural and social environment. Is the organization ready for change in this dynamic environment? Do individuals feel personally responsible for business innovation? Can individuals and organizations learn quickly from their experience? Does the organization leverage innovative ideas and the spirit of entrepreneurship? These are some of the important conditions of mature organizations.

COMMUNICATIONS
- Understanding of Business by IT
- Understanding of IT by Business
- Inter/Intra organizational Learning/Education
- Protocol Rigidity
- Knowledge Sharing
- Liaison(s) effectiveness

COMPETENCY/VALUE MEASUREMENTS
- IT Metrics
- Business Metrics
- Balanced Metrics
- Service Level Agreements
- Benchmarking
- Formal Assessment/ Reviews
- Continuous Improvement

GOVERNANCE
- Business Strategic Planning
- IT Strategic Planning
- Organization Structure Reporting
- Budgetary Control
- IT Investment Management
- Steering Committee(s)
- Prioritization Process

IT BUSINESS ALIGNMENT MATURITY CRITERIA

PARTNERSHIP
- Business Perception of IT Value
- Role of IT in Strategic Business
- Shared Goals, Risk, Rewards/Penalties
- IT Program Management
- Relationship/Trust Style
- Business Sponsor/ Champion

SCOPE AND ARCHITECTURE
- Traditional, Enabler/ Driver, External
- Standards Articulate
- Architecture Integration:
  - Functional Organization
  - Enterprise
  - Inter-enterprise
- Architectural Transparency, Agility, Flexibility
- Manage Emerging Technology

SKILLS
- Innovation, Entrepreneurship
- Culture Locus of Power
- Management Style
- Change Readiness
- Career Crossover Training
- Social, Political, Trusting Interpersonal Environment
- Hiring and Retaining

17

Ephraim R. McLean and Scott L. Schneberger

Information Technology Human Resource Strategies

: Chapter Summary

1. Information technology is getting cheaper, while IT labor is becoming more expensive, especially as a portion of the total IT budget. But if IT is to rise to the challenge of being an enabler—and, indeed, a shaper—of overall business strategy, then the role of skilled IT professionals in achieving this goal becomes even more critical than it has been in the past. With new technological developments being announced at an ever-increasing rate, the half-life of the knowledge base of the IT specialist is constantly shrinking. Existing workers are struggling to stay current, and new workers are not being trained fast enough to meet the demand. This trend is likely to continue into the foreseeable future.

2. The human capital dimension of information technology becomes even more complex with the globalization of business. With the Internet, IT workers can now be anywhere in the world. The workers can come to the work—electronically—or the work can come to the workers, with various offshore programming powerhouses emerging and multinational development teams presenting their own special management challenges.

3. Managing and motivating IT workers requires special attention to the unique characteristics of these IT professionals. Research has shown that they differ in significant ways from other types of professionals, and these differences offer both challenges and opportunities to human resources (HR) and IT management. High growth needs and low social needs, among others, must be accounted for in order to achieve a motivated IT workforce.

4. Behavioral research also offers additional insights. These theories contend that all human behavior is caused by a sense of need, is goal-oriented, and is motivated by perceived motivators. Maslow's hierarchy of needs theory and Herzberg's hygiene and satisfiers factors each contribute to our understanding of the causes of motivation and worker satisfaction. Companies that are able to attract and retain skilled IT workers through enlightened HR practices gain a source of competitive advantage.

5. Finally, a number of strategies and approaches are available to the human resource function within companies to address the IT staffing challenge. These include the resource-based view, the uncertainty-reduction strategy,

the portfolio-management strategy, and the expertise-oriented view of HR. Each approach has its strength and weaknesses and needs to be tailored to the circumstances and culture of the organization. Also, the HR function itself is going through a fundamental change, mirroring the expanded role that the IT function is experiencing.

: *Introduction*

Since the earliest days of electronic computing, companies have gained some degree of corporate advantage by strategically applying the right capital to the right information technology. During the 1960s, those who could afford large mainframe computers, computer operations rooms filled with skilled technicians, and programmers for key business computer applications found they could significantly reduce corporate costs and processing times compared to the manual methods used by competitors. In the 1970s, companies that correctly identified new computer applications for operational purposes brought localized, midsized computing to bear for specific competitive advantages. In the 1980s, firms that saw the potential for personal computing and applied information technology to the desktop began to reap increased gains in business productivity and bolster their strategic advantage by improving internal processes through networking systems and improving automated process flows. Finally, in the 1990s and leading into the 2000s, companies have sought to overtake competitors by leaping into e-business technology to stake their claim in the New Economy. During these hectic years, especially for those making strategic business and IT decisions, it was a wild ride with some huge payoffs—and some huge costs.

One overriding trend during this period was the lowering, if not elimination, of technological entry barriers. Except for isolated patented technology, information technology (IT) became an increasingly cheap and prevalent commodity. Computing hardware costs fell roughly 50 percent every 18 months for the same processing and storage capability. Complete enterprise-wide computer software applications have now become off-the-shelf items that are configured—not developed—to meet corporate needs. Moreover, business computer system packages have become available to anyone, anywhere in the world through Internet web services. Today, information technology by itself is increasingly a level playing field, where you can't win by just showing up.

A key point of this chapter is that competitive advantage in future business environments will come not from applying corporate capital to the right information technology but by applying the right *human* capital to information technology. This human capital includes all IT professionals as well as all corporate users of information technology. Winning in this environment won't depend on whether you have all the IT tools; for very little cost, future business computing technology will be ubiquitous and relatively cheap. Successful IT competitive strategies will depend more on *how* information technology is applied than to *what*. And how it is applied will depend on corporate human capital recognizing opportunities, innovating, identifying potential solutions, making decisions, and executing them with sound action. This chapter focuses, in short, on the human side of information systems. In some ways, applying the right human capital is more difficult than applying the right information technology. There are five fundamental challenges in strategically selecting, acquiring, and utilizing human IT capital:

1. Information technology capabilities are advancing at exponential rates; human IT capabilities are not.
2. Human capital and the corresponding labor markets are very different from financial or technological capital markets because humans have hopes and dreams, perceptions, intangible needs and desires, and choose to act from moment to moment. Moreover, human capital with the skills needed to ensure business success will not likely ever be a commodity; indeed, human IT capital is likely to be continually scarce as information technology incessantly improves at rapid rates.
3. IT people appear to be appreciably different from other professionals in terms of their goals, needs, and motivation. Thus, this dictates specialized strategies for managing and measuring IT human capital.
4. Human resource (HR) management is itself undergoing essential changes. HR organizations need to take into account how information technology affects their operations and processes.
5. Organizations are becoming increasingly global; social, political, legal, and cultural differences can be substantial, demanding new approaches to deal with them.

Although these challenges can be formidable, we think that each challenge also presents an opportunity for organizations to capture competitive advantage through sound, effective IT human resource strategies. This chapter includes a closer examination of the challenges noted earlier, and examination of some of the foundational theories on human resource management, and our recommendations on responding to these challenges.

: IT Human Challenges

Information Technology Advances

Moore's Law[1] states that computer processing capability doubles approximately every 18 months—a trend that has held remarkably constant for over 30 years. Even more remarkable, however, are its economic effects. The U.S. Federal Reserve chairman, Alan Greenspan, has credited Moore's Law for raising U.S. productivity an entire percentage point per year; the U.S. Commerce Department has said IT accounted for 35 percent of the U.S. economic growth in 1998 (Greenspan, 2002). Computer processing that used to cost millions of dollars to purchase and millions of dollars to house now costs less than a thousand dollars and can be carried in a briefcase—allowing companies to buy increasingly more computer power for the same amount of money and switch computer purchases from capital expenditures to operational or expendable expenses. As computer prices continue to fall, however, labor costs continue to rise; information systems have an inverse cost curve compared to the people these systems are supposed to make more productive. One might wonder, with such an inverse cost curve, why computer-based information systems aren't replacing workers en masse. On the contrary, the extraordinary rate of technological change seems to breed new jobs faster than it replaces older ones.

But the other side of this rosy economic coin is the fact that the people who design, develop, market, install, maintain, acquire, implement, operate, and use these information systems must keep up with incessant technological changes and improvements. They must have the foundational education to understand the underlying technology; they need specific training in each new technology; and they need to understand the new or evolving intended purpose of applying this technology. Compounding these learning needs is the short half-life of the knowledge itself—about three years. (For instance, in three years, half of what one knows about computer networking technology will be obsolete.) Computer networking producers, for example, use a rule-of-thumb that every new product has a marketable life of about two years before it must be improved or replaced. This requirement for continual education and training, constrained by the short window of opportunity and payoff, present significant barriers to finding good IT workers in the labor market.

Human IT Labor Markets

The effects of this rising business demand for IT labor has, for the most part, shown the classic supply-and-demand relationship of the general labor market model. Although supply, IT labor, and demand by organizations for this labor are determined independently in more or less free markets, the supply of IT labor has responded to increased organizational use of, and demand for, computers by directly raising the price for IT labor through increased wages, and indirectly increasing the supply as the price of IT labor rose and the field became more attractive to those entering the workforce. The factors of IT labor *demand* include the increases in demand for new information technologies skills and decreases in demand for older technology experience, competitive forces and the economic environment, and the retraining and use of current employees. The factors of IT labor *supply* include the quantity and quality of IT educational programs, the perception of workers of labor trends, compensation incentives, and recruiting strategies; and the number of workers entering and leaving the field.[2]

But these markets are not totally free—immigration laws, for example, can hinder free movement of labor; supply reactions to demand can take time; and demand for certain types of IT labor changes as the business use of the technology changes. As a consequence, the supply and demand for IT labor tends to go through up-and-down cycles. When the price and supply movements stop cycling, economists say, the market has reached equilibrium. If anything, however, the IT labor market appears to be in a continual state of *dis*equilibrium—mostly because of the high rate of technological change.

For example, the mid-1990s was seen as a period of very high demand and very short supply. Large and medium size businesses were implementing enterprise resource planning (ERP) systems. Businesses were hastily trying to prepare for potentially disastrous "Y2K," or Year 2000, problems. And "new economy" initiatives were budding and escalating at unprecedented rates. There were abundant stories in the general press, and in the IT press in particular, about the extent businesses would go to find, hire, and keep IT labor, offering new IT graduates salaries higher than their supervisors, flashy cars, vacations, work arrangements reminiscent of dorm life, and—especially with Internet start-ups—stock options. The U.S. Bureau of Labor annually posted dire warnings about IT labor shortages and the possible consequences for future national growth. The U.S. Congress sought to increase the number of H-1B visas available to foreign technical workers to help meet an estimated shortage of 350,000 IT workers.

By the end of 2001, however, job cuts of IT workers had reached nearly two million, with the layoffs fairly evenly distributed across the computer industry except for telecommunications and Internet-related jobs, where they were abnormally high because of the glut of broadband communications capability and the "dot-com" financing implosion (DiSabatino, 2002). Except for technical superstars, the recruiting cornucopia was empty. Job fairs weren't pulling people off the street; they were crammed with laid-off workers and hopeful recent graduates eager to sign for more modest compensation packages. Only a few job types are hiring now with raises: salaries for database managers are up 4.8 percent over 2000; for disaster recovery specialists, up 3.1 percent; and for enterprise resource integration managers, up 2.9 percent (Fox, 2002).

With technology rapidly changing and market-driven technology standards continually evolving, how can IT executives ensure they have the right people in the right places at the right time to maximize the potential of IT? And what sort of people are we talking about—these IT professionals?

IT Professionals

IT professionals—people whose primary job tasks involve acquiring, developing, managing, and maintaining information technology or information systems—appear to have unique characteristics beyond the field of knowledge they hold, are an increasing part of IT budgets, and are becoming increasingly specialized.

Research conducted by Couger in the 1980s showed that IT professionals had higher perceptions of skill variety than the average of all other professions for which there were data. Their sense of task identity and task significance was likewise higher than all other professions (Couger & Zawacki, 1980). Programmers and analysts had the highest sense of professional autonomy and the need for feedback than all other professions. And all types of IT personnel felt a higher than average sense of satisfaction about their tasks and work. IT professionals also showed a very high need for personal growth and development, higher than the average levels of all other professions, and therefore had a high potential for being motivated. By contrast, IT personnel also had very low social needs, felt less satisfaction about working with others and with supervisors, and believed they received less feedback on their work. And IT professionals were often more loyal to their profession than to their company (although primarily during periods of high demand for, and short supply of, IT professionals).

With new collaborative-networked technologies, new software development paradigms, and more global operations, IT workers are also becoming increasingly collaborative and distributed. Software engineering teams can be distributed globally, working on projects asynchronously through Internet connections. Virtual teams can form, collaborate, develop, and then disperse when the product is digitally delivered. Given the time zones worldwide, projects can be worked on continuously, handed off with the daily western passage of the sun. The very technology that improves corporate business productivity can improve IT productivity: virtual collaboration, e-mail, online conferencing, group decision support systems, and group online communications.

IT professionals appear to represent a growing portion of IT budgets. In the early 1970s, IT labor accounted for about 30 percent of a typical IT department budget; by 1980, they accounted for about 50 percent; and, in the 1990s, they were above 50 percent. Historically, the largest single lifetime cost of an information system was software maintenance; and by far the major cost of software maintenance is labor. This escalation in IT labor costs can be explained by two other trends: the continual downward cost curve of computer hardware (and therefore its lower percentage of the IT budget), and the acute and chronic shortages of IT labor (with a consequence of rising salaries).

But it can also be partially explained by the increased specialization of

IT labor. As new computer technologies are discovered, developed, and used in the marketplace, new technical specialists are required. In the 1970s computing world of mainframes, there were generally three main programming specialists: operating system, application, and communications. Today there are dozens: programmers for client applications, client interfaces, server applications, network operating systems, server operating systems, client operating systems, and so on. In 1995, an analysis of over 1,000 job postings in a major southern city revealed 29 different IT job types advertised. Within each type of job, there were numerous specialties—15 different kinds of programmers alone (McLean & Schneberger, 1997)!

These factors present significant challenges to formulating and executing HR strategies for IT labor. IT labor is scarce, becoming more crucial for corporate operations, and becoming more specialized.

Human Resource Management

Human resource (HR) management and strategy are undergoing significant functional changes, both in general and as it relates to IT personnel management. Only in the early 1980s did companies begin to create HR strategies linked to their corporate strategies. Before then, HR management was an administrative task aimed at minimizing cost and improving efficiency for internal customers; now it is more often seen as a strategic function for providing value to external customers. HR management and strategy has moved from being operationally reactive to strategically proactive. HR departments have been redesigning their processes, deploying specialized HR information systems or functionality, and building strategic partnerships with internal business units. An axiom of modern HR strategy is that business managers (including Chief Information Officers, or CIOs) need to play a pivotal role as *drivers* and *deliverers* of corporate HR policy.

Based on surveys of HR managers, the difficulty of attracting and retaining top talent continues to be a key human capital concern as labor is increasingly mobile and willing to change employers for potential short-term and long-term gain. The Bureau of Labor Statistics has reported that the U.S. will experience a total labor shortage of about 10 million workers by the year 2008 (Fyock, 2001). As we pointed out earlier, the difficulty in attracting and retaining IT personnel has been acute, most of the time. In 1997, the Office of Technology Policy estimated that, through 2006, there will be approximately 138,000 new IT jobs yearly, while the Information Technology Association of America found that nearly 10 percent of all U.S. IT positions were already unfilled—approximately 350,000. Those vacancies were observed across industry types, size, and region. Moreover, the problem is not confined to the United States; Western Europe was estimated to have a shortage of 850,000 IT sector jobs (including computer-literate clerical workers), with Germany alone having a shortage of approximately 75,000

IT professionals. It has been estimated that the European Union has lost over $100 billion in gross domestic product because of IT professional shortages. Moreover, IT labor tends to have high turnover rates (between 25 percent and 35 percent in *Fortune* 500 companies, higher than other corporate positions), these figures suggest attracting and retaining IT workers should present an acute and chronic problem for HR and IT managers (Hayes, 1998).

A survey of 32 companies in 1998 found that successful IT retention efforts relied on measuring performance, strong compensation and benefit packages, favorable work arrangements, recurring and current training and development, clear career development paths, clear advancement criteria, active management presence and leadership, a sense of corporate community, comfortable corporate lifestyles, and employment stability (Agarwal & Ferratt, 1998). It has been noted anecdotally that some companies ignore the experience of older IT workers for the up-to-date technical training of new workers; but we believe this trend, if it was prevalent, will reverse as team-building skills, system integration experience, and business knowledge become more important to meeting corporate and customer needs than just technical skills.

Globalization

Organizations are becoming ever more global; language, social, political, legal, educational, and cultural differences among IT workers and between IT workers and their corporate characteristics can be substantial. Computing and communication infrastructures worldwide vary noticeably, not only in technical standards and compatibility but also in mere presence. And, while communication networks like the Internet go a long way to standardizing and connecting computing worldwide, corporate IT problems are still heightened by distances; equipment installation, training, configuration, and troubleshooting across the globe can be problematic.

Ordinary human IT capital challenges are exacerbated by these additional hurdles and the complexity of either compiling a comprehensive, global IT strategy, or weaving a complex series of regional or country-specific strategies into a harmonious whole. It is understood that enforcing technical standards—especially those from the marketplace—can be much easier than enforcing human standards laden with historical precedents and cultural expectations. To some extent, these problems can be ameliorated by simply giving global IT workers tasks without direct oversight; they can complete the tasks within their own cultural boundaries and strengths without having strict, homogenized HR policies. But, as global interplay rises, corporate work independence will likely diminish. A sound, effective IT HR strategy must face global differences and opportunities.

: *Foundational Theories*

In developing thorough and effective IT human capital strategies, foundational theories can guide corporate management, in particular, theories about human behavior and human resource management strategy.

Human Behavior

At the core of human labor behavior are theories about human motivation. These theories by and large assume that human behavior is caused by a sense of need, is goal-oriented (to satisfy the need), and is motivated by perceived motivators. While there have been dozens of foundational theories, primarily in the fields of psychology and sociology, they can be thought of as falling into two main camps: primary or physiological needs, such as those common among all animals including man; and secondary or learned needs, which can be different even among members of the same species. These two camps also can be organized in different theoretical frameworks: internal and external, mechanistic or cognitive, or content and process. The latter theoretical framework will be used here, as it was the model for seminal research in the 1980s on IT workers by Couger and Zawacki (1980).

Process motivational theory is based on people behaving to meet their perceived needs as a continuous flow of interrelated activities. Under this theme, there are three prevalent theories: stimulus, equity, and job characteristics. *Stimulus theory* is based on the simple concept of reward and punishment; people will seek rewards and avoid punishment. Rewards and benefits, sometimes called "carrots" and "sticks," can be short-term or long-term, mild or intense, regular or random. *Equity theory* is based on the concept that rewards and punishments are relative, not objective; people will judge the merit of rewards and punishments at any given moment within many contexts and therefore will be less consistent than otherwise might be expected. *Job characteristics theory* presumes five core characteristics of jobs that motivate human labor behavior: skill variety, task identity, task significance, autonomy, and feedback. The higher the degree the person identifies with perceived benefits from these characteristics, the greater the person will be motivated to work.

Content theories focus on single points in time—assuming that human behavior is a conglomeration of moment-to-moment perceptions, feelings of want, decisions about how to best fulfill those wants, and even simply reactions to events. The first core theory in this group is the need or *self-actualization theory* espoused by Abraham Maslow (1954). In this perspective, people have a hierarchy of needs (ordered from bottom to top): physiological, safety, social, esteem, and self-actualization. People seek to satisfy lower levels before higher levels, but lower levels need not be satisfied entirely before higher levels come into play. Also part of this theory is that a satisfied need is no longer a behavior motivator; and as an individual moves up the hierarchy, it becomes progressively more difficult to satisfy the individual's higher-level needs. The second content theory is Herzberg's *motivation-hygiene theory* based on a two-factor approach: minimizing dissatisfaction and maximizing satisfaction, simultaneously (Herzberg, Mausner, & Snyderman, 1959). Dissatisfaction occurs when basic maintenance or "hygiene" needs, such as job security or pay, are not met, while satisfaction involves achieving motivational or intrinsic needs such as achievement, advancement, and authority. In motivation-hygiene theory, while both needs are addressed, the greatest motivation comes from the "satisfiers." It might be worth recalling at this point that IT workers tend to have (among other characteristics) very low social needs and very high self-fulfillment needs; thus, they are likely to be very high in Maslow's hierarchy of needs and therefore more likely to be motivated by satisfiers than by basic or intrinsic needs.

Human Resource Strategy

Like human behavior theory, there are a number of varying theories concerning human resource strategy, including resource-based view, uncertainty, portfolio, and expertise.

In *resource-based view* (RBV) human resource strategy theories, a firm's ability to generate revenue depends on its human resources—its employee competencies (i.e., knowledge, skills, and attitudes) to meet challenges, make decisions, and carry out strategic plans successfully. These core competencies can also be used to differentiate firms; one organization's monopoly of particular human resource competencies can be used as a barrier (or human capital advantage) against competing organizations. But, while these competencies are vital, they are also elusive to identify, measure, protect, and alter. HR strategies, therefore, focus on finding, retaining, and positioning the firm's human resources to best fulfill corporate goals—as well as measuring HR management success with feedback from practice. HR practices such as personnel flow management, organizational structure, and culture are based on an RBV perspective of HR strategy. And not only is the firm's strategy likely driven by external conditions but also the HR strategy is affected by economic conditions, employment markets, education standards, legal frameworks, and so on.

Uncertainty HR strategies are not focused on maximizing personnel competencies, but reducing uncertainty, instability, and chance. These strategies seek to meet reasonable risks with the lowest attendant corporate costs or further risk. Inherent in this theoretical approach are practices such as formal orders, established procedures, contractual arrangements, and less personal autonomy. Uncertainty HR strategies appeal to workers' commitment, responsibility, and loyalty, and include many measures of effectiveness to gauge performance and achievement. They assume that a perfect mix of human resources and external events is unlikely; human resources need to be tightly controlled to maximize gain with minimal cost.

Portfolio HR strategies are based on the concept that a corporation has a portfolio of different activities, functions, and operations—and the demands and opportunities of one part of the portfolio need to be balanced against the needs and opportunities of the other parts. This is similar to an investment portfolio of stocks and bonds, high risk and low risk, short term and long term, and so on. A portfolio HR strategy might balance the personal needs of the individuals versus the business needs of the corporation, the cost efficiency of infrastructure activities with the potential effectiveness of research and prototyping, and the experiential breadth from continual job rotation versus the skill depth from vertical placement. Optimal balance of human resources is the goal.

In the *expertise-oriented view* of HR management, human resource strategies seek to maximize the efficient and effective output of established employees. HR practices seek to germinate human productivity, create an internal environment that will nurture and support employee creativity and activity, match employee strengths for symbiosis and resonance, support formal and informal networking and communications, and measure success more by corporate performance than by individual performance. In this sense, HR practices seek to inspire and empower employees more than regulate them.

There also are two primary global HR strategic theories: collectivist and relativist. The *collectivist view* is that what is best for the corporation is best for the workers; the more efficient and harmonious the corporate activity, the better the bottom line and the better off will be the employees. HR practice with this perspective is highly centralized and based on low costs, efficiency, consistency, standards, best practices, and interoperability. The other theoretical perspective, the *radical relativist view*, presumes that the effectiveness of a particular HR practice depends on how well it matches a regional, national, or local value system. In this sense, what's good for the local workers is good for the global corporation. Implicit in this view is that global HR strategy should be made up of many local strategies for each cultural environment as opposed to one, centralized global strategy based on efficiency, best practices, or simply ethnocentrism. Culture is thought to include knowledge, belief, art, morals, law, customs, and any other capabilities and habits of a society that are guided by values. Corporate HR strategies under this perspective should adopt the management approaches of the country in which they operate, not impress corporate approaches on global workers. In essence, "When in Rome, do as the Romans do."

: Conclusions

The development of new information technologies, and their use in an ever-expanding array of business applications, has created a severe challenge for managers in all parts of the organization—IT, HR, and general management. With the exception of a few economic downturns, most of which have been fairly short in duration, the demand for skilled IT workers has continued and grown unabated for over 40 years. And the growth has been in both depth and breadth; depth in the increased amount of training required to become proficient in some aspect of computing, and breadth in the rapidly expanding number of areas of specialization. As a result, it has produced a shortfall in the number of skilled IT workers available to meet the demand. Although estimates of the size of this shortfall vary, none deny its existence, the present downturn in 2001–03 notwithstanding.

In response, a number of approaches have been, and are being, tried. One is to import IT workers from abroad under an expanded H-1B visa program. Congress has twice raised the limit on the number of foreign workers allowed in this county in recent years at the urging of high tech companies and industry groups.[3] A corollary of this is to send the work abroad. Offshore outsourcing is becoming increasingly attractive in such places as India and Russia, where well-trained computer professionals are available at a fraction of their cost in the United States. Managing such global networks of development teams, however, requires special care and attention. The entire life cycle, from initial specifications to documentation and maintenance, must take into account language, culture, reward systems, and other differences.

Critics of this use of foreign IT workers, whether they are located here or abroad, claim that we are over looking domestic solutions. Older workers, with outdated skills, are being laid off rather than being retrained and re-skilled. "You can't teach old dogs new tricks" captures this philosophy. But oftentimes these workers possess other advantages gained over a number of years such as knowledge of, and loyalty to, the company. It is in the retraining of these experienced but not technically current employees that a partnership between the IT and HR functions can be particularly effective.

At the entry level, more is needed at the university and technical school levels. Both more degree-based and continuing education is needed. But IT and computer-science faculty are in short supply and the production of Ph.D. graduates, like the IT field in general, is not keeping up with the demand. A combined effort of the federal government, state and private universities, and the computer industry is needed to address this issue.

Another solution is to attempt to slow down the pace of technical change. Driven by vendors anxious to sustain their growth with a flood of new products and system upgrades, many of dubious business value, companies are faced with a continuing training problem for both users and IT professionals alike. If the time between releases could be lengthened, even by a few months, and the upgrades and patches could be batched, a substantial saving in training costs could be realized.

All of these points offer ways of meeting the increased demands for IT professionals, but they must be coupled with retention strategies for the IT employees that are already in place. What motivates them to stay—or to leave? In this regard, behavioral theories from psychology and sociology offer us some insight.

The basic work of Maslow and Herzberg and the applied work of Couger offer us some guidance. Maslow's hierarchy of needs suggests that lower levels of need (like an adequate salary or an attractive workplace) once satisfied no longer serve as a source of motivation; and attempts to use these lower levels as motivation levers will be unsuccessful. This is similar to Herzberg's hygiene factors. If a hygiene factor is not met (like an inadequate salary), then it will cause dissatisfaction and possible intentions to leave. But satisfying a hygiene factor does not serve as a source of motivation. Often it is the job itself that serves as this motivation. As Herzberg observes: "If you want people to do a good job, give them a good job to do."

Couger and others have identified what some of these job-centered motivating factors are: skill variety, task identity, task significance, autonomy, and feedback. To the extent that managers can positively influence these job factors, a more committed workforce will result. Couger's research also found that IT professionals have job-related needs that distinguish them from the general population. Their achievement and growth needs are among the highest ever measured, while their need for social interaction is among the lowest. The latter suggests that using team-based approaches to system development, particularly those involving representatives from the user community, may be problematic. The former points to the need to provide for training and exposure to the latest technology, even if there is no current business need for such technology. This desire to continually learn new things makes the staffing of areas such as systems maintenance particularly difficult. It is here that long-time, experienced IT employees, however, may prove to be a valuable asset to companies.

Finally, it is important to recognize the HR function as a vital partner in attracting and retaining skilled IT employees. Just as the IT function within organizations has become increasingly more strategic and critical to the business success of the enterprise, so, too, has the HR department become a more strategic player—both in its innovative uses of information technology in support of its own activities, and in its role in providing the skilled IT workers needed by the organization. As stated at the outset, "successful IT competitive strategies will depend more on *how* information technology is applied than to *what*. And how it is applied will depend on corporate human capital." Understanding and utilizing this human capital is at the heart of achieving business success.

▪ Notes

1. Gordon Moore, former CEO of Intel Corporation.

2. In 2002, the Commission on Technology, Gender, and Teacher Education reported the female portion of the U.S. IT workforce had shrunk from 40 percent to 20 percent in the previous 15 years.

3. 195,000 for 2002 and 2003, but reverting to 65,000 in 2004 without further legislation.

▪ References

Agarwal, R., & T. W. Ferratt. (1998) "Recruiting, Retaining, and Developing IT Professionals," *Proceedings of the 1998 ACM SIGCPR Conference,* 292–302.

Couger, J. D., & R. Z. Zawacki. (1980) *Motivating and Managing Computer Personnel.* New York: Wiley.

DiSabatino, J. (2002) "Report: Job Cuts in 2001 Rearch Nearly 2 Million," *Computerworld (on-line),* Jan. 3.

Fox, P. (2002) "Some Sanity Returns to IT Hiring," *Computerworld (on-line),* Jan. 14.

Fyock, C. (2001) "HR Strategies: Tried and True, Plus Some New," *HR Magazine,* 46(10), 157–60.

Greenspan, A. (2002) "Productivity," remarks at the U.S. Department of Labor and American Institute Conference, Washington, Oct. 23.

Hayes, F. (1998) "Wanted: True Believers," *Computerworld,* 34(4), 8.

Herzberg, F., B. Mausner, & B. B. Snyderman. (1959) *The Motivation to Work* (2nd ed.). New York: Wiley.

Maslow, A. H. (1954) *Motivation and Personality.* New York: Harper and Row.

McLean, E. R., and S. L. Schneberger. (1997) *ICAPP Strategic Industry Needs Assessment: Information Technology.* Atlanta, GA: Board of Regents of the University System of Georgia, Dec.

VIII

Aligning This Book

18

Jerry Luftman

Strategic Alignment as a Process

: *Chapter Summary*

1. Alignment is about process. It's about what *all* management does together to achieve its business objectives. IT strategic alignment focuses on the activities that all management performs to achieve cohesive goals across the IT and other functional organizations (strategic business units; e.g., finance, marketing, human resources, manufacturing). Therefore, alignment addresses both how IT is in harmony with the business, and how the business should, or could be in harmony with IT.

2. Alignment evolves into a relationship in which IT and other business units adapt their strategies together. Achieving alignment is evolutionary and dynamic. It requires strong support from senior management, good working relationships, strong leadership, appropriate prioritization, trust, and effective communication, as well as a thorough understanding of the business and technical environments.

3. Achieving and sustaining a high level of alignment maturity demands focusing on maximizing the enablers and minimizing the inhibitors that cultivate alignment. It is a continuous process. It combines all of the ideas presented in this book.

4. As business and technology have become increasingly intertwined, strategic alignment continues to be a major corporate issue. The emergence of IT from the back room to the forefront of business brings the alignment issue under the spotlight like never before. The potential efficiencies and competitive advantages afforded by technology have become crucial.

5. In many respects, alignment boils down to the effectiveness of the interpersonal relationships among business and IT managers. Effective IT leaders must be privy to senior business management's tactical and strategic plans. They also must be present and play an active role when corporate strategies are discussed. Additionally, business managers must be involved with IT as they derive IT strategies.

6. IT and business must work together to develop an integrated strategy that addresses the important problems and opportunities of the firm. This relationship must continue to effectively identify and carry out the plans and realize the value.

: *Introduction*

As conveyed throughout this book, one of the most important objectives for IT management in the twenty-first century is to be architects of alignment linking business and IT. The metaphor of architecture is chosen because IT strategy is not just about technology; it is about the purposeful creation of integrated environments that leverage human skills, business processes, organizational structures, technologies, competencies, and industry direction to transform the competitive position of the firm. Naturally, offering new products and services via information technology is another important transformational vehicle. Considerable recent research has shown that the effectiveness of the linkages relating IT and business are critically important to sustaining competitive advantage in today's hyper-competitive global markets. When these areas are aligned (e.g., integrated, in harmony), a company's ability to respond to increasingly uncertain and evolving markets (the external environment) is significantly enhanced; sometimes to the level where companies can define entirely new markets or set the standard of excellence in their industry.

As architects of alignment, IT management plays a pivotal role as they have the responsibility to consider the organization across functional and process boundaries. These boundaries should be expanded to include external partners and customers. In this role, IT managers need to:

- Be knowledgeable about how the new IT technologies can be integrated into the business (including customers/clients and partners) as well as among the different technologies and architectures.
- Be privy to senior management's tactical and strategic plans.
- Be present when business strategies are discussed.
- Understand the strengths and weaknesses of the technologies in question and the corporate-wide implications.

It is important for business and IT managers to understand that alignment is about the evolution of a relationship between business and IT, and how the organization can leverage information technology. Alignment is a process that is enabled or inhibited by a number of factors that are experienced every day. Recent research into the factors that enable or inhibit alignment based on survey responses from senior business and IT managers show that there are six key enablers to alignment as well as six corresponding inhibitors to alignment (table 1.1). Managers should especially note that several of the attributes that enable alignment also show up as inhibitors to alignment. The enablers and inhibitors identified in the original research have not changed, as the research continues.

Achieving and sustaining alignment requires conscious attention and focus by IT and functional (strategic business unit; e.g., marketing, research and development, finance) management to enhance the enablers of alignment and minimize alignment's inhibitors. When formulating an IT strategy, management cannot consciously design for alignment. Alignment is, rather, a consequence of sound processes, practices, and evolving human relationships that embrace mutual understandings of goals, value, culture, and capabilities that leverage the development of strategies that can ultimately coadapt to changing situations. IT strategies that focus merely on technology and ignore the partnership and communications aspects of the business-IT relationship inevitably fail. Alignment is an ongoing process.

The process must focus on all six strategic alignment maturity assessment criteria to be effective. The thought leaders contributing to the insights presented in this book recognize that there is no one answer. They present many ideas and approaches. Some are new; some are not. The dominant theme of this book is that *all* of these factors must be understood and regularly worked on to ensure alignment and the innovative business transformations that it can deliver.

Scope and architecture is the only technical criterion included in the alignment maturity assessment. It is important to recognize that, as with the other criteria; executives must have an appropriate understanding and strategy that addresses how the business can leverage these technologies. IT executives have the responsibility of providing business executives with the appropriate level of understanding while focusing not on the technology, but how the business can leverage the technology.

⦂ Today's Business Environment

To better understand why alignment between business strategy and IT strategy is critical not just for competitive advantage, but for business survival, organizations need to understand the forces that shape the business environment. Today's business environment can be best characterized as one of increasing globalization, increased competitive pressure, frequent mergers and acquisitions, rapidly changing technology, and evolving patterns of consumer demand. Change is now the norm rather than the exception. Many of these changes come as the result of events never anticipated. Organizations must learn to quickly adapt to these changes or face extinction (at worst) or assimilation (at best) by competitors that can emerge anywhere in the world. In short, the predictability of the business environment has dramatically declined while its complexity has simultaneously accelerated.

Competitive advantage in this turbulent environment is no longer just about having the best products or the lowest prices, but about having:

- Unsurpassed relationships with customers and suppliers.
- Unique and adaptable business processes.
- The ability to harness the information and knowledge of the firm's employees and partners to continuously create new, hard to duplicate products and services.

Organizations need to become "change leaders" merely to survive in the twenty-first century business environment.

: Strategy—A Definition

The word strategy is derived from Greek, and it means "the art of the general." Until recently, even in the English language, strategy was a military term. It has only been since the 1960s that the business world has adopted the term.

Strategies are business decisions taken at particular points in time by different people in response to sets of perceived environmental factors. Strategy is about making choices that include:

- Selection and priorities of business goals.
- Choice of products and services to offer.
- Approach to obtain the competencies necessary to attain critical success factors.
- Design and configuration of policies that determine where and how the firm positions itself to compete in its markets.
- Appropriate level of scope and diversity (e.g., specialization).
- Design of organization structure, processes, and policies used to define and coordinate work.

The integration and coordination of these choices makes them a strategy. Integration and coordination of the choices is key to survival of the enterprise.

Another definition of strategy is offered by Drucker (1998): "Every organization operates on a *Theory of the Business*—a set of assumptions as to what its business is, its objectives, how it defines and measures results, who its customers are, and what its customers value and pay for. A business strategy converts this *Theory of the Business* into action by enabling an organization to achieve its goals in an increasingly unpredictable business environment."

: IT Strategy

IT strategy is a set of decisions made by IT and functional business management that either enable or drive the business strategy. It leads to the deployment of technology infrastructure and applications, and human competencies that will assist the organization in becoming more competitive. IT strategy must be concerned not just about technology choices but also about the relationship of technology choices to business strategy choices. The selection of appropriate technologies can, in many situations, have substantial influence on, or even drive, the transformation of the business strategy. As discussed in chapter 4, it is not the technology alone that brings these benefits. It is the business processes that are changed by leveraging information technology that provide the business value. That is why a strong IT-business partnership is critical. Neither IT nor the business can do it alone. Their strategies must be aligned.

: *IT and Business Transformation*

In the formulation of an IT strategy, IT can drive business transformation, as well as enable transformation. The evidence that IT can transform business has been amply documented. In the role of transformation driver, the IT strategy becomes the business strategy, offering novel and competitively differentiating ways of doing business. In its role as transformation driver, IT can create and exploit new markets, link customers more tightly to the firm, and define new standards of operational excellence for the industry. Examples of firms that have used IT as a transformation driver include Dell, Cisco, Schwab, and Amazon.com—all of which have established the operational process "bar" over which all potential competitors must now jump to even consider competing in their markets.

Another, earlier example of IT as a transformation driver is the Sabre Group, formerly the American Airlines reservation system. Initially a proprietary reservation system for American Airlines flights, Sabre's accommodation of flight information from other airlines eventually opened the way for it to become a flight booking system for the airline and travel industry. Sabre's value grew to the point where the value of its information content (and the driving information technology) exceeded the value of American's flight operations assets. Eventually, Sabre Group was formed as a company independent of American Airlines, with Sabre firmly established as an industry standard.

In its role as an enabler of transformation, IT's capabilities to interconnect people and processes, span organizational (and interorganizational) boundaries, and quickly bridge geographical distances, can help organizations explore new markets and customer segments, create new processes, and provide a critical supporting role in the implementation of business transformation strategies. An excellent example of IT as an enabler of transformation is Federal Express's use of IT to track packages, which supported its revolutionary concept of airline hubbing for overnight package delivery. This process innovation redefined the small package delivery business and put the U.S. Postal Service at a severe competitive disadvantage.

Another example of IT as a transformation enabler is *USA Today*'s use of new communications technologies and graphics information management technologies to support what is now a national newspaper. *USA Today* transformed the processes involved with producing, printing, and distributing a daily newspaper to a national and international readership through the deployment of IT.

Unfortunately, IT can also be an inhibitor to business transformation. This situation occurs through a couple of mechanisms:

1. *When the IT strategy is not aligned with the business strategy*: just as a sound business strategy must take into account both external positioning in the marketplace, as well as the internal arrangement of its organizational structure and competencies, IT strategy must also reflect a firm's positioning in the external IT marketplace and the configuration of its internal IT infrastructure and architecture.

2. *Overemphasis by IT management and business management on technology*: the focus of transformation can be misdirected away from changing and transforming critical business processes to the implementation of technology infrastructure for its own sake. Part of this is because of communications issues between the different "cultures" of management.

The components of the strategic alignment model were shown in figure 1.1. It is the relationships that exist among the 12 components of this model that further define business-IT alignment. The components of this model, in concert with the enablers/inhibitors research (Luftman & Brier, 1999), form the building blocks for the strategic alignment maturity assessment. Aligning these components focuses on the activities that management performs to achieve cohesive goals across the information technology and other functional organizations (e.g., finance, marketing, HR, manufacturing). Alignment maturity evolves into a relationship in which the function of IT and other business functions adapt their strategies together.

Decades have passed. Billions of dollars have been invested in IT. Alignment—applying IT in an appropriate and timely way, in harmony with business strategies, goals and needs—remains a key concern of business executives. Alignment addresses both how IT is integrated with the business, and how the business should/could be integrated with IT. Frustratingly, organizations seem to find it difficult or impossible to harness the power of IT for their own long-term benefit, even though there is worldwide evidence that IT has the power to transform whole industries and markets.

Remember, alignment provides the means for a firm to maximize its IT investments and achieve harmony with its business strategies and plans. Alignment is important to firms for many reasons. The major reason is to ease the development and implementation of cohesive organization and IT strategies that facilitate the firms' ability to meet its goals. By understanding and leveraging the business-IT relationship, organizations can concentrate on the application of IT to enable or drive the business strategy. This harmony can be extended and applied throughout the organization as new opportunities are identified.

Traditional methods for developing business strategies have failed to take full advantage of IT. Information technology is frequently treated as a "cost center" or viewed as an "expense" rather than an enabler or driver of business value. Strategic alignment sheds new light on IT and its role in the development of business strategies. It considers the strategic fit between strategy and infrastructure as well as the functional integration of business and IT.

Alignment of IT strategy with the organization's business strategy is a fundamental principle that has been advocated for over 15 years. IT investment has been on the rise for years and managers are looking for ways in which this vital resource can be successfully managed and integrated into the organization's strategies. IT managers must be knowledgeable about how these new technologies can be integrated into the business (in addition to the integration among the different technologies and architectures) and must be privy to senior management's tactical and strategic plans. IT and business executives must be present when corporate strategies are discussed. IT executives must be able to delineate the strengths and weaknesses of the technologies in question and understand the corporate-wide implications.

⁝ *Strategic Alignment as a Process*

The approach applied to attain and sustain business-IT alignment focuses on understanding the alignment maturity, and on maximizing alignment enablers and minimizing inhibitors. I have used a six-step approach (Luftman & Brier, 1999) designed to make strategic alignment work in any organization. This process mirrors traditional strategic planning, and incorporates an organizational assessment using the strategic alignment model. The six steps are:

1. Set the goals and establish a team (including sponsor and champions)
2. Understand the business-IT linkage (As-Is To-Be assessment)
3. Analyze and prioritize gaps
4. Specify the actions (project management)
5. Choose and evaluate success criteria
6. Sustain alignment

The process begins by *setting the organizational goals and establishing a team.* The importance of setting a clear direction or goal(s) for the organization prior to selecting technologies and how they will be applied cannot be overlooked. Too often the tendency is to seize on a new IT product or service without giving full consideration to its strategic fit to a business plan. The more appropriate approach is to initially ask some questions related to specific organizational goals. Is the organization trying to improve:

- products and services?
- customer relationships?
- competitive position?
- costs and quality?

For the Charles Schwab Corporation, the business focus for many years has been to lower their operational costs and offer superior service at lower prices to their investors. Their traditional investor seeks discount brokerage services and is unwilling to pay for investment advice. In the late 1990s, Schwab shifted toward delivering customized information to the investor as quickly as possible. In so doing, the company converted to a full-service brokerage firm. Through the years since it was incorporated in 1971, the company has been a leader in using IT as an important tool in meeting changing but well-defined business goals.

The steps taken to set the goals, market the objectives of the assessment, and negotiate for an executive sponsor, business champion, and team are crucial. Senior executive support must be obtained (the number one enabler identified in my research). The highest-level business executive representing the organization being assessed should be the sponsor. Selecting a cross-functional team consisting of from 6 to 12 executives from the major business units and IT is the next part of this step.

The team typically would report to the senior executives that report to the sponsor. If the sponsor was the CEO, the team would comprise senior vice presidents. Their credibility and knowledge of the business are key. They also must be open to new ideas and be willing to take a holistic view of the organization. IT's involvement in the development of the strategy is essential (the second highest enabler identified in the research). The critical first steps in the planning process are to ensure that the right team is committed and that they clearly understand, and are in agreement with, the goals of the business. Although there are times when IT is or should be the driver of business strategy, experience indicates that business goals must be clearly specified and understood before proceeding in the alignment analysis.

The second step in the process is to *understand the linkage between IT and the business*. The organization must understand the current and future business and IT environments by assessing the twelve strategic alignment components (see fig. 1.1). This relationship is derived from an analysis of the current ("As Is") and future ("To Be") states for each of the 12 components of strategic alignment.

First, focus on the current state for each of the 12 components. Then focus on the future state for each of the 12 components. Do not put time constraints when discussing the future. Brainstorming techniques work well. If the team comprised senior VPs, each would discuss, from their respective points of view (e.g., marketing, finance, R&D, engineering, manufacturing, HR, IT), the current and then the future state of business scope, competencies, governance, and so on. The individual team members' point of view and discussions that ensue provide the dynamism that results in a powerful list of opportunities and problems. A skilled facilitator can prove invaluable during this brainstorming session. These discussions promote IT's understanding of the business, while promoting the business's understanding of

IT (the third highest enabler identified in our research). This mutual understanding results in greatly improved relationships across the different organizations (the fourth highest enabler identified in our research).

When deriving a strategy for an entire firm, initially do this As-Is To-Be assessment for each of the functional organizations independently. Then get knowledgeable representatives from the different organizations together to derive a corporate view of the strategy. This produces both individual business unit strategies and a corporate strategy. Naturally, the subsequent steps are also done for both the individual business units and the overall corporate strategy.

Analyzing and prioritizing the differences (gaps) between the current and future states of each of the 12 alignment components (fig. 1.1) will provide the major content of the business and IT strategies. This is the third step in the process. Ask team members to suggest opportunities and problems. A full day is usually necessary to do this part of the assessment. In sessions that have been conducted, the discussion is kept free flowing rather than restrictive. Most executives find it helpful to discuss the results with their staffs and then return a week later for another full day of brainstorming with the assessment team. The gaps (which are candidates for projects) and their value are described in business terms. Focusing on these gaps leads to a prioritized identification of IT projects that can leverage business opportunities (the fifth highest enabler identified in my research).

To prioritize the gaps as candidates for projects, a simple table used in scenario planning (fig. 18.1) can be applied. It evaluates the likelihood that the event (the gap that will be considered as a project candidate) will occur

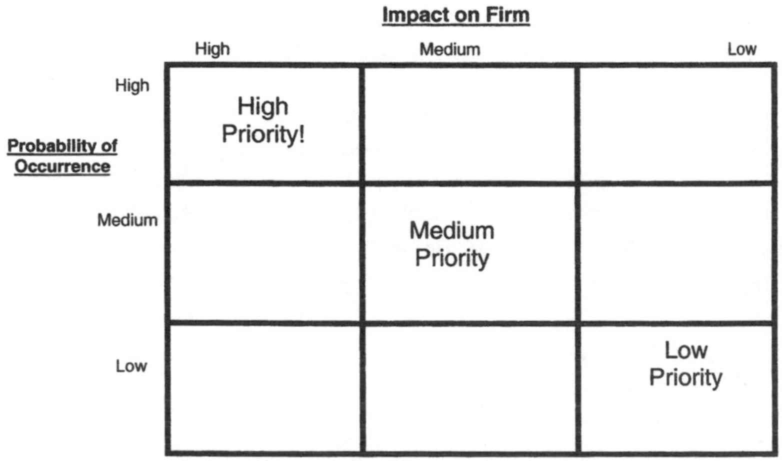

Impact on Firm

	High	Medium	Low
High	High Priority!		
Medium		Medium Priority	
Low			Low Priority

Probability of Occurrence

Figure 18.1. Scenario analysis matrix

and the implications it will have on the organization. The ensuing priorities are identified based on the placement of the gap (project candidate) in the scenario analysis matrix in figure 18.1.

Take each gap that has been identified and ask the team to place it in the table. The gaps that demand high priority are those that are likely to occur and likely to have a major impact on the business: the upper left box. Those gaps become the high priority project candidates. The gaps that fall in the low priority box are not regarded as important project candidates. Those projects that fall in the medium priority box need additional discussion to identify which gap will be included as project candidates that are recommended and those that will not be carried forward. Using this approach in concert with the portfolio management approach described in chapter 4 is very helpful.

The prioritized list of projects is reviewed with the sponsor and the senior executives for approval. A business member from the team should do the presentation. In almost all cases, approval is obtained for several of the high priority projects and the executive team walks away with a much better appreciation for IT. The presentation also should be used to communicate with the rest of the organization.

For Charles Schwab, the step of examining how IT can enable distinctive competency is straightforward. Schwab has a history of relying on technology to provide top customer service and to lower costs. To meet the customer need of retrieving stock quotes and placing orders rapidly, Schwab introduced TeleBroker, a fully automated telephone system, in 1989. As newer IT capabilities became available through the years, Schwab analyzed how these technologies might help to meet their business goals. Some examples are Equalizer, a software product that allows personal computer users to trade stocks online, and StreetSmart, the first Windows-based software to provide online trading of bonds, equities, and mutual funds.

The fourth step is to *specify the actions* necessary to carry out the recommendations. Frequently, the focal areas for the actions to be taken are in the infrastructure (fig. 1.1) domains of the strategic alignment model. For either business or IT, three areas to consider are the policies to be set, processes to be developed or redesigned, and the skills to be acquired. After this analysis has been completed, the next questions pertaining to project management that must be answered include:

· What are the deliverables?
· What has to be done?
· What is the completion date?
· Who is responsible?
· What are the risks?

In building an infrastructure for IT through the years, Schwab was able to capitalize on previous technological capabilities as new technology initiatives were introduced. The Schwab Mutual Fund OneSource program, introduced in 1992, enabled customers to purchase mutual funds much more easily than was possible previously. Customers could now purchase from their own brokerage account using any of Schwab's trading interfaces, including TeleBroker and StreetSmart.

After the strategy has been set and the action plan has been specified, the next step is to *choose and evaluate success criteria*. This necessitates revisiting the strategic goals and selecting the measurement criteria to apply in assessing the implementation of the project plans. Some frequently used criteria are:

- Sustainability—the ability to preserve an advantageous market position.
- Flexibility/agility—the potential for revision in strategic choices.
- Economics—the financial analysis of the tradeoffs among varying dimensions of value.

Having established a sound business strategy through the years, Schwab had to evaluate its strategic choices. In 1995, when the Internet began to have a profound effect on the economics of the brokerage industry, e.Schwab was introduced. This new service allowed investors to obtain account information through the Internet. During the last four years, Schwab's embrace of this technology has resulted in a transformation of its business. Schwab has become an information provider in addition to a transaction processor. In so doing, the "no-frills" discount broker is becoming a full-service brokerage firm. In 1998, e.Schwab was eliminated and replaced by www. schwab.com.

Some problems just won't go away. Why are so many of the inhibitors (table 3.1) IT related? Obtaining IT-business alignment is a difficult task. The last step in the process, *sustaining IT-business alignment*, is even more difficult. To sustain the benefit from IT, an "alignment behavior" must be developed and cultivated. There are several significant behavioral traits (see fig. 18.2) characteristic of organizations that have linked IT and business strategies. By adopting these behaviors, companies can increase their potential for complete alignment and improve their ability to gain business value from investments in IT.

As is true for all functions (e.g., finance, marketing, HR) of a business, the strategy for IT should be a major component of the business strategy. At United Services Automobile Association, USAA, in San Antonio, Texas, strategic alignment is critical to success. According to CEO Robert Herres, "Technology forces us to think about how and where our processes intersect. Alignment across businesses is critical for us because our goal is to exploit the efficiencies of centralized information management while we decentralize service delivery."

An unrelenting focus on customer needs has never been more critical than it is today. IT can play an important role in attracting and keeping customers, and the results should flow to the bottom line. The Charles

> Successfully aligned organizations are those that concentrate on:
> · Allowing for IT and business capabilities to be weighed equally.
> · Developing the skills necessary for success.
> · Empowering workers in a team-based environment.
> · Gaining agreement on outcomes required from the business processes.
> · Instilling a sense of urgency in managing IT-enabled projects.
> · Leading in the deployment of IT to create customer value.
> · Nurturing a culture of open human communication.

Figure 18.2. Behavioral traits characteristic of organizations linking IT and business strategies

Schwab Corporation story is one of transforming an industry. The effect of schwab.com has been to make Schwab a player in full-service brokerage. "The transforming event," according to co-CEO David Pottruck, "is the ability to deliver personalized information to the customer in real time, at virtually no cost."

Frequently, the latest technology instinctively becomes the solution. Successful firms resist this trend. Instead, they begin by deciding what results they must have from the business strategy and business processes. It is then that technologies are weighed along with other resources as possible solutions. Much of the potential for success has to do with governance. IT governance, described in chapter 7, plays a significant role in prioritizing IT initiatives as well as sustaining aligned business-IT organizations.

⁝ Relationship Is the Key

Alignment might succeed without many factors, but a climate that fosters a close relationship is an absolute necessity. In my study of IT management practices in over 50 firms, I concluded that the building of effective relationships with line managers is imperative for successful IT organizations. IT personnel at all levels must develop strong, ongoing bonds with line managers. Only through these relationships can the necessary communications, partnerships, measurements, skills, and governance occur to ensure that both business and technology capabilities are integrated into effective solutions for each level of the business. These are the elements of alignment maturity.

Skills in project management are always important for success in IT implementation, but for these relationships to endure, skills in people management are more critical than ever. The skills that organizations need to get IT projects completed have assumed new dimensions. This is a major shift for most IT professionals. Technical skills have always been the pre-eminent requirement in staffing. But IT education in many organizations now includes interpersonal skills such as active listening, marketing, nego-tiation, and team building.

I have applied this six-step process with hundreds of firms. Sessions are designed to educate cross-functional teams about strategic alignment, assist them in assessing the "gaps" between their current and future states, identify project priorities, leverage the enablers, address the inhibitors, and under-stand the maturity of the organizations alignment. Participants have received more than just education about alignment. They leave with a greater appre-ciation for IT, develop stronger credible relationships and lines of commu-nication, and achieve harmony among business and IT requirements. Com-bining previous strategic alignment research with the validated enablers and inhibitors, and the alignment maturity assessment, has proven to be most efficient and effective.

⦂   Conclusions

Strategic alignment is an ongoing process. It has remained a major issue for over 15 years. There appears to be no single strategy or single combination of activities that will enable a firm to achieve and sustain alignment. Tech-nology and the business climate are changing far too quickly for this to occur. The 12 components of alignment are in constant flux and their in-terrelationships are as unique as the companies that follow them. The ena-blers and inhibitors to achieving alignment have remained consistent, how-ever, over the past 10 years. This chapter has described a six-step technique that has been successfully applied to treat alignment as a process by assessing the components and focusing on the enablers and inhibitors. Using this approach along with focusing on improving the organizations alignment maturity are effective vehicles to prepare for the challenging future.

Executives should work toward minimizing those activities that inhibit alignment and maximize those activities that bolster it. They should con-centrate on improving the relationships between the business and IT func-tional areas, work toward mutual cooperation and participation in strategy development, maintain executive support, and prioritize projects more ef-fectively. IT executives *can* be successful business leaders and keep their or-ganizations in constant harmony by continuous focus on the enablers and inhibitors described in this chapter.

Alignment is a dynamic, complex process that takes time to develop and even more effort to sustain. Companies that have achieved alignment can facilitate building a strategic competitive advantage that will provide them with increased visibility, efficiency, and profitability to compete in to-day's changing markets. Sustaining this relationship, however, is more difficult than achieving it. The importance of cooperation among business and IT to maximize investment in technology remains clear. As IT plays an increasing role in defining corporate strategies, its correct application will facilitate a more competitive and profitable organization. The careful assessment of a firm's alignment is important to ensure IT is being used to appropriately enable or drive the business strategy.

⁝ References

Drucker, P. (1998) *Peter Drucker on the Profession of Management.* Boston: Harvard Business School Press.

Luftman, J., & T. Brier. (1999) "Achieving and Sustaining Business IT Alignment," *California Management Review,* 42(1), 109–22.

Index